HIDDEN HISTORY

ANCIENT ALIENS
AND THE
SUPPRESSED ORIGINS
OF CIVILIZATION

ALSO FROM VISIBLE INK PRESS

Alien Mysteries, Conspiracies, and Cover-Ups
by Kevin D. Randle
ISBN: 978-1-57859-418-4

Angels A to Z, 2nd edition
by Evelyn Dorothy Oliver, Ph.D., and James R Lewis,
Ph.D.
ISBN: 978-1-57859-212-8

Armageddon Now: The End of the World A to Z
by Jim Willis and Barbara Willis
ISBN: 978-1-57859-168-8

The Astrology Book: The Encyclopedia of Heavenly
Influences, 2nd edition
by James R. Lewis
ISBN: 978-1-57859-144-2

The Bigfoot Book: The Encyclopedia of Sasquatch, Yeti,
and Cryptid Primates
by Nick Redfern
ISBN: 978-1-57859-561-7

Conspiracies and Secret Societies: The Complete Dossier,
2nd edition
by Brad Steiger and Sherry Hansen Steiger
ISBN: 978-1-57859-368-2

The Dream Encyclopedia, 2nd edition
by James R Lewis, Ph.D., and Evelyn Dorothy Oliver,
Ph.D.
ISBN: 978-1-57859-216-6

The Dream Interpretation Dictionary: Symbols, Signs,
and Meanings
by J. M. DeBord
ISBN: 978-1-57859-637-9

The Encyclopedia of Religious Phenomena
by J. Gordon Melton
ISBN: 978-1-57859-209-8

The Fortune-Telling Book: The Encyclopedia of
Divination and Soothsaying
by Raymond Buckland
ISBN: 978-1-57859-147-3

The Government UFO Files: The Conspiracy of Cover-Up
by Kevin D. Randle
ISBN: 978-1-57859-477-1

Hidden Realms, Lost Civilizations, and Beings from Other
Worlds
by Jerome Clark
ISBN: 978-1-57859-175-6

The Horror Show Guide: The Ultimate Frightfest of Movies
by Mike May
ISBN: 978-1-57859-420-7

The Illuminati: The Secret Society That Hijacked the
World
By Jim Marrs
ISBN: 978-1-57859-619-5

The Monster Book: Creatures, Beasts, and Fiends of
Nature
by Nick Redfern
ISBN: 978-1-57859-575-4

Real Aliens, Space Beings, and Creatures from Other
Worlds
by Brad Steiger and Sherry Hansen Steiger
ISBN: 978-1-57859-333-0

Real Encounters, Different Dimensions, and
Otherworldly Beings
by Brad Steiger with Sherry Hansen Steiger
ISBN: 978-1-57859-455-9

Real Ghosts, Restless Spirits, and Haunted Places, 2nd
edition
by Brad Steiger
ISBN: 978-1-57859-401-6

Real Miracles, Divine Intervention, and Feats of
Incredible Survival
by Brad Steiger and Sherry Hansen Steiger
ISBN: 978-1-57859-214-2

Real Monsters, Gruesome Critters, and Beasts from the
Darkside
by Brad Steiger and Sherry Hansen Steiger
ISBN: 978-1-57859-220-3

Real Vampires, Night Stalkers, and Creatures from the
Darkside
by Brad Steiger
ISBN: 978-1-57859-255-5

Real Visitors, Voices from Beyond, and Parallel
Dimensions
by Brad Steiger and Sherry Hansen Steiger
ISBN: 978-1-57859-541-9

Real Zombies, the Living Dead, and Creatures of the
Apocalypse
by Brad Steiger
ISBN: 978-1-57859-296-8

ABOUT THE AUTHOR

Jim Willis earned his master's degree in theology from Andover Newton Theological School, and he has been an ordained minister for more than forty years. He has also taught college courses in comparative religion and cross-cultural studies. His background in theology and education led to his writing twelve books on religion, the apocalypse, cross-cultural spirituality, and the mysteries of the unknown. His books include Visible Ink Press' *Ancient Gods: Lost Histories, Hidden Truths, and the Conspiracy of Silence; Supernatural Gods: Spiritual Mysteries, Psychic Experiences, and Scientific Truths;* and *Lost Civilizations: The Secret Histories and Suppressed Technologies of the Ancients.* Willis resides in the woods of South Carolina with his wife, Barbara.

HIDDEN HISTORY

ANCIENT ALIENS AND THE SUPPRESSED ORIGINS OF CIVILIZATION

Jim Willis

VISIBLE INK PRESS

Detroit

**HIDDEN HISTORY:
ANCIENT ALIENS
AND THE
SUPPRESSED
ORIGINS
OF CIVILIZATION**

Visible Ink Press®
43311 Joy Rd., #414
Canton, MI 48187-2075

Visible Ink Press is a registered trademark of Visible Ink Press LLC.

Most Visible Ink Press books are available at special quantity discounts when purchased in bulk by corporations, organizations, or groups. Customized printings, special imprints, messages, and excerpts can be produced to meet your needs. For more information, contact Special Markets Director, Visible Ink Press, www.visibleink.com, or 734-667-3211.

Managing Editor: Kevin S. Hile
Art Director: Mary Claire Krzewinski
Typesetting: Marco Divita
Proofreaders: Larry Baker and Christa Brelin
Photo Research: Barry Puckett
Indexer: Shoshana Hurwitz

Cover images: Shutterstock.

ISBN: 978-1-57859-710-9

Cataloging-in-Publication Data is on file at the Library of Congress.

10 9 8 7 6 5 4 3 2 1

TABLE OF CONTENTS

THE BIG PICTURE: ORIGINS OF THE COSMOS

BEGINNINGS: THE EMERGENCE OF LIFE

EMERGENCE: THE FIRST HUMANS

EXPANSION: THE FIRST PIONEERS

POSSIBILITIES:
WHERE ARE WE AND WHERE ARE WE GOING?

DEDICATION

To those who march to the beat
of a different drummer.
May your kind increase!

ACKNOWLEDGEMENTS

Thanks to Dr. Ioannis Syrigos, director of *Ancient Origins* magazine, for his permission to use extensive portions of the article he wrote that is quoted in the section of this book called *Expansion: The First Pioneers*. As of this writing, the problems outlined in this chapter are still ongoing.

Thanks also to Waziyatawin. Her experience in trying to bring Dakota sensibilities to academia, outlined in the chapter about oral tradition (p. 297), is heart breaking, but, somehow, hopeful as well. As long as there are people like her involved in the struggle, there is hope.

For many years now, Sandy Kransi has been my go-to biology expert. Now it is my privilege to add Oné Pagán to the team. His book is listed in the bibliography. Don't miss it. It's a great read!

Kevin Hile and I have worked together on four books for Visible Ink Press. A writer is only as good as his editor. Thanks, Kevin.

Speaking of Visible Ink Press, a book comes together because a lot of people work behind the scenes to bring it about. Thanks to all who produced this one.

The world owes a great debt to Graham Hancock, Andrew Collins, and many of their colleagues. For many years they have marched to the beat of a different drummer, fighting the good fight for truth and historical accuracy while risking reputation and economic gain as a result. Their books are listed in the Further Reading. Please read them. You'll be glad you did!

Photo Sources

Alexthegreatg13 (Wikicommons): p. 158.

Bjoertvedt (Wikicommons): p. 287.

Cpt. Muji (Wikicommons): p. 239.

Crux007 (Wikicommons): p. 40.

Dbachman (Wikicommons): p. 169.

EmDee (Wikicommons): p. 21.

Maximilian Dörrbecker (Chumwa): pp. 236, 237.

Fremont Culture Art: p. 132.

Future of Humanity Institute: p. 55.

Joan Halifax: p. 12.

Heinrich Harder: p. 182.

Hughes Television Network: p. 291.

Kartik (Wikicommons): p. 4 (left).

Bob King: p. 48.

Leonid Kulik: p. 250.

Library of Congress: p. 354.

Los Angeles County Museum of Art: p. 244.

Museo Nacional de Historia, Mexico: p. 225.

NASA: pp. 29, 76, 356.

NASA/JPL: p. 312.

NASA/JPL/University of Arizona: p. 313.

National Archives and Records Administration: p. 140.

National Institute of Standards and Technology: p. 34.

National Library of Australia: p. 285.

National Library of Medicine: p. 233.

NMB (Wikicommons): p. 280.

Bengt Oberger: p. 59.

PhotoColor (Wikicommons): p. 70.

Saqib Qayyum: p. 274.

Heironymous Rowe: p. 310.

Science magazine: p. 167.

Sergiodlarosa (Wikicommons): p. 184.

Shutterstock: pp. 8, 10, 14, 23, 25, 28, 30, 32, 37, 39, 46, 52, 57, 60, 62, 67, 77, 80, 81, 84, 87, 93, 97, 99, 102, 104, 118, 120, 122, 125, 129, 136, 143, 156, 165, 171, 174, 175, 179, 188, 191, 194, 196, 200, 201 (map), 206, 207, 212, 214, 217, 220, 223, 224, 227, 229, 231, 245, 256, 257, 268, 270, 272, 275, 278, 284, 292, 293, 303, 315, 318, 320, 322, 325, 327, 329, 346, 352, 361, 364, 367, 370, 373, 377, 379, 382, 384, 385, 397, 400, 405, 407, 409, 411, 413.

Smithsonian Institution: p. 27.

Ryan Somma: p. 201 (inset).

Pierre Stromberg: p. 295.

Svenska Familj-Journalen: p. 350.

Tamm E, Kivisild T, Reidla M, Metspalu M, Smith DG, et al. (2007) "Beringian Standstill and Spread of Native American Founders." PLoS ONE 2(9): e829: p. 305.

Sven Teschka: p. 134.

Tamiko Thiel: p. 20.

Jose Bernardo Troncoso: p. 185.

U.S. Geological Survey: p. 248.

Robert Wilson: p. 4 (right).

Public domain: pp. 110, 127, 138, 152, 178, 210, 289, 299, 333, 335.

Introduction

"Know thyself!"

These words were inscribed in the court of the Temple of Apollo at Delphi. They were later quoted and expanded by the Greek philosopher Socrates. He used them to highlight the fact that, in his opinion, "the unexamined life is not worth living."

The phrase prompts some inevitable questions. Do we, both as individuals and collectively as members of the human species, really know who we are? Do we know where we came from or how we originated? Do we understand our place in the great scheme of things?

We like to think we do. After all, we have been immersed in the human mythos from our conception. We have been told a story and taught rudimentary history. In school we were tested to make sure we learned the basics. As such, most of us are at least somewhat educated, modern, seemingly productive members of the human race.

But underneath much of the accepted, unexamined blather of twenty-first-century pseudo-sophistication lies a deep, abiding secret. Much of what we have been taught is wrong, some of it is misguided, a portion of it is a blatant lie intended to keep us in line, and a good deal of it has been, for reasons we shall soon explore, suppressed.

Historical Examples

Before you shrug your shoulders, scoff out loud, and arrive at the inevitable conclusion that the last paragraph is utter nonsense, consider a few facts:

- Quantum mechanics, although counterintuitive, seemingly impossible, and maddeningly difficult to grasp intellectually, is currently the most tested and consistently substantiated phenomenon in the history of science. Not once has it been proven false. Even Albert Einstein, one of the greatest theoretical physicists who ever lived, refused to accept quantum reality until his initial emotional response was finally overcome by complex mathematical equations. The theory claims, among other things, that the basis of everything is, in the end, nothing, even though a reality called "nothing" probably doesn't exist. What do you do with information like that?

- In this scientific age of materialism, we have reduced virtually everything down to its core, peered into the very heart of the atom, traveled to the nether regions of human consciousness, and plumbed the depths of creation itself. Yet, in defiance of all claims of intellectual rationality, polls show that religion, superstition, and belief in alien intervention and psychic abilities still thrill us and form the basis of what many folks believe to be true. Why? What is it about these subjects that is so compelling that it causes people to innately believe in mystery and mysticism despite their most rational intentions?

- If you talk to your friends and associates, most of them probably won't recognise the names Alan Guth or Leonard Suskind, even though they are among the most important theoretical physicists and cosmologists of our day. The same goes for Paul Dirac and Richard Feynman. Working independently over the course of a few decades, they helped develop what is now a standard theory about the very early universe. In spite of the fact that they explored what may turn out to be the central phenomenon that makes everything we know possible, they are virtually unknown to most people. Yet the same people who are not familiar with the names of these great intellectuals universally recognize the names of Merlin the Magician and Gandalf the Wizard, who are both fictional characters.

How Do We Know What We Think We Know?

Sometimes our language betrays us. Consider the following well-known and oft-employed phrases:

- "I refuse to believe it unless I see it for myself!"
- "You'll never convince me...."
- "That's unbelievable!"
- "You won't believe what just happened!"

The hidden truth in all these statements is that most of us are creatures of personal experience. We may claim to be rational. We may consider ourselves openminded. We may honestly think we are receptive to proven facts and figures. Nevertheless, many of us still accept things as true only if they fit into our current worldview and system of beliefs, which are universally formed through personal experience and conversion, not education.

In order to accept something, we usually need to personalize it. So if we don't see a flying saucer with our own eyes, if we don't undergo a transcendent experience, if we don't personally engage in a psychic phenomenon, we have a hard time accepting it. After it happens, we become believers for life, but no book, no TV show, no story, will, in and of itself, really convert a skeptic. As far as worldviews go, we are, each of us, our own judge and jury. If we experience something as true, we call it a belief. If we don't, we label it faith. In the court of modernity, belief trumps faith every time.

That's why it's so hard for many people to accept the idea that life simply doesn't work the way we think it does and that most of what we believe to be true is really an illusion. It also explains why the real story behind much of our history is so often suppressed. If self-appointed, accredited gatekeepers of education want to promote their own worldview, which they honestly believe to be true, it only makes sense that they keep opposing ideas hidden from the students they are trying to educate. Why muddy the waters with evidence that conflicts with orthodox opinion? That's why academics often express disdain for TV shows. They can control what is said in their classrooms. They can't control the content of the History Channel.

Beginning in April 1989, a growing group of protestors in China began demonstrating for basic human rights. The demonstrations culminated in what we in the West commonly call the Tiananmen Square protests in Beijing. In mainland China this is referred to as the June Fourth Incident.

To this day, in China, you won't hear a single mention of the event if it presents even a shadow of criticism of the Chinese government. The entire news media suppresses every TV show, every Twitter feed, every Facebook reference, and every social media contact or email that talks about what happened there. As far as the Chinese government is concerned, the whole thing never occurred. If they can keep their citizens from knowing about it, it never happened.

We in the West, who have seen the pictures and heard the reports of the students who were there, know better. If no one knows about it, however, it never took place.

This is a deplorable situation. In order to be free, people need to know the truth. We can justly criticize the Chinese government for such suppression. The truth, however, is that this kind of behavior goes on, to a greater or lesser extent, everywhere, including in the United States.

The reason Jack Nicholson's character from the movie *A Few Good Men* was able to create a now-famous catch phrase "You can't handle the truth!" is that so many people in positions of power—political, religious, or academic—really believe it when it comes to dealing with the public.

As a former college professor, I've seen this play out in academic institutions. While talking to experts in various fields, I have grown used to hearing similar stories of suppression. While reading about suppressed histories, I have come across horror stories of broken and shattered lives, some of which I will share in the following pages. Sometimes it isn't convenient, for a host of reasons, for scholars and specialists to reveal anomalies in their fields of study. Fear is a great motivator, and it has been (and apparently still is) used to suppress inconvenient truths.

How do we open our eyes to possibilities that might explain questions that are so troublesome they are often, intentionally or not, hidden from us and tacitly banned from our educational facilities? Like children, we allow the "adults" of the entrenched culture to "protect" us from inconvenient truths that they feel we might not be able to handle. When politicians pivot away from embarrassing questions, we can usually spot the subterfuge. When seemingly very smart academic or religious specialists imply they know more than we do, however, we assume our questions are silly and will only serve to reveal our ignorance.

It takes courage to say, "This may be a stupid question, but...." Consider a few examples:

- Before the 1960s, experts "knew" there had been no American pre-Columbian contact with European cultures. We were told it was not possible to cross the North Atlantic in boats available to seafarers of that day. If high school students like me even brought up the possibilities, we were told to refer to our textbooks. There we would find the orthodox opinions of the experts. But then came the discovery of a Viking settlement at L'Anse aux Meadows in Newfoundland. In just a few short years, once the doors—and, more importantly, minds—were opened, it began to appear that Scandinavians came early to the American party.

Perhaps Dr. Albert Goodyear, who pushed back dates for the first Americans even further by at least 35,000 years with his excavations at the South Carolina Topper archeological site, said it best: "You don't find what you're not looking for."

- Before 1994 we "knew" that the agricultural revolution and subsequent experiments in civilization began in Mesopotamia about 6,000 years ago. To suggest anything other than that was to earn ridicule and scorn from established professors. Even Egyptian culture could not have been more ancient because it was an established fact that no one anywhere else in the world had the technology and sophistication to build great, stone structures such as the pyramids. Then came the discovery of Göbekli Tepe, built at least 6,000 years earlier, and suddenly the world of traditional archeology was turned upside down.

- As the nineteenth century drew to a close, physicists believed they had pretty well figured out the nature of reality. The natural world had revealed its secrets. It consisted of matter (the stuff of the cosmos) and fields (the cosmic ocean in which the stuff floated). That was about it. The laws of gravity governed both. It was at this time that a young man named Max Planck was faced with a decision. He was a gifted pianist with a promising future, but he was fascinated by physics as well. Coming to a crossroads that would determine what he would do with his life, he consulted one of his professors. He was told, "Physics is finished, young man. It's a dead-end street! You'd be better off becoming a concert pianist." Max, as it turns out, refused the advice, which turned out to be the best decision he ever made. He was awarded the Nobel Prize in 1918. By 1925, classical physics pretty much fell apart in terms of scientists keeping their grip on what was until then called reality. The quantum realm had conquered the field.

Suppressed History

These few examples illustrate a central premise of this book. When we talk about "suppressed" history, we are not demeaning the progress and intention of science in general. It is, and will probably always remain, a superb method of shining the light of knowledge into the darkness of ignorance.

No, the problem is not science, *per se*. It's how science is often presented.

Established teachers, writers, and professors are human. They have to deal with their own human frailties. One of those frailties is ego. Once scholars are convinced by a particular bit of orthodoxy, it's hard for them to admit they were wrong when new light illuminates the truth. The problem is compounded after textbooks are published and reams of material are distributed. When you test students on something and insist that they parrot back to you what you have taught them, it can be humiliating to later say, "Sorry about that. I was wrong." It's far easier to suppress new evidence and hope it will go away. It's not that a secret cabal exists that deliberately withholds evidence and distorts knowledge, although that has happened in the past and undoubtedly continues to this day in some areas; it's just that humans don't like to admit that they're wrong.

Take the famous example of the first people to come to North America. Fifty years ago, almost every history textbook used in public schools throughout the United States taught that the human race spread out around the world from its genesis in Africa. In the 1950s, this "Out of Africa" theory had only recently, and with much controversy, replaced the belief that the human race began in the Fertile Crescent's Garden of Eden. Much later, the story continued, a thousand-mile-wide land bridge connected Siberia to Alaska, and a corridor through the glaciers opened up for a time, allowing humans to follow migrating herds of mammoths and other now-extinct species right into the heart of the virgin American continent.

I remember well the excellent pictures that I devoured in my fifth and sixth grade history texts. They have stayed with me for more than sixty years. That shows how easily young minds can be molded, and once shaped, they are difficult to reconfigure.

A few years later, during the early 1970s, we were told that because humans were such efficient hunters, they killed off the great megafauna of North America. Their primary weapon was the Clovis projectile point. Carbon dating of mastodon kills near Clovis, New Mexico, provided a time frame of between 8,000 to 13,000 years ago. Because this was the earliest clear indication of human activity in America, it was assumed that these were the first people to enter the North American continent.

"Clovis First" became the basic orthodoxy. Anyone disputing it was not just confronted, they were ridiculed in classrooms and in print. Quite a few archeologists went to their graves feeling humiliated, their reputation in tatters.

Those who fought on, refusing to suppress evidence that wouldn't stay buried in sites such as those found in Chile, Pennsylvania, Virginia, Oklahoma, and South Carolina, didn't conform to traditional guidelines. Reputable archeologists at those sites and others seemed confident they were dealing with material much older than a mere 8,000 to 13,000 years.

They were subsequently derided and mocked. To this very day, there are a few archeologists who warn their doctoral students to suppress any pre-Clovis evidence they unearth because it might ruin their careers if they make their discoveries public.

Eventually, some obstinate specialists persevered and raised doubts in the minds of a new generation of archeologists. Clovis First is no longer universally accepted. Fresh ideas and new avenues of entrance into the Americas are now acceptable.

Those who tout the march of science point to examples such as this as proof that the scientific method works. It takes time, they say, but it is a sure thing. New ideas *will* see the light of day. Patience is a virtue. Fresh ideas require fresh evidence.

All that is true, but it is hardly a comfort to those who went to their graves feeling humiliated and rejected.

What this means is that common courtesy in academia is not only polite, it is essential. Although most folks don't like to admit it, the field of science is as drenched in ego and ideology as the field of religion. When *facts* confront each other, they can be compared and contrasted. When *ideologies* collide, too often the human thing to do, unfortunately, is to denigrate your opponent's character rather than their argument.

Niels Bohr once called Richard Feynman an "idiot" right in front of a gathering of the greatest theoretical physicists in the world to whom Feynman had just introduced his now-accepted theory of electrodynamics.

Hugh Everett's Many Worlds theory is probably as important as Einstein's theory of relativity, but Everett died a tragic death after years of being blackballed from the world of physics.

Warren K. Moorhead was told his ideas were preposterous, and he was quickly laughed off the archeological stage when he first suggested that a maritime archaic civilization existed in Maine as early as 5,000 years ago. He died thinking he was a complete failure. Although he was right, and is now considered a genius, it is a matter of public record that no archeologist has yet officially apologized for destroying Dr. Moorhead's life.

Suppressing history is not science. Using the tools of ridicule and humiliation when confronting innovative solutions to weak historical arguments is not helpful. Indeed, it only creates dissension and polarization. Not every conjecture is true just because it is new, but it ought to at least be treated with respect because it just might be a harbinger of the next breakthrough.

Clarifications

In this book we're going to explore some big ideas, many of which were met with ridicule when first introduced but that might provide answers to perplexing questions. Most have been suppressed in the sense that they have yet to enter the mainstream. Some suggest the work of natural forces that have yet to be fully understood. Others are much more suspicious because they postulate that we are not alone in the universe or, even more controversially, the multiverse.

This takes us into the field of study now popularly called "ancient alien theory."

Before we begin, we'll need to make clear what we mean when we use the words "ancient" and "alien." If your thoughts immediately turn to little green men in flying saucers, you need to reboot your mental software. It's obsolete. You might want to update to a new way of understanding what many scientists, cosmologists, philosophers, and even theologians now consider to be a basic, fundamental fact of nature:

We are not alone, and we never were.

We have a cosmic purpose beyond that which is immediately apparent to our five senses.

This theory is no longer the exclusive domain of metaphysics, religion, and the supernatural. If you have trouble with that, you need to get over it because it becomes more obvious every day that the filters of our five senses keep us isolated from the fact that most of what goes on in the universe takes place beyond our ability to physically perceive it.

Psychics, working only with the tools of their highly trained intuitive abilities, have long known this to be true. Religious scholars have been writing about angels from a parallel dimension called Heaven for thousands of years. Mystics and shamans have been communicating for millennia with entities from other worlds.

Until recently, we didn't have the computer-driven skills to explore those worlds. Now, given the eleven dimensions of string theory, radio telescopes that penetrate to the event horizon of our universe, mathematical equations that take us where no one has gone before, and the worldwide sharing of experiences old and new that speak of long-forgotten, ancient mythologies that reveal historical truths, new vistas have opened up.

When we use the word "alien" today, it is no longer limited to nuts-and-bolts spaceships, although it certainly includes them. No, "alien" also refers to that which is outside the perceivable range of our five senses. Because it is outside normal experience, it is "alien" to us. That's all. What else can we call it?

The bottom of the sea, where we have never been able to go before, is an "alien" environment. The Moon and Mars, both of which we have visited with the aid of technology, are "alien" bodies in space. We thus need to rethink our use of the word "alien." It's a good word. Let's not surrender it just because it's been ridiculed and suppressed.

Similarly, the word "ancient" needs a new definition. We used to think that pre-agricultural civilizations were ancient. We used to think that a five-billion-year-old planet is ancient. We used to think that a 13.8-billion-year-old universe is ancient. Now we wonder what happened *before* the beginning and even what came before that. New ideas about the nature of time and space are pushing "ancient" towards "eternity" and "infinity."

"Ancient alien," therefore, refers to forces—and possibly even hard-to-imagine sentient entities—that are outside our normal perception realm and incredibly old by earthly standards.

What this means is that, given this definition, if you agree that "In the beginning, God created the heavens and the earth," then you believe in an ancient alien. After all, you can't get more "ancient" or "alien" than God.

At Christmas time, if you sing "Hark! The Herald Angels Sing," you believe in ancient aliens. How else do you describe vocalists from another dimension?

If you contemplate Vishnu sitting on the cosmic ocean while dreaming the world into existence, you believe in ancient aliens.

If you suspect that an angel named Gabriel appeared to the Old Testament's Daniel, the New Testament's Virgin Mary, and the Qur'an's Mohammad, you believe in ancient aliens.

If you accept Schrödinger's idea that things in the quantum world can only come about in the presence of an observer, you believe in an ancient alien of some kind. Who else was there to observe the Big Bang?

It's as simple as that. Don't let prejudicial semantics get in the way. Penetrate to the core of religious reality and you will find an ancient alien, whatever its name. The universe is a big place. There's plenty of room for mystery beyond our ability to understand it.

The multiverse is even bigger. Contemplating the mysterious origins of an infinity of space and time can keep you awake at night. But the temptation to throw your hands in the air and walk away from the task of trying to understand is the one certain way to halt progress and the relentless sweep of science. We wouldn't have come this far if something didn't intend us to continue, even if that something is only human curiosity. As far as we know, we are the only creatures on the planet with the will to think about who we are and the imagination to project those thoughts into the future. Suppressing even the most outlandish thoughts won't take us further down the road.

Our Method

In order to begin the quest, we have set for ourselves, we'll start with big ideas about the cosmos itself. Then we'll move on to the beginnings of life, eventually progressing to the human race and its developing civilizations. At each stage of the journey we'll first examine the prevalent, orthodox, standard view currently in vogue. Then we'll proceed to look at alternative theories: first those that find their impetus in nature itself and then those that move to the possibilities of ancient alien intervention, always remembering how we just defined the phrase "ancient alien." It's a huge, loaded subject that needs to be examined, not suppressed.

At the end of this journey together we will arrive at a new beginning, a starting point from which we can all continue our own research, and a "big idea" about why we are here at all. Hopefully, this survey will spark fresh ways of thinking and allow us to build on the work of those who have come before.

Sometimes, in order to see farther into the future, it helps to stand on the shoulders of giants. What we are about to do is explore the work of those giants. They have much to teach us. Let's begin!

THE BIG PICTURE:
ORIGINS OF
THE COSMOS

PRIME THEORY

THE BIG BANG

In 2007 a comedy named *The Big Bang Theory* debuted on CBS TV. It starred Jim Parsons as Sheldon Cooper and Johnny Galecki as Leonard Hofstadter, two brilliant but socially challenged physicists, along with a cast of off-beat characters who help them adapt to the morass of twenty-first-century popular culture. When the show became a hit, its very name catapulted the primary theory of how the universe began into the popular consciousness. The term "Big Bang" was coined by Sir Fred Hoyle, an English astronomer and cosmologist, in 1949 and has been well-known to astrophysicists ever since, but it took the TV show to make it a part of everyday contemporary language. If you Google "Big Bang Theory" these days, you'll discover that half the references relate to the scientific theory, and half to the TV comedy.

The first use of the phrase "Big Bang Theory" was derisive in nature. When Hoyle first used those words, it was as part of a BBC radio broadcast on astronomy. He didn't accept the fact that the universe had a beginning, other than by the hand of a god he came to believe in only later in his life. Instead, he believed in what is called the Steady State Universe, a concept we'll tackle later in this chapter. When he said the universe began with a "Big Bang," he meant to belittle the concept. Now it has come to be accepted by the great majority of astrophysicists.

The basic concept is that the universe we look at today through our powerful radio telescopes and the vast technological resources now available to scientists everywhere began some 13.8 billion years ago when an almost infinitely small, infinitely hot, and infinitely complex singularity that contained the potential for everything that is, suddenly exploded. As it expanded it carried all of space and time with it.

We can never see this event, of course. We can only imagine it. It became apparent when astronomers first recognized that every galaxy and every star in the universe is racing away from one other in every direction. If you draw a series of dots on the surface of a deflated balloon, and then blow it up, you'll have a good mental picture of the process. Imagine a film showing this expansion, and then play the film backward in your mind. Everything that is moving out and away will now be moving closer and closer together, until eventually it all meets at one point. That point is called a singularity.

Ultimately, the only way to describe the process is through mathematical formulas, but the leftover cosmic radiation can be detected as an "echo" or "afterglow" throughout the universe. It is known as cosmic microwave background.

This cosmic microwave background was discovered by accident. In 1965, Arno Penzias and Robert Wilson worked for Bell Telephone Laboratories in New Jersey. They were building a radio receiver and couldn't eliminate a hissing sound that pervaded their work. They tried everything to get rid of it, even resorting to sweeping out the antenna equipment because they thought pigeons had left droppings in the works. They killed what turned out to be innocent pigeons and cleaned up their mess, but the noises persisted.

American physicist and radio astronomer Arno Penzias (1933–; left) and astronomer Robert Woodrow Wilson (1936–) received the 1978 Nobel Prize in Physics for their discovery of the cosmic radio background radiation indicative of the Big Bang.

Meanwhile, however, Robert Dicke led a team of researchers at Princeton University who were studying the problem of cosmic microwave background, now called CMB. When he heard about the problem Penzias and Wilson had encountered, he wondered whether they might be hearing the leftover noise that emanated from the original big bang at the beginning of the universe.

After a thorough study both teams published papers in the *Astrophysical Journal* in 1965 and a new theory was announced.

From pigeon poop to the origin of the universe. That's how science works sometimes.

The cosmic radiation background was brilliantly photographed and rendered by NASA's Cosmic Background Explorer, the COBE, in the last decade of the twentieth century. By now, most people have seen subsequent photographs, even though they may not understand exactly what they are looking at. The work continues through the European Space Agency's Plank satellite, which, in 2013, calculated the age of the universe at 13.82 billion years old.

Still, though, many questions remain. The Big Bang Theory says something "banged," and estimates when, but what banged? And why? How did it bang? What came before the bang? And how did it get so big so fast?

Many religionists were quick to jump on the bandwagon because a big bang sounds suspiciously like God saying, "Let there be light." But there are problems with this concept.

First of all, the light didn't show up for at least 380,000 Earth years after the initial explosion. In the first second of the beginning of the new universe, its surrounding temperature measured an astounding 10 billion degrees Fahrenheit, or 5.5 billion degrees Celsius. All kinds of neutrons, protons, and electrons were careening about, forming a kind of cosmic cloud that gradually either combined or decayed as the universe cooled. Light wasn't yet visible. It took at least 380,000 years for light, or photons, to become visible. When they did, and not until, they formed the cosmic microwave background.

But the complex math required to understand all this raises even more questions. There is a lot of energy left unaccounted for in the visible universe that we study today. Only about 5 percent of it is made up of such things as planets, stars, and galaxies. Where's the rest of it?

This leads to now-famous theories about dark matter and dark energy. The math says they're there, somewhere. We just can't see it with the technology now available to us.

Other questions persist as well. According to traditional physics, nothing can travel faster than the speed of light. Albert Einstein himself discovered the speed limit. Light travels at 186,000 miles (299,792 kilometers) per second.

To get a mental handle on this, think about it this way. If you set out to travel around the world, moving at the speed of light, you could follow the equator seven and a half times around in one second. Remember that, on your next coast-to-coast, five-hour (not counting a layover in Atlanta) airplane flight.

To make matters worse, since its inception, the universe has undergone what physicists call "epochs." But to make the math work, many of these epochs were contained within the first second, that's right, "second," of its existence. As a matter of fact, current theory holds that more happened in the first second after the big bang than has happened in the last 13.8 billion years.

Skipping all the math, here's a quick run-down of the history of the universe:

Zero to 10^{-43} seconds: *The Planck Epoch*

Very little is known about this time period. It's about as close to "in the beginning" as we will ever be able to go using today's knowledge. Einstein's General Relativity formulas propose a gravitational singularity, but it might be that the four fundamental forces that govern everything in existence (electromagnetic, weak nuclear, strong nuclear, and gravitational) were all somehow unified at this point, held together in perfect symmetry. Picture a sharp pencil standing on its point. It looks great, but you know it can't last. Rather quickly, something has to give.

Picture a sharp pencil standing on its point. It looks great, but you know it can't last. Rather quickly, something has to give.

How big was the universe back then? Not big enough to even imagine. Technically, estimates run to an area described as one Planck Length. That's 10^{-20} times as big as a proton. As for its temperature, you wouldn't want to vacation there. It's so hot that at that temperature the laws of physics cease to exist.

10^{-43} to 10^{-36} seconds—*The Grand Unification Epoch*

The main event during this epoch was that the force of gravity separated from the other three forces, which remained unified. The very earliest elementary particles and antiparticles began to form.

10^{-36} to 10^{-32} seconds—*The Inflationary Epoch*

This may be the hardest epoch to understand. Somehow the strong nuclear force asserted itself and separated from the pack. The universe underwent such an expansion that to call it "rapid" is a bit silly. In a fraction of a second, much faster than the speed of light allows, the universe expanded from an infinitely small point to the size of a grapefruit.

How? No one understands. Why? That's even murkier, but the expansion is still going on today. It's just not happening so fast.

10^{-36} to 10^{-12} seconds—*The Electroweak Epoch*

All kinds of weird, exotic particles interacted during this epoch. They're called W and Z bosons, and the newly discovered Higgs boson. This formed the now-famous Higgs field, which slows down particles so that their energy becomes mass, allowing the future formation of the material universe that we all know and love. In other words, energy was now converted to mass, thus making possible Einstein's great equation, $E = mc^2$ (Energy equals mass times the speed of light squared).

10^{-12} to 10^{-6} seconds—*The Quark Epoch*

Now things start to get familiar. The universe cooled down to a mere 10 quadrillion degrees so the four familiar forces (remember them from the Planck Epoch? Electromagnetic, weak nuclear, strong nuclear, and gravitational) that govern everything we know could now begin to work their magic. It still was a pretty formidable place. Quarks, electrons, and neutrinos formed in huge numbers and began to collide, annihilating each other, but by a mysterious process called baryogenesis, one quark in every billion pairs survived.

Why is this important? Because they soon combined to form matter.

10^{-6} to 1 second—*The Hadron Epoch*

During the Hadron Epoch the temperature of the universe cooled to a balmy trillion degrees. This allowed quarks to form hadrons such as protons and neutrons. When electrons began to collide with protons, they fused together to form neutrinos that had no mass, but could travel through space freely, if you consider that by this time space was only a little bigger than the size of a basketball. Still, though, even given the limited room to maneuver, they reached nearly the speed of light. They continue their explorations to this very day, but now they have a lot more room to maneuver. The only rule they follow is that their overall charge and energy must be conserved.

INTERMISSION

We have now been through the first six epochs in the history of the early universe, which is, in Earth time, only one second old. How big was it back then? Consider this fact. Our Milky Way Galaxy is about 100,000 light years across. In other words, it takes a beam of light only 100,000 years to travel from one side to the other. The whole observable universe didn't reach this size until it was about three years old.

The Milky Way galaxy where Earth resides consists of hundreds of billions of stars, including our sun.

But here we run into a real problem. As we'll soon learn, the question about size is pointless because the universe may not have a measurable boundary. And remember that the "universe" itself is not really expanding. It's the space inside it that is pushing everything apart.

It might be a good idea to stop at this point and get things into some sort of perspective. We accept all these facts and figures because a few very intelligent people agree that they are true. Those people teach at places such as Cambridge and MIT, so we have to have faith that they know what they're talking about.

But at the risk of inserting a grain of grit into the grindings of this huge, academic, justifiably impressive machine, we need to ask a few questions. They are questions that Albert Einstein struggled with for much of his life:

- Is there still room for common sense in cosmic speculation, or will common sense prove to be an illusion?

- If so, how did something so fundamental, something that shaped our very existence as a species, prove to be a mirage?

- Has common sense been leading us down a blind alley all this time?

Theoretical physicists are just folks. They are all very bright, of course, but they come with their own set of preconceived opinions, egos, and prejudices. They have logged countless hours studying very complex mathematical equations. They have spent a lot of money and labored long in the academic vineyard to obtain their prestigious and justifiably earned right to be respected and admired. They are very intelligent and undoubtedly know more than almost everyone else about the mystifying enigmas of origins.

And that's a problem when it comes to the idea of suppression of knowledge. Scientists don't set out to keep secrets. That goes against the very principles upon which their life is based, but as they learn more and more, studying an extremely complicated and specialized body of evidence, the further they progress the fewer people they can talk to who understand what they are saying. Because they are people, just like everyone else, is it any wonder that they might occasionally get frustrated and belittle mundane arguments they long ago surpassed? And in their frustration, can we blame them if they sometimes snap out in anger and belittle someone who is struggling with questions that they grew tired of explaining when they taught first-year graduate students?

In this case, suppression is not deliberate. It is not done out of malicious intent. It is simply a human reaction to a frustrating dilemma.

But the history of science is also littered with the detritus of ideas we once "knew" to be true and protected with vigor in an attempt to shore up a professional reputation. Big Bang theory is no different. It's obtuse and simple at the same time. Anyone can imagine it without really understanding all—or even some—of the mathematical ins and outs. Is it true? No one knows. Once we accept it, it becomes very easy to suppress anything else. And, as we shall soon see, there are many alternative theories put forth by equally smart people.

That being said, now that we are armed with at least a modicum of cautious skepticism, we can continue.

One second to three minutes—*The Lepton Epoch*

We now enter an epoch that is all of three minutes, minus one second, long. Most of the hadrons and antihadrons have collided and annihilated each other, so leptons and antileptons now dominate the material substance of the universe. Electrons and positrons are free to collide. When they do, energy is freed up in the form of photons. When the photons collide, they form pairs of electrons and positrons.

Three minutes to 20 minutes—*A Time of Nucleosynthesis*

Spring comes to the early universe. The temperature falls to a billion degrees or so, and atomic nuclei begin to form through a process called nuclear fusion, but, as is often the case with Spring, its time is short. After 20 minutes or so it becomes too cool for fusion to work, and things begin to take on a semblance of what we might begin to call normalcy.

From three minutes to 240,000 years—*The Photon Epoch*

It is now summer in the universe. It fills up with plasma—kind of a thick soup of electrons and atomic nuclei. Photons rule in terms of energy output. There is still a lot of contact between photons, electrons, and atomic nuclei, but things are relatively calm.

240,000 to 300,000 years—*Let There Be Light!*

It's a nice day in the universe. Temperatures fall to about 3,000 degrees, roughly the current temperature that we find on the surface of the sun. All sorts of things can now happen, but the most important, at least from our perspective, is this: Light begins to shine!

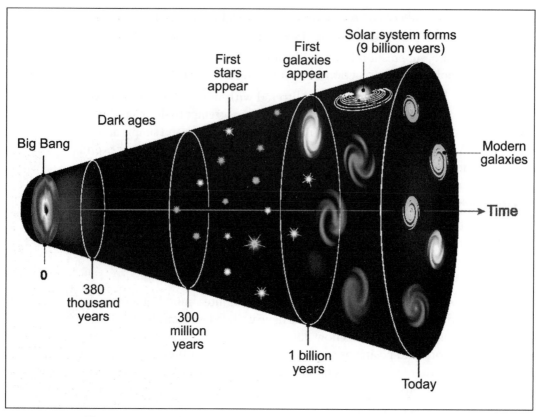

The universe as we know it took billions of years to form as matter and energy gradually resolved themselves into stars, planets, solar systems, and galaxies.

Ionized hydrogen and helium atoms begin to capture the odd electron and hold it in orbit. A process called recombination begins. The importance of this is that the electric charge of the electrons is neutralized. Now that electrons have recombined with atoms, the universe becomes, for the first time, transparent, as it were. Light now shines in the darkness. It is the earliest epoch we can observe. Photons are now free to move about; the same photons that we have discovered make up the cosmic background radiation. In other words, this is the first universe we can begin to observe and study. It consisted of a dim fog formed by about 75 percent hydrogen and 25 percent helium, with just a pinch or so of lithium thrown in for good measure.

300,000 to 150 million years—*The Dark Age*

Just when things started to get interesting, winter descended upon the universe. For a little less than 150 million Earth years there were photons around. In other words, there was light, but no stars had formed yet. The light was diffused, and activity slowed way down. It would have been a boring time to be around, and mysterious "dark matter" ruled the day, but expansion continued, as it does to this day, so it was only a matter of time until things picked up.

150 million years to 1 billion years—*Re-ionization*

The first step forward began when quasars formed as gravity began to collapse pre-structures into themselves. This caused intense radiation levels that re-ionized their surroundings. Hydrogen, having already gone through a metamorphosis a few epochs ago, changed once again.

The universe reversed course and changed back to consisting of a sort of ionized plasma. Small pockets of these gases began to clump together and collapse under the weight of gravity. They soon became hot enough to trigger nuclear fusion again, and the first stars were born. They had relatively short life spans, but they were big—at least a hundred times bigger than our sun. Cosmologists call them metal-free Population III Stars. Eventually they were followed by Population II and finally Population I Stars, each class being formed by the material left behind when the earlier population stars, called supernovas, collapsed under their own weight. Clumps of these stars formed around each other, drawn together by gravitational forces. They formed clusters, and then super clusters.

> The universe reversed course and changed back to consisting of a sort of ionized plasma. Small pockets of these gases began to clump together and collapse under the weight of gravity.

8.5 to 9 billion years ago—*Home at Last*

Finally, our solar system emerged out of the chaos. Our sun was formed—a rather late generation star that incorporated the collapsed, exploding material from generation after generation of stars that previously existed, had their day in the sun, so to speak, and then imploded. Our solar system, formed by more exploding debris, formed about 5 billion years ago. All in all, it took between 8 and 9 billion years after the Big Bang to make our 'hood. It still wasn't ready for us. That took a lot more time and is another story that we'll explore later, but in the end, out of nothing—something, and out of chaos—order. Or at least what we call order.

Meanwhile the universe continues to expand, but so does the number of questions:

EXPANSION

Take the matter of expansion, for instance. The universe is expanding. That we can measure, but only recently have we come to understand that the expansion, driven by forces unknown, is speeding up. Eventually, if things continue on as they are now, we won't be able to see faraway galaxies. They will have outdistanced their own light waves. Our telescopes won't be able to bridge the gap between them and us.

Then what happens? Are we destined to live in a cold, uncommunicative cosmos that, because of unmanageable distances, couldn't answer our questions even if it tried? And if the universe continues to expand, what is it expanding into? By definition, it can't be expanding into space because space itself is what is expanding. How are we to conceive of space expanding into "nothing," or, more accurately, "something" that doesn't yet exist?

Of all the questions that drive cosmologists nuts, this is one of the biggies. Because it is so intuitive, it is the one most often asked by laypeople. That can make even the most balanced physicist a bit testy at times.

The answer depends on astronomical philosophy, not science. It demands more faith than evidence, and that's anathema to a proper scientist. If space has a boundary, then there must somewhere be an edge where space ends and "nothing" begins, but what is the nature of "nothing?" So it's common to say, as did Stephen Hawking, that space has no boundary. Here the scientist usually tries to employ a visual aid of some kind. He or she might roll a piece of paper into a tube and talk about something called curved space, that eventually folds in on itself, but the illustration doesn't really work because the piece of paper obviously exists to our eyes as existing "in" something, even if only the environment in which it is used to illustrate the idea of "nothing."

In short, it's a maddening question because no one knows the answer, or even if the question itself is valid. To journey very far into these kinds of thought patterns can lead to madness. Are we to live forever frustrated by questions that haunt our existence but are destined to remain beyond our reach? Will the curiosity that lifted us up from the world of animals and that drove our evolution turn out to be our undoing?

Author and scholar of mythology Joseph Campbell (1904–1987) talked of a universe that was not the first but just a reincarnation of many past universes.

No wonder we can safely talk about suppressed histories. Who wants to even bring up a subject for which there is no answer? It is far easier for the professor-in-charge to leave the question unasked and then patronize the poor layperson who does so, acting as if the question is really dumb.

If that has ever happened to you, take comfort in a famous quote from Joseph Campbell: "The psychotic drowns in the same waters where the mystic swims." Don't be afraid to be a mystic!

THE MULTIVERSE

In 2014, Alan Guth, one of the principle architects of inflation theory, said that most models of inflation lead to the idea of a Multiverse, rather than a Universe.

To better understand what he meant, picture a pot of water on a hot stove. As it begins to boil, bubbles form. As we have just seen, right after the Big Bang, during the Inflationary Epic, the universe expanded exponentially at a rate much faster than the speed of light. A point, or perhaps field, of unimaginable energy that still existed only as potential was somehow triggered by something—no one knows what—that caused space and time to grow, virtually instantaneously, into the material that built the universe we view today.

If the Inflationary Epic produced what we call space/time, it must have also produced other space/times. In other words, bubbles formed in what we just called a "field of unimaginable energy," just as they do in a boiling pot of water. The water is the field of energy. The bubbles are universes. Each one became a potential space/time cosmos.

Ours is one of them, but just one of many. Hence the term "Multiverse," rather than "Universe." The bubbles might have merged, grew bigger, and eventually popped. Some were very big, and others were quite small. The big ones formed by absorbing adjacent bubbles. Some lasted a long time. Others popped right away.

If we evolved in any one of those bubbles, we would be unaware of the fact that adjacent bubbles were following their own evolutionary paths. They might come and go rather quickly, but what is time compared to forever? If we live in a bubble-type universe that lives and dies over a few billion years, that seems like an immensely long time to us, but what are a few billion years when it comes to eternity? Eternity isn't just a long, long time. Eternity has nothing to do with time. Time exists within eternity. How can we creatures of time possibly get our minds around a concept like that? It's quite literally impossible for us, and its very frustrating to think we might be surrounded by separate universes that we will never be able to comprehend, let alone contact.

A brahma and the lotus illustrate the infinite cycle of the creation of galaxies.

INFLATION/DEFLATION

A third set of questions revolve around the idea of inflation. Did inflation happen once? Is it still going on? Or is it cyclical? Will the universe someday "deflate?"

In other words, what we call the beginning, or the Big Bang, might have been a unique event, but it is conceivable that a Big Bang happens over and over again. Although it is almost impossible to imagine, there might never have been a first cause that produced a first Big Bang.

Or, to tweak the idea just a bit, perhaps the universe has undergone many inflationary periods. Maybe we just happen to be living in one such phase. Perhaps countless other universes have appeared and eventually produced a thinking species such as us, who contemplated this same question. It's similar to the movie *Groundhog Day*, in which Bill Murray wakes up each morning to face the same day over and over again. Except in this case, a "day" lasts for billions of years.

In other words, the universe itself might be merely a reincarnation of countless previous universes. Joseph Campbell once described this theory using the classic cycles of Hinduism called *Samsara*:

> Vishnu sleeps in the cosmic ocean, and the lotus of the universe grows from his navel. On the lotus sits Brahma, the creator. Brahma opens his eyes, and a world comes into being. Brahma closes his eyes, and a world goes out of being. The life of a Brahma is 432,000 years. When he dies, the lotus goes back, and another lotus is formed, and another Brahma. Then think of the galaxies beyond galaxies in infinite space, each a lotus, with a Brahma sitting on it, opening his eyes, closing his eyes....

> —Joseph Campbell, speaking to
> Bill Moyers in *The Power of Myth*

This old, old spiritual wisdom and insight now seems to have been given flesh and blood through the discoveries of cosmology. All that we call "normal" might be merely a segment of an eternal unity. It is a snapshot—a still photo that is part of an ever-turning movie reel, and we are but small characters in the plot of a supernatural drama, connected on every level but unable, in our present material form, to understand the whole story.

THE PROBLEM OF QUANTUM OBSERVATION

Quantum theory itself raises more questions. To paraphrase a very difficult subject, a basic tenant of quantum reality is that the observer creates reality.

For all our lives we have been taught that we live "in" a universe that exists "out there" whether we are around to observe it or not. When we die, the universe continues without us.

But as counterintuitive as it sounds, the truth seems to be that nothing happens at the quantum level without an observer. Scientists say it doesn't happen until somebody measures it.

This is the idea that gave Einstein fits. "Do you mean that the moon isn't there unless I look at it?" he once famously asked.

Brian Greene, in his book *The Fabric of the Cosmos*, pointed out that "when we measure an electron's position we are not measuring an objective, preexisting feature of reality. Rather, the act of measuring is deeply enmeshed in creating the very reality it is measuring."

In other words, it's not that measuring an electron reveals either its location or its velocity, depending on the method you employ. No, observing it brings it into existence. *Where* was it before someone looked at it? *What* was it before someone looked at it? The best we can say, given the limitation of language, is that it was a "wave function," a probability, a possibility, even a thought. When someone observed it, it "collapsed" into what was observed.

Now comes the big question. In order for the initial singularity to collapse into the visible universe, it could only have happened in the presence of an observer of some kind. If that rule is broken, quantum mechanics falls apart. Did consciousness of some kind exist before the initial singularity—the Big Bang?

It had to! Where else do quantum particles come from? If particles come into existence only when intentionally observed, who or what was present at the Big Bang to cause the initial singularity to collapse into material existence?

Where does anything come from? Where does anything go? Energy somehow became reality. An observing consciousness brought about material existence.

How can we accurately perceive that which is beyond our ability to intellectually grasp? Can we trust our mathematics? Can we accept what seems so outside our experience? It's a problem because if Quantum Theory is correct, it automatically assumes a Consciousness preceded creation, and that sounds suspiciously like either a religious concept or, at the very least, an alien alternative concept, depending again on how we define "alien."

THE MYTHOLOGY OF SCIENCE

Where does all this leave us?

Make no mistake, science and the quest for understanding are wonderful things. Science drives us forward and makes possible a way of life unprecedented in the history of the human race. It reveals heights of knowledge our grandparents never dreamed of.

But science, as close as it comes to reality, needs to be kept in balance. Just because something is "true" today doesn't mean it will stand the test of tomorrow's new evidence.

Scientists are ordinary people who need to consider the possibility that they might have, without realizing it, formed an ideology that could compromise their objectivity. They need to demonstrate humility, just like everyone else.

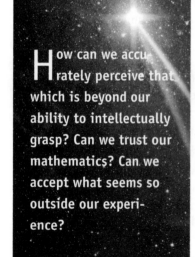

How can we accurately perceive that which is beyond our ability to intellectually grasp? Can we trust our mathematics? Can we accept what seems so outside our experience?

As in every field, there are a few scientific rock stars who deserve special consideration because of their talent and insight, but ego-based ideology is a constant threat. Cosmologists and theoretical physicists who study origins need to remember that what they reveal is a story—a mythology that attempts to explain the origins of the Universe, or Multiverse. It might be the most accurate story going right now, but it is still a story. No one was there to see it happen and, as we have just seen, it's a pretty fantastic tale.

Besides that, there are other stories that might be equally plausible. Some of them are based on hard evidence, put forth by scientists with credentials just as impressive as those who came up with the idea of a Big Bang at the beginning of time. Others are more speculative. Some are new, others are as old as the first people who looked up at the skies and wondered.

One of my favorite speeches of all time was given by Robert Jastrow, an eminent American astronomer, physicist, and cosmologist, in his response to receiving an award for discovering the background radiation that appears to prove the theory of an initial Big Bang:

> At this moment it seems as though science will never be able to raise the curtain on the mystery of creation. For the scientist

who has lived by his faith in the power of reason, the story ends like a bad dream. He has scaled the mountains of ignorance; he is about to conquer the highest peak; as he pulls himself over the final rock, he is greeted by a band of theologians who have been sitting there for centuries.

Those are good words to remember!

NATURAL ALTERNATIVE THEORIES

Now that we've studied the prime origin theory accepted by most cosmologists today, let's look at other theories in contention, any one of which could suddenly inflate in acceptance and replace the Big Bang Theory. Some of them are variations on a theme. Some are from a totally different perspective. All are fascinating! As we begin, we have to do so with an advance warning or two.

First: These are very advanced theories that, to fully understand, require a degree of study, experience, and specialized knowledge that, quite frankly, most of us who haven't spent a lifetime taking and teaching advanced math courses really can't fully understand. They require a nuance and talent that are very rare. For most of us, advanced mathematical formulas don't jump off the page and become full-blown, visualized theories. If we think simple common sense will suffice in the extremely rarified air of advanced quantum physics, we just sound silly to those who know what they are talking about. Many of us wouldn't last a week in even a graduate-level physics program.

Second: These ideas are, in a sense, suppressed, but not by design. Scientists want their ideas out there. They don't do advanced cosmology and then deliberately keep their ideas to themselves out of some kind of feeling that the public is not ready to take on their findings. There is no deep, secret, scientific cabal out there intent on deception for some reason.

But the theories are suppressed just the same because if you want to understand the latest ideas in cosmology you have to work at it. They don't fit on a bumper sticker and you can't just Google "Superstring Theory," read an article, and understand the concepts.

In 1996, David L. Goodstein and his wife wrote a book called *Feynman's Lost Lecture: The Motion of Planets around the Sun*. In that book he wrote:

> [Richard] Feynman was a truly great teacher. He prided himself on being able to devise ways to explain even the most profound ideas to beginning students. Once, I said to him, "Dick, explain to me, so that I can understand it, why spin one-half particles obey Fermi-Dirac statistics." Sizing up his audience perfectly, Feynman said, "I'll prepare a freshman lecture on it." But he came back a few days later to say, "I couldn't do it. I couldn't reduce it to the freshman level. That means we don't really understand it."

So we can't really file these theories away under "Suppressed Origin" theories, implying some kind of malicious intent. They are not being suppressed as part of someone's hidden agenda. They are out there and accessible. It's just that only a few people really understand them in the detail they deserve, so they remain outside the parameters of popular table talk.

Nevertheless, we're going to try to at least present some of them so that anyone who is interested can pursue them. At minimum, we can try to describe them in popular terms, employing well-known illustrations and concepts, to at least whet the appetites of those who are interested. To some laypeople, even these brief summaries will seem hopelessly technical. To others of a scientific bent, they may prove cringe-worthy in their simplified misconceptions.

With that caveat, we proceed.

QUASI STEADY-STATE

In 1948, Fred Hoyle, Hermann Bondi, and Thomas Gold proposed what was then a fairly radical view about the origins of the universe. To put it simply, there was no origin. They called their theory the Steady State Theory and claimed that the universe had no beginning. It always was and always will be.

In some ways, it was an attempt to avoid what some scientists later began to call the "slippery slope of intelligent design." In other words, if there were no beginning, there was no need for a God. This concept effectively separated science from religion.

Theoretical physicist and author Richard Feynman (1918–1988) was corecipient of the Nobel Prize for Physics in 1965. Only after his death, however, did his name become known outside of academic and government circles.

In order to adopt this theory, you had to accept on faith that the universe was infinitely old. As a matter of fact, the word "old" doesn't really apply because how can something with no beginning and no ending even have an age? It simply is. If you try to get your mind around that idea you'll soon discover that it takes a lot of what sounds suspiciously similar to religious faith. Many people who believe in an eternal God do so because that's one of the only ways to explain how everything began. If "this" caused "that," what was the first "this"? The easiest way to answer the question is to say, "In the beginning, God...."

Logically, following this train of thought, an eternal God, or Consciousness, or the Ground of Being, or some other theological proposition, always existed and brought the universe into existence from nothing. The principle was called, in Latin, *ex nihilo*, or "out of nothing."

The centerpiece of the Steady State Theory was that even though the universe was expanding, its density remained constant because matter is constantly being created to compensate for its expansion.

Many in the religious establishment, of course, rose up in righteous indignation, but the scientific community was quick to jump on board partly because it eliminated the need for a first cause. In other words, God.

The idea of an expanding universe, however, had been around ever since Georges Lemaître, a Belgian Catholic priest, first proposed it in 1927. It had become quite popular. As a matter of fact, it was while defending his Steady State Theory that Hoyle coined the derisive term Big Bang. He thought that by belittling it in this way he could gain some points in the popular press. Ridicule has long been used as a way to make the opposition appear foolish while suppressing their ideas.

By the mid-1960s, most cosmologists were convinced that the age of the universe was finite. It had a beginning and will probably have an end of some kind. There had

Belgian astronomer and cosmologist Father Georges Lemaître (1894–1966) was a Jesuit priest who remains notable for observing that nearby galaxies were moving away from us. This led to the idea that our universe is expanding, as later confirmed by Edwin Hubble.

been too much evidence accumulated by this time to deny it, but Hoyle and some new colleagues went back to the drawing boards and managed to put together a modification of their original theory that could account for the new microwave background information that produced the now famous "echo" throughout the universe.

They called their new theory the Quasi Steady-State Theory and put forth the idea that the new evidence could be proof of what they called "creation events," or what appeared to be discrete explosions that occur throughout the entire universe in "creation centers" of dense matter and strong gravitational forces. According to Hoyle, powerful creation events are rare, but one of them took place between 10 and 15 billion years ago. That's the one that produced us. Our neighborhood of the universe expanded rapidly and that's what we now measure, mistaking it for the beginning of the entire universe.

Small creation events are still taking place, according to this theory. We mistake their true reality, calling them quasars and radio waves from distant galaxies. The theory goes into a lot of technical matters involving light elements such as hydrogen, helium, and lithium. It claims that in the present day we don't yet have the technology to measure the gravity waves generated by these small creation events, but someday we will.

Hoyle never claimed to have the final answer to the question of origins but intended "to open the door to a new view which at present is blocked by a fixation with big bang cosmology."

Right now, the Big Bang Theory holds sway. Most cosmologists are pretty confident the Quasi Steady-State model won't topple the edifice of current understanding. The microwave background itself, they claim, is the strongest argument of the accepted theory.

There are still quite a few scornful barbs aimed back and forth. Proponents of what Hoyle once famously derided as a "Big Bang" accused him of "not having done his homework," which was a pretty disrespectful insult to be leveled at an eminent physicist such as Fred Hoyle. He may have disagreed with the primary cosmological myth, but he certainly produced a lot of evidence to back his claims.

Hoyle may be wrong, but demeaning personal comments are really inexcusable in scientific debate, no matter how frequently they are used. There are better ways to treat a respected colleague, even though Hoyle initially started the fight with a disrespectful comment of his own that happened to become the popular name of the very theory he was trying to discredit. Outright scorn is a tactic of suppression. There are more constructive ways to debate in public.

ETERNAL INFLATION

The Big Bang Theory has been verified in many of the areas it can be verified—that is, with math and observation, limited though such methods may be, but it has a few problems. In attempting to answer some of those problems, the road led to many offshoots and variables. Old inflation, as well as chaotic, new, extended, double-law, hybrid, natural, BBI, and assisted inflation, are just a few of them. We'll look at a few of these in a minute, but for now we'll zero in on a hotly contested theory called the Eternal Inflation Theory.

We have already looked at the idea of inflation—the sudden period of exponential growth, much faster than the speed of light, in which the universe expanded to immense proportions. The math seems to indicate that inflation began at a defined instant in the past, for whatever reason, but there doesn't seem to be any reason for it to stop, so questions arise. Does it, indeed, stop? Or does it stop in some local areas and continue throughout the rest of the universe?

In addressing these questions, the Eternal Inflation Theory says that the initial inflationary period goes on forever throughout most of the universe, but slows down in localized spots, sometimes visualized as bubbles. Each bubble is a universe unto itself. We live in one of them and call it "the" universe. If intelligent life arose in an adjacent bubble universe, they would call theirs "the" universe. And because this happens a lot, maybe even an infinite number of times, the whole thing must be called a *multi*verse, rather than a *uni*verse. Picture our boiling pot of water again, filled with bubbles. Each bubble is an independent universe, which may even be governed by completely different rules of physics.

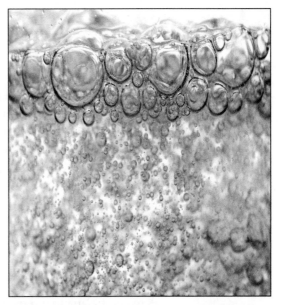

Will we ever be able to interact with any of these hypothetical universes? Sad to say, the answer—at least physically—is almost certainly "no" because the space between them is still expanding much faster than the speed of light.

At this point we face a serious problem. For many decades now, scientists have worked hard to keep religion out of science. The idea of a God is untestable and unprovable because God, by God's very nature, must exist outside the arena that science is exploring. Therefore, scientists at cosmological convention after convention

A multiverse of bubbles illustrates the Eternal Inflation Theory, which describes a reality in which each bubble is a universe unto itself.

have laid down a basic ground rule that any opinions that can't be measured, tested, and checked out by others is not allowed on the dais. Religionists have pointed to a lot of circumstantial evidence, but that was not permitted. It had to be real and provable or it didn't count.

Now we have a scientific theory about origins that lies beyond the rules of physics, and a multiverse that has only circumstantial mathematical evidence, but we can't go out there and obtain samples, look at them under a microscope, and measure them, knowing full well that *our* physics might not be compatible with *their* physics.

Are we still doing science, or have we strayed into the religionist's field of mythology, and possibly even theology? After all, if we compare the words "Unknown Forces" or "Consciousness" to the word "God," the arguments sound strangely similar. Have science and religion, long travelling separate roads, now merged onto the same freeway? Any theory that uses the word "Eternal," as in "Eternal Inflation," or "Creation," as in "the moment of creation," sounds pretty religious to most folks who don't know any better.

Where does modern science stop and religion begin? If inflation has a beginning, but continues on forever, it sounds suspiciously like the Christian Doxology: "As it was in the beginning, is now and ever shall be; World (or universes) without end." And a universe that has no boundary sounds a lot like the scientific principle put forth by King Solomon in I Kings 8:27, when he said, "Behold, the heaven (universe) and heaven of heavens (multiverse) cannot contain thee."

It's enough to make a scientist shudder. Do I hear an "Amen?"

A MIRROR UNIVERSE

In an episode of the popular *Star Trek* television show, James Kirk and several of his officers visited a parallel universe in the year 2267. It coexisted with our universe, occupying the same space but on a separate dimensional plane. It was called the mirror universe because it was just like the prime universe, only backward, as if viewing things in a mirror. Good people there were bad people here, and vice versa.

It was highly entertaining, similar to the concept explored in the Superman "Bizarro" world, which was resurrected on an episode of *Seinfeld* in 1996. Everything was backward, which made for some interesting times, but, of course, it was all fictional.

Might it be possible that such a universe could exist?

A team of Canadian researchers led by Latham Boyle, Kieran Finn, and Neil Turok, from the Perimeter Institute for Theoretical Physics in Waterloo, Ontario, have explored just that possibility. Surprisingly, their theory, as strange as it may sound at first, explains some real problems with the Big Bang Theory. According to Turok: "It's very dramatic. It completely runs counter to the way that physics has been going for the last 30 years, including by us. We asked ourselves, could there not be something simpler going on?"

There are two possibilities inherent in this theory. Let's take them one at a time:

Scenario #1: A Previous Universe

The first theory proposes that our universe emerged from a previous existing universe, different because everything was reversed. Hence, a "Mirror" universe. Particles now were antiparticles then. Time ran backward. If you spilled some soup, it would be seen as flowing from a puddle on the floor into the soup bowl, much like a movie being played backward.

It all sounds strange to us, but the people there, growing younger every day, would see it as normal. It's as if our universe, following the normal

Canadian researchers suggest our present universe exists as the reverse of a previous universe: just like looking into mirror, everything is reflected backwards.

expanding rules of time, would reach the end of its cosmic bungee cord and reverse itself, flowing backward. Effects would become causes. It's not that the previous universe would be different from ours, it's just that it would be a mirror image that gave birth to its opposite.

Scenario #2: An Opposite Universe

This idea is even simpler to imagine. Think of two universes exploding from the Big Bang, but moving in opposite directions through time, one forward, the other backward. This picture allows for some creative explanations to some pretty fundamental problems.

Again quoting Neil Turok, "Theorists invented grand unified theories, which had hundreds of new particles that have never been observed. String theory with extra dimensions, multiverse theories. People just basically kept on inventing stuff. No observational evidence has emerged for any of it."

According to this theory, the first second of the universe would become much simpler. There would be no need to add on theories about a multiverse and extra dimensions, dark matter, and super string theories.

According to Latham Boyle, "Suddenly, when you take this symmetric, extended view of space/time, one of the particles that we already think exists—one of the so-called right-handed neutrinos—becomes a very neat dark-matter candidate. And you don't need to invoke other, more speculative particles."

Boyle, Finn, and Turok say this theory grew out of what they considered to be "bizarre add-ons" proposed by physicists to justify the Big Bang Theory. They had even helped develop some of them, but you are probably thinking by now that this is pretty bizarre, too. Nevertheless, they say their theory, unlike the Big Bang Theory, has the benefit of being able to stand up to testing. This will certainly be needed if doubters are ever going to be convinced. It's hard to imagine life being lived backwards, but to be honest, anyone living in a hypothetical mirror universe and reading about this theory would probably think that what we experience is rather strange.

To begin to grasp the concept we really have to begin with the idea that, believe it or not, our conception of time is an illusion.

In 1987, British astrophysicist Arthur Eddington coined the phrase "arrow of time" to describe the nature of time as we perceive it. In 1992 his idea became the subject of a two-part *Star Trek: The Next Generation* episode called *Time's Arrow*. The crew of the USS Enterprise goes back in time to discover information in the past that had already been deposited by them from the future. Needless to say, this produces some interesting plot twists.

But Arthur Eddington is the very same man who also once said, "The universe is not only stranger than we imagine, it is stranger that we *can* imagine." Nowhere is his assertion more compelling than when it comes to experiencing what he called the "arrow of time." From our perception, time flows from the past, through the present, and into the future. It seems obvious to us. We can't really imagine any other way to describe it. This is Eddington's "arrow of time," moving from a starting point into the future.

But for decades now, physicists have been suppressing an astounding fact. There are no fundamental laws of physics that unequivocally demand time works this way. Einstein's theories of special and general relativity and the newly discovered equations of quantum reality, Newton's theories about gravitation, and Maxwell's theories of electrodynamics work just as well whether time flows forward or, from our perspective, backward. It doesn't make any difference. The reason we perceive of time as an

Astrophysicist Sir Arthur Eddington (1882–1944) was knighted in 1930. He was a leader in the physics of relativity and coined the phrase "arrow of time."

"arrow" moving forward is because that's the way it seems to us. Any other conception just seems silly, but mathematically, it's only one way to perceive it. After all, we can play a digitally recorded event backwards. Why not time?

Julian Barbour has done more work on the subject of time than anyone. When my wife and I wrote *Armageddon Now: The End of the World A to Z* back in 2005, we examined his work in detail. In his words: "Time is not something that pre-exists. The direction and flow of time we have to deduce from what's happening in the Universe. When we look at it that way, it's natural to say that time begins at that central point and flows away in opposite directions."

From our perspective, causes produce results. Break an egg and it scrambles. That's because we live in a universe governed by basic laws of entropy.

But if time can move backward as well as forward, there could very well exist a universe in which, from our perspective, effects produce causes.

To us, a Big Bang produces a universe, but the laws of physics say it is perfectly permissible to say that a universe might produce a Big Bang. If such a universe exists, and if life develops within in, they would insist that what we experience is silly.

In 2014, Julian Barbour and some of his colleagues published a paper in the *Physical Review Letters* that described how they ran a computer simulation that seemed to indicate that the so-called "arrow of time" is governed by grav-

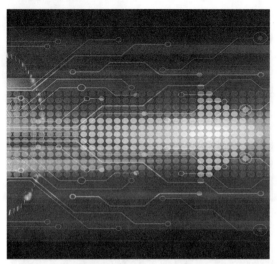

Sir Arthur Eddington's "arrow of time" is a phrase he invented to explain the perception of time by humanity.

ity, not thermodynamics. When gravity acted on 1,000 particles and drew them all together, they wound up at a point Barbour called the Janus Point, which were really points with the smallest possible distance between them.

"It's the simplest thing," says Barbour. "You start at the central Janus point where the motion is chaotic—that's like the Greek notion of primordial chaos—but then in both directions you get this structure forming. If the theory is right, then there's another universe on the other side of the Big Bang in which the direction of experience of time is opposite to ours." In one universe, the film runs forward. In the other, it runs backwards.

How many of us have observed that we would like to live our life over if we could know what we know now? Well, here's a chance to do just that. Life would no longer be wasted on the young. The older we get, the better we would feel. The more we age, the healthier we would be. From a biological standpoint, it would prove to be a big improvement. For that reason alone, this theory is worth keeping around, whether or not it is ever proved.

Others have speculated about the idea of time flowing backward. T. H. White's *Once and Future King*, for instance, explains Merlin's ability to divine the future by assuming that he is actually living his life backward. He can tell the future because he has already lived it.

The 2008 movie *The Curious Case of Benjamin Button* was loosely based on a short story by F. Scott Fitzgerald. It tells the story of Benjamin Button, played by Brad Pitt, who was born as an old man and gradually, as the story unfolds, keeps getting younger.

These literary and film explorations, however, don't really illustrate the problem of the "arrow of time." In a mirror universe, everything moves backward, not just people. Merlin the Magician and Benjamin Button are portrayed as living backward in a forward-moving universe, but in the mirror universe, their surroundings are also moving backwards. Anyone who evolved in such a universe would be completely unaware of any sense of moving backward in time. In their universe, that's just the way things work.

The whole picture of an egg reassembling itself after being broken is not really a good metaphor, but it's hard for us to picture *any* metaphor of a universe in which time moves diametrically opposite to anything we've ever imagined. Once again, this is an idea that only a mathematician can really fathom.

Of course, just because the math works in two directions doesn't mean any such place really exists. The best we can say is that it is mathematically possible that such a universe *could* exist, so the whole idea of time moving backwards is not new, but it is now receiving new attention due to the mathematics of a mirror universe.

COLLIDING IN HIGHER DIMENSIONS

If moving backward in a time dimension is difficult to imagine, how about tackling a dimension of space that we will never be able to see or experience? Things are about to get even more interesting.

One of the most intriguing theories to come out of quantum mechanics studies is an idea called string theory. The idea is that at the basis of everything there are tiny, vibrating strings of energy that come in an infinite number of shapes. For a while it was hoped that this would fulfill the quest for the famous GUT theory, the holy grail of quantum physics. GUT stands for "Grand Unification Theory," the theory that would unite all that is known about physics on both the classic and quantum levels.

In his book *A Brief History of Time*, Stephen Hawking closes with words that have now become famous to those who are engaged in the illusive quest for a grand unification theory:

> If we do discover a complete theory, it should in time be understandable in broad principle by everyone, not just a few scientists. Then we shall all, philosophers, scientists, and just ordinary people, be able to take part in the discussion of the question of why it is that we and the universe exist. If we find the answer to that, it would be the ultimate triumph of human reason—for then we would know the mind of God.

String theory has been around for while, but it has yet to fulfill its promise. Some theorists are beginning to think they need to start looking elsewhere. Nevertheless, there are some intriguing concepts that

British physicist Dr. Stephen Hawking (1942–2018), probably the most well-known scientist after Albert Einstein, urged a greater understanding of a theory of unifying all the forces of nature.

have come to light. One of them is the idea that we live in a multiverse consisting of at least eleven different dimensions.

We are all familiar with three spatial and one time dimension. Height, width, breadth, and time are part of everyday life. That leaves seven more. Six of them consist of "strings" of energy that are so small and curled up into such infinitesimal tiny rings that for all practical purposes, unless we are involved in some pretty intense mathematical exercises, we might just as well ignore them. That leaves one more, and it's a doozey.

Picture everything you know and have ever experienced, including height, width, breadth, and time, as existing on a flat hyper-surface called a "'brane," short for membrane. This is the universe we all know and love. Right next to us is an extremely thin layer of another dimension, and on the other side of that is another 'brane that could conceivably have evolved just like we did and be filled with sentient beings who are also wondering about the make-up of the multiverse. (If you want to leave out the sentient beings, that's okay. The theory works whether they are there or not. I just threw them in to make things interesting.)

Even though the two 'branes are separated by a tiny, tiny spatial dimension, like two pieces of bread making up a sandwich that has a spatial-dimension filling, these 'branes have familiar properties. They have momentum, they consist of energy, and they are very excitable. Quarks, electrons, and leptons move along them, causing a disturbance in the force. Every few trillion years or so these 'branes smash together and then bounce away from each other. The last time they did this in our neighborhood, at least the last time with which we are familiar, was about 13.8 billion years ago. We call it the Big Bang.

While the term "Big Bang" has come into general exceptance, the wording was first used to denigrate the idea of a sudden beginning of everything.

When this happens all kinds of energy rushes out from the spot where they collided. Eventually things start to settle down, the energy takes on mass and becomes matter, one small piece of which becomes a home for an (arguably) intelligent race of beings able to contemplate their origins. Just a microscopic distance away, the other 'brane experiences the same thing, but the sentient beings living on each 'brane are completely unaware of the existence of the other. All we can see and experience are things that move along the four dimensions of height, width, breadth, and time. So close—and yet so far!

Now go back to the energy of the dimension that separates the two 'branes—

the "filling" in the 'brane sandwich. This energy takes over and forces the two 'branes apart, kind of like a reverse field of gravity. It forces the 'branes to stretch and expand. According to the theory, this dimension, or force, is what we now call dark matter. We know it's there. We know it's forcing our universe to expand, but we can't see it, so we call it "dark."

Meanwhile, back at the 'brane, trillions of years go by and each 'brane stretches out, relaxes, and becomes a kind of flat surface. The 'branes are once again parallel and empty. Then there is another disturbance in the force. The "dark matter dimension" causes the 'branes to come together and collide again.

And the wheels on the bus go 'round and 'round and the process begins once more and continues forever. It's not a disturbance in our 'brane that causes the collisions to occur, it's the Dark Matter dimension that holds the fate of the 'branes in its proverbial but eternal hands. Our familiar four dimensions eventually stretch out and become smooth and restful. It's the dimension in the middle that causes what we call creation, again and again, cycle after cycle. We happen to live in a convenient time during one of these endless cycles. A trillion years in the past, or a trillion years in the future, conditions for life as we experience it won't be right. Biological life will cease to exist until the next Big Bang starts things up again.

To further complicate things, though, Big Bangs might occur all along the surface of the 'branes, causing multiple bangs and thus multiple universes on the surface of the same, perhaps infinite, 'brane, but they happen so far apart that for our purposes they can't be experienced. All we can do is measure the spatial variations and temperature differences left over from previous bangs in our cosmological vicinity.

One of the aspects that might prove to be measurable, however, is a phenomenon called gravitational waves. The idea is that when the 'brane collisions, or Big Bangs, happen, they create fluctuations of space-time itself. These are gravitational waves, and scientists hope to, one day soon, be able to create experiments that will predict, identify, and measure these waves. If they succeed in their quest, this theory will take on even more weight. Until then, it's just another intriguing theory.

Once again we have to ask the question. When we explore areas we cannot measure, observe, or identify, are we still doing science, or have we moved into the arena of metaphysics? That's why theoretical physicists want to develop methods of experimental research that can be conducted at places such as the Large Hadron Collider in Europe. Until then, even ideas as lofty as this remain speculative. Only experimental, verifiable evidence can keep these ideas firmly entrenched in the scientific camp.

GRAVITY OVER THE RAINBOW

So far, except for the Quasi Steady-State Theory, all the ideas we've looked at began with a bang. Space had a beginning at a particular time, roughly 13.8 billion years ago.

But what if the universe had no beginning? In the relationship we now call Space/Time, what if time has the dominant position? What if space exists inside of time, so to speak? What if time indeed reaches back toward infinity, with no starting point? In other words, what if infinity means an infinity of time with no beginning and no end?

That's a hard concept for our minds to grasp, but it is, indeed, a logical consequence of an idea called Rainbow Gravity.

Clara Moskowitz, in an article published by *Scientific American* on December 9, 2013, described such a universe. Her basic idea is that gravity has a different effect on various wavelengths of light. In other words, as light photons travel through space, all the colors of the rainbow respond in different ways to the force of gravity, depending on their vibrational energy.

According to Einstein's equations concerning general relativity, gravity "warps" space itself. Picture a bowling ball suspended on a tightly stretched bed sheet. No matter how tightly you try to hold the four corners of the sheet, the bowling ball will depress it, causing it to sag. Anything surfing along the sheet will follow the sag. It's path will be curved, or "warped." This includes light waves. They will follow the curve of space caused by anything with a heavy gravity quotient. If they are moving quickly, they will follow the warp but have enough speed to exit the sag and keep going. If they are moving more slowly, they will be caught in the sag's vortex and be drawn inward toward the center.

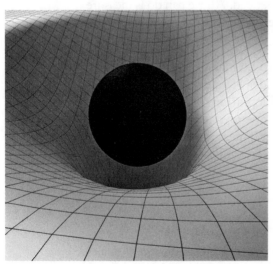

Now it gets interesting. Light particles are energy. They will respond to gravity according to the density and vibrational frequency of each color of the rainbow. Red has a higher frequency than blue, for instance. Particles with different energies will experience different gravitational pulls, causing different apparent space/times. Different frequencies, in other words, correspond to different energies, so light particles, or photons, will travel on slightly different paths through space, affected by the warp of the particular gravitational field through which they pass.

This "bowling-ball-on-bedsheet" illustration shows the concept of how Einstein theorized gravity warps space, causing light waves to follow the curve of space.

The effects are extremely small, of course, so we don't notice them when we look at light emanating from stars or galaxies, but bursts of energy, seen as light, will reach our eyes at slightly different times even though they started from the same place. If we had instruments sensitive enough to measure these discrepancies, which we don't, it would appear as if the source of the energy sent them out at slightly different times.

One observer might report an exploding gamma-ray burst, for instance, as occurring at a specific time, depending on the frequency of the light they were measuring, and another observer, measuring the same event at a different frequency, would report that the same event occurred at a different time. The speed of light is always the same, of course, but because gravity affected each wavelength differently, the individual wave lengths traveled different warped paths, some a bit longer than others, and so gave the appearance of leaving their source at different times.

It would be the same as if two runners, running exactly the same speed and the same course, arrived at the finish line at different times because one ran down the exact center of the track while the other cut off the tangents at each curve.

This leads to two different ways to interpret the data.

1. In the first scenario, retracing time backwards implies that the universe gets denser and denser but never quite reaches a starting point at the same time. The early arrivals will have to wait for the latecomers who traveled farther, and by the time they all get there, the ones who arrived first will have dissipated their energy.

   Think of it this way. You want to walk from point A to point B in a series of journeys. In each journey, you walk exactly halfway from where you are to where you want to wind up. You'll never reach point B because no matter how close you get you can always divide the remaining difference exactly in half. Eventually you'll be dealing with some pretty small distances, but mathematically you can always divide the remaining distance in half.

2. In the second scenario, the universe reaches infinite density, but eventually plateaus. There is never a singularity, a starting point. Time eventually plateaus as well of course, because space/time is one entity.

These are interesting mathematical conundrums, but is there any substance here?

Sabine Hossenfelder, of the Frankfurt Institute for Advanced Studies, is blunt in stating her opinion. "It's a model that I do not believe has anything to do with reality."

And that's the central problem with some of these relatively unknown ways of conceiving the early universe. They are esoteric, to say the least. A few people get really interested. The majority simply ignore them. The result is suppression. No one does it on purpose. Maybe there's a good reason to consider them mathematical semantics and even rather silly. If you tried to teach students every crazy idea that got published in a scientific journal, you'd never reach the end in an average lifetime.

But once in a while, a crazy idea, such as quantum physics, for instance, turns out to be true, even if an Albert Einstein, for example, tries to suppress it.

It's a problem.

THE SLOW THAW

The standard model of creation says the universe began very dense and very hot, and then it got bigger and cooled down. What if the reverse was true? What if it instead is slowly emerging out of an empty, cold, deep freeze?

In 2012, physicists from the University of Melbourne proposed that the universe had its beginnings when it went through what they called a phase shift, a transformation similar to a solid turning into a liquid. Right now, we're in the midst of that transformation.

At first, the idea didn't gain much traction in the scientific community, but it has been recently upgraded a bit by Heidelberg University's Christof Wetterich. According to him, the universe is not expanding. It's just putting on weight.

Gabriel Popkin, in an article published by *Science News*, tried to explain the concept. According to him, we don't know whether or not the mass of particles in the universe has always remained constant because all we can measure, given today's level of science, are the corresponding ratios between different masses. We can't be sure that the weight of the masses themselves has always been constant.

Think of it this way. In a vault in France there is stored what is called a standard kilogram. Everything on Earth is measured and rated according to how it compares to this standard weight.

Now, what if the weight of this standard measurement is changing, and we

This polished cylinder, made of 90 percent platinum and 10 percent iridium alloy, is 1.5 inches in diameter and 1.5 inches high, being an exact copy of the international prototype kilogram kept at the International Bureau of Weights and Measures (Bureau International des Poids et Measures) in Sèvres, France.

don't realize it? If it's getting slowly heavier, and we don't notice it, then everything else we measure will also appear to be getting heavier. We can't tell it's happening because everything we weigh is being compared to one standard. If the standard weight that we call a kilogram is quietly getting heavier, everything compared to it will seem to be getting heavier.

What Wetterich is saying is that if the mass of particles in the universe appears to have been increasing, it might be because the radiation in the early universe, the standard unit against which we measure everything, makes it appear as if it were a lot hotter than it really was, giving a false impression.

The level of radiation may be changing. We can't be *sure* it's constant. All we can do is *assume* that it is. In other words, if the ruler we are using to measure the mass of the universe, radiation, is changing, it will throw off all our calculations. If that's the case, the universe isn't expanding. The yardstick by which we measure the expansion is actually shrinking. It's as if someone is sneaking into the vault in France and slowly changing the weight of the standard kilogram.

I face this same problem when I try to tune my guitar. Invariably I find the string that is out of tune, and then tune the rest of the guitar to it. In this metaphor, radiation is the string that's out of tune in the cosmic guitar, and we are tuning our whole cosmology to it.

The bottom line is that we don't need to pack all the matter of the universe into a single, hot, dense singularity. The universe instead might be a cold, deep space, stretching back to an infinite past. It's just now starting to thaw out.

Will we ever have the technology to check out Wetterich's figures? No one knows. We certainly aren't there yet but stay tuned.

A Cyclic Universe

If we stop to think about it, there are two basic ideas about the universe that can keep us awake and staring at the ceiling at night.

The first is that the universe had a beginning. Immediately our minds jump to the next logical question: What came before that?

The second is even more mind-blowing. What if the universe never had a beginning? The contemplation of eternity is not conducive to restful sleep.

Thinking about the second of these ideas brings us to the concept of a cyclic universe. This is a model that proposes the universe is simply a living example of a huge, self-perpetuating machine that regularly "breathes" in and out, forever. It undergoes endless repetitions of expansion and cooling, each cycle marked by a big bang followed by a big "crunch."

There are three assumptions needed to describe these cycles.

- First, what we call the Big Bang is not the beginning of space and time. Instead, it represents a moment when gravitational energy pulls everything together. It's difficult to imagine all the matter in even the relatively small visible universe we observe with the naked eye drawn together into an infinitesimally small point, but if it happened, the heat due to friction alone could not be measured by any device we have. The best we can do is write down a 10 followed by a long string of zeroes and say, "That's it!" If that ever happened in the universe of physical matter, something would have to blow. That "something" is what we call the Big Bang.

- Second, after the bang, as radiation energy exploded outward, there would have come a time of gradual cooling. Expansion would eventually lead to what we see now. We are in an expansion stage and will continue for billions of years.

- Third, somewhere in the neighborhood of 10^{12} years or so, things will start to pull together again, and the process will start to crunch down on itself. Time and space will reverse, rushing together instead of pulling apart. Eventually another Big Bang will occur, and the process will start all over. According to this view, it's been going on forever. And will continue forever. That's right—forever. And ever. Worlds without end. Amen. That thought can keep you up at night.

Practically speaking, until recently both the Big Bang and the Cyclic Universe theories fit all the observable data scientists have collected so far. No one knows what happened before the initial bang, so whether it was preceded by a previous universe was anyone's guess. The only way to go about proving either one is to figure out where the universe is going. If gravity is sufficient to pull things back together, the cyclic universe has a good chance of being the right guess. No less an intellectual giant than Albert Einstein thought this was the case, and he was convinced only after his beloved steady state universe was disproved by expansion arguments.

But lately new evidence has surfaced that questions the cyclic hypothesis. According to the Second Law of Thermodynamics, entropy must increase, not decrease. This would imply that each successive cycle would grow longer and increase in both strength and size. Extrapolating backwards, given an unending series of cycles, much earlier cycles would have been shorter and smaller, until eventually there would come a time when energy would not have been sufficient to produce a universe. An eternal series of cycles doesn't work if there was an initial cycle. That would bring us right back to the same point. "What came before the first one?"

Until 2011, that was the way things stood, but with the discovery of dark energy that grew out of a survey of more than 200,000 galaxies and figured in data from 7 billion years of cosmic time, it now seems as though dark energy, called "dark" because we can't see it, is pushing the matter in the universe apart at an increasing rate. Gravity doesn't seem strong enough to be able to gather it all back together again.

Earlier, when we looked at the higher dimensions of string theory, we tried to picture a multiverse consisting of flat membranes lined up like a loaf of sliced bread, each slice separated from its neighbors by a field of dark energy. When they collide they produce a Big Bang, and the process goes on forever. This might be a more up-to-date way of describing the old Cyclic Universe theory.

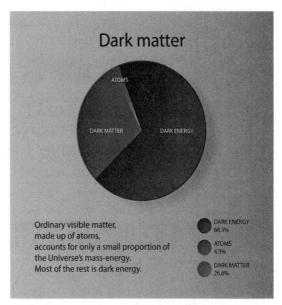

Dark matter

ATOMS

DARK MATTER   DARK ENERGY

Ordinary visible matter, made up of atoms, accounts for only a small proportion of the Universe's mass-energy. Most of the rest is dark energy.

DARK ENERGY 68.3%
ATOMS 4.9%
DARK MATTER 26.8%

Dark energy makes up almost 70 percent of the mass of the universe.

There is quite a history behind the problem of whether or not gravity is sufficient to overcome the outward expansion force of the universe. Way back in 1917 Albert Einstein was so troubled by the failure of math to explain the problem of gravitational force that he introduced what he called a "cosmological constant" into his equations to make them work. He later called this his greatest blunder. He came to believe he had manipulated the math to make it fit the practical world. He had a picture of a static universe in his head and didn't want to change his ideas to fit the facts of an expanding universe.

But later theorists, after Hubble's work in 1931 confirmed an expanding universe, accepted the plain and observable facts. Until the 1990s they accommodated Einstein by assuming his cosmological constant was zero. Even folks who never got past algebra know that all kinds of neat things can be manipulated if you multiply by zero.

But in 1998, when evidence accumulated that the universe is expanding at an accelerating rate, Einstein's old idea of a non-zero cosmological constant was dusted off because it made things work. The result of that discovery was what we now call dark energy—so called because it's there and it works, but we can't see it.

Einstein used the Greek letter lambda (λ) to stand for his cosmological constant. Now it symbolizes dark energy in modern equations. So far it's strictly a mathematical construct, and beyond the range of any modern technology to actually see, but it works, so it must be there. As a matter of fact, it seems to compose some 68 percent of the mass/energy of the universe, functioning as sort of anti-gravity. It's a force that pushes and repels rather than pulls and attracts.

The reason we don't hear more about all this is because of the mind-boggling complexity of doing the kind of math required to understand what has been called the "cosmological constant problem." It's one of the great unsolved mysteries in science.

Physicists argue endlessly about all this and most of us are left shaking our heads and asking who could possibly care. After all, life offers a lot more urgent set of daily problems to think about, but we ignore these arguments to our own detriment because solving this problem holds the key to a full understanding of how we got here, and thus who we are in the great scheme of things. Until more research reveals greater depths of understanding, all most of us can do is wait for the experts to hash it out some more.

WHITE HOLES AND ALTERNATE UNIVERSES

Have you ever opened up a set of Russian dolls? One doll is hidden inside an identical doll, and then another, and another. In an article published in *National Geographic News* on April 12, 2010, that's the illustration used by Ker Than to describe a theory that says our universe might be nested inside a black hole, which might be a part of a larger universe. If that theory proves to be the case, black holes might turn out to be doorways into alternate realities.

The basic idea, simplified, of course, is that all the matter a black hole gathers due to immense gravitational forces doesn't just collapse into a single, infinitely dense point. It spews forth from the bottom of the black hole, emerging through a "white hole" into another reality.

Einstein theorized that whenever matter in a single region becomes too dense, as it might in a black hole, it would create a singularity. Singularities are infinitely dense and infinitely hot, yet they take up no space. It's an idea that is suggested by a lot of mathematical evidence but makes no practical sense at all.

Enter white holes. If there is no "bottom" to black holes, but rather a "white hole funnel" into another reality that can spew forth all the matter sucked into the top, then there need be no infinite, hot, dense singularity at all. Instead, the matter entering a black hole becomes the building blocks of a universe forming on the other end.

In effect, the black hole becomes similar to what sci-fi enthusiasts would call a wormhole—a tunnel through space—but it emerges into a totally different reality.

This might explain some real difficulties arising from traditional theories about the formation of the universe. For instance, cosmologists theorize that our universe began with a singularity, but where did the singularity come from? How did it just appear out of the blue one day?

One explanation might be that everything in our universe was funneled here from an alternate reality. It consists of material that was sucked into a black hole over "there," and then spewed out "here." In other words, at the heart of our universe was a white hole, not a singularity.

There are other intriguing ideas suggested by this theory. Nikodem Janusz Poplawski is a Polish theoretical physicist who is widely known as a champion of this

Some people believe a black hole might function as a space tunnel—or wormhole—to another reality.

theory. He burst into public consciousness when his work was outlined in a 2011 episode of *Through the Wormhole*, hosted by Morgan Freeman. In 2015, *Forbes* magazine voted him one of the five scientists in the world most likely to become the next Albert Einstein. Besides his alternative ideas concerning black hole singularities, he points out that his theories might also answer a central question concerning gamma ray bursts.

No one really knows what gamma ray bursts are. They originate at the very fringes of the observable universe and seem to be associated with supernovas or the explosions of stars in galaxies located almost unimaginable distances away from us, but no one really knows if this is the case or not. The simple truth is that their origins are a mystery. Poplawski theorizes that they might be discharges from alternate universes, the result of matter being sucked into a black hole and funneled through a white hole into ours. In his words: "It's kind of a crazy idea, but who knows?"

How do you test such a massive idea?

Now it gets difficult.

Black holes rotate. If our universe was "born" inside a revolving black hole, then we must have inherited our parent universe's rotation. If we can someday find a way to prove that we rotate in what he calls a "preferred direction," it would support Poplawski's theory.

How do we do that? I haven't the faintest idea. I have to take him at his word because he's a lot smarter than me.

Polish physicist Nikodem J. Poplawski has theorized that mysterious gamma ray bursts might emanate from an alternate universe.

Poplawski goes further into the scientific/philosophical, metaphorical wormhole, however. According to the accepted standard model of the creation of our universe, after the Big Bang the curvature of the universe increased. That was all of 13.8 billion years ago. By now, sufficient time should have elapsed so that the universe should have curved in on itself to the point where we should be sitting on the surface of a closed, spherical universe, but we're not. The universe seems to be flat in every direction. What happened? To make matters even more difficult to understand, data examined from light created very near to the beginning of time and space indicates that right after the Big Bang, things were fairly uniform in terms of temperature. Objects we observe way out on our opposite sight horizons of the universe must have once been close enough to interact and blend together, kind of like adding cream to your morning coffee and watching it disperse throughout the whole cup.

As we have seen, cosmologists chalk this all up to something called inflation. By this they mean that things had a chance to mix together in the first microseconds after the Big Bang and then were carried outward in a sudden, mind-blowing expansion event. The cream and the coffee, already mixed, expanded together.

It's a great idea, and currently holds the number one position on the cosmic origins hit parade, but is it true?

Poplawski questions some accepted interpretations, which say that inflation was caused by something called "exotic matter." That's a theoretical substance that repels rather than attracts, like gravity. He thinks exotic matter might have its origin when massive stars in alternate realities collapse, forming black holes. They became, in effect, worm holes into our reality. "There may be some relationship between the exotic matter that forms wormholes and the exotic matter that triggered inflation," he claims.

Is any of this possible? Yes. Is it probable? Maybe. Is it provable? Not by a long shot. Is it interesting? You bet! Is it worthy of further study? Absolutely! It might bring us closer to the basic questions that haunt our waking dreams:

"How did we get here?" "What's the meaning of it all?" assuming it all has meaning.

Damien Easson is a theoretical physicist at Arizona State University. He sums up the whole issue very succinctly: "What is new here is an actual wormhole solution in general relativity that acts as the passage from the exterior black hole to the new interior universe. Is the idea possible? Yes. Is the scenario likely? I have no idea, but it is certainly an interesting possibility."

The idea of a parent universe giving birth to an infant universe is interesting, but it faces a fatal flaw when it comes to describing our origins. In effect, all it does is kick the proverbial can down the road. If a parent universe gave birth to us, where did the parent universe come from? Somewhere, back in the mists of eternity, there had to be a first universe. Where did that one come one from?

Once again, we're left with a mystery. Perhaps it's time to cease our survey of natural alternative theories and look elsewhere. With this in mind, we now enter the field of:

> The idea of a parent universe giving birth to an infant universe is interesting, but it faces a fatal flaw when it comes to describing our origins.

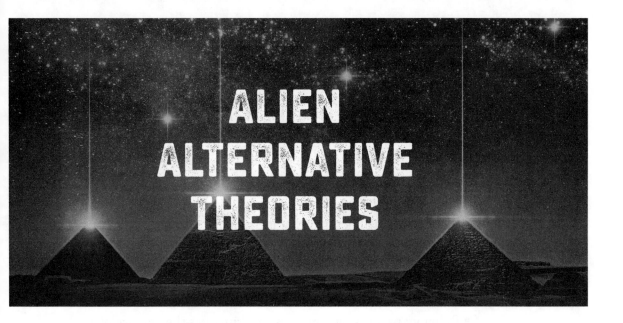

ALIEN ALTERNATIVE THEORIES

If the universe, or the multiverse, wasn't created by forces we have labeled "natural," maybe we need to turn to theories that can only be characterized as "supernatural."

Once again we need to remind ourselves that we are employing words often misused in the popular media. It might prove helpful to reread the introduction to this book. There we made some basic assumptions:

- "Alien" doesn't necessarily refer to little green men from outer space.

- "Alternative" simply means adopting a theoretical world view that includes the possibility of alternate realities that exist outside our normal perception realm.

- "Theories" refers to gathering facts and thinking outside the box about what they mean.

Thus, *alien alternative theories* are no more outlandish than quantum mechanics. If they explore possibilities that might explain reality, they deserve some time in the sun.

Some of these theories are brand new and have been popularized by movies such as *The Matrix* and *The Terminator*. Others are as old as the Bible. All imagine a greater reality that exists outside our normal waking consciousness. A few go further than examining causes and effects. Some imply purpose, an idea usually missing from the scientific concepts we have looked at so far. In other words, we are about to enter an arena that goes beyond asking "How and When?" and raise the questions, "Who and Why?"

That's a place most scientists fear to tread, but, as we shall soon discover, there are people who have been surveying that domain for millennia.

METAPHYSICS, SPIRITUALITY, AND RELIGION

At the heart of the so-called debate between science and religion lies a simple ideological conflict. Is there a God? Is there a Consciousness that intends, creates, and pervades the universe? Is there a First Cause?

First, some definitions:

- Metaphysics: a philosophy that is essentially a theory of reality that examines existence and the very nature of things.
- Spirituality: tends to personalize reality, often imaging an intelligence bigger than ourselves that exists outside our perceived consciousness.
- Religion: narrows, systematizes, and ritualizes the practice of spirituality.

All three ask some simple questions. Did thought and intention bring about the cosmos? Is there a universal Mind of some sort that sought to take on material substance? Or did everything we know and experience come about through the process of natural law?

On these questions hang the very nature of the conflict.

The science/religion debate is not really about facts versus faith. It's not about what we know versus what we believe. It's about conflicting ideologies. How we approach the issue is of paramount importance.

In July of 1633, Galileo Galilei faced the most momentous decision of his life. The man Albert Einstein would one day call the father of modern science, the same one Stephen Hawking would claim was responsible for the birth of contemporary physics, had to choose between science and religion. If he chose science, he would be tortured to death. If he chose religion, he would have to publicly recant what he privately knew to be true and then spend the rest of his life under house arrest.

In those days the Roman Catholic Inquisition held Europe under total control. Anyone who disagreed with church doctrine was in danger of being turned over to the authorities of the church, who also held sway over the political establishment.

The Inquisition had a unique method of operation. First, the defendant was declared guilty by the local bishops and church hierarchy. Then came the trial, the only purpose of which was to give the guilty party a chance to recant. Often this second phase was accompanied by fiendish torture that led to death. If the victim recanted he, or, in some cases, she, was still killed, but at least, went the thinking, they had the solace of knowing they would be divinely pardoned and could still enter heaven after appropriate fees had been paid by their relatives and loved ones.

Galileo's crime was that he supported a rather new scientific theory that had earlier been championed by Nicolaus Copernicus. It was called helio-centrism. This was the view that the sun was the center of the universe and that the Earth revolved around it in orbit. Most educated people of the time knew this could not be true because the Bible, in Psalms 93:1, 96:10, and I Chronicles 16:30, stated quite clearly that "the world is firmly established; it cannot be moved." Psalm 104:5 definitively declared, "the Lord set the Earth on its foundations; it can never be moved." If that weren't enough, Ecclesiastes 1:5 settled the issue in words anyone could understand: "The sun rises and sets and returns to its place."

In those days, for every good Christian and for every scientist since Aristotle, the matter couldn't be any more settled. Geocentrism was definitely the order of the day. That is, the sun revolves around the Earth. *We* are the center of the universe. Therefore, Galileo was guilty of heresy.

True, there was a lot of political infighting and back-room dealing going on behind the scenes. Galileo, after all, was a friend of the pope, but on June 22, 1633, the Inquisition issued its verdict. Galileo was found "vehemently suspect of heresy" for believing that the Earth actually moves. He was told to "abjure, curse, and detest" such an opinion. The next day, following his decision on pain of torture to recant his heresy, the death sentence was commuted to house arrest and he was ordered to never publish any such material again for the rest of his life. (Which, thank goodness, he ignored. He still had some of his best work ahead of him, including the work that nominated him as "the father of modern physics.") His books were ordered burned. (But many had already been smuggled out of the country, much to the benefit of the scientific community.)

Thus it was that, faced with torture and death if he stuck to his scientific principles, he publicly recanted, but legend has it that as he signed the accursed document prepared by the Inquisitors, the papers that confirmed the obvious dogma that the Earth was fixed at the center of God's universe, he muttered quietly, *E pur si muove!* ("And yet it moves!").

It is probably only coincidental irony that years later, long after Galileo's death and subsequent exoneration, his body was finally transported to a place of honor in the Basilica of Santa Croce. During this move three fingers and a tooth were removed from his corpse. That is why, to this day, an exhibit at the Museo Galileo in Florence, Italy, features a unique display. It's the middle finger from Galileo's right hand.

Most people think he probably would have approved.

The church moved slowly to admit its wrongs. The cascading Protestant Reformation and internal strife eventually caused the Inquisition to lose its stranglehold on the scientific community. There were pockets of resistance, of course, and they were not limited to Catholic circles.

In 1692 more than two hundred people, mostly women, were accused of witchcraft in Salem, Massachusetts. Twenty were executed in the resulting hysteria. Officially, the power behind the trials was the secular state, but it was universally acknowledged that the clergy supported that power. After those trials—and maybe even *because* of those trials that were closely observed by Puritan preacher Cotton Mather—the church lost most of its power to so flagrantly and abusively dominate scientific research.

It's fashionable these days to say that science and religion eventually came to an "agreement." Science would henceforth study the material world while the church would stick to matters of spirit, ethics, and morals. Although that is certainly a politically correct way to parse the resulting truce, it's not quite true. It is much more accurate to say that science demanded the respect it was due, displayed the equivalent of Galileo's middle finger to established religion, and the church was powerless to do anything about it.

The trial of Galileo (1564–1642) in Rome led to his being found "suspect of heresy" by the pope. He was consequently forced to recant his statement that Earth revolved around the sun.

Given the sweeping tide of history, church authorities eventually tried to reconcile their errors, but in typical ecclesiastical fashion it took a while. In 1741 Pope Benedict XIV authorized the publication of Galileo's complete scientific works. In 1758 the study of heliocentrism was removed from the church's famous *Index of Prohibited Books*. In 1990, Cardinal Joseph Ratzinger, who would later become Pope Benedict XVI, recognized that the whole Galileo affair was "a symptomatic case that permits us to see how deep the self-doubt of the modern age, of science and technology, goes today," whatever that means. One wonders what Galileo would have thought of such an interpretation.

On October 31, 1992, Pope John Paul II expressed regret for how the whole case was handled and confessed to Catholic Church "tribunal errors." But it was a matter of too little, too late, and everybody knew it.

For the most part, the negotiated truce between science and religion still holds. Religion is thought to deal with ethics and morals—with "ought to" statements. We "ought to" deal with others in a moral, upstanding way. We "ought to" help the poor and downtrodden. We "ought to" obey God's laws, whatever individual religions conceive them to be. Why? For the most part it's because God said so in some revealed text. Hence the popular bumper sticker: "God said it. I believe it. That settles it!"

Science deals with facts—with "is" statements. Its methodology consists of a sure-fire system to arrive at the truth:

- Ask a question

- Research your material

- Form a hypothesis

- Conduct controlled experiments to test your hypothesis

- Analyze your results and compose a theory

- Subject your theory to peer review

Using this method, it can be fairly conclusively stated that grass is green due to chemical processes involving chlorophyll. The speed of light is 186,282 miles per second. It is a fact that the entropy of a system approaches a constant value as the temperature approaches absolute zero.

No faith or revelation is required. Anyone, anywhere, can try to duplicate your results. If successfully defended, your theory becomes established dogma until proven otherwise. It will never be stated as a completed Truth with a capital "T" until all the possible facts are accounted for. In other words, never, but it will be recognized as pretty darn close to fact.

So, for example, Darwin's "theory" of evolution by means of natural selection is just that—a theory, but pretty much everyone in the scientific community, at least until relatively recently, agrees that it's a pretty accurate description of how we got here. It was the closest thing to "fact" anyone else had ever come up with. To say it is "just" a theory is to completely miss the point of how science works. It was a theory that best summed up the available evidence. Even though it is constantly being tweaked and molded, the difference between accepted theory and established fact is, for the most part, merely one of semantics.

Lately, however, the winds of change seem to be blowing across the no-man's land separating science and religion. Historical dividing lines drawn in the sands of time are blurring a bit. It is now popular in some circles to draw conclusions that indicate our religious ancestors were somehow able to intuit what modern scientists have now begun to systematically describe. In other words, the world of science sometimes seems to blend into what we have traditionally called metaphysics, religion, and spirituality. Indeed, reading some of the really cutting-edge scientific theories that push the boundary of traditional cosmology, it's sometimes tough to see where science ends and metaphysics begins.

Vishnu dreaming the universe, the intentional observer needed to bring life into being, is the creation belief of the Hindu religion.

If the universe began, for instance, with a Big Bang, but quantum theory says that nothing can occur in the material realm without the presence of a conscious observer, that sounds suspiciously similar to "In the beginning ... God said let there be light ... and God saw that it was good." In other words, God was the observer. There was no one else around at the time.

If intentional observation is needed for anything to happen, the ancient Hindu Rishis were right on the money when they pictured Vishnu dreaming the world into existence. Take away the religious metaphors and the acts they describe sound pretty modern.

Perhaps we all might benefit by reading again the old texts after first shedding our preconceived prejudices. There might indeed be "gold in them thar hills."

That being said, are there other concepts that explain the creation of our universe that substitute another entity for a supreme God or gods of some sort?

A DIGITALLY SIMULATED UNIVERSE

I remember it as though it were yesterday. In the early 1980s I first felt the video vibe, and it terrified me. Pac-Man had come out in 1980, followed by Ms. Pac-Man in 1981. That's the version that created all the waves in the American arcade market. Sometime after the first home version came out, I walked into a room filled with people who were playing Ms. Pac-Man on their television. I was a video game virgin with a fairly well-attuned spiritual antenna, and for the first time in my life I experienced the frenzy of a room full of gamers. You could cut the hysteria with a knife. I had never felt anything quite like it. A disturbing feeling of almost uncontrolled tension, mixed with something I didn't quite understand at the time, was palpable. I somehow sensed that something new had captured human consciousness, and I had to get up and walk out. I was simply too uncomfortable.

Now, more than thirty years later, the amount of sophistication found in video games has changed so much and extended so far that if you wanted to fly from then to now over the gaming landscape you would have to change planes in route. That's how much things have evolved. The present-day animated characters so familiar to modern gamers have become so realistic, and computer-generated imagery (CGI) effects so lifelike, that it's almost impossible to tell where reality ends and make-believe begins. From the first *Star Wars* series to the second, Yoda went from being a puppet embracing a warm human hand to being an entity who could bounce around a room with more grace than Mikhail Baryshnikov. It's amazing.

But some experts are beginning to wonder. If computer-driven effects and artificial intelligence (AI) have come so far in just a few short years, where will it end? What's possible? Will the characters someday become so life-like that they will actually become sentient, independent entities?

Now take it one step further. Has it already happened? Are we and the whole universe in which we live, in fact, an elaborate digital game programmed by some future kid fooling around with a quantum computer in his basement? Does that explain why, when you look deeper and deeper into the world of matter that appears so real and solid to us, when you eventually get down to the building blocks of everything, they turn out to look suspiciously like pixels on a screen? Is that why chaotic things happen? Is that why we sometimes feel so out of control? Is that why random super villains rise up from time to time and lead willing armies into senseless wars that no one really wants to fight? Is it all a game?

To some theorists the question is no longer *if* it might be possible to someday produce a digitally simulated universe filled with digitally simulated people. The question is, has it already been done, and are we the final result? Are we living in an illusion, programmed by somebody who is playing God? Did it begin when a future programmer wrote his program and switched it on for the first time? And will it end when his mother calls him upstairs to eat supper?

Or how about this one? Are we a computer-generated program launched by a future scientist who just wanted to know what would happen if he programmed in a universe driven by evolution? Where would it go? Turn it on and let it run for while. The result is us. "Wow! Look gang! Evolution can produce sentient life! That should earn me a doctorate!"

Most people, upon confronting this theory for the first time, react with predictable laughter, followed by an immediate look of terror in their eyes. "It can't be! Can it? No! But what if…?" Even Dr. Neil deGrasse Tyson, the popular author, speaker, TV host, and head of the Hayden Planetarium, agrees that this is a distinct possibility.

Video game artificial intelligence sequences are built on a very complex pattern of "if/then" sentences. "If this, than that." Picture a flow chart and you'll come pretty close. *If* the character does this, *then* the result will be that—and so on. It's all based on programmed computer codes, executed line by line. Following these codes, robots function very much like human beings, reproducing human actions one step at a time, only a lot faster.

But now more complex behaviors have been programmed, powered by today's supercomputers. They will soon be followed by tomorrow's quantum computers. In a few short decades, maybe even years, experts believe they will be able to program robots and screen images that will function in virtual reality and be almost indistinguishable from humans.

These creations won't follow line-by-line sequences of code. They will be so sophisticated that they will "think" on the fly, so to speak. They will analyze how a certain input code corresponds to certain outputs in human behavior, and then immediately respond with human-like motions. Essentially, they will be creating their own programs—their own flow charts—in the moment. The programmers will no longer be in control. They will have handed over the programming to their artificially intelligent hosts. The AIs will have learned how to imitate human behavior. They will still respond to lines of code, but they will have written those lines themselves.

If that happens, will the computer-driven artificial intelligences become self-aware? Will they be, in other words, sentient beings?

No, they will still respond to digital codes. If you ask them, "Who are you? Where did you come from?" they will only respond by mimicking observable human responses.

"Whew!" we say. "That's a relief!"

But here's the problem. This is exactly how the human brain works. It sends out electrical impulses, creating chemically induced emotions, based on either imagined or actual previous experiences. Our brain-codes work something like this, absurdly simplified, of course: See the tiger. Hear the tiger growl. Panic! Fight or flight? If fight, then produce weapon. If flight, jump and run!

See? You're following a flow chart of "if" statements, coded into your nervous system. Some of us are coded for bravery, others for cowardice. (Or, perhaps, intelligence. Your explanation will depend on how you're programmed.) Some will fight. Others will run.

We think we are self-conscious, independent entities, but we're wired just like supercomputers. We respond just like robots to external stimuli. We think we are acting independently, in the moment, but we might just be following a sequence of codes.

This raises an essential question. Is consciousness produced in the mind? Is it a byproduct of electrical impulses and chemical responses? If so, we might, indeed, be either independent individuals or software-controlled, artificially intelligent, sentient creatures.

Or did consciousness come first? Are we a product of consciousness? In other words, are our brains producing or interpreting consciousness? Is the computer responding to its own programming? Or is it preprogrammed to respond in a particular way?

I once had a conversation with a man who was very much interested in this subject. He was trying to describe to me how far the computer/MP3/hand-held/Kindle/smartphone/gizmo culture had evolved since the internet went public back in the 1970s. After conveying to him my fear of losing my work if my computer ever crashed, he informed me that he could throw his entire computer in the nearby lake and not lose a thing.

I told him I've had the same thought many times, but, "Where's all your information, your pictures, your tunes?" I asked. "How do you back them up?"

"They're in the cloud," he said.

"What cloud?" I inquired.

That was my introduction to what everybody else in the world but me, apparently, understood. I looked it up online, thereby using "the cloud" to tell me what "the cloud" is. Here's what I discovered:

> In the simplest terms, cloud computing means storing and accessing data and programs over the internet instead of your computer's hard drive. The cloud is just a metaphor for the internet. It goes back to the days of flowcharts and presentations that would represent the gigantic server-farm infrastructure of the internet as nothing but a puffy, white cumulonimbus cloud, accepting connections and doling out information as it floats.
>
> —Eric Griffith in *PC* Magazine: www.pcmag.com

When I read these words it sounded to me as if we humans had invented a "cloud" technology that duplicated how the universe really works. According

Cloud computing is a recent technological invention, but it happens to also reflect how the universe functions.

to the ancient Hindu mystics, all the information (or what we would call "bits" today) is out there in what they called *Akasha,* a Sanskrit term. Today we call it consciousness. We access it through our brains, the "hardware" of the analogy. The "software" corresponds to the various religious/philosophical outlooks we espouse. We even call it the same thing—"memory."

The analogy is perfect, except that *our* cloud, the internet, is a human invention. The *real* cloud is Consciousness. In other words, we have created robots and artificial intelligence in *our* own image. Using the cosmic cloud as a model, we created artificial life forms called video characters that think and act according to our bidding. If we ever do manage to create a completely artificial sentient being (like the android Data of *Star Trek* fame), we will have mimicked the exact same structure of intelligence that we now experience here in our material world.

"But wait a minute!" you exclaim. "We were the ones who placed the information in the cloud in the first place. The information was already there before the artificial life form we created ever evolved."

Exactly! First the cloud, then the artificial life form. First Consciousness, then humanity. First the information, then the download. First the future programmer, than our universe. The future creates the past, which we, who are playing the game, experience as the present.

"But the internet cloud is a product of intelligence," you insist. "It had a creator. Us!"

Right, with one important difference. Consciousness didn't just *have* a creator. Consciousness *is* the Creator. And then we came along, made in the image of the Creator, and were able to not only access the information, we were able to do it in full consciousness while being aware of the fact that we were doing it! Consciousness accessing consciousness while being fully conscious. That's what it feels like when you live inside a digitally programmed computer program.

"Now, hold on," you shout. (By now you're getting excited.) "The 'information' that you're talking about isn't really hanging around in a 'cloud.' It exists in millions of computers that are sitting around out there in every country on Earth. It's accessed by an electromagnetic, quantum infrastructure grid that connects every computer on the internet to every other computer. It's real. It's a verifiable fact!"

Exactly! Each and every human being, everything in all of creation, is connected. It all exists in a universal field, an "information" field that Carl Jung labeled the collective unconscious and Ervin László, reverting to ancient Hindu Sanskrit, dubbed the Akashic field. It is a power field, the ground of our being—a mystical field that is at the same time magic and real.

Einstein accessed it. (What do you think he was doing when he engaged in "thought experiments?") Did Newton and Socrates and Brahms and Mozart and the builders of ancient monuments and Hindu mystics and every other genius who ever lived.

What goes around comes around. We, the participants and recipients of Consciousness, have invented our own version in our own image.

The ironic thing is that most people today are just about as ignorant of all this as their computers are ignorant of *their* own individual identity. At least I don't think computers are aware that they exist. Not yet, anyway. (Maybe the next upgraded models will be. Sometimes I think mine already knows.) And if we ever do build artificial intelligence able to obtain consciousness, that is, awareness of its own existence, than AI will have completed the journey that our first ancestors began when they stood up, walked over to the nearest fruit tree, and decided to "fill the Earth and subdue it."

Now comes the big question. If we ever will be able to accomplish this feat, who is to say that it hasn't already been done and we, including our whole universe, which is the backdrop of our existence, aren't the product of this programming?

Are we "living the dream," the product of a future computer's generated artificial reality? At this point, we just don't know for sure. A very good case could be made that our explorations into the very nature of the universe, from its beginning to the present day, look suspiciously like a computer-generated video game, down to the very pixels that form the substance of what we call matter. We even fall asleep every night so that we can be defragmented and processed, while our dreams produce a "memory loop" of what has happened to us.

But if we stop to ask whether we should continue along the path of creating artificial intelligence, we might come to the realization that if we stop now, we might be short-circuiting our very future—that is, the future existence of a programmer who created us in his or her image.

That's exactly the conundrum posed by Preston Greene, an assistant professor of philosophy at Nanyang Technological University in Singapore. In an article entitled *Are We Living in a Computer Simulation? Let's Not Find Out*, published in the *New York Times* on August 10, 2019, he revealed that some top researchers in the fields of social and natural sciences have been quietly studying this problem in depth.

The whole project came about by accident. The researchers had set out to "try to answer questions about our world: What causes war? Which political systems are the most stable? How will climate change affect global migration? The quality of these simulations is variable, since they are limited by how well modern computers can mimic the vast complexity of our world—which is to say, not very well."

The project managers realized that to obtain the accuracy they needed they were going to have to ramp up their computers to a much higher degree. Currently that wasn't possible, but one day, and one day soon, it would be, given the progress computer technology was experiencing.

Then the light bulb went off. It wasn't possible now, *but very soon it will be!* That's what set them off. They began to imagine a future of technological innovation.

In Greene's words, "What if computers one day were to become so powerful, and these simulations so sophisticated, that each simulated 'person' in the computer code were as complicated an individual as you or me, to such a degree that these people believed they were actually alive? And what if this has already happened?"

That led to the 2003 prediction by philosopher Nick Bostrom that we might already be living in such a simulated world. He puts it this way:

> If people eventually develop simulation technology—no matter how long that takes—and if they're interested in creating simulations of their ancestors, then simulated people with experiences just like ours will vastly outnumber unsimulated people.

> If most people are simulations, the odds are good that we ourselves are simulations. Our world would be just one simulation of many, perhaps part of a research project created to study the history of civilization.

George Smoot, Nobel laureate in physics, estimates the ratio of real to simulated people might be as high as 10^{12} to 1.

This led to an interesting experiment conducted in 2012. Although it was, by necessity, a very complex experiment, the bottom line goes something like this.

Some of the simulations carried out on modern computers used to study the cosmos produce what are called "distinctive anomalies." That's a technical term for glitches. Specifically, they appeared while studying simulated cosmic rays. Physicists who detected these glitches, or anomalies, began to think that we might be able to detect comparable anomalies that occur in the universe. If they did, that would be evidence that we are actually living in a simulation.

University of Oxford philosophy professor Nick Bostrom considers it possible that our world might one day have more simulants than humans.

By 2018 Professor Smoot had garnered enough evidence to officially declare, "You are a simulation and physics can prove it!"

So far, confirming experiments have not been conducted. Preston Greene hopes they never are. He has come to the conclusion that if the truth is discovered, one of two things might happen.

The first is quite boring. The second would be catastrophic.

Think of it this way. What if experiments prove we are *not* living in a simulated universe? That would be met with a gigantic ho-hum and "I told you so!" from the assembled multitudes and be forgotten by tomorrow morning.

See? Boring.

But what if we are?

Greene uses the analogy of current scientific studies that employ placebos and projects moving forward in time. If patients learn whether or not the pill they have been taking is real medicine or a sugar pill, the experiment becomes worthless. The whole procedure is immediately scrapped.

He thus argues that it would be crucial to future scientists that we do *not* discover whether or not we are living in a simulation. If we find out, the whole experiment falls apart and a future someone will pull the plug, ending everything we know, or think we know, about who we are. The result would be the annihilation of our existence.

One of two things would happen. The results would prove utterly boring, or we would be suddenly be destroyed. Either way, why try to find out? There might be value in the results, but why take the chance?

Here's another way to look at it. Suppose scientists working at the Large Hadron Collider, the giant European particle accelerator, announced that "this experiment is unlikely to succeed in producing an interesting result, but if it does, it may cause the annihilation of our universe." Would it be a worthwhile experiment?

It's worth thinking about.

INTERVENTION FROM BEYOND, PART I: SPACE

In this chapter, and the next two, we're going to go where cosmologists fear to tread, and with good reason. If an entity or entities unknown, and here you can insert the notion of God, or gods, or the Force, or something quite beyond our ability to conceive, exists and created our universe, there is absolutely no way of proving it with the traditional tools of science. That is a given, but just because we can't conceive of something doesn't mean it isn't there. And therein lies the central problem between science and religion, metaphysics, or spirituality of any kind.

To put it in a nutshell, when we talk about belief systems involving anything beyond our ability to prove, versus fact-based systems we can measure, we have moved out of the arena of reasoned discoveries and into the arena of differing ideologies. Two people can sometimes debate facts and still remain friends, but when ideologies enter the picture the atmosphere often gets rather murky.

People believe what they want to believe. That forms their ideology. Then they gather facts to support that ideology. This is exactly the opposite of how science is supposed to work. Unfortunately, scientists, being human, often operate in precisely this fashion. Many a scientific fact has been suppressed because it didn't fit into the current ideological niche. Witness the whole Clovis First ideology that held sway for fifty years in American archeology.

The same goes for politics. Conservatives and liberals lob supposed facts across the great gulf that separates them and can't understand why their counterparts on the other side can't see what seems, to them, as plain as day.

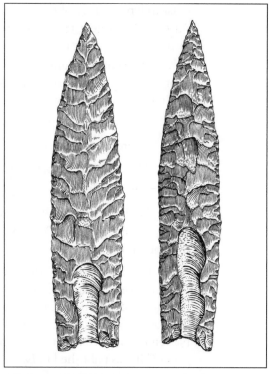

The spearheads of the Clovis people (named for the place of their discovery in New Mexico). Studies at the turn of the twenty-first century revealed that this single group was not the first to populate the Americas almost 13,000 years ago.

Within religions, members of one sect cite holy texts that, for them, settle any issue once and for all. They can't comprehend how people on the opposite side seem so blind.

Atheists compile what, to them, seems like irrefutable evidence that a god cannot exist. Believers shake their heads in amazement at what they consider to be woeful ignorance and lack of faith.

In any battle between ideologies, facts don't matter much. The thing that changes people's mind is not an intellectual decision, but rather a moment of conversion. Only after an "Aha!" moment does a liberal become a conservative, an atheist become a believer, a Catholic become a Protestant, or a Clovis First archeologist become a radical diffusionist.

If you don't believe it is possible for this universe of ours to have been created by an outside entity of some kind, you might want to skip the next three arguments. Or at least you'll probably read them with an inner smile and wonder at their naïveté. If you, on the other hand, believe in God or gods who exist independently of the universe, you will probably accept one of the ideas set forth but reject the other two. It's not my intention to change anyone's mind. I'm just trying to be thorough and present the viewpoints.

If an entity or entities unknown created the universe in which we live, it or they are alien to our understanding and are either eternal or incredibly ancient. Hence, we now jump into the waters of ancient alien theory.

Where could such an entity come from?

There are three possibilities.

This first one is that they come from space itself.

That idea is going to need some fleshing out. How could space be created by an entity from within the space it is supposed to have created?

Let me explain. Or rather, let me defer to a few others who have tried to explain it.

Caleb Scharf is an astrophysicist. He holds the title of director of astrobiology at New York's Columbia University and studies consciousness in both humans and machines. His book *The Copernicus Complex: Our Cosmic Significance in a Universe of Planets and Probabilities* is listed in the back of this book. In November of 2016 he wrote an article entitled "Is Physical Law an Alien Intelligence?" It was published in *Nautilus* magazine, and he almost certainly regretted it as soon as it came out. The response, much of what was extremely critical, was overwhelming. Soon after he had to write another article in which he said he was merely putting forth what to him was an intriguing idea. He didn't intend it to be a scholarly article subject to peer review, but whatever he intended, it certainly struck a chord.

He began by quoting Arthur C. Clarke's famous dictum that any advanced technology is indistinguishable from magic. "If you dropped in on a bunch of Paleolithic farmers with your iPhone and a pair of sneakers, you'd undoubtedly seem pretty magical, but the contrast is only middling: The farmers would still recognize you as basically like them, and before long they'd be taking selfies, but what if life has moved so far on that it doesn't just appear magical, but appears like physics?"

From there he began to speculate. Since so many have taken his idea seriously and run with it, I feel free to do the same. It leads to an interesting idea.

Simply put, what if the beautiful, mathematically complex universe in which we live is, itself, it's own intelligent designer? What if the laws of physics, both classical and quantum, are not simply functions of how the universe operates? What if they rather demonstrate its very personality? Could it be that in a short time we will become, like Scharf's Paleolithic farmers, so used to the idea of mathematical perfection that we will cease to be amazed and start seeing it for what it is?

As Scharf himself puts it:

After all, if the cosmos holds other life, and if some of that life has evolved beyond our own waypoints of complexity and technology, we should be considering some very extreme possibilities. Today's futurists and believers in a machine "singularity" predict that life and its technological baggage might end up so beyond our ken that we wouldn't even realize we were staring at it.

Others have approached, albeit cautiously, a similar idea. Max Tegmark of MIT, for instance, believes that "our external physical reality is a mathematical structure." (His book *Our Mathematical Universe* is listed in the Further Readings.) In other words, mathematics does not merely *describe* the universe. The universe *is* mathematics, and human beings are, in his words, "self-aware substructures."

At the risk of oversimplifying the work of these brilliant men, think of it this way.

Suppose the universe is a physical structure, the "body," if you will, of a conscious intelligence that sought to take on material form? According to this line of thought, we are very small cells of that immense body who have evolved the ability to consider such things as existence itself. When we study physical laws that seem somewhat miraculous, we have simply discovered the personality of our host. That's the way it functions.

To explore a little further, I'm going to pause for a moment to consider another line of evidence that goes way beyond anything Scharf and Tegmark brought up. They would probably steer clear of this observation, but I find it intriguing, so here goes.

Going back to the time of Pythagoras, Greek philosophers have postulated what they called "mathematical entities." The formal term is "mathematical monism." What they meant was that nothing exists except mathematical objects.

That sounds rather strange to non-mathematical minds who struggled with algebra, but it's intriguing to note that the

Physicist and cosmologist Max Tegmark is a professor at MIT and scientific director of the Foundational Questions Institute that researches today's big questions, including the issues involving the potential risks of advanced artificial intelligence.

The archeological site Göbekli Tepe, located atop a mountain ridge in the Anatolia region in Turkey, has been determined to be over 11,000 years old. Who constructed it remains a mystery.

idea jibes with the experience of ancient shamans, who long ago learned to journey to mystical realms outside normal reality. And what did they often encounter on these journeys? Geometric, or mathematical, shapes that seemed to form the basis of the reality they were encountering. They even considered these shapes to be portals into other realms.

When the old shamans returned from these trips, they taught their tribes to re-create some of these shapes on the ground. As I discussed in my books *Ancient Gods* and *Supernatural Gods*, all around the world we find megalithic structures built along strict geometrical shapes. Recent discoveries in the Amazon, now made possible through the use of ground-penetrating radar, reveal not hundreds, but thousands of these structures. Squared circles, mathematically precise lines that follow exact true north/south and east/west alignments, pyramids, triangles, and complex shapes were imitated way before societies became familiar with geometry and advanced math.

Did the original builders, through strictly psychic means, encounter the true nature of the universe? And did they duplicate that nature on the ground? Is that the answer to the mathematical precision of structures such as Giza and Göbekli Tepe? In other words, did the universe reveal itself through intuition to the ancients long before we blundered onto the secret through our left-brain intelligence? Is that the secret to the nature of reality? Is that why so many of the geometric megaliths seem to be associated with the soul's journey after death? Does math lead us out of the labyrinth of life?

Many scientists are willing to consider the Gaia hypothesis—the idea that our planet is a living, breathing, connected entity in and of itself. Can we now extend that idea to the whole universe? Did an intelligence far beyond our ability to comprehend somehow "decide" to take on material form, and the laws and rules we are now exploring were the chosen means to express the personality, the essential "is-ness," of that form?

If this is so, as crudely as I have put it, what does that mean about our place in the universe? Returning to the words of Caleb Scharf:

The universe does funky and unexpected stuff. Notably, it began to expand at an accelerated rate about 5 billion years ago. This acceleration is conventionally chalked up to dark energy, but cosmologists don't know why the cosmic acceleration began when it did. In fact, one explanation with a modicum of traction is that the timing has to do with life—an Anthropic argument. It's a stretch, but maybe there's something about life itself that affects the cosmos.

This is mind-bending stuff. It's a modern, scientific attempt to explain old realities held by religionists and others who subscribe to a metaphysical ideology. There's no way, given our present technology, to ever prove any of this. People either believe it or they don't, but one thing becomes clear as we consider ideas such as this. It's entirely possible that the equations so beloved by theoretical physicists might not just *describe* life. Life itself may *be* in the equations.

INTERVENTION FROM BEYOND, PART II: TIME

"Time is the school in which we learn. Time is the fire in which we burn."

These words were written by Delmore Schwartz in the poem "Calmly We Walk through This April's Day." In it, he questions the idea of time, but does he go far enough?

We usually think of time as an entity in itself. We "have" it, we "run out" of it, it "stands still," or it "rushes by." We experience it as a river that runs from the past, through the present, and into the future. We use time to measure how old the universe is. We say the universe was created 13.8 billion years ago, as if the universe cared whether or not it had anything to do with how many times our puny Earth has revolved around our average sun. We even use time to measure how far light travels in a second, as if the idea of an artificially contrived second was some kind of universal constant.

Time marks our days and has for a long time. I've written a few books about megalithic cultures. Those are the folks who built places like Stonehenge in England. One of the popular theories about stone circles is that they were elaborate ways to measure time. The builders would watch for the sun as it rose every morning and mark where it came up. Then they would delineate the places where it stopped at its southern and northern extremities, the solstices.

Some archeologists claim they needed to do this because the ancients wanted to know when to plant their crops. I don't buy that because there are easier ways to mark such things that don't involve moving megaton boulders all around the countryside, but many experts seem to think places like Stonehenge were observatories designed, among other things, to measure time.

Some archeologists speculate that Stonehenge served as an observatory. If true, it would be the oldest time-keeping device in the world.

If our megalithic ancestors were that concerned about time, they've had centuries to pass the tendency down to us, and they've done it very well. From measuring time by the season, we soon moved to measuring it by the month. Then those months were divided into weeks and days. Finally, the days, which only had three times to remember—morning, noon and night—were divided into hours, minutes and seconds. We've now reached the point where we're wound up so tight that we pick our supermarkets by how fast we can get through the checkout counters.

Think how pervasive the whole system is. We get used to time before we go to school. TV programs last an hour, with commercials every few minutes. We have designated mealtimes. Then, when we go to school, classes are exactly forty-seven minutes long. Psychologists spend a "50-minute hour" with their patients. Most of us wear digital watches so we can't tell time anymore. All we do is read numbers.

Now that I'm getting older, I find my bedtime is moving up. The other night I felt really tired and wanted to go to bed, but I looked at the clock and realized it was only 7:00, so I figured it was too early. It took ten minutes of nodding off before I realized I had turned over my bedtime to an external clock rather than an internal one.

When we go to work, many of us punch in at a time clock and work at a job that pays us to produce so many pieces of work at exactly a predicted amount of time. We check out at the same time every day, having worked exactly eight hours, no more (or we get overtime) and no less (or they dock your pay). And then, when we finally retire from the rat race of time, what do they give us? Ha! A watch.

But what if time is something completely different from our normal perception of it?

In Marcel Proust's seven-volume novel *In Search of Lost Time* (also translated as *Remembrance of Things Past*), he relates a story of suffering that befalls the hero of the book. Many, many pages later the hero resolves to write a book, which turns out to be the book you have been reading.

The novel is based on a theory that has come to be called the *Participatory Universe Theory*. It proposes that time is a self-sustaining loop: that the universe creates us, and we in turn create the universe. If the universe had an initial existing state, none of this would be possible, but, as we have seen, according to many cosmologists the universe never *had* an initial existing state. It is eternal. It had no beginning—no starting point. The Big Bang that began *our* universe was one of an infinite number of Big Bangs. Something came before. And before that. And before that. Forever. There is no boundary that marks the beginning. According to this theory, time does not exist. There is only an ever-present, eternal experience of "now."

What if something exists "above" the reality of time? How can we who have been born into its illusion possibly conceive of such a thing?

Try thinking of it this way. When you attend the performance of an absorbing stage play, the objective concept of time outside the theater ceases to exist for you. You get totally wrapped up in the experience of the actors. For a while, it feels as though you exist in their time, not yours. Eventually, no matter how many years the action of the drama portrays, the play ends and you return to your normal concept of time. The author of the play has tricked you. He made you feel as though what you were participating in was more real than the ticking of the watch on your wrist. For a few hours you were outside and above the standard of time as it appeared on the stage.

Now consider this. What if life in the universe is a play written by a playwright who lives forever? What if, as actors, we are so much in character that we are not aware that time as we know it exists only between curtain calls? After the curtain falls and the lights come on, we enter a totally different kind of reality.

If we hold to this theory, we find ourselves very close to the parameters of religion and an eternal God who writes the play. Of course, if we choose to fiddle a bit with the controls, we can tweak the concept of God.

Some of you might not be comfortable with a traditional religious concept of God, so, try this on for size. It's a theory called the *Observer-Created Universe Theory*. It builds on the idea in quantum physics that says nothing happens in the material world without the presence of an observer. In this theory, we are the observers. We, as living entities, observe the universe. It then becomes *our* universe.

Because we are in this universe, we select the path our universe took in order to produce *us*.

What this means is that the concept of time is turned around to work in our favor. The present determines the past. We observe in the present and that fixes the past on a course that leads to us.

The only thing that makes this theory work is the basic assumption that there is no "past" in the first place. There is no future. There is only the ever-present "now." The idea that time flows in a river from the past through the present into the future is an illusion. It may well *feel* that way to us. It *appears* to be the way time rushes by, but that's not the case at all.

Now take the theory forward another step. Imagine that you, or perhaps even the whole human race, are a playwright engaged in writing a play that explains how we got to be playwrights in the first place. We imagine the actors, the dialogue, the sets, and the props. After all this we sit back to await opening night and begin to watch the play unfold.

Like Marcel Proust in his famous novel, we have written ourselves into the play and assume the leading role. We not only wrote the play, we are acting in it. And because we are good actors, we totally lose ourselves in the part. We are absorbed by the people in the drama and forget that we are merely actors on a stage.

"All the world's a stage," said Shakespeare, "And all the men and women merely players; They have their exits and their entrances." He was mimicking this theory.

When the play is over, we take our bow and make our exit. Only then, when the lights come on at the end, do we realize that we have participated in a drama starring us. We wake up and come "back to reality."

But what is that reality? The part we played on stage was that of an actor in a drama. Who was the author of the play? We were! The other actors in the play, if they had known you wrote the drama in the first place, would have probably considered you to be a god, a being from "outside," able to control events at will and direct the whole production.

If any of this is true, and of course it's all highly speculative, then the identity of God is now apparent. God is us. Is that what the Old Testament psalmist meant when he said, "Know ye not that ye are gods?" We wrote the play and are now living it out. We're such good actors, and live so totally in character, that we don't realize it. When the time comes for us to take the final curtain call at the end of the drama, we will have arrived back at the beginning of the play and realize the play is over. In some cases, it was a comedy. Sometimes, sad to say, it was a tragedy. Hopefully it will have been a resounding success.

If any of this is true, our universe is the backdrop for a play of cosmic proportions, written by one who stands outside of time as we know it. To again quote the Bard, "Life's but a walking shadow, a poor player, that struts and frets his hour upon the stage, and then is heard no more. It is a tale told by an idiot, full of sound and fury, signifying nothing."

A bit gloomy, perhaps, but worth considering when time seems to pile up on us.

INTERVENTION FROM BEYOND, PART III: DIMENSIONS

We now find ourselves well within the boundaries of traditional monotheistic religion. If our universe was created by an intelligent entity from another dimension, it is very similar to saying, "In the beginning, God created the heavens...." It might sound foreign to some believers, especially those who are Jewish, Christian, or Muslim, to refer to God as "an intelligent entity from another dimension," given the years and years of doctrinal teaching, art, music, and other cultural baggage we have inherited, but that is essentially what the Bible says in its opening lines.

Using the Bible as a guide for the moment, although it is by no means the only text considered sacred by those who believe in an extra-dimensional god, if we read the words of the original authors and impose upon them a twenty-first century vocabulary, we arrive at a hypothesis that sounds something like this:

> God is a hyper-dimensional entity that exists outside the dimensions of our universe. This entity created both the spatial and temporal dimensions that form our material parameters. Because this entity exists above and beyond the dimensions that limit our perception realm, it is able to understand, or in our words, "see," everything that happens to us and everything else. Because time is simply a dimension, this entity can see both past and future, and is able to interact anywhere within this universe, both in space and in time.

In other words, to quote from Robert Browning's *Pippa Passes*: "God's in his heaven, all's right with the world."

Notice how this definition answers a few important questions but raises a lot more. Accepting this theory answers questions about miracles, for instance. When things happen that defy physical laws, it is because God is interacting with the universe from "outside," so to speak.

But this explanation opens up a Pandora's box of problems:

- Why does God interact sometimes and not others? What triggers such interactions? Does God have favorites?

This takes us into the sticky wicket of theodicy, that branch of systematic theology that tries to understand how a good God can allow evil in the world. If evil is real, either God allows it, in which case God is not good, or God is not powerful enough to prevent it, in which case God is not omnipotent. Seminarians have been struggling with this one for millennia. All kinds of explanations have been offered. So far, none have proved powerful enough to stop the discussion.

- What is the true nature of God?

The God of the Old Testament is, in the words of Exodus 20:5, "a jealous God, visiting the iniquity of the fathers on the children to the third and the fourth generation of those who hate him."

This is completely different from the sentiments of the New Testament. Consider this verse from the Sermon on the Mount in Matthew 5: "Love your enemies. Bless those who curse you. Do good to those who hate you and pray for those who mistreat you and persecute you."

The usual way of explaining these contradictory descriptions is to say that God is good—perfect, as a matter of fact—but God's ways are mysterious and far beyond our ability to understand.

But if God is understood to be an entity from another dimension, maybe that entity is not perfect. Maybe the entity has mood swings, just like us. After all, we are said to be created "in his image." If that is the case, things might not be as calm and in control as we sometimes think they are. And that opens up even more problems when it comes to arriving at a definition of ethics or morality.

We like to think such things are patterned on the will of a good God, but what if our Creator isn't that way at all? It gives new meaning to the familiar words: "Thy will be done on Earth as it is in heaven." What if that turns out to be the central problem of history? What if things on Earth really *are* the way things are in heaven? What if the jealous God of the Old Testament really *is* the guiding principle for things on Earth?

- Does God really punish those who oppose God? Is there an eternal hellfire reserved for the wicked, or, even worse, for those who may be good but have never, either through ignorance of the truth or inaction, chosen to believe in God?

The reality of hellfire has always been a powerful stimulant. Listen to these words the famous New England revivalist Jonathan Edwards preached in Enfield, Massachusetts, on July 8, 1741. He called his sermon "Sinners in the Hands of an Angry God":

> There is no want of power in God to cast wicked men into hell at any moment. Men's hands cannot be strong when God rises up. The strongest have no power to resist him, nor can any deliver out of his hands. He is not only able to cast wicked men into hell, but he can most easily do it…. Though hand join in hand, and vast multitudes of God's enemies combine and associate themselves, they are easily broken in pieces. They are as great heaps of light chaff before the whirlwind; or large quantities of dry stubble before devouring flames. We find it easy to tread on and crush a worm that we see crawling on the Earth; so it is easy for us to cut or singe a

slender thread that anything hangs by: thus easy is it for God, when he pleases, to cast his enemies down to hell.

Edwards was never able to finish his sermon that day. So great was the weeping and wailing in the congregation that pastors felt the need to go down and walk among the congregants, praying and consoling them. It helped spark the Great Awakening in New England and is still a popular theme of those who follow in the footsteps of modern evangelists, such as the late Billy Graham.

But how does this doctrine of fear and eternal torture fit into a theology of forgiveness and hymns sung to "gentle Jesus, meek and mild?"

It's a problem.

Putting aside the God of the Bible, is there room for an extra-dimensional intelligent creator, who is not so much personality as mind? Is such a creator better described as a field of consciousness, divorced by its sheer infinite size from the reality we normally perceive?

Theologian Jonathan Edwards (1703–1758) preached hellfire and brimstone sermons to his New England congregation. How does using religion to incite fear fit into the idea of a kind and loving Jesus?

Stephen Hawking spent much of his life searching for what physicists call the *Theory of Everything*. This is the grand unification theory that unites the fields of classical and quantum physics. Ervin László claims to have found it. It lies at the center of his Akashic Field Theory, released to the world in his 2004 book, *Science and the Akashic Field: An Integral Theory of Everything*.

László was born in Budapest, Hungary, in 1932. He has written more than seventy-five books and published hundreds of scientific papers. He is a serious scholar who is well-respected by those in various scientific communities such as philosophy of science, integral theory, and systems theory. When he talks about "developing a holistic perspective on the world," a view he labels "quantum consciousness," he speaks with the authority of a man well-versed in multiple disciplines.

When I wrote about him in my book *Ancient Gods*, I said these words:

Using math and the tools of the physicist, [László] claims to have discovered a field of "in-formation" that he calls the zero-point field—a place (which is really not a "place" at all) from which all energy "forms" existence. Existence, then, is constantly being formed. It is "in-formation." The zero-point field is Ground Zero in terms of being that particular point from which every single ripple of quantum energy originates. It is the mysterious field that eludes and tantalizes the scientists at CERN's Large Hadron Collider in Switzerland. It is home—the "mind of God"—the place that is both originator and receiver of particles that spring into existence from "nowhere" and go back to "somewhere" just as quickly. It is our home as well—the Alpha and Omega, the beginning and the end, of our existence.

Could it be that László's "mind of God," a phrase used by both Albert Einstein and Stephen Hawking, is just that? Can the "intelligent entity" worshipped by much of the world for thousands upon thousands of years, the entity called "God," actually be understood in terms acceptable to scientists or those who consider themselves to be atheists? Is there an intelligence outside the universe, dimly recognized and intuited since humans first stood upright and began to develop a capacity for symbolic, religious thought? Has the problem between science and religion all this time not been about substance as much as semantics? Are they both talking about the same thing but just using different metaphors?

If any of this is true, and if a new generation of both scientific and spiritual thinkers can put behind them all the cultural baggage that has littered the playing field for lo these many years, we might be on the breakthrough of a new and powerful understanding of reality, no longer bound by prejudicial language and hyper-critical opinions.

That would be a breakthrough indeed, for it would mark a new level in our evolution. I wrote about this evolutionary leap in my book *Faith, Trust, & Belief*:

> Solutions to our problems do not lie in technology and innovation, although they will be necessary tools. No, the only real solution lies in a change of heart. Human beings must experience a breakthrough of the spirit. We must pierce the illusion and connect with the Reality that is, rather than the reality that appears to have surrounded us. The future hangs in the balance. It's that serious. The hope of the world lies in our ability to create new life, new ways of doing things, new ways of thinking. We need, all of us, spiritual growth and a change of direction.

If a super-intelligent, hyper-dimensional entity—"God" if you will—exists, and is the source of reality, we will never contact or unite with it using the tools of the scientists. The very best scientific research can offer is a collection of circumstantial evidence, but given the spiritual history found in virtually every culture on Earth, such an entity seems to *intend* that we connect with it. Why else do we find religious thought so compelling? Why else do we keep returning to the spiritual quest?

Of course, if you don't look for something, you won't find it. Those who espouse the idea that "God created the heavens …" will keep reminding us to continue the search.

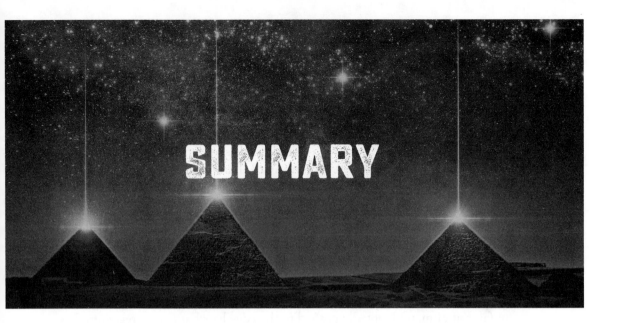

SUMMARY

Where did the universe come from?

After covering a plethora of ideas, some accepted by mainstream cosmologists and others not, all we can say for sure is that no one knows. That doesn't mean there is a lack of opinion. Far from it. Strident voices have arisen from all sides, some heaping absolute scorn on those who disagree with them.

And that's the problem, isn't it? When people want answers to deeply felt questions, they tend to clump around ideologies that, according to them, best encompass the given facts, but, in truth, ideologies are based upon gut feelings as much as anything. When other facts cloud the issue, the tendency is often to suppress them, acting as if they are not important. That's why it took so long for the Big Bang theory to fight its way to the top of the heap, clawing its way over everything from the religionist's "God created" to Einstein's Steady State. Then, when most everyone finally settled on the fact that the universe began with a bang, it took a lot of effort for other variations and some of the totally different theories we have examined to find their place in the sun. Some of them seem to be succeeding quite well and threaten to replace the Big Bang theory. Others are still struggling.

What is missing in the debate right now is not a new fact or theory, although that will definitely help shape the ongoing search. What is missing is humility. Outshouting an opponent does not move the argument forward. Suppressing an opponent's research doesn't help either.

In 1904, Austrian physicist Ludwig Boltzmann attended a conference that brought together the leading experts of his day in order to discuss, among other things, atomic theory. Boltzmann's ideas now form the basis of much of what is known about thermodynamics, but he was at the conference for another reason. His goal was to defend the idea, around since the time of the Greeks, that the atom was at the root of everything.

Present at the conference were two other physicists who disagreed. Wilhelm Ostwald and Ernst Mach thought atoms were nothing but a theoretical construct. In other words, according to them, atoms didn't really exist. Using their own phrase, the two of them were there to bring about the end of "the old atomic-mechanistic world picture."

When the conference was over, many attendees thought Ostwald and Mach had carried the day. They were ready to move on from atomic theory. After much name-calling and ridicule, the atom was pronounced dead. It was great sport, and a good time was had by all.

Except for Boltzmann. Two years later, distressed by what he felt was unfair criticism, undoubtedly pushed to the edge by what is now recognized as bipolar disorder, Boltzmann hanged himself.

His death was undoubtedly one of the great tragedies of science. Were his ideas, today respected and almost universally accepted, worthy of so much scorn that they should prematurely hasten the death of a brilliant man?

The history of science, and, to be fair, many other fields as well, is littered with such events. Let's call this behavior by its rightful name—bullying. A bully seeks to suppress an opponent—to cover up inconvenient facts. We often hear that in order to succeed a person has to have "thick skin." If a scientist presents a new idea for consideration, he or she will need courage to face up to the coming storm of ridicule such ideas generate.

But why? If only "thick-skinned" researchers survive, doesn't that mean that the course of evolution itself will select for such people and eliminate any sensitive, "thin-skinned" scholars? And what, in heaven's name, does being "thick skinned" have to do with intelligence? Maybe that's precisely the problem with the progress of the human race when it comes to understanding who we are. Maybe we have elimi-

Austrian physicist Ludwig Boltzmann (1844–1906) fiercely debated that atoms did exist, an unpopular scientific view at the turn of the last century.

nated the best and brightest among us, allowing only those whom evolution has programmed to shout the loudest and thus carry the day.

Alfred Wegener, for instance, was the one who first conceived of an idea he called *Kontinentalverschiebung*. That means continental drift. He was met with such violent ridicule that his peers in the American Association of Petroleum Geologists convened a conference for the sole purpose of discrediting him, but his work now forms the basis for the theory of plate tectonics.

No one remembers who else attended that conference. Wegener is lauded as a genius, but what cost was he forced to pay for his insight?

Every one of the theories we have examined so far has been the victim of vicious attacks by those who ought to know better. Every theory has faced ridicule in the world of academia. Maybe time will prove them all wrong. Maybe the real answer to the question of origins has already been discovered but has been suppressed because somebody didn't want to put it out there and face what will surely be a firestorm of criticism.

During the time of Isaac Newton, many secretly agreed with his ideas but kept quiet so as not to face the Inquisitors.

There were quite a few scientists who kept silent so as not to be accused of disagreeing with the great Albert Einstein.

How many archeologists uncovered evidence that discredited the "Clovis First" model that held sway in American archeology for fifty years, but were afraid to publish their evidence for fear of losing funding?

The field of cosmology is no different. Something significant happened 13.8 billion years ago. No one knows for sure what it was, but to suggest a novel idea is to submit to ridicule for sure. And the bigger the idea, the louder the ridicule.

Dr. Stephen Fleischfresser lectures and writes about the history and philosophy of science. In the summer of 2018, he wrote an article for *Cosmos 77* called "Head-to-Head: When Scientists Do Battle," in which he outlined the history of some of the tragic battles similar to those we just referenced. It is a sobering read and makes one wonder how much further along we would be had we learned along the way to simply demonstrate human decency and encouragement instead of suppression and ridicule. What if we could someday learn to treat one another with respect instead of derision? It might change the future of our race.

BEGINNINGS: THE EMERGENCE OF LIFE

The Great Chasm

Before we can begin to explore the emergence of life in the cosmos, we have to answer another question: What is life?

Life is usually defined as a condition that separates animals, plants, and microorganisms from inorganic matter. Animals and plants grow, reproduce, carry on functional activity, and continuously change until they die.

That sounds rather simple, doesn't it? So what's the problem?

Well, here it is. Like everything else in the world of matter, life is composed of energy that, on this side of the newly discovered Higgs Field, takes on mass in the form of atoms. Atoms combine to form the 118 types of elements listed on the periodic table, and not all of these are the exclusive province of life.

Carbon, for instance, seems to be a particular favorite of living things, but it can also form objects like diamonds, which certainly add to the luster of life but are not themselves alive. How does it happen that carbon can sometimes reach such a degree of complexity that it is able to bestow life and all of its prerequisites to creatures such as humans in all their cellular glory? How does a carbon atom become alive and form self-replicating DNA that can be passed along to offspring? Diamonds can't do that.

In other words, life, complete with consciousness in all its self-aware glory, is composed of lifeless atoms. How did that happen? Atoms and molecules, no matter how complex, are not alive. The cell is the actual fundamental unit of life. The frontier between life and non-life is between atoms/molecules and the cell, but nobody knows where that frontier may lie! Our task now is to survey some different theories and hope to at least direct the search down productive avenues.

The basic question we need to ask is this: Is life on Earth a lucky, once-in-a-trillion occurrence or is it somehow an inevitable consequence of the laws of nature? If life was a statistical fluke, then the universe is probably a pretty dull place, but if it occurs naturally, or even supernaturally, then we are probably not alone and it's just a matter of time before we encounter it elsewhere out there among the stars. If the great chasm that exists between chemistry and biology is a simple traverse, the universe is probably full of life. If not, not.

Back in 1953, Stanley Miller and Harold Urey conducted a famous experiment that sent shockwaves through the religious community. Until then, the answer to how life began was thought to be a simple one. God did it. No matter what your religious persuasion, it was a pretty safe bet that science was never going to produce life. That was thought to be a one-off miracle. Period. The chasm between life and non-life was too great to be bridged by any other means.

But Miller and Urey designed an experiment wherein a beaker was filled with a mixture of gases thought to be similar to those that made up the atmosphere of the very early Earth. They were suspended over a small flask of water, which represented the early oceans, and then zapped with an electric spark, which duplicated lightning.

After letting things continue for a week, they examined the contents of the beaker, only to discover that some organic amino acids had formed a kind of scum along the edges. From this experiment was born the idea that some of the chemical components of life could arise through natural processes. Mind you, nothing crawled out of that beaker. They had not created life. All they had done was to show that the chemicals needed to produce life had formed, but it was still an important experiment.

It was, of course, met with derision. Most new ideas are. The British astrophysicist Sir Fred Hoyle led the charge. He was famously quoted as saying that the appearance of life on Earth would be the equivalent of a tornado sweeping through a junkyard and somehow assembling a Boeing 747.

Chemist Stanley Miller's (1930–2007) experiments on the primitive origins of life wrought the creation of the term "prebiotic soup."

The story of the Miller–Urey experiment didn't end in 1953. As material continued to be refined over the years, including additional data by Miller himself, who tested various gaseous mixtures, scientists learned that the mixture of gases they used, mostly methane and ammonia, didn't exist in sufficient quantity on Earth at the time life was supposed to have originated. The atmosphere at that time was made up of carbon dioxide and nitrogen. In 1983 Miller repeated the experiment, correcting for the new information. It turned out to be a dud. Very few amino acids were formed. The religious establishment breathed a great sigh of relief. God seemed to be back in the creation business, His competition now safely eliminated.

But the rejoicing in the camp of the creationists didn't last long. Jeffrey Bada was a protégé of Stanley Miller, and in 2011 he conducted the experiment again, this time correcting some flaws in Miller's technique. The results duplicated the 1983 experiment, but this time there was a sufficiency of amino acids.

In contrast to Bada's work, many scientists believe that amino acids were not formed on Earth but rather arrived here as passengers on a passing comet or meteorite. We'll have a lot more to say about that later. However the amino acids came to be, once biological life began, the process of evolution could now begin in earnest on Planet Earth.

In all the confusion arising in the battle between the "Only God could do it" folks and the "Give nature credit" camp, a substantial truth seems to be suppressed.

Here's the problem. There is a huge gap between a self-replicating cell, complete with DNA that can be passed on to offspring, and an inert, nonliving piece of matter, even if it contains all the essential chemicals. For matter to take on life, a tremendous number of things have to fall into place at the very same time. One depends on all the others. They all have to come into existence together. There is no time or room for gradual evolution because until everything works just right, there will be no offspring to pass on the parent's DNA.

Try this experiment. Pull up YouTube, the History Channel, or some other network that features science documentaries. Type in something like "How Did Life Originate." You'll pull up hundreds of TV specials. They will be brimming with breathless talking

A world of science-related entertainment and information is available 24/7, but there is still no credible explanation of how matter first took on life.

heads, some of them quite famous, marveling about the various places life could have come from. There will be spectacular special effects depicting the early Earth, deep ocean rifts, bubbling cauldrons of steam, or vast ice fields.

They will be immensely entertaining, but they will all share one thing in common. From the opening credits to the final theme song, not once will some reputable scientist say he or she knows how life bridged the great gap, either here on Earth or in some faraway galaxy.

We now come to the essential theory of how life began. It's accepted by virtually everyone, from every field of science. We know that the great chasm between life and nonlife was somehow bridged. We know approximately when it either occurred on Earth or arrived here from somewhere else. We know it happened because the proof is that we are here. We know the mechanism behind how it accomplished its great evolutionary journey from then to now.

But how did it happen? How was the great chasm bridged? How does nonlife somehow live?

No one knows. Here's the bottom line: There is no Prime Theory of "Beginnings: The Emergence of Life."

NATURAL ALTERNATIVE THEORIES

The World of RNA

There are lots of theories propounded and many ideas being discussed. Here are a few of them.

For those who took biology classes a long time ago and haven't kept up on the latest breakthroughs, or for those who missed class on the important days, we need a quick review of how life differs from nonlife.

Ribonucleic acid (RNA) is present in all living cells. It acts as a kind of go-between, picking up instructions from deoxyribonucleic acid (DNA) that carries genetic information. Everyone knows what DNA is because Abby Sciuto used it for more than a decade to solve crimes for the *NCIS* television team. DNA is why blue-eyed kids spring from blue-eyed parents and basketball players often produce tall children.

Why do you have blond hair? Because your DNA, inherited from your parents, predetermined you to have blond hair. How did the cells of your body get the message? RNA told them to do it. To be technically correct, RNA carries the instructions from DNA to "control the synthesis of proteins." But sometimes RNA oversteps its bounds a bit and actually carries genetic information itself. It works by informing cytoplasm, the jelly-like solution composed mostly of water, salts, and proteins that fills each and every one of your cells, how to go about doing its job when it comes to reproducing itself and passing along genetic information.

Got that? Neither do I, but that's what I learned when I read a whole lot of books that you now don't have to read. You can thank me later. Although one I do recommend that you pick up right away is a book called *Strange Sur-*

DIFFERENCES BETWEEN DNA & RNA

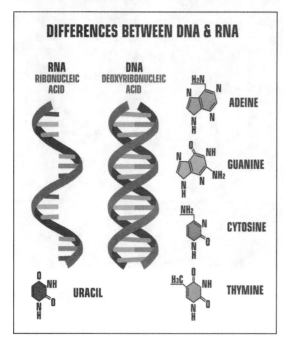

RNA
RIBONUCLEIC
ACID

DNA
DEOXYRIBONUCLEIC
ACID

ADEINE

GUANINE

CYTOSINE

URACIL

THYMINE

The differences in the structure of the DNA and RNA molecules are illustrated here. DNA determines genetics, and RNA instructs the body.

vivors: How Organisms Attack and Defend in the Game of War, by Dr. Oné R. Pagán, professor of biology, blogger, writer, and obvious lover of the natural world in all its mystery. It's a great read. (You'll find it listed in the Further Reading.)

In Dr. Pagán's words:

Sadly, this (the mystery of how life began) is one of many mysteries that we have little hope of ever solving completely. This key moment happened about three and a half billion years ago, giving geology plenty of time to erase any evidence that might tell us how life got its start. And this is assuming that life started here on Earth!

The point of this little excursion into an unsolved mystery is that somehow, somewhere, sometime long ago in Earth's history, or maybe even somewhere else in the universe before the Earth was formed and ready to support life, chemistry made the jump to biology, bridging the great chasm. If we're going to examine how that happened, we have to know at least a little about this stuff.

A long time ago, the Earth reached a Goldilocks zone, neither too hot nor too cold (although the indications now are that that zone is a whole lot bigger than we once thought) and the miracle took place. Life arose from nonlife. That means the conditions, however horrendous they might now appear, were ripe for the jump to occur. It was a very big jump. Even, as some have said, almost insurmountable. Whatever the process, it must have had something to do with RNA, a molecule that has been around for a long time and does all sorts of amazing things at the cellular level.

When biologists talk about RNA they use words such as "catalytic activity," "protein molecules," and "enzymes." I bring this up because it points out that life, even at the primitive levels found in early Earth history, is an extremely complex thing. RNA must have been around since the beginning.

But even here there is a lot of argument. Some researchers believe life began with simple molecules and later evolved into RNA. A few others, however, hold that a lot of different environmental conditions could have come together in a perfect storm to produce a complex scenario conducive to the development of RNA. In other words, what might have happened is essentially the creation of organic minerals, forming a kind of waiting room wherein prepared, ready, and willing material was ready to leap across the chasm separating life and nonlife when conditions were right.

All this is extremely technical stuff. Biology is a highly complex discipline. Can we ever learn to generate RNA-based life in the laboratory and then let it proceed down the path that leads to biological evolution?

Well, maybe, but it sure seems to be a long way off right now. It's important research, however, because it leads to answers about life in the whole universe, not just life on Earth. Obviously, the process occurred. We are living proof. Somewhere, somehow, it happened. If it is an extremely rare occurrence, happening on Earth only, the universe must be a pretty sterile place, but if nature produces the great leap naturally, chances are that the universe is full of life.

Which is the case? So far, all we can say is, stay tuned.

FIRE AND ICE

In the last section we put forth the idea, long held by many in the field of biology, that assumes life originated in what has been described as "primordial soup" when amino acids formed in a thick environment of water, methane, ammonia, and hydrogen after the whole mixture was sparked by lightning. Lightning certainly qualifies as the heat and sparks used in the famous Miller–Urey experiment of 1953, but there are possibilities involving heat and the origin of life that don't depend on electrical discharges.

A relatively new theory suggests that life may have originated, and maybe still is originating, deep in the ocean within warm, rocky structures called hydrothermal vents.

On April 9, 2014, the Woods Hole Oceanographic Institute published the results of research conducted by geochemists Eoghan Reeves, Jeff Seewald, and Jill McDermott, who were the first to test an idea that was first proposed in 1977, when scientists discovered colonies of biological communities clustered around seafloor hydrothermal

A 3-D rendering of a hypothermal vent of the kind found at the bottom of the ocean. Despite the lack of light, an entire, thriving ecosystem was discovered around these vents.

vents, thriving far from sunlight. It turns out that such environments provide an ideal incubation laboratory because they contain the soup necessary for the emergence of microbial life that could later evolve into the rich ecosystem we enjoy today.

Were extreme places such as these the place that life emerged? If so, the possibilities are good that other planets could duplicate this same kind of environment throughout the universe. The key to the process is something called methanethiol. Could this be the key chemical needed to bring forth life? Is this the substance that bridges the great gap between life and nonlife?

As it turns out, no. The new study found that methanethiol is not found in quantities once thought. Maybe RNA and then DNA didn't come first in the quasimagical jump to life. Instead, methanethiol might be a byproduct of microbial life that has already formed.

Eoghan Reeves puts it this way: "Maybe methanethiol just wasn't a good starter dough. The hydrothermal environment is still a perfect place to support early life, and the question of how it all started is still open."

Simply put, this theory challenges the whole idea about life not existing until fully functioning DNA arrives on the scene. It would be extremely difficult to imagine life consisting of anything other than information-storing molecules along the lines of our DNA. This is an extremely complex system that would have had a hard time seeing the light of day without a lot of things happening coincidentally all at the same time.

But maybe life isn't just about replicating information and passing it along to offspring. Maybe there's another process at work. Assembling new proteins and building cells requires a lot of energy. Is there a simpler life form that could have existed until all the complex processes were ready to step into the spotlight of life?

This is difficult stuff to deal with. Cells use energy from food to push protons, composed of hydrogen atoms, into a sort of reservoir contained by each cell membrane. Eventually, what we wind up with is more protons on one side of the membrane than the other. Then, just like a power dam built on a river, the protons flow back through molecular-sized "turbines" embedded within the membrane. This generates the kind of energy used to fuel the rest of all the cell's activities.

Maybe, however, life could have made use of other energy sources, such as heat, electrical discharges, or even radioactive minerals. If so, any energy source, such as those found in deep hydrothermal vents, might be of service. As a matter of fact, such vents may be the only other source of energy where such effects could be harvested.

Is this how nonliving molecules bridged the great gap? At least it's a possibility, say the authors of the new study.

But fire and heat may not be the key to discovering the origins of life. Instead of life forming in the oven, it may have formed in the freezer.

Colin Barras, writing in the February 26, 2016, edition of the *New Scientist* daily bulletin, reports that this might, indeed, be the case. It turns out that at the time life supposedly formed on Earth, our planet might not have been the hellhole that it was thought to be. It might instead have been a giant snowball.

This theory results from an analysis of 3.5 billion-year-old rocks discovered in South Africa. This, you will remember, was exactly the time when life was thought to have first seen the light of day. The Earth was supposed to have been pretty hot back then, but a careful study of the rocks from that time indicate that the oceans might have been about the same temperature as is found today. Perhaps even colder. And there may have been ice present.

Quite a few climatologists doubt the evidence, but, as we have seen time and time again, scientists love a good fight. There is a growing voice in the scientific community, however, that asks whether life could have formed in the more stable conditions of frozen water rather than the volatile conditions of volcanic vents. Indeed, the world of RNA hypothesis could really have benefitted from such conditions. Ice slows the breakdown of fragile molecules, giving them more time to do their molecular thing.

Or, perhaps a compromise could be considered. What if life formed in hot, hydrothermal vents emptying into cold seas?

Back in 1972, the same Stanley Miller we mentioned earlier had placed a vial containing a mixture of ammonia and cyanide in ice. He carefully tended it for the next 25 years, telling almost no one about it. Once in a while, he had added dry ice to make sure the concoction kept at a constant minus 107 degrees Fahrenheit. The temperature was chosen because it was the same as Europa, the icy moon of Jupiter. This sample was just one of many he had hidden away at various temperatures and climatic conditions. He wanted to cover all the bases.

His former student, now a colleague, Jeffrey Bada, was the one who checked out the frosted vial on a morning that was to become famous. Something had happened. Miller was reportedly calm, cool, and collected, but Bada recognized right away that the formerly colorless mixture of ammonia and cyanide was now obviously coloring one of the numerous cracks in the ice. Both men immediately recognized that they were looking at the building blocks of RNA and DNA and the beginnings of what could be protein.

Criticism immediately followed their announcement, and the argument continues to this day, but a growing number of scientists have long thought cold conditions make more sense than warm or hot when it comes to producing life, at least in terms of chemistry. Back in 1982, in his novel *2010: Odyssey Two*, Arthur C. Clarke pinpointed ice-covered Europa, one of the

Jupiter would look something like this if viewed from the surface of its ice moon, Europa. Author Arthur C. Clarke said Europa could have originated life, a theory backed up by an experiment involving dry ice conducted by Dr. Stanley Miller.

moons of Jupiter, as a place life could originate in our galaxy. Maybe we need to dust that novel off and read it again.

One thing is certainly clear. If an icy world is needed to produce life, the universe has a lot of those conditions to spare. The chances of finding it among the stars would take a giant leap forward if that proves to be the case.

MOLECULES WITH FEET OF CLAY

So far, we've seen that life might have begun in fire. It also might have begun in ice. Now we come to a third possibility. Did life begin in clay?

The Bible claims that this is where humans came from. Genesis 2:7 says humans were created from the "dust of the ground." The Hebrew word translated as "dust" is *afar*, but that doesn't help us much. It's true that *afar* can also be translated as "mud," but it also encompasses "lichen," "grass," or even "stones." Besides, the Bible only uses *afar* when it refers to human beings. According to Genesis 1, life itself, including everything from plants to animals, was created from nothing. *Ex nihilo* is the phrase usually used, meaning "something from nothing." The religious interpretation that was in place for millennia, at least in the west, is not much help in this case.

To get from clay to life itself, and then to humans, we have to go to Cornell University and a team of biochemical engineers who wrote an article for the November 7, 2013, online edition of *Scientific Reports*, published by Nature Publishing. To make a long story short, although clay appears to be a sterile blend of minerals, it could have been the medium in which complex biochemicals combined to make life possible. Dan Luo, professor of biological and environmental engineering at Cornell, put it like this: "We propose that in early geological history, clay hydrogel provided a confinement function for biomolecules and biochemical reactions."

For those who didn't follow the particulars in that last sentence, here's the layman's synopsis. Clay forms a *hydrogel*. That's a medium that contains microscopic spaces that can soak up liquids, much like a sponge. Over the course of billions of years, all the stuff needed to produce life might have been held in suspension, so to speak, and thus protected until the miracle occurred. Somehow a cell membrane formed, in which life could have been generated.

In the two last sentences we used a "can," a "might have," a "somehow," and a "could have." That sounds, to untrained ears, pretty "iffy." Needless to say, though, a lot of research went into the process and we don't want to belittle the work lest we be guilty of the same kind suppression by disparagement argument we have aimed at others.

Here is the basic problem that led to the experiment. Yes, chemicals could have formed in an ancient primordial soup, but given the vast expanse of the ancient oceans, how could they have managed to come together at just the right time and place to form life?

It's a dilemma, but if they could have been trapped in ancient clay until, by chance, a membrane somehow formed to separate them out from everything else and contain them together in a small space, it would have formed a closed medium in which to work the magic.

To add a little more mystery, clay apparently formed at about the same time cell-like structures first appeared. Coincidence? Well, we'll see. To see where this ends, follow the Cornell University's Center for Materials Research Shared Facilities, supported by the National Science Foundation. They have a long way to go, but they do important work.

BURIED AT SEA

On May 22, 2019, Carl Zimmer, writing in the *New York Times*, reported that scientists in the Canadian arctic recently discovered the world's oldest known fungi fossils. That might not seem important at first, but it

Yes, chemicals could have formed in an ancient primordial soup, but given the vast expanse of the ancient oceans, how could they have managed to come together at just the right time and place to form life?

opened up a big mystery concerning how life evolved in the oceans and then spread to land.

It works like this. Most of us might not have much interest in mushrooms beyond putting them on a pizza, but when it comes to Mother Nature, fungi are huge. We've identified more than 120,000 species so far, as compared with only 6,400 species of mammals, for instance. Their success lies in their diet. Fungi don't absorb sunlight, like other plants do. Instead, they put out enzymes that break down cells, even rocks, which the fungi then devour. This makes them pretty versatile critters. Remember that the next time you hike past a stand of vicious toadstools. Some fungi, given a chance, even prey on humans, both living and dead, a fact noted time and time again in sci-fi movies about spores invading the Earth.

Way back in the early 1900s, scientists found fungi fossils in Scotland that had fossilized, turning into stone. They were about 407 million years old. Ever since then it has been assumed that fungi and plants came to shore from the oceans at the same time, working together to transform barren rocks into a soil capable of supporting life. Because of this assumption, all fungi were thought to have shared a common ancestor that existed about 407 million years ago.

But when modern DNA tests were used on the new discovery, the numbers indicated that the ancient fungi's common ancestor lived closer to a billion years ago. That leaves a 600-million-year gap in the record, providing all kinds of time for interesting things to happen. The fossils weren't much bigger than bacteria. Does that have implications concerning how early life formed on the planet?

The ancient fungus is called *Ourasphaira giraldae*. You might be hearing about this in the near future. A lot of research needs to be done, but the implications concerning the formation of early life are intriguing. Up until now, the oldest known plant fossils were thought to be some red algae that are about 1.2 billion years old. Apparently, fungi have a long and illustrious ancestry.

Remember that when you eat your next pizza. You're eating ancient history.

THE GAIA HYPOTHESIS

In the 1970s, the chemist James Lovelock and microbiologist Lynn Margulis proposed that planet Earth contained so many interlocking systems that depend upon each other, and are so closely integrated, that they form a single, complex, self-regulating system that maintains the conditions for life. Resurrecting an ancient name for Mother Earth, they called their idea the Gaia Hypothesis, following the suggestion of the novelist William Golding.

The hypothesis suggested that the best way to study life as we know it is to face the fact that, in terms of function, the Earth exhibits all the elements that we recognize as a single, interlocking organism. The biosphere and the evolution of life-forms contribute to the stability of global temperature, ocean salinity, oxygen in the atmosphere, and other factors that figure into an explanation and understanding of such things as habitability and the sustainability of life itself.

❂ The theory was initially criticized, ridiculed, and suppressed but has now been proven so conclusively that the proposition is currently studied by geophysicists, Earth system scientists, biochemists, ecologists, and philosophers.

The Gaia Hypothesis is that Earth is a living, breathing single organism composed of systems that rely on one another.

In layman's terms, the Gaia Hypothesis says that the Earth is a living, breathing entity much like the human body, with its various systems and organs, and needs to be treated as such if humans are going to survive.

It's a wonderfully comforting theory because it makes science become much more holistic than it usually proves to be. Rather than following the principles of dissection and compartmentalization so common to many scientific disciplines that follow the principle of reductionism, it unites various disciplines after centuries of division.

It fits in with the truly spectacular pictures we have of the Earth as viewed from space. In those wonderful images, our planet is not divided by lines on a map, check points, barbed wire, or political ideologies. It is one living, blue, splendidly shining whole. We see land and ocean, continents and ice caps, mountains and rivers, rain forests and deserts, clouds and rainbows. We see every element contributing to the whole. It is unimaginable to leave any piece out and still have a whole. To say Earth doesn't "think" is to ignore our part in the greater scheme. After all, our brains can't function without other organs of our bodies.

Those who picture the Earth just as a provider of resources (the "Drill, baby, drill" folks) obviously object to this hypothesis. After all, if humans want cheap gas, they certainly don't want to be stopped from having their way with the Earth, and to hell with any Arctic caribou that may stand in the way!

But to those who view life from a broader perspective, it makes perfect sense. When you stub your toe, your whole body hurts. When part of the body suffers, you hurt all over. In the same way, when people destroy part of our habitat, even if they, personally, never go there, they are destroying part of a living, breathing organism called Gaia.

It makes a difference in your thinking when you start to throw trash out of your car window. In the words of James Lovelock himself:

> It may be that one role we play is as the senses and nervous system for Gaia. Through our eyes she has, for the first time, seen her fair face and in our minds become aware of herself. We do indeed belong here. The Earth is more than just a home, it's a living system and we are part of it.

What does this mean in terms of the formation of life? It means that we can't separate life from nonlife anymore than we can separate the importance of our fingernails from our red blood cells. They are different from one another only in terms of their function within the whole. Life is evolving, but it didn't begin a few billion years ago. It began with the earliest formation of planet Earth. Everything is dependent upon everything else.

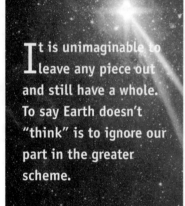

It is unimaginable to leave any piece out and still have a whole. To say Earth doesn't "think" is to ignore our part in the greater scheme.

This is a religious concept as much as a biological one, so now it's time to begin to look at ideas about the origin of life that take us outside the rational, left-brained, scientific method. These are also the ideas most often suppressed in the arena of academia.

In 1987, the microbiologist Graham Bell wrote these words: "I would prefer that the Gaia hypothesis be restricted to its natural habitat of station bookstalls, rather than polluting works of serious scholarship." The microbiologist John Postgate went even further in *New Scientist*: "Gaia—the Great Earth Mother! The planetary organism! Am I the only biologist to suffer a nasty twitch, a feeling of unreality, when the media invite me yet again to take it seriously?"

Ideas such as these to the contrary, we now enter areas of study that cannot be dissected and put under a microscope, but although science once ridiculed the idea of a living, breathing, live entity called Gaia who is an integral whole, evolving with a definite purpose, it's becoming harder to defend such a position.

Adam Frank, an astrophysicist at the University of Rochester, put it this way: "It's definitely time to revisit Gaia." He was echoed by David Grinspoon of the Planetary Institute: "Life is not something that happened *on* Earth, but something that happened *to* Earth.

We now turn our eyes away from the material Earth and begin to ask searching questions about what lies beyond the reach of our telescopes, microscopes, and mathematical equations. We will even begin to confront some questions that are no longer simply ethical or moral in nature, an arena that is usually considered the "proper place" for religion.

If we are only one part of a greater whole, and if we are one intelligent organ of a greater reality, if we are a part of Gaia, then what are we doing, not just to the planet, but to ourselves? If human beings are the evolving brain of an organism called Gaia, is that brain functioning properly? Maybe we don't need a physician as much as a psychologist.

Those are the kinds of questions we need to keep in mind when we look outward, and sometimes inward, for the origins of life.

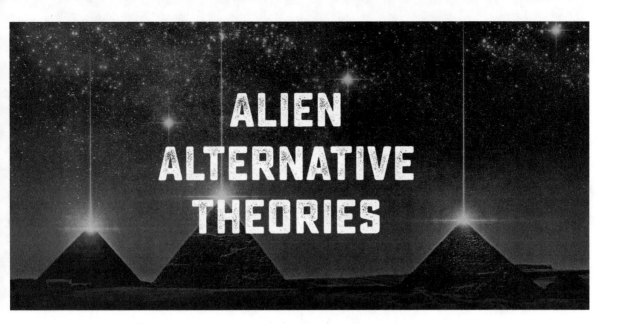

ALIEN ALTERNATIVE THEORIES

BIOLOGICAL SETI AND PANSPERMIA

Are we alone in the universe? Is there life out there among the stars? The answer to these questions could be closer than we think. Instead of looking "out there," maybe we need to look "in here"—in the very cells of our body. Rather than those cells being stamped with a label that says, "Made on Earth," they might have been manufactured, or at least invented, in space somewhere "a long time ago in a galaxy far, far away."

Here's the question, expressed in the most succinct way I know to phrase it. DNA is code. Bill Gates has described it as being more complex that any software so far invented. It thus stands astride the dividing line between the digital world and the biological world.

If this is so, who programmed the code?

What scientists are looking for is an intelligent signal embedded in genetic code. It would probably be mathematical in nature and something that cannot be attributed to Darwinian evolution. Vladimir I. shCherbak of al-Farabi Kazakh National University of Kazakhstan and Maxim A. Makukov of the Fesenkov Astrophysical Institute call the search "Biological SETI." They claim that they have a better chance of detecting such a signal than those who are engaged in trying to decipher radio signals from space in a relentless search for extraterrestrial life.

In the journal *Icarus*, they put it this way:

Once fixed, the code might stay unchanged over cosmological timescales; in fact, it is the most durable construct known. Therefore, it represents an exceptionally reliable storage for an intelligent signature. Once the genome is appropriately rewritten, the new code with a signature will stay frozen in the cell and its progeny, which might then be delivered through space and time.

To acknowledge hypothetical genetic code messages properly, strict rules of conduct have been formulated for their search. Any signal must be statistically relevant. It must have a high degree of probability. It must possess what is called "intelligent-like features that are inconsistent with any natural known process." In other words, researchers will need to prove that the signal was deliberately placed in living cells by an intelligence that expected us to someday find it.

Makukov and shCherbak claim to have already hit a rich vein of information. According to their interpretation, genetic code "appears to have been invented outside the solar system several billion years ago."

This immediately brings up the theory of Panspermia.

There are only two ways life could have begun on Earth. Either it originated here, or it was brought here.

Most scientists who study such things operate on the assumption that somehow, someway, something happened right here on Earth that managed to work the magic. It must have been part of a universal process, eventually understandable to science, built into the very fabric of the cosmos, thus capable of repeating itself on planet after planet throughout the universe.

There are current theories, of course, that attempt to explain it, but the simple truth, as we have already seen, is that no one really knows how it came to pass that one day inorganic material suddenly developed the capacity to manufacture reproducing cells complete with DNA that could guide the course of evolution. Although there have been many experiments that seek to unlock the mystery of life, we just don't have any clear, definitive explanation yet.

The easiest way—or perhaps we should say the most comfortable way—to explain our ultimate origins is to theorize that life *here* was seeded from life out *there*. In other words, cellular life developed somewhere, somehow, in the universe and was then brought here on some interplanetary transport, be it comet, asteroid, or even space dust. Once it arrived on a suitable planet, full of all the right building blocks that could nurture and sustain its existence, it began to flourish, evolving from single cells to what we see all around us today.

Panspermia means "seeds everywhere." Probably the first to think along these lines was Anaxagoras, a Greek contemporary of Socrates, but Aristotle, part of the same crowd, disagreed. He thought life came about by a process he called "spontaneous generation."

Science sided with Aristotle for more than two thousand years, until Louis Pasteur performed an experiment in 1864 that proved Aristotle and everyone else had been wrong the whole time. Although a few diehards tried to hold on by saying life had begun on Earth spontaneously one time by accident before settling down into an observable process, they couldn't save the theory. It died a quick death even though there were no other ideas around that could better explain the problem.

Where and how had life come from nonlife?

There is always the religious hypothesis, of course. "God did it and that settles it!" But science is understandably reluctant to go there.

The path of least resistance seemed to involve kicking the can down the road, or at least off the planet. In other words, we may not know how life developed out *there*, but we can guess how it came to be *here*. Life arrived on an interplanetary visitor that collided with Earth in the distant past after surviving a long journey during which

French chemist and microbiologist Louis Pasteur (1822–1895) is best known for discovering how heat can kill food-spoiling organisms (pasteurization). He also showed that life could not have originated through spontaneous generation.

it lay dormant, awaiting a good environment. The theory works because it seems a logical, safe way to explain things. After all, no one was around billions of years ago to check it out.

That's a good middle-of-the-road theory, halfway between "God did it" and "Ancient aliens produced it." It's feasible and it works. It seemingly solves the problem of life on our planet in the same way anthropologists solve the problem of how a particular continent became home to a particular group of people. "We're not going to discuss human origins in general," they say. "We're just going to talk about how humans got *here*."

But this leads to an inevitable question. What if DNA-carrying bacteria were *deliberately* sent here? What if an ancient civilization faced extinction due to, for instance, its star going nova or another cosmic catastrophe? Such a scenario is usually confined to the sci-fi genre, such as a famous *Star-Trek: The Next Generation* episode (*The* "Inner Light") wherein Captain Jean-Luc Picard finds himself living an earlier, parallel life on a planet that is about to be destroyed. The inhabitants send out a "message in a bottle" to whomever might come across it so that they won't be forgotten.

A surprising number of scientists are willing to consider such a thing. They reason that so-called "junk DNA," the 97% of DNA that we can't figure out, really contains coded messages that tell us who we are and why we are here. In other words, we are the aliens.

DNA Doctors

Rather than life being randomly deposited here, what if an alien presence came and deliberately seeded our planet for the express purpose of producing life on what was, up to then, a barren rock? After all, when we talk about "terraforming" Mars so as to make it habitable, isn't that exactly the same idea?

On July 30, 2018, Bill Steigerwald and Nancy Jones, writing on the official NASA website from the Goddard Space Flight Center in Greenbelt, Maryland, wrote an article with a rather startling headline: "Mars Terraforming Not Possible Using Present-Day Technology."

The shocking part of the article was not that it isn't feasible for us to terraform Mars—that is, make it habitable for human occupation—but rather that it is not feasible *given today's technology*. Here's the conclusion to that article: "Taken together, the results indicate that terraforming Mars cannot be done with currently available technology. Any such efforts have to be very far into the future."

In other words, "We'd do it if we could, but we can't yet. Wait for a few years!"

> How can it be that, on the one hand, we belittle thoughts of alien intervention on Earth when it comes to the origin of life, relegating it to the arena of science fiction, and then, on the other hand, talk about doing it ourselves in the future?

How can it be that, on the one hand, we belittle thoughts of alien intervention on Earth when it comes to the origin of life, relegating it to the arena of science fiction, and then, on the other hand, talk about doing it ourselves in the future? Given the gist of the NASA article, this conversation is apparently being held at the very highest levels of those involved with space exploration. It seems the very essence of hypocrisy to privately plan the very process we publically deride. That is the essence of suppression.

If preparing a planet for habitation by our species is something we would consider, even if "far into the future," it is not that big a jump to think that other species, older and more advanced than us, could have come to the same conclusion. The only fly in the proverbial ointment is the matter of distance. Mars is not very far away, relatively speaking. Once the technology exists, we could travel there easily in a few months, depending on how far apart our two planets are at the time.

Other planets would present far larger obstacles to overcome, but certainly an alien species with the ability to transform life on a planet would have sufficient technology available, even given our current understanding of the laws of physics, to overcome that obstacle.

Space exploration essentially began with the launch of Sputnik, in October of 1957. That was only a little more than sixty years ago. Since then we have launched Voyager I, which has now entered interstellar space. If we can make that kind of progress in such a short time, who knows what might be possible in a few more years?

Let's go even further out on a limb. Given that Mars once had a far different environment than it has now, could it be that life on Earth was actually seeded from Mars? Are we, in effect, Martians? Are we "ancient aliens?" It's just not that fantastic a statement anymore. Apparently, people in the upper echelons of science are saying such things to each other. Maybe they need to say it to us as well.

PHYSICAL INTERVENTION

That being the case, is there any evidence of ancient alien activity on Earth? Is there anything in our history that points to the startling conclusion that life as we know it came about as the direct result of past ancient alien intervention?

Yes, there is. I believe we can find three lines of evidence that point to the fact that our ancestors believed that entities beyond the confines of the boundaries of our planet played an important role in the origins of life.

Evidence in Religion

The first line of evidence can be found in ancient religions that have been around for thousands of years.

Religions of all types are steeped in dogma and tradition, so it's hard to break free of cultural baggage and consider religious mythology with fresh and inquiring eyes, but when we make the effort, surprising insights come to light. What if the ancients were intuitive enough to remember things that we, in our rush to systematic, left-brained thinking, have forgotten? What if they understood things we have confined to the dustbin of superstition and ignorance? Might their stories, found in what we now call religious texts, reveal profound truths that have been hiding in plain sight all these years?

Religions of all types are steeped in dogma and tradition, so it's hard to break free of cultural baggage and consider religious mythology with fresh and inquiring eyes, but when we make the effort, surprising insights come to light.

We have already touched on some of these questions. Let's explore them in more detail.

Is this the first universe, the first cosmos, to exist? If not, did our distant ancestors know it? They might not have had access to our radio telescopes and space probes, but did they utilize another means of perceiving what modern cosmology is just discovering? Did the old ones *intuit* what we have *deduced*?

Way before we learned anything about big bangs, infinite multiple universes, and quantum theories that render our rock-solid material surroundings into sensory illusions, had our ancient ancestors already come to the same conclusions that our cutting-edge physicists are now beginning to explore? And are those conclusions found hidden in the great religions of the world, buried deep beneath the doctrinal rubble that covers over most religious traditions?

Let's begin with one of the most ancient world religions still in existence.

The principle creation metaphor of Hinduism, one of the world's oldest religions, goes something like this:

> Brahman meditates on the lotus blossom growing from the navel of Vishnu, who sleeps on the cosmic ocean made up of the remains of the last universe before this one. When Brahman opens his eyes to look around, a world comes into existence. One day in the life of Brahman is four billion, three hundred and twenty years, or one world cycle. Then he closes his eyes and the world disappears. When he opens them again, another cycle begins. All this goes on forever.
>
> —Jim and Barbara Willis in *Armageddon Now*

That sounds suspiciously like a poetic interpretation of the latest version of *Multiverse* or *Membrane* theory, but it is a story that has been told and retold for 5,000 years! And it is not the only one. Stories very much like this have been conveyed down through the centuries all over the world. When freed from the physical shackles of the body, the mind can, and often does, penetrate areas where even telescopes and particle accelerators cannot follow. Do our religious traditions illustrate this fact?

The ancient Hindu *rishis* (wise men) did not follow the path of math and science. They followed their intuition and inner guides to the Source. They called it the Akashic Field. In the words of the *Rig Veda*: "Sages who searched with their hearts discovered that what exists is akin to the non-existent."

By "searching with their hearts," the Rishis found "what exists." The Hindu expression for the material world is *Maya*, which means illusion. In other words, everything that we think is "real" is, at its root, an "illusion"—not what it seems.

Consider a story familiar to most Western believers. Most Jews, Christians, and Muslims have all read the opening verses of the book of Genesis. What happens when we convert the poetry of the Bible to more modern vocabulary? A word-for-word translation doesn't really work because poetry conveys images, not facts, but when we substitute the words "Conscious Energy" for "God," when we throw in a reference to the Higgs Field, through which energy takes on mass, when we compare the "days" of the Genesis account roughly to the epics of the Big Bang theory, and when we allow the imagination of 5,000-year-old intuition to run free, it's not that hard to reconcile the poetry of Genesis with the theories of science.

Rishis (shown here near the Ganga River in Varanasri, India) are not men of science but rely on intuition in their search for the origins of existence.

There is no way we can authentically step back into the shoes of the ancient ones. We don't know what they were thinking and feeling, but we can look at the traditions that grew out of their experience, the religions they began, the "culture" that formed around the "cult," and possibly discover clues about what they knew.

Earlier we looked at the possibility that our cosmos is not the first cosmos. This is classic Hinduism. We saw as well that life on our planet might have arisen somewhere else. Are we just the latest, most evolved, sentient beings to come down the pike or have there been others? And, as unbelievable as it sounds, have those "others," and here you can insert the word "gods" if you like, attempted to leave clues behind so that intelligent beings in the *next* cosmos, perhaps *our* cosmos, can discover them when a species arises that is smart enough to find and interpret them? Did the ancient ones explore the answers to these questions using methods and employing abilities that have atrophied in us, due to disuse? If so, then we are now *discovering* these concepts, not *inventing* them.

If quantum theory, for instance, is true today, it was just as true in the time of the ancients. If it proves to offer adequate explanations of how the cosmos came to be, that explanation was just as available to the old ones. They might not have had the use of our modern scientific toys, but they may well have had other means at their disposal—intuitive methods we are just now beginning to acknowledge. Those methods could very well have been preserved in what we now call religion.

Albert Einstein and Stephen Hawking were forced to resort to religious language when they sought to discover, in their words, "the mind of God."

> **M**ass and energy are the same thing. Life is a swirling mass of energy that came from somewhere, no one really knows where, and eventually winds up somewhere else, or perhaps back where it began.

Lately, Ervin László resurrected the Hindu term *Akasha* when he needed to explain a universal field of consciousness that is "in-formation."

These are the questions that religions were first invented to explore, yet here they are, the subject of scientific investigation.

The "mass" of the material world, of life itself, the "*m*" of $E = mc^2$, is really energy—the "*E*" of the equation. Mass is energy. Energy is mass. Mass and energy are the same thing. Life is a swirling mass of energy that came from somewhere, no one really knows where, and eventually winds up somewhere else, or perhaps back where it began. Before Einstein's equation, mass was *some*-thing. After, it was seen to be *no*-thing. Dspite what our senses tell us, life is really an illusion. With one simple equation, $E = mc^2$, Einstein concluded that mass (*m*) and kinetic energy (*E*) are the same thing, since the speed of light (c^2) is constant. In other words, mass can be changed into energy, and energy can be changed into mass. And it's not a matter of one *becoming* the other. Both are present and equal *at the same time*.

How did it all begin? No one knows. The religious answer is just as valid as the scientific one. God, aka The Great Mystery, is still at the beginning of the equation.

Do we owe our very being to the collapse of another whole cosmos? Have there been previous universes? Was there any time? Was there any space? Was there anything at all? If so, what was it? Has a previous cosmos passed on to us some bit of information that we someday might come to learn is responsible for our very existence? Is that not a definition of the word "God?"

These are religious questions—the greatest origin questions of all. They go back to the time when, "In the beginning," the whole Cosmos began. Physicists lose sleep over this stuff, but they keep trying to figure it out with mathematical computations that grow more and more complex. Brane Theory, String Theory, Big Bang Theory, Multiverse—it seems as if the list grows every year. It turns out that even scientists have molded themselves into "denominations."

Our question is this: Could it be that religion and science are actually on the same quest but using different methods? Neither set of methods is sufficient of and by itself, but if they join together, might they be able to go where previously we have never gone?

The problem is that the religionist and the scientist don't talk together very much. They don't respect each other enough, but if each learns the other's language and respects the findings inherent in the methods of the opposing disciplines, interpreting those findings within accepted parameters of language and tradition, who knows what might become possible?

Evidence in Stone

The second line of evidence that life is the creation of entities beyond the confines of the boundaries of our planet is to be found in the edifices of Earth and stone built by our ancient ancestors. If there is a universal doctrine found in ancient religion, it is this: "As above, so below." They believed the origin of life on Earth was to be found in the heavens, and they attempted to reproduce that reality on Earth. Echoes of this belief are to be found even in modern religions. Every Sunday, Christians recite what is called in some traditions, the "Our Father," and in others, "The Lord's Prayer": "Thy will be done on Earth as it is in heaven."

Pyramid builders of the past were obsessed with the idea that life came from the stars. In China, the Xi'an Pyramids mimic the alignment of Orion's belt, as do the pyramids of Teotihuacan in Mexico and the ones found on the

This is the Pyramid of the Sun as seen from the Pyramid of the Moon in Teotihuacan, Mexico. It was built by people who looked to the stars for answers.

Giza plateau in Egypt. These are just some of the hundreds and hundreds of ancient monuments built to point to the heavens while identifying astrological data found in the night sky.

Sometimes, for reasons that defy logic, the ancients even went deep underground to reproduce the heavens on the ceilings of caves. Why? No one knows, but it might have something to do with the Shamanic tendency to visualize a world above and a world below this one.

Obviously, something was going on in their minds that we have forgotten. Perhaps it's because we are no longer creatures of the darkness, able to easily see and access the stars. Our lives are so lit up and illuminated that we have lost contact with the heavens, but our ancestors knew. They understood.

To make a long story short, we don't know what they were trying to convey, but the labor they undertook proves beyond a shadow of a doubt that they were trying to preserve something that was very important to them. If we are ever going to understand where life came from, maybe we need to recapture at least the essence of their worldview.

Evidence in Story

The third line of evidence that life is the creation of entities beyond the confines of the boundaries of our planet is to be found in the world of mythology—the world of stories.

Michael Witzel, a linguist and philologist from Harvard University, is a bit of a synthesist. He has employed the techniques used in molecular genetics, anthropology, and archeology to make a rather radical proposal.

In his book *The Origins of the World's Mythologies*, he puts forth the argument that because many myths from cultures that have never been in contact with one another share so many similarities in terms of similar story lines, plot twists, and central characters, they might have had a common origin. Given great amounts of time and retelling, the stories change over the years, but because they came from a common source, whether they are mythologies from India, Japan, Greece, Egypt, Mesopotamia, or the Americas, they retain some of their essential character.

When geneticists or archeologists find similar traits in their studies, they assume a common ancestor. Could the field of mythology demonstrate this same kind of connection? What if a common ancestor once told a tale about the creation of life. His ancestors took this tale with them as they dispersed throughout the world, modifying it over thousands of generations, but keeping the central focus.

Why is this such a radical theory?

Because, say the critics, in order to locate the common ancestor, you have to go all the way back to Paleolithic times. Witzel believes that our first ancestors—at least a hundred thousand years ago and maybe a lot longer than that, going all the way back to whoever the "African Eve" might have been—told the first stories that are still remembered today. In other words, just as apes and humans had a common ancestor whose traits and DNA we shared long after that ancestor had disappeared from Earth, our linguistic DNA, so to speak, reveals our connections to the very first *Homo sapiens*. Witzel suggests there was a "proto-language" from which all languages have evolved, and ancient origin myths and stories are the proof of his theory.

If he is right, then it appears that the key to deciphering the first examples of symbolic thinking, found in great painted caves and rock art around the world, is to understand that they were early attempts to unlock the meaning of life. Our ancestors asked the same questions we ask. "Who are we? Where did life come from? Where are we going? What's it all about?"

Witzel indentifies an early split in our linguistic family tree that divided humankind into what he calls the Laurasian mythological branch, found in Europe, Asia, and the Americas, and the Gondwanan mythological branch, the oldest of the two, found in sub-Saharan Africa and in an arc across to Australia. In his words:

> Witzel suggests there was a "proto-language" from which all languages have evolved, and ancient origin myths and stories are the proof of his theory.

Laurasian myths share a common storyline that tells of the creation, in mythic time, of the world, of several generations of deities during four or five ages, of the creation and fall of humans, and finally of an end of the universe, sometimes coupled with the hope for a new world. Laurasian mythology was successful as it put essential questions and answered them in a satisfactory way. It asked the eternal questions—"Where do we come from? Why are we here? Where do we go?"—and answered them by stating that we are descendants of the gods, who on their part have evolved from early generations and ultimately from the universe itself, whose ultimate origin is prominently debated.

Gondwanan myths, meanwhile, are notable for their lack of a narrative about creation and the origin of the universe. In these more ancient, "southern" myths, the Earth and Universe are supposed to pre-exist and their main focus is on the creation of humans and their culture. Often the creator in Gondwanan mythology is a deus otiosus, or "idle god," who withdraws back into the sky after the act of creation.

This is a fascinating theory for many reasons, but primary among them is that the implied truth might have had insights into our origins that far surpass our own.

Take the flood myth found around the world, for instance. It is a universal theme and implies a memory of an actual event that was witnessed by our ancestors. It might be the most ancient memory found in our psychological DNA. The same holds true for stories about "heaven and Earth," about primordial darkness and chaos, about slaying dragons or serpents, and gender-based gods who came from afar to begin life on this planet. If these stories revolve around a kernel of historical truth, amplified and augmented, of course, they might illustrate memories more than made-up stories.

If your knowledge of mythology is limited to hearing a few Joseph Campbell videos or watching the latest Marvel Comics movies featuring Thor and Loci, here's a quick course in Mythology 101. It's a fascinating subject and deserves a lot more attention in high schools and colleges that tend to emphasize math and science over the humanities.

Myths about the creation of the universe and our place in it are called Cosmogonic Myths. Although we tend to treat them with a bit of disdain these days, especially when it comes to carrying any kind of useful scientific meaning, in their original forms and cultures they were considered to be prime vehicles for expressing profound truths about the nature of life. They might never have been taken literally in the sense of conveying real history, but they were considered expressions of great wisdom. Thus, animals talk, the gods walk among humanity and talk to them, order evolves out of chaos, and heroes arise and perform great acts of courage. What was important wasn't that they described actual history. Their meaning was what set the myths apart. They were meant to be poems, not prose. They produced *images* of truth and reality, not *descriptions* of them. They didn't tell you what life was. They told you how to live it. They didn't describe how atoms form cells. They conveyed what it felt like to be human.

Noah's ark floating across a water-covered Earth is the Christian version of the flood myth ... or perhaps memory of a time of a great water-borne catastrophe.

In the words of Mircea Eliade:

Myth narrates a sacred history; it relates an event that took place in primordial Time, the fabled time of the "beginnings." In other words, myth tells how, through the deeds of Supernatural Beings, a reality came into existence, be it the whole of reality, the Cosmos, or only a fragment of reality—an island, a species of plant, a particular kind of human behavior, an institution.

Astronomers today study cosmology, using the tools of rational empiricism. That's the theory that all knowledge is derived from sense-experience. This is an important field of study, but it's not the only one and often doesn't go far enough.

What is missing is the concept of etiology. That involves looking for the *cause* for something that goes beyond the physical. It's the acknowledgment that there are things going on in the universe that are beyond the capacity of our senses to fully incorporate.

Think of it this way. Empiricism tells you how a symphony is composed. Etiology tells you that it's beautiful. Empiricism tells you the universe began with a Big Bang. Etiology tells you it has meaning. That's the difference between cosmology and cosmogony.

In much of today's world these distinctions are simply not understood. Myths meant to invoke the magic of life are instead studied to work out a rational reason why God exists.

No wonder not many people read Michael Witzel's book of origin myths. We no longer understand how to read a myth, let alone interpret it correctly. We twist a myth into a scientific straitjacket and wonder why it doesn't fit.

There are, however, categories of myths that prove useful when it comes to understanding the intent of the original author.

- *Ex nihilo* myths: We've already talked about this one. These are myths that say life arose from nothing. God created it. The most well-known *ex nihilo* myth is the Genesis account of the creation of the world.

- *World parent* myths: This is the idea that creation occurred because two primeval parents either gave birth to the cosmos or were somehow separated and caused the creation of everything that is. The best-known version is probably the union of Father Sky and Mother Earth.

- *Emergence* myths: In these myths, life emerged from another, usually previous, world. The most well-known example is probably the Hopi emergence myths that describe three previous worlds. As each was destroyed in turn, the people found their way into a new creation.

- *Earth diver* myths: These are stories that depict a supreme being sending a messenger, usually an animal, into primal

Turtle Island, a Native American creation myth, speaks to the creation of the Americas.

waters. The animal returns with sand or rocks that become the foundation for habitable land. According to many Native American creation myths, the Americas, often referred to as Turtle Island, were formed in this way.

What these myths tell us is that our ancestors were interested, probably very early in our species' history, in how life began. It may sound as if they simply engaged in fanciful storytelling as they sat around an evening fire, but they were serious. They wanted to know who they were and why they were alive, able to ask such questions. We may not think they got very far, but, when you come right down to it, do our modern scientists really know any more than our ancient ancestors did?

• How did life arise from nonlife? No one knows.

• Did life arise on this planet or was it brought here from somewhere else? No one knows.

• Does life have a purpose or are we a cosmic accident? No one knows.

• Is humankind following a pre-ordained path toward an ultimate end? No one knows.

Rather than calling mythology less than scientific and relegating it to the back seat of the academic automobile, perhaps we should rather begin really teaching it. We need to elevate it, not suppress it. It might lead to a brand-new way of understanding what life really is. Right now, we're allowing the halls of scientific academia to pull all the strings, but as Dr. Phil used to famously say, "How's that working for you?"

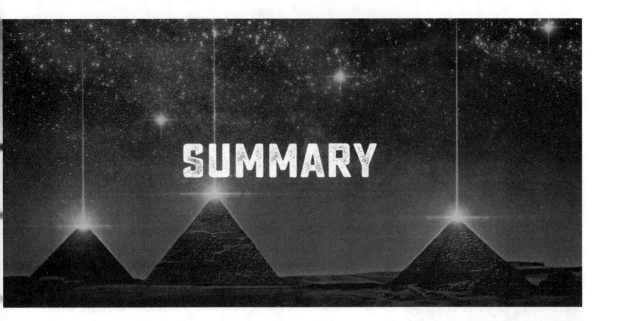

SUMMARY

There is a big gap between life and nonlife, and we're not even close to filling it yet. One of the big surprises I received when researching this chapter was to consult with a number of biology professors, one of whom has been my go-to resource in matters biological for many years. When I asked her to read some of my results concerning this gap, she was quite frank about the chasm between chemistry and biology. What bridged that gap? In her opinion, it was God. This was someone who has taught biology all the way up through the college level and has read most of what has been written about some very complex issues. She knows the ins and outs of all the arguments and is quite used to students sitting in her classroom, laptops at the ready to catch her whenever she might slip up. Yet she still believes, after a lifetime of study and teaching, that only divine intervention can bridge the chasm between life and nonlife.

She obviously can't teach that in a public school. The ACLU would jump on her with both feet if she did. Academics are simply not allowed to bring divine intervention into the classroom. It's not scientific.

But, when you come right down to it, if the facts point to a god, it's not scientific to ignore the facts just because they indicate a road you don't want to travel because it might lead to something you don't believe in.

The problem, of course, lies in the loads and loads of baggage with which we have encumbered any belief in other dimensions and alternate realities. That baggage is called religion. We have so stigmatized words such as "God," "heaven," and "spirit" that to use them in polite company these days is to invite ridicule. It might be polite ridicule, but it is ridicule, just the same. When it comes to the consideration of who we are and how life emerged, we often eliminate the very real possibility of supernatural origins right off the bat.

But things may be changing. New ideas in physics and cosmology give us a language in which we can convey theories about hidden dimensions and alternate realities without resorting to words that no longer ring true. We can talk about parallel dimensions without using the word "heaven." We can talk about intelligent entities outside our perception realm and never once say the word "angel." We can bring up the concept of conscious intelligence and universal intention without using the word "God." We can study psychic phenomenon without resorting to the word "miracles." Such language allows us to discuss what we previously declared to be off limits because we no longer need to tie a religious tradition and primitive dogma to our thoughts about what might exist out there on the other side of the Higgs field.

> New ideas in physics and cosmology give us a language in which we can convey theories about hidden dimensions and alternate realities without resorting to words that no longer ring true.

As a result of all this new openness, both the field of science and the field of religious study can breathe the fresh air of intellectual freedom. People from both sides can now talk to each other. Granted, there is a long way to go. We can't expect centuries of conflict and distrust to fade away overnight, but maybe, just maybe, the windows have been opened a crack. When a scientist can study alternate realities without being labeled a "believer" by some who scorn traditional religion, and when a religionist can think in terms of God being the ultimate ancient alien without being kicked out of church, suppression of opposing ideas is no longer possible.

The key, of course, is respect. Suppression thrives when respect dies. Honesty, following the facts even if they overthrow cherished prejudices and lead to places we don't want to go, and acknowledging the magic inherent in the honest study of life's mysteries, is a spiritual quest as well as an academic exercise. May they both thrive together in the light of wisdom as well as knowledge. Because in the end, they are probably the same thing.

EMERGENCE: THE FIRST HUMANS

PRIME THEORY

LUCY THE *AUSTRALOPITHECUS AFARENSIS*

Human genetics is a fascinating science. Accepted current research suggests that every human being on Earth is descended in an unbroken line, traced through our mothers in a genetic system called matrilineal descent, from one woman who lived in western Africa some 200,000 years ago. She was given the rather catchy nickname "Mitochondrial Eve," named after her genetic lineage and biblical counterpart. Unlike her counterpart, however, no one suggests that she was the only woman who lived at the time. The human population numbered in the tens of thousands back then. Other women alive no doubt passed on their lineage to people living today who carry their genes, but at some point in the long human history since then, each of their lines of descent failed to generate a reproducing female, thus breaking the mitochondrial line. In order for the genes carrying this mitochondrial material to continue into the future, the offspring of these women had to, at some point, mate with the descendants of Mitochondrial Eve, the African matriarch of us all. Mutations have occurred, obviously. We share different color skin and eyes, for instance, but according to the "Out of Africa" theory, every person alive on Planet Earth today is, in one sense, African beneath the surface.

All this biology, however, still doesn't answer two questions. What makes us human and how did we get that way?

Is the answer to be found in our biology or our physical actions? In other words, are we human because of what we *are* or what we *do*?

If we became human when we started to walk upright, then it can be said that our transition from ape to human took place some six million years ago, but if we became human when ancient upright walkers started to have legs mechanically similar to ours, then, according to Smithsonian studies, that would make us some three million years old.

If we became human when we tamed and utilized fire, we are about 350,000 years old.

If we became human when we started to bury our dead with grave implements, signifying religious thought or a belief in an afterlife, then we are about 100,000 years old as a species.

If we search out the very earliest example of symbolic thought, meaning cave paintings and rock art, it was only about 40,000 years ago when we began to hit our stride, although that number is being pushed back almost daily.

What makes us human and how did we get that way? It depends entirely on who is asking the questions.

The interesting thing is this. Recent discoveries always seem to push the dates back further in time. Anthropologists today think our species is much older than did their counterparts of a 100 years ago, or 50 years ago, or even 20 years ago.

What that implies is that if we were sitting, perhaps even dancing, around a fire in the Middle East at least 350,000 years ago, if we were building boats and making voyages across large expanses of water 130,000 years ago, if we were using tools and depositing them all over the world at least 100,000 years ago, we have had plenty of time to develop cultures that are now lost to history. We are an amazing species!

But we have to begin somewhere, so, if you haven't met her yet, let me introduce to Lucy.

In 1974, paleontologist Donald C. Johanson and his team were working in Ethiopia, searching for evidence of early humans. Little did they know they were about to have even their fondest dreams realized. They managed to uncover about 40 percent of an early female human ancestor who lived about 3.3 million years ago. For a while, later researchers even thought they found her baby, but after careful analysis, the "baby" turned out to be about a hundred thousand years older than her "mother."

Lucy's skeleton, officially *Australopithecus afarensis*, is over three million years old and resides in the National Archeological Museum in Madrid, Spain.

In the end, the discovery of both skeletons proved the existence of a human ancestral species now called *Australopithecus afarensis*. At a party thrown to celebrate the discovery, the young researchers kept playing the Beatles' rendition of *Lucy in the Sky with Diamonds*. Hence, the old girl was given a new name—Lucy. It stuck. To this day she remains Lucy the *Australopithecus afarensis*, the "upright ape."

Lucy has a combination of both ape and human features. Her spinal column indicates that she walked upright, but she was only about three and a half feet (107 centimeters) tall. Males were probably a bit larger. She had an ape-like head, with a low, heavy forehead, and a jaw that jutted out. Her wisdom teeth had grown in and her skull had grown together, so she was probably an adult. Her brain was about the same size as a chimpanzee's.

All in all, Lucy is usually cited as our oldest known predecessor. Her offspring, it is thought, probably evolved into our ancestors.

But there are problems that are associated with this scenario. Although the facts are often suppressed, consider a few anomalies in the anthropological record that indicate real human beings are a lot older than Lucy.

- From *The Geologist*, December 1862: "In Macoupin County, Illinois, the bones of a man were recently found on a coal bed capped with two feet of slate rock, ninety feet below the surface of the Earth. The bones, when found, were covered with a crust or coating of hard glossy matter, as black as coal itself, but when scraped away left the bones white and natural." But the coal deposits that had formed over the bones were proved to be at least 286 to 320 million years old. Although any evidence from that long ago is rather sketchy, that is, at least, an eye-opener.

- In Foxhall, England, in 1855, a human jaw was found in a quarry at a level of sixteen feet (4.88 meters) underground. Soil comparisons indicate the jaw was at least 2.5 million years old. American physician Robert H. Collyer described the Foxhall jaw as "the oldest relic of human existence." It appeared to be quite modern, displaying none of the ape-like qualities one would expect in such an ancient specimen. Many dissenters simply ignored the evidence because it didn't fit accepted chronologies.

- Researchers discovered a fully modern human skull in Buenos Aires, Argentina. It was lying in an Early Pliocene formation and suggested the presence of modern humans in South America between 1 and 1.5 million years ago. The modern appearance of the skull didn't fit conventional thinking about human origins, so it was simply discounted, even though the skull was found in Pre-Ensenadean strata, which dates back more than a million years. This is called "dating by morphology," a process that disregards all other data, no matter how credible, simply on the grounds that "this artifact can't be here because it's not supposed to be here!"

- In Paris, Eugene Bertrand, while digging in 1868 in a quarry on the Avenue de Clichy, found parts of a human skull, along with a femur, tibia, and some foot bones. The geologic soil layer was dated to approximately 330,000 years ago. This created problems for scientists because when Neanderthals were finally accepted as ancestors of modern humans, an idea that eventually was discredited, it was difficult to explain why a modern human skeleton could predate Neanderthals.

- In 1911, an anatomically modern human skeleton was discovered by J. Reid Moir beneath a layer of glacial boulder clay near the town of Ipswich, England. It was discovered at a depth of 4.5 feet (1.37 meters) between a layer of clay and glacial sands, dated by the British Geological Survey as being as much as 400,000 years old. The find was rejected by the specialists of that day. In their words: "Under the presumption that the modern type of man is also modern in origin, a degree of high antiquity is denied to such specimens."

- A hill called the Colle de Vento is situated in Castenedolo in the Swiss Alps. Millions of years ago, during the Pliocene epoch, layers upon layers of mollusks and coral were deposited in what was then a warm sea. In 1860, Professor Giuseppe Ragazzoni traveled there to explore the deposits. He later wrote: "Searching along the bank of coral for shells, there came into my hand the top portion of a cranium, completely filled with pieces of coral cemented with the blue-green clay characteristic of that formation. Astonished, I continued the search, and in addition to the top portion of the cranium I found other bones of the thorax and limbs, which quite apparently belonged to an individual of the human species." Geologists and anthropologists of that time, of course, rejected the evidence. They were thought to be a modern burial that intruded themselves into ancient strata. Ragazzoni was, quite understandably, upset with the reception his discovery received, but even more discoveries were located in the same strata. Eventually he contacted Professor Giuseppe Sergi, an anatomist from the University of Rome. In 1883, Sergi wrote: "The tendency to reject, by reason of theoretical preconceptions, any discoveries that can demonstrate a human presence in the Tertiary is, I believe, a kind of scientific prejudice. Natural science should be stripped of this prejudice. By means of a despotic scientific prejudice, call it what you will, every discovery of human remains in the Pliocene has been discredited."

Today most anthropologists are tempted to disregard evidence such as this because it is thought to be old and outdated. Because of such prejudicial suppression, the "Out of Africa" evolutionary theory still reigns supreme when it comes to human origins.

But without discounting the facts of evolution, is it driven by forces that are not quite so prosaic? Are there alternatives out there? Indeed, there are. Here are a few of them.

NATURAL ALTERNATIVE THEORIES

THE ANTHROPIC PRINCIPLE

Earlier, when we looked at origin theories about the cosmos, we introduced Sir Fred Hoyle and his Steady State hypothesis. To quickly recap, in 1948, Hoyle was promoted to Lecturer in Mathematics at Cambridge. He published two papers on steady-state cosmology that year, in which he presented a serious alternative to the Big Bang theory. His theory wasn't based on any recently collected data. Indeed, most of the work being done at that time supported the newly developed Big Bang theory that had rapidly taken over the science of cosmology. No, his problem was that he found the very idea that the universe had a beginning to be philosophically troubling.

That led him to speculate about human life on Planet Earth. Eventually he proposed what is now called the Anthropic Principle. His theory is based more on philosophy than science, but modern quantum physics seems to follow a similar tendency. Its basic tenet is that the universe cannot exist without a consciousness to observe it.

How could the universe be so well balanced as to fall within such a very narrow band of laws that just happen to define the boundaries of human beings and their thought processes? It seems very unlikely. Therefore, Hoyle proposed that human beings originated and evolved within the universe because this is the kind of universe in which they could originate and evolve.

It seems like circular reasoning, but it makes sense, in a philosophical kind of way.

There are currently two accepted variations on Hoyle's original theme.

The first is called the Strong Anthropic Principle (SAP to those in the know) and is championed by Frank Tipler and John Barrow. They believe that the universe is somehow compelled to produce conscious life. In other words, the universe *intended* us. We are its reason for being.

The second variation is called the Weak Anthropic Principle (WAP). Its chief cheerleader is Brandon Carter. He believes the universe is fine-tuned to our specifications because of what he calls selection bias, or even *survivor* bias. In other words, only in a universe that is capable of supporting life will life arise. There might be many other universes out there beyond our perception range in which we could never have come to pass, but this one happened to have suited a particular type of sentient consciousness, so here we are.

> When [Hoyle] began to think along these lines, he was an atheist, but he soon began to believe that the guiding hand of God was behind the whole thing.

This kind of theorizing had a profound influence on Hoyle. When he began to think along these lines, he was an atheist, but he soon began to believe that the guiding hand of God was behind the whole thing. This line of thought eventually led to the concept of what is now called "Intelligent Design," a designation adopted by conservative Christian theology because it was more accepted by the evolution camp with whom they had been arguing ever since the Scopes Trial. We'll have a lot more to say about that later. To Hoyle, the statistical improbability of carbon-based life forms such as humans was too much to overcome. He couldn't imagine such an event without help from outside.

But before we jump right to supernatural theories about the origin of life, are there others to consider that are a bit closer to home?

Of course!

IF AT FIRST YOU DON'T SUCCEED...

It is theoretically possible, given the open-ended aspect of eternity, that the rise of something similar to intelligent, conscious humanity has already happened an infinite number of times and will continue to happen forever. In other words, every possible sentient, life-sustaining universe that *could* ever be, *will* be, given enough time.

Now we'll go a little further out on the proverbial limb. Suppose you someday invent a time machine and travel back into history. There, you change something. When you return back home, cause and effect will ensure that everything is different. You have altered the time-space continuum. The slightest change can produce unimaginable consequences. What if you somehow interfere with your parents ever meeting each other? You'd never have been born, but you obviously were born because you were able to go back into your past.

Before you think this is just another *Back to the Future* scenario, remember that the very latest, up-to-the-minute projections based on Einstein's space/time theories seem to indicate that it might be possible to travel back in time, though probably not forward.

What might that mean? Just this. If a future time traveler went back to pay our ancestors a visit, he might change the reality we are currently enjoying.

Now, what if this has already happened? What if a future someone already launched a new timeline, an alternative reality, and you're living in it? In other words, our origins came about because of a future time traveler.

And if that isn't enough to keep you up nights, could that future time traveler actually be the supreme being people worship today? Could the "God" of religion actually be a time traveler from the future who came back to "in the beginning" just to change the way the world works?

YOU AMONG THE STARS

Here's another possibility.

If the universe is infinitely large, and the elements that compose it are finite, there are only a limited number of ways to combine finite elements within an infinite space. Sooner or later some combinations are going to repeat or start to look similar to others. If you go out on a trip amongst the stars and travel far enough, you're bound to come across areas that look very much alike.

What this means is that although your body is composed of a huge number of chemicals and other stuff, somewhere out there is someone who looks and acts a lot like you because the chemicals that make up them have arranged themselves in the same way that they made up you. You have a twin. There's no other way to say it. There is a planet like Earth with people who look like us. We think *we* are the reality and *they* are copies, but they think *they're* real and *we're* the copies. If they traveled here, they would be amazed to find a species that looks just like them.

It sounds fantastic, similar to a sci-fi writer's fevered dream, but mathematically it works. This view says we are not unique at all. We arose here on Earth, but somewhere out there we can find a copy. It's only a matter of space, time, and statistical probability.

BIOCENTRISM

In 2009, Robert Lanza and Bob Berman wrote *Biocentrism: How Life and Consciousness Are the Keys to Understanding the True Nature of the Universe*.

If the universe is indeed infinite, yet there are only a finite number of ways to organize the elements within it, then it is possible that eventually these patterns repeat, that there could be a second Earth or even a second, twin you.

They followed this up in 2016 with *Beyond Biocentrism: Rethinking Time, Space, Consciousness, and the Illusion of Death.*

The basic premise of their books was that "life is not an accidental by-product of the laws of physics. Nor is the history of the universe the dreary play of billiard balls [i.e., cause and effect] that we've been taught since grade school." Instead, they offered a radical new way of looking at the rise of humankind.

In short, the universe cannot be understood without including the presence of biology. The universe does not create life. Life creates the universe, which is not a byproduct of physical laws. Life creates the physical laws. The sweeping conclusions found in these books challenge the concept of death, as well as changing the way people should think about time, space, and consciousness.

In Lanza's words: "A full understanding of life cannot be found by looking at cells and molecules through a microscope. We have yet to learn that physical existence cannot be divorced from the animal life and structures that coordinate sense perception and experience."

In a plain and simple statement of fact, Lanza places biology "above the other sciences in the attempt to solve one of nature's biggest puzzles, the theory of everything that other disciplines have been pursuing for the last century. Such a theory would unite all known phenomena under one umbrella, furnishing science with an all-encompassing explanation of nature or reality."

Now that's confidence!

What is the theory called biocentrism? How can we understand it if we lack Lanza's experience and specific knowledge? Consider this.

Each theory we have discussed so far about the creation of the universe, life on Earth, and the rise of humankind has this in common: We are the ones making observations. We supply names for that which we observe and write the stories that wind up in textbooks. What if reality lies in the subjective observations we have rather than in the objective objects we describe? What we are describing is our own nature, not an objective reality.

Think about it in simple terms. We say that the moon is so many miles or kilometers from Earth at any given time, and to reach it takes so many days and hours. Once stated in those terms, we accept the results and think no more about it. That's an objective fact.

But how far is a mile or a kilometer? How long is a day or an hour? Those are human-calibrated measurements, not some objective fact. A 24-hour day exists only in our reality. It is based on our planetary experience. We set the parameters and determine the rules. And the same thing holds true for everything we measure and observe.

> René Descartes once famously said :.. "I think, therefore I am."... Although many have since argued with his supposition, what he did was to acknowledge the importance, perhaps even the primacy, of consciousness.

René Descartes once famously said, *Cogito, ergo sum* ("I think, therefore I am"). Although many have since argued with his supposition, what he did was to acknowledge the importance, perhaps even the primacy, of consciousness. We can talk all we want about a mysterious "ether" that, up until a few years ago, filled space. We can speak with reverence about Einstein's space/time or hypothetical, convoluted string theories. We can imagine membranes and parallel universes, but these are all constructs invented by the human mind. No one knows if they really exist. Still, our tendency is to imagine them and then accept their objective existence. In truth, they really exist in our minds—in our consciousness. They are located within us, not "out there" somewhere.

In Lanza's words: "When science tries to resolve its conflicts by adding and subtracting dimensions to the universe, like houses on a Monopoly board, we need to look at our dogmas and recognize that the cracks in the system are just the points that let the light shine more directly on the mystery of life."

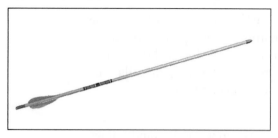

Is the arrow at rest or in flight? If an object is found to be in a specific location, that object must be at rest, or so said Greek philosopher Zeno of Elea, who showed that motion is therefore impossible.

Ultimately, it's the observer who creates reality and our conception of it. It's not something we discover. It's something we create by looking at it with a particular frame of mind and experience and then describing it.

We've already pointed out that the universe exists with very close tolerances regarding human life. A little too much of this or too little of that and we would cease to exist. Why? Because the universe is a construct of consciousness. Without human perception there would be no reality. Until we observe and describe something, for all practical purposes it isn't there. The universe seems to have close tolerances because those tolerances are the ones within our perception realm.

This is hard stuff. It can seem as though we are just using semantics to tout some newfangled idea, but consider this thought experiment.

If you watch an arrow launched from a bow, it appears to fly through the air from here to there. That seems patently obvious.

But think about this. Twenty-five hundred years ago, a brilliant philosopher by the name of Zeno of Elea came up with a paradox he called The Arrow. He started at a perfectly logical point. Nothing can be in two places at once. Thus, at any given time during its flight, the arrow is in one specific location.

Now it gets tricky. If the arrow is in a specific location, it must be at rest. That means that at any and every moment of its flight, the arrow is at rest. The only logical conclusion, then, is that motion is impossible. How could the arrow be in motion if it is always at rest?

What that means is that motion is impossible. The arrow can't fly from here to there because at any and every moment it's not going anywhere. Motion is an illusion, a product of our minds.

Time, therefore, cannot be an absolute reality. It needs consciousness to make it happen. And consciousness needs biological entities to produce its magic—the magic that we call reality.

Before you dismiss this concept out of hand, this is exactly what quantum reality says. The uncertainty principle says that a particle does not exist outside the study of an observer. We make choices all the time. Without those choices there is no determination of the position anything occupies or the speed at which it is moving.

If you're frustrated by all this, take comfort in the fact that Einstein couldn't accept it either. At least not at first. It took him a long time. His space/time was totally incompatible with quantum theory.

And make no mistake about it, it is incompatible. It works in a practical way, however, so we accept both Einstein's classical physics and quantum reality. Both are true *if* we stick to the purposes for which we use them, but don't forget that the choice to employ one or the other is made by a biological entity—us! We choose. Once again, a biocentrist view of the universe is in play.

Let's sum things up in this fashion. Human beings arose because they are the only biological, thinking animals that can describe the elusive substrata of conscious activity. Using this way of thinking, do universes exist that are empty of biological creatures that observe them? No, they don't.

Would they exist if we could somehow travel there? Yes, they would. Because we would then be introducing a thinking, biological creature into the equation who can observe, report, and define.

So if they didn't exist before they were observed, did they just pop into existence when someone asked about them and imagined them? Or, as Einstein famously said, "Is there no moon unless somebody looks at it?"

It's kind of like the Zen question, "Is there sound in the forest when a tree falls if nobody is there to hear it?"

Biocentrism says, "Not only is there no sound without an observer, there is no tree!"

In short, we are dealing with a totally counterintuitive idea—the fact that there is no reality outside of ourselves, in which we live, move, and have our very being. That's an illusion. It's a powerful illusion, and our senses rebel if we consider anything else than its deceptive power, but it's an illusion just the same.

At least, it is according to Robert Lanza. Let's give him the final say:

> Despite such things as the development of superconducting super colliders containing enough niobium-titanium wire to circle the Earth 16 times, we understand the universe no better than the first humans with sufficient consciousness to think. Where did it all come from? Why does the universe exist? Why are we here? In one age, we believe that the world is a great ball resting on the back of a turtle; in the next, that a fairy universe appeared out of nowhere and is expanding into nothingness. In one age, angels push and pummel the planets about; in another age, everything is a meaningless accident.... Consciousness cannot exist without a living, biological creature to embody its perceptive powers of creation. Therefore, we must turn to the logic of life, to biologic, if we are to understand the world around us.

THE MARCH OF EVOLUTION

Michael J. Behe is one of the most controversial biochemists in America today. Stephen Colbert called him "The Father of Intelligent Design." The *New York Times Book Review* says his books about the shortcomings of Darwinian evolution are "close to heretical." Richard Dawkins calls him a "maverick." In 2005, when asked to testify in the *Kitmiller v. Dover Area School District* trial, the court found that "Professor Behe's claim for irreducible complexity has been refuted in peer-reviewed research papers and has been rejected by the scientific community at large." Loved by Evangelical "Young Earth" folks, who believe the world was created just a few thousand years ago, he is reviled by the great majority of the scientific community. His Wikipedia page biography describes him as "an advocate of the pseudoscientific principle of intelligent design," and even his own biology department at Lehigh University, where he a professor, repudiated his views.

How did he come to occupy this treacherous position of both love and hate?

Basically, he claims that biochemical structures are too complex to be a product of evolutionary mechanisms and must be a product of Intelligent Design. To most scientists, that is simply a scientific-sounding way to say "God did it."

He calls his position "Irreducible Complexity," and he has paid the price for making his views known to the wider world in a series of books beginning in 2006 with *Darwin's Black Box: The Biochemical Challenge to Evolution*, and continuing through 2019, with the publication of *Darwin Devolves: The New Science about DNA That Challenges Evolution*. His argument is that the latest scientific discoveries uncover a startling fact that has been ignored and suppressed by traditional academic evolutionary science. Darwin's "mechanism" that pushes biology is actually a process of *devolution*, not *evolution*.

Behe says it like this: "Darwin's mechanism works chiefly by squandering genetic information for short-term gain." In other words, evolution can change things, making them appear different, but it can't create anything at the genetic level.

Charles Darwin (1809–1882) is sometimes called the "Father of Evolution," but biochemist Michael J. Behe says "Father of Devolution" is a more appropriate title because evolution can only change, not create.

To those who teach in mainstream schools, this is heretical, especially when it comes from the mind of someone who knows the scientific lingo, has all the right credentials, and knows how to push all the right buttons. He is able to speak in detail, and even eloquence, about "progenitor fibrinogen genes in echinoderms." He understands more about *Escherichia coli* experiments than many of his detractors. Phrases such as "chloroquine resistance" and "trichromatic vision in primates" are his bread and butter. What layman wouldn't be impressed?

According to Behe, if we are ever going to understand how life arose and eventually produced us, Darwinian evolution won't explain much of anything. Only an intelligent mind, he says, can produce intelligent life.

To put it in its simplest terms, natural life could never have arrived without supernatural help. When it comes to how life bridged the gap between chemistry and biology, let alone how human beings came to be, God did it. No other scientific theory explains it adequately.

I cannot overstate the rancor Behe has generated in the scientific community. Those who argue with his thesis usually spend more time assassinating his character then his ideas. Venom almost drips out of your computer when you begin to read the arguments that "conclusively and completely discredit his books, once and for all." The trouble is that whenever Behe appears at a function to argue his case, the place is sold out weeks in advance. A lot of believers love him.

And that's the problem. His theory of Intelligent Design and Irreducible Complexity has been completely co-opted by the religious right. He quickly became the darling of the creationists.

The second theory that forms the creationist's philosophy involves William Dembski's ideas about Specified Complexity. That's the theory that, in his words, says, "Something that's specified and complex is by definition highly improbable with respect to all causal mechanisms currently known."

What that means is that there are gaps in the evolutionary process that cannot be explained. How did a creature suddenly develop eyes, which are highly complex and need a lot of features to come together all at the same time in order to work? Statistically, it seems highly improbable for a lot of different things to occur at the same time just by chance.

Critics call this a "God of the gaps" theory. In other words, when science can't explain something, someone decides that God must have stepped in to bridge the gap. To such people, this "proves" the existence of God. To others, the fact that we don't understand something yet doesn't prove that we won't someday. That's the kind of search that makes science work. The search for missing knowledge is the key to the scientific method.

On the other hand, Dembski sounds like he's on to something when he points out the fact that scientists are committed to what he calls methodological materialism. Most scientists are wedded to the idea that there is a rational, natural cause for every effect. If a supernatural entity does exist, they'll never find it because their very method eliminates even the idea of the supernatural. If you refuse to consider a possibility, that possibility will never be found.

What does all this mean? Science cannot prove that God exists. Neither can it prove that God doesn't exist, but Creationists can't prove God exists either. Folks on both sides of the argument have already formed their own ideology. In that regard, both scientists and religionists believe what they believe because of their own faith in what they believe in.

Critics call this a "God of the gaps" theory. In other words, when science can't explain something, someone decides that God must have stepped in to bridge the gap.

Once again, we are dealing with ideologies, not facts. And a clash of heartfelt ideologies often leads to attacking your opponents' characters, not their arguments. That's why the venom flows so freely when it comes to discussing the books of Michael J. Behe or the lectures of William Dembski. They both bring up ideas that could undermine the currently accepted ideas about how humans came to be on Planet Earth. Evolutionists feel threatened, sometimes justifiably, but when you kick your opposing theorists out of the club, you are guilty of suppressing the very ideas that might provide a breakthrough to our knowledge.

On the other hand, creationists are not being honest either. They too often are quick to couch outdated and oppressive doctrines in spruced-up scientific garb so as to hide their real agenda.

It's a huge problem, and one that won't go away quickly. The Discovery Institute's "Scientific Dissent from Darwinism" list now has well over one thousand Ph.D. signatures attached to it, so it's not fair when his critics say Behe is on a "lonely and quixotic quest." That's simply not true. Even Werner Heisenberg, a life-long Lutheran who was a giant among theoretical physicists, once famously said: "The first gulp from the glass of natural sciences will turn you into an atheist, but at the bottom of the glass God is waiting for you."

The idea of humans evolving from the natural world, following the principles of natural selection in which the fittest survive to reproduce, is still on the march. Perhaps a much better tactic, however, would be to show a little more respect and a little less rancor on both sides. Setting up straw men and then knocking them down in front of an audience that understands neither the complexities nor the hidden agenda of an opponent is no way to make progress. Only at the end of the journey will we know who was right and who was wrong. Until then, a dose of humility in the face of a great mystery will go a long way.

PANPSYCHISM

Move over survival of the fittest. Step aside gradual evolution through adaptability and random mutations. There's a new player on the scientific/philosophical block. It's called panpsychism, and it threatens to challenge absolutely everything we think we know about what the universe is and our place in it.

On the simplest level, panpsychism makes the astounding claim that the universe, rather than being a sterile backdrop in which materialistic "stuff," such as human beings, evolves and develops, is instead a web of consciousness that brought about everything that is. This way of thinking is nothing new for those who follow metaphysics and some ancient religious systems. The idea of an Akashic Field has been around for millennia, but for scientists operating within the parameters of mathematics and the scientific method, to give such a theory a name and subject it to peer-reviewed papers is a breakthrough. What panpsychism says is that the universe itself might be self-aware and that human beings arose out of that awareness.

Zen masters for thousands of years have said that everything is one, but to give this concept official-sounding labels such as "entanglement" and "proto-consciousness fields" is quite shocking. It means that lines of inquiry that have traditionally moved along two separate roads, called metaphysics and science, may have now merged into one superhighway.

Christof Kock of the Allen Institute for Brain Science, a Seattle-based, independent, nonprofit medical research organization dedicated to accelerating the understanding of how the human brain works, has been designing experiments that define consciousness. His results indicate that biological organisms are conscious if they are capable of changing their behavior when confronted by new situations, but if a system is able to act upon its own state and, in effect, determine its own fate, it is conscious even if it is not biological or organic.

Although he has yet to present his ideas in the form of a formal "Theory of Mind," it is still a fascinating conjecture that has many theoretical physicists rereading traditional religious systems of thought and wondering if the ancients intuited what modern mathematicians have finally deduced. With more experimentation, panpsychism might produce repeat-

Which is the way? The only way to determine is through thoughtful listening and reasoned discussion.

able observations that could lead to fully developed scientific theories about the nature of a universe that intentionally produced us. It might also help understand our unique place in a cosmos that has developed biological entities that are able to comprehend and become conscious of themselves as separate and individual beings.

To fully understand what this means we first have to differentiate panpsychism from other traditional systems of religious thought.

The first systematized religion was very probably what is now called animism. This was the belief that everything is "animated" by fully developed, conscious, and intelligent spirits that eventually came to be known as gods. This differs from panpsychism in that panpsychists shy away from the idea that human-like, and especially godlike attributes live within disparate objects found in nature.

The distinction is important. When the ancient Greeks, for instance, wrote that "everything is alive," it sounded like panpsychism, but they still viewed the universe as a stage upon which animated entities and objects played their part, rather than saying that the universe itself was the author of the play.

Pantheism came closer to the idea when it claimed that everything, collectively, is God, but it didn't go so far as to define the nature of mind and individual entities that make up creation. Baruch Spinoza, the great Jewish-Dutch Sephardic philosopher, considered God and the cosmos to be one but

The ancient Greeks such as philosophers Plato (left) and Socrates believed the universe to be a stage upon which the drama of life was enacted.

didn't speak to the nature of mind itself, so some panpsychists claim him as their own and others don't.

The philosophical/religious system called panentheism surmises that God penetrates everything. According to this worldview, a single, unified God is omnipresent as spirit in all things, but panpsychists argue that this doesn't really represent their views because the concept of "God within something" downplays the notion of the thing itself being a whole and unique expression of universal mind.

These distinctions are subtle. The average layperson probably thinks such semantics get in the way of understanding, but science is complex. To the true scientist/philosopher, specifics are important. If the basic, underlying concept of panpsychism is that all things are an expression of a mindlike quality, or even that all things *possess* a mindlike quality, such minute differentiations are important.

The word "panpsychism" was first coined back in the sixteenth century by Francesco Patrizi, an Italian philosopher. He combined two Greek words, *pan*, meaning "all," and *psyche*, meaning "mind," to describe his belief that all things have a mindlike quality, but this definition is so general in scope that it took until recently for scientists to employ it. What, after all, does "all things" mean? And what is "mind?" Are rocks conscious? Does an electron possess a mind? Until we can agree on definitions for those two concepts, further research is futile.

But panpsychism moves the discussion away from objects and places it instead directly on the fabric of the universe itself. It is the cosmos that is mind, not the objects in it. They merely reflect the greater reality. Sir James Jeans, an English mathematician, astronomer, and physicist, perhaps said it best back in the 1940s: "The universe looks more and more like a great thought rather than a great machine."

It's important, however, to keep reminding ourselves that all this discussion about who first started thinking along the lines of panpsychism theory detracts us from what is really important. The point is not that the modern theory of panpsychism may not, indeed, be very modern. The

Renaissance thinker Francesco Patrizi (1529–1597) of Italy coined the term "panpsychism," meaning all materials have an element of conciousness.

point is that the theory has now bridged a great gulf that, until recently, separated science from philosophy, metaphysics, and religion. It is now officially a cross-discipline field of research. This is extremely important. It tells us that specialists from different academic disciplines are searching for the truth about our ancient origins and that their research is beginning to converge. If panpsychists can bring all things in both the material and the mental realms together under one roof, some startling conclusions come to light:

- First: "Mind" is inherent in all things. It is not injected into them or imposed upon them. They are expressions of mind itself.

- Second: That means "mind" has a focus to it. There is purpose and direction. The universe is not a cosmic accident. Its structure is not accidental, and its unity is real.

- Third: The ancients were right when they intuitively grasped the fact that a forest, for instance, is not just a bunch of trees. It is an entity unto itself, with a unique personality or spirit. It consists of a multitude of systems, such as trees, plants, animals, rocks, and atmosphere, but together all these systems make up one bigger system. And forests are part of a greater system called Planet Earth, which is part of an even greater system called the Milky Way galaxy, and so on, all the way up to a universe, which could very well be part of an even greater system called a Multiverse. In other words, everything is one. It is thus imbued with purpose and direction because it is all an expression of Universal Mind.

People who believe in a God are now saying, "I told you so!" Nonbelievers may like the concept of panpsychism but feel uncomfortable because they instinctively feel that something so complex cannot be contained within the rather simplistic parameters of traditional religious understanding. It is not hard to understand why there is still a great deal of conflict swirling around this whole topic. It comes with built-in dissension.

Perhaps the easiest way to put the two views into context is to reduce the whole problem to two distinct ways to view the universe.

The panpsychism view is that mind came before the universe and the universe is a self-realization, or manifestation, of that mind. "Mind" is therefore distinct from "brain." Our brains are receivers, not originators, of mind.

Think of a radio. Radio waves permeate our existence but we're not aware of them until we tune into the correct frequency to pick up the signal. In this illustration, "mind" is the radio wave. "Brain" is the radio receiver.

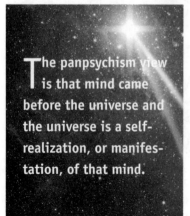

The panpsychism view is that mind came before the universe and the universe is a self-realization, or manifestation, of that mind.

The opposing view is called emergentism. This is the view that a mindless universe came first. Mind somehow emerged from it at a later, unknown time. "Mind" is therefore a product of evolution. Chance rules the universe, and we are the lucky beneficiaries of that chance.

Emergence theory holds sway in the halls of academia these days. The problem is that it is very difficult to explain how mind managed to emerge in biological entities. Most physical attributes, such as eyes and ears, for instance, are simply genetic reconfigurations of things that existed before. Parents pass them on to their children.

But mind isn't a biological constant. A human egg, as far as we can tell, doesn't have a mind. A newborn baby does. How and when does such a miracle take place?

In 2006, Galen Strawson wrote a groundbreaking article called "Realistic Monism: Why Physicalism Entails Panpsychism." Not too many people read it because it appeared, to the best of my knowledge, only in *Oxford Scholarship Online*, but in it he argued that there is one ultimate reality to the universe. "Mind" seems to be part of this ultimate reality, but "mind" consists of mental stuff, which cannot arise from nonmental stuff. Therefore, the one reality and "mind" must be identical. In his words: "Brute emergence is by definition a miracle every time it occurs." Given the universality of mind, that's a difficult fact to swallow.

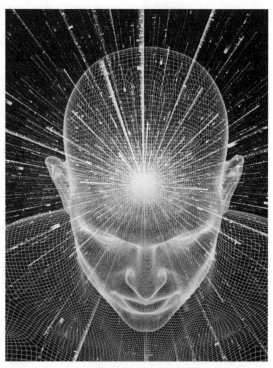

From a strictly rational viewpoint, therefore, the concept of panpsychism has to be at least entertained in any honest scientific/philosophical system of thought. If Strawson is correct, our ancient ancestors once again seem to have anticipated modern scientific thought. What they intuited with their right brain we are figuring out with our left.

Why is this important? Simply this. The world is a complex place. Sometimes we feel overwhelmed. It seems we are living insignificant, pointless lives that are bereft of meaning and purpose, but if we are a product of Universal Mind that has been, so far at least, 13.8 billion years in the making, we matter. We are important! What seem to be significant political divisions are, in the long run, insignificant. If enough

The Universal Mind is the concept that everything in our universe is one.

of us take the long view, we can rise above them and get about the important business of fulfilling our potential. And that's no small thing!

Panpsychism is, at its root, about something that is very close to metaphysics, or twenty-first-century spirituality. It is not about religion, although many religious concepts have found their way into the discussion. It doesn't have a lot to say about theology, although theology may be important in the search for knowledge about the ultimate Mystery that is called God, Jehovah, Allah, Brahman, Manitou, the Great Spirit, Creator, the Ground of our Being, Eternal Consciousness, and many, many other names.

Instead, the scientific/philosophical study of panpsychism is a search for that which is common to every human being who has ever lived and who ever will live. Whether we consider our worldview to be sacred or secular, religious or humanist; whether we eagerly await the newest scientific discovery or spend our days dreading the next disclosure that might undermine our faith, we share something with every other human being on Earth. We are alive. Vibrantly alive. Mysteriously alive. We live and breathe and swim in an ocean of spirituality. We are not only one with Universal Mind, we are a product of it. We thus have immense value.

Think of the words great religions have used to describe spiritual attributes: compassion, goodness, love, joy, peace, everlasting life. Think of the ways the ancients linked spirit with the environment and how indigenous peoples around the world see the handiwork of spirit in their surroundings. Ancients listened for the "music of the spheres," the song of the heavens. All we have to do is substitute the words "Universal Mind" for "Spirit" and we immediately enter into a common system of thought. Universal Mind is no longer pictured as a remote being "out there." It is now a universal construct "in here."

Spirituality is thus our connection with that which makes us distinctly human. Love is spiritual. Compassion and empathy are spiritual. When human beings treat each other with respect, they practice spirituality.

Love, faith, hope, trust, and respect are rock-solid real. People have died for them. They rule history, but they cannot be taken apart, broken down, and studied under a microscope. Religions often corral spirituality within systems and doctrines, but spirituality refuses to conform to rules. When a soldier, out of compassion and in spite of his training, passes up a chance to shoot a helpless enemy, he exhibits spirituality. When a victim forgives her assailant, she exhibits spirituality.

Spirituality is about music, not spreadsheets. It is about understanding and compromise, not rules and regulations. It is poetry, not prose, but it can infuse spreadsheets, rules, regulations, and prose with meaning. In the end, what gives life purpose and makes it worth living is our universality and oneness, the very essence of panpsychism. And that is our hope.

ALIEN ALTERNATIVE THEORIES

ZECHARIA SITCHIN AND THE COMING OF THE GODS

Are human beings a designed species? Were we deliberately engineered for a purpose?

According to Zecharia Sitchin, that's exactly what we are.

In 1849, while searching through the Library of Ashurbanipal in what is now Morsul, Iraq, Austen Henry Layard made what was to prove a significant discovery. He found a significant portion of a 3,800-year-old manuscript containing a Babylonian creation epic called *Enûma Elis*. It told the story of a god named Marduk, sometimes called Nibiru, who had created humans as a slave race, whose purpose was to serve the gods. A team of "Watchers," also referred to as "Holy Ones," was assigned to supervise the work force. These "watchers" were given the title Anunnaki. There were some 600 of them, half serving in heaven and half on Earth. Marduk, the one who engineered the slave race of humans, was the son of the god named either Enki or Ea, the "God of the Waters."

Scholars eventually decided that the generic meaning of Anunnaki was simply a word that mean "gods of heaven and Earth," or possibly "angels of heaven and Earth."

The late Zecharia Sitchin disagreed. In his opinion, "Anunnaki" didn't mean "gods of heaven and Earth" at all. That was a mistranslation. A better rendering was "those who from heaven to Earth came." And "Marduk" wasn't quite right either. Sitchin preferred "Nibiru." And that wasn't just the name of the chief god. It was the home planet of the Anunnaki. According to his translation and interpretation, the inhabitants of Nibiru had created a slave race to mine gold, which was needed back on their home planet in order to seed their atmosphere from time to time. All that was needed was a little genetic manipulation. The human race thus came into existence. What had previously been a primate life form was created with a few tweaks of their DNA.

Erich von Däniken latched on to Sitchin's work and popularized it with his immensely successful book, *Chariots of the Gods?* in 1968. That book launched the Ancient Alien Theory movement and the rest, as they say, is history.

Sitchin was a scholar. Although he worked outside his field of training, he was one of a small handful of people who could read Sumerian. It was only natural that his followers trusted him when it came to translations of esoteric texts. His book, *Genesis Revisited*, which presented ancient mythology in a new light and re-energized the study of megalithic ruins scattered around the globe, never quite caught on like von Däniken's. Indeed, von Däniken was ridiculed by conservative academia. In 1968, before the advent of the History Channel, to suggest that we may have been visited by ancient aliens, including the Anunnaki, was considered outlandish.

Now, however, "Ancient Aliens" is a common phrase. Although neither Sitchin nor von Däniken coined it, both the phrase "Ancient Alien Theory" and the name "Anunnaki" are well known.

Anasazi pictographs on the wall of Sego Canyon in Thompson Springs, Utah, could support the views of author Zecharia Sitchin that Earth was visited by rulers from other planets or dimensions.

What Sitchin theorized, in a nutshell, was that so-called mythical gods and goddesses were not simply made-up beings or figments of the fertile imaginations of an ancient priestly class. Instead, they were physical kings and rulers from other planets, dimensions, or even time zones. Their status was misrepresented over the course of centuries, resulting in an expansion of legends and stories that grew into religions, and then myths. Eventually the legends grew until, in Sitchin's hands, and later, von Däniken's they became visitors from outer space who traveled here in their "chariots of the gods."

Later writers considered them to be humans, perhaps the survivors of a great cataclysm that destroyed their civilization here on Earth, as is claimed by scholars such as Andrew Collins, who traces them to ancestral Solutreans, a very Earth-bound human culture who survived the great cataclysm of the Younger Dryas Event.

It's easy to suppress information about the Anunnaki, relegating their existence to the area of superstitious nonsense. Most traditional scholars do just that. They are extremely frustrated when college students who have watched the latest *Ancient Alien* TV episode start asking questions. These classroom discussions are often filled with disdain and ridicule, but it's difficult to ignore the texts. The ancients seemed to take them quite literally. And when the subject matter spills over into accepted and revered religious traditions, the whole subject can get a bit uncomfortable.

Lots of people hold the Bible in great respect, for instance, even if not many have read it. When folks do dig into it, and come across something like this, what are priests, rabbis, and ministers supposed to do?

> When men began to increase in number on the Earth, the sons of God saw that the daughters of men were beautiful, and they married any of them they chose…. The Nephilim [most translations use the word "Giants"] were on the Earth in those days—and also afterward—when the sons of God went to the daughters of men and had children by them. They were the heroes of old, men of renown.
>
> —Genesis 6:1–6

Who were these "sons of God," who fathered the mysterious "giants," or "Nephilim?" Were they the Anunnaki, the "heroes of old, men of renown?" The Old Testament text comes from roughly the same geographical location as the earlier Babylonian and Sumerian stories. Were they all related? Are they religious myths or historical legends based on fact?

And what about the oldest religious text yet discovered, the famous *Epic of Gilgamesh?*

Here we read that Gilgamesh, king of Uruk, and Enkidu, a wild man who was created by the gods, were engaged in a long friendship.

Wait! "A wild man who was created by the gods" is featured in the world's oldest epic poem? What are we supposed to do with information like that? Do we simply ignore it because it sounds utterly preposterous in this day and age?

Before the internet, teachers and professors could rest fairly easily in the knowledge that their students might not hear about any of this. Suppression was the name of the game. Now it's a lot harder.

Zecharia Sitchin has passed on. Erich von Däniken is getting on in years but has not lost his vitality. He is still a featured speaker at conventions. It might yet prove that they will have the last laugh when it comes to understanding the truth about human origins.

JEHOVAH AND THE DEMIURGE

Author Erich von Däniken 's *Chariots of the Gods?* (1968) was an immensely popular and controversial book.

Enûma Elis and *The Epic of Gilgamesh* weren't the only texts to come out of Mesopotamia. In 1912, a group of five text fragments was discovered in Egypt. They had originated in the "Land between the Rivers" but had somehow been transported to the archives of the Egyptian king Amenophis. They were called the Amarna texts and told a unique human origin story.

As we have just seen, according to Sumerian mythology, human-like gods called Anunnaki had initially come to mine resources that were needed on their home planet. Now, with the creation of a human labor force, their duties changed. They now ruled over what was, for all practical purposes, a human slave race. Their base of operations was Mesopotamia, the land between the Tigris and Euphrates rivers. In the *Epic of Gilgamesh*, the world's first epic poem, it was identified with Eden. *Eden*, in Sumerian, means "steppe" or "plain."

Here's a portion of one of those fragments that I covered in detail in my book, *Lost Civilizations*. It is transcribed from a story called *Adapa and the South Wind:*

When the gods, like men,
Bore the work and suffered the toll,
The toil of the gods was great.
The work was heavy, the distress was much.

The chief god, Anu, recognized that things couldn't continue as they were, so he commissioned his son, Enki (Ea), and his daughter Ninki (Enki's half-sister) to do something about the problem.

Their solution was to create humans by sacrificing a god, mixing his body and blood with clay, and forming the first human being made in the likeness of the gods.

You have slaughtered a god together
With his personality.
I have removed your heavy work.
I have imposed your toil on man....
In the clay, god and man
Shall be bound
To a unity brought together;
So that to the end of days
The Flesh and the Soul,
Which in a god have ripened—

That soul in a blood-kinship be bound.

According to the Amana texts, the first humans were incapable of reproduction. Some modification was needed. Eventually the first fully functional man was developed and named Adapa. His story continues in the text fragment called *Enki and the World Order.*

Enki's half-brother, Enlil, is about to become very important in the suppressed history of three great world religions, but to understand how he figures into the biblical account familiar to Jews, Christians, and Muslims, we need to set the stage.

Enki, it seems, decided that the gods needed to supervise the world, or it would descend into chaos. Human beings weren't capable of managing themselves, so Enki appointed various gods to oversee such activities as utilizing water to irrigate crops, building cities, herding livestock, domesticating animals, and, most important according to the texts, "managing" women.

To read the Sumerian Eden story side by side with the Genesis Eden story is very instructive. The biblical Eden arose much later, but in many ways, they address identical issues. Even if we consider them to be only simple metaphors that describe actual historical events, such as the agricultural revolution and the birth of civilization, they point out that our ancestors had a profound understanding of philosophy and psychology. They are, in many ways, very similar accounts.

But in a major way, they are quite different. To understand this difference, we turn to the work of a French scholar named Anton Parks. He offers a lifetime's worth of study, working with Sumerian texts that have even been translated into French.

According to Parks, the Sumerian texts picture human beings living in a kind of concentration camp. In the Bible, they live in a Paradise.

In Parks' translation of the Sumerian texts, God doesn't plant a garden for humankind in which he "walks in the cool of the evening." His version says the gods "came in strength from beyond time. They were carried, one day, by the rebellion of the universe."

Parks' gods, the *Annuna* (Anunnaki), were very real entities from beyond, who represented two distinct regimes, one patriarchal and one matriarchal.

Enlil was the patriarchal, evil god, whose only purpose was to enslave the human race.

Ninki, sister to Enki, represented the feminine presence. She was often pictured as a reptilian figure. Parks goes so far as to contend that she may have been the inspiration for the serpent in the Eden of Genesis.

Here's why that distinction is so important. If Parks is right, and the Sumerian texts are to be taken literally, then the Genesis serpent wasn't evil at all. In his version, the serpent, later called "that old devil" by the Christian author of the *Book of Revelation*, was actually trying to free humankind by offering them the gift of the knowledge represented by the tree that bore the fruit of the knowledge of good and evil. She wanted them to eat of the Tree of Life and "be like gods." It was a good thing she was doing, not a bad one. This is the exact opposite of what is taught in monotheistic religions that follow the teachings of the Bible.

Since history is written by the winners, however, the story we are so familiar with is fake news—the truth turned on its head. Enlil lost the first battle. He wasn't able to prevent the new human race from a major step in their development. He didn't stop them from eating the fruit of the tree of the knowledge of good and evil.

One interpretation of the Adam and Eve story is that the serpent was trying to free, not enslave, the first couple by offering them the gift of knowledge.

But he could cast humans out of the garden before they ate of the tree of life. So that's exactly what he did. Humans were thrown out of Eden.

In other words, the familiar words of Genesis are actually the story of how Enlil disguised himself as God in order to continue his original intent of creating a slave race.

That might explain the curious way in which Genesis emphasizes the fact that two angels, wielding flaming swords, were placed at the entrance to Eden. They were there to make sure that humans never attained the godhead and eternal life.

It has been said that the smartest thing the devil ever did was to convince humans that he didn't exist. This reading of the Sumerian myth goes one step further. It says that the smartest thing the devil ever did was to convince humans that he was God.

According to Anton Parks, YHVH of the Bible, often translated into English as "The Lord," is not really the God who created humanity. That honor falls to Enki and Ninki. Their original creation was, in the words of the Bible, "very good."

But rather than being the hope of the world, the "God" of the Bible is actually Enlil, the one who stepped in and enslaved humankind. His title is the Demiurge. His goal is a patriarchal system of rule that wants to suppress freedom, especially the freedom of women. He doesn't want equality. He wants subservient slaves. He doesn't want creative, right-brained, intuitive thinkers. He wants left-brained, obedient servants who are forced to work each and every day. Remember that during your Monday morning commute! It makes you wonder if Enlil has actually succeeded in his mission.

This reading explains the difference between Genesis 1 and 2, where everything is "very good," and Genesis 3 and onward, where all hell breaks loose.

To sum this up in the simplest possible way, Parks' version of the original Sumerian text says that humans were upright-walking animals who were modified through DNA manipulation to fill the role of slaves and workers. According to Parks, the word *Adam* in Sumerian means "animal." *Eden* consists of the words *E*, meaning "home," and *den*, which means "life." The *Satan* in Sumerian is a title that means "the Administrator." In English, it can also be translated as "the Accuser of the Brethren."

Ninki, the "serpent" of Eden, elevated humans after their genetic manipulation made them intelligent, thinking, elevated animals. She bestowed upon them the gift of wisdom—of knowing good and evil, right and wrong.

Although she won this stage of the battle for humanity, Enlil still carried the day when he drove humans out of Eden and forbade their return.

Here's the bottom line. According to this reading of the story, the God who monotheists have been worshipping for the last 5,000 years is not Jehovah, the creator God. He is Enlil, the patriarchal Demiurge—Satan himself.

This radical approach explains some curious biblical stories that theologians have been arguing about for thousands of years.

- Why did the God of the Old Testament send a flood to destroy humankind so soon after creating them? How did they go so wrong so quickly?

- Why did God command the Israelites to kill innocent Canaanite women and children?

- How could the God of peace be used to justify such things as the Crusades and the Inquisition?

- Why does the Old Testament God seem so bloodthirsty and the New Testament God encourage the idea of the Prince of Peace?

- How could the author of 1st John in the New Testament declare that "we know we are of God and the whole world is in the hands of the evil one" (1 John 5:19)? Did he somehow recognize the truth?

Even though morality is important to us, which is another way of saying that we know the difference between good and evil, we still seem suspended in a divine battle of competing spiritual forces. We still need to "earn our daily bread by the sweat of our brow." It's just that we have turned our curse into a search for meaning. We want to get back to Paradise. We exhibit both the grace of the gift of Ninki and the snare of Enlil, the Demiurge.

The year 1945 saw the accidental discovery of a cache of texts in Nag Hammadi, Egypt. They are called the Gnostic texts and seem to indicate that the Gnostics, an early Christian sect that was declared heretical by the Roman establishment, actually agreed with this reading of the biblical account. The church suppressed their scriptures, burning them in order to make sure no one could ever read them. Only one of them, the Gospel of John, made it into the New Testament, and even that's a questionable Gnostic text.

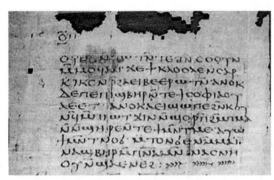

One of the discoveries at Nag Hammadi was this fragment of the Gnostic Apocalypse of Peter, part of Codex VII that is now preserved at the city's library.

But some of the scrolls were secreted away and hidden. Because of this relatively recent discovery, we now know that to the Gnostics, wisdom, or "Sophia," represented a feminine energy that refused to be kept buried. She was Ninki, the Creator, the *logos*, or Word of God.

The Gnostics seem to have believed that they were engaged in a cosmic battle that is still being played out in our day, even though we have long forgotten that we are part of an eternal conflict between good and evil.

But have we completely forgotten? Does our subconscious still remember? Whenever we joke about having an angel on one shoulder and a devil on the other, whispering in our ear, are we acknowledging the presence of Ninki and Enlil?

When we refer to "Mother Earth," the creation of Sophia, the goddess of wisdom, are we reminding ourselves that although our day-to-day existence may be ruled by the Demiurge, within that battle we still recognize a divine spark that must not be put out?

The Demiurge may dominate our day-to-day reality, which we acknowledge whenever we say, "The devil made me do it." But Eden still awaits if we can only persevere. We all long for a better life that always seems to be just beyond our grasp. We all long for a return to Paradise but are frustrated by the two angels of death who guard the entrance with flaming swords. It appears we can't return to Paradise without dying first.

This reading of the texts is a completely different reading than the biblical account many of us grew up with, but whether we read it allegorically or historically, it still causes us to pause and think about what we believe and why we believe it. If it contains any historical truth at all in its portrayal of human origins, it is worth our consideration.

DISCOVERING ALIENS IN THE MIRROR

Do aliens exist on planet Earth?

"Yes!" say a growing number of people. And we look at them every day when we look in the mirror. To paraphrase Pogo, "We have met the alien and he is us!"

Do we descend from the stars? Do we owe our lives to creatures from off our home planet?

On May 18, 2019, a group of researchers from various disciplines including biology, history, astrophysics, psychology, and sociology met in Paris for the biannual meeting of the Messaging Extraterrestrial Intelligence International (METI), a nonprofit research organization. Workshops centered around the theme "What Is Life? An Extraterrestrial Perspective."

- Are extraterrestrials staying silent out of concern for how contact would impact humanity?

- Do we live in a "galactic zoo?"
- Should we send intentional radio messages to nearby stars to signal humanity's interest in joining the "galactic club?"
- Will extraterrestrial intelligence be similar to human intelligence?
- Did life get to Earth from elsewhere in the galaxy (interstellar migration)?

Many of the discussions centered around what is commonly called the Zoo hypothesis. This is an idea first put forth in the 1970s. It suggests that aliens might be watching and protecting us. In other words, Earth might be a kind of cosmic zoo, kept either as a source of entertainment or enlightenment by aliens. With more than 4,000 planets charted in the Milky Way galaxy alone, it seems plausible to think that at least some of them might be home to an intelligent species such as ourselves, only much more advanced.

This begs the question, why haven't we heard from them?

Well, maybe we have. Maybe they even engineered our very existence in the distant past. Like any good science experiment, you need to watch the results to see how everything comes out. Hence, the Zoo hypothesis.

To put this into perspective, let's survey some background.

We'll begin with what some scientists call the Great Silence. This stems from the famous Fermi Paradox, first suggested by Enrico Fermi back in 1950. Basically, he posed a simple question: "Where is everybody?"

If alien life is statistically highly probable, why haven't they contacted us? Why is there only a great silence? Are they out there but, for some reason, maintaining their privacy? Have they just not discovered us yet? The universe is, after all, a big place. Maybe they haven't detected us yet. Or maybe there is some kind of Star Trekian "Prime Directive" that forbids first contact until the subject species is deemed ready. Maybe we are simply biologically incompatible. If European contact with Native

Noted for making the first nuclear reactor possible, Italian American physicist Enrico Fermi is also famous for the paradox named after him in which he wondered why humanity has not been in contact with intelligent alien life.

Americans led to their near extinction because of the introduction of diseases for which Indigenous people had no immunity, then perhaps contact with aliens could prove fatal to both humans and aliens alike.

If the Zoo Hypothesis is correct, is there anything we can do about speeding up the process of contact?

Well, the truth is that we are already doing it. We've been sending radio signals into outer space ever since the early twentieth century. As for TV, well, *I Love Lucy* broadcasts that travel into space may not be a sign of intelligent life, but at least it demonstrates a certain mastery of technology.

Jean-Pierre Rospars, the honorary research director at the Institut National de la Recherche Agronomique and co-chair of the METI workshop, puts it this way: "Cognitive evolution on Earth shows random features while also following predictable paths … we can expect the repeated, independent emergence of intelligent species in the universe, and we should expect to see more or less similar forms of intelligence everywhere, under favorable conditions. There's no reason to think that humans have reached the highest cognitive level possible. Higher levels might evolve on Earth in the future and already be reached elsewhere."

For those who feel more comfortable with math and science rather than philosophy, consider the Drake Equation. That's an attempt to beef up the Fermi Paradox with mathematical equations and numbers. The equation comes right out of the SETI Institute's search for radio signals that might indicate intelligent life in the universe.

Here's the equation: $N = R \times fp \times ne \times fl \times fi \times fc \times L$

It breaks down like this:

N = The number of civilizations in the Milky Way Galaxy whose electromagnetic emissions are detectable.

R = The rate of formation of stars suitable for the development of intelligent life.

fp = The fraction of those stars with planetary systems.

ne = The number of planets, per solar system, with an environment suitable for life.

fl = The fraction of suitable planets on which life actually appears.

fi = The fraction of life bearing planets on which intelligent life emerges.

fc = The fraction of civilizations that develop a technology that releases detectable signs of their existence into space.

L = The length of time such civilizations release detectable signals into space.

Got that? One word of caution. At the METI workshop, emphasis was given to the last three factors. They represent not just the number of worlds that harbor intelligent life, but how long they last. In other words, there is a built-in assumption, from practical Earth experience, that industrial civilizations tend to blow themselves up before they get smart.

Nicolas Prantzos, director of research of the Centre National de la Recherche Scientifique, puts his hopes in radio astronomy more than actual physical contact, given the immense distances involved, but he is holding out for eventual first contact just the same. As he puts it: "It appears that although radio communications provide a natural means for searching for extraterrestrial intelligence for civilizations younger than a few millennia, older civilizations should rather develop extensive programs of interstellar colonization. This is the only way to achieve undisputable evidence, either for or against the existence of extraterrestrial intelligence, within their lifetime."

> Evolution might take very different pathways on very different planets. Just because we behave in a certain way doesn't mean aliens will follow suit.

On the other hand, why should we assume that if other species exist they might be even remotely similar to us? Evolution might take very different pathways on very different planets. Just because we behave in a certain way doesn't mean aliens will follow suit, but it's typical for human beings to be arrogant and judge situations by our own experience. It's a trait that often gets individuals in trouble when they assume someone will react a certain way in a situation just because that's what *they* would do.

Roland Lehoucq, an astrophysicist at the Commissariat à l'Énergie Atomique, puts it succinctly: "The environment on an exoplanet will impose its own rules. There is no trend in biological evolution: the huge range of various morphologies observed on Earth renders any exobiological speculation improbable, at least for macroscopic 'complex' life." He went on to discuss "our persistent anthropocentrism in our understanding and description of alien life" and "how difficult it is for humans to imagine extraterrestrial intelligence radically different from ourselves."

Much of what we have just learned about the 2019 METI workshop is due to concise and helpful reporting from Jamie Carter, writing for *Forbes* magazine. His entire report (available online at https://www.forbes.com/sites/jamiecartereurope/2019/03/18) is well worth the read. He sums up the entire conference rather succinctly: "In short? We're too self-obsessed to even imagine extraterrestrial life, let alone find and communicate with it, and if there's not going to be proof within our lifetimes, we're not much interested in looking. Is there intelligent life out there? Probably, but we'll probably never find it."

In other words, when you look in the mirror do you see an alien?

Who knows? But at least there are reputable scientists tying to find out.

There are other avenues being pursued. An op-ed column in the June 10, 2016, edition of the *New York Times* was entitled "Yes, There Have Been Aliens." It was written by astrophysicist Adam Frank from the University of Rochester. He is the author of the book *Light of the Stars: Alien Worlds and the Fate of the Earth.*

In his article he put forth a rather startling suggestion: "While we do not know if any advanced extraterrestrial civilizations currently exist in our galaxy, extraterrestrial civilizations almost certainly existed at one time or another in the evolution of the cosmos. The degree of pessimism required to doubt the existence, at some point in time, of an advanced extraterrestrial civilization borders on the irrational. We now have enough information to conclude that they almost certainly existed at some point in cosmic history."

He goes on to say that "10 billion trillion planets exist in the right place for nature to have at it. Each world is a place where winds may blow over mountains, where mists may rise in valleys, where seas may churn, and rivers may flow. When you hold that image in your mind, you see something remarkable: The pessimism line represents the 10 billion trillion times the universe has run its experiment with planets and life."

It is quite likely there is intelligent life out there, but it is questionable whether we will ever find it. It is also possible there were advanced civilizations millions of years ago that are now extinct.

When you consider that two planets within our own system, Earth and Mars, both have climate zones where, for at least some of their existence, "winds blew over the mountains and mists rose in the valleys," you've got to concede that he makes a good point.

As we have seen when we looked at the prime theory of human origins, studies in genetics seem to indicate that every living human being on Earth is descended from a single woman called "Mitochondrial Eve." She lived about 200,000 years ago. At about that time, something happened. We don't know what it was, exactly, but something certainly kicked in. Was that "something" due to alien intervention? If it had been anatomically and biologically possible, even a single act of intercourse with an alien might have done the trick. A single change in a single gene would have been enough to get the process started. It might have occurred naturally, but maybe not. The truth is, no one knows.

On the other hand, there have been at least six mass extinctions on Earth that we know about. Any one of them would have thrown an existing species back into the stone age, assuming they had already passed through that age and evolved into advanced culture. If that were to happen to us, everything we know about space travel, radios, Twitter, and Facebook would be lost overnight. We would become simply another species that didn't make it.

Given that possibility, is it any wonder that an alien species might want to hold off awhile to see what the future holds before they introduce themselves?

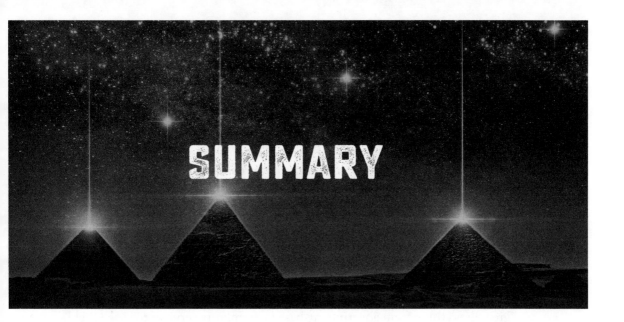

SUMMARY

As we sum up all this information about human origins, where does it leave us? What do we really know about who we are as a species, where we came from, and how we got here, let alone where we're going?

In the end, of course, each one of us needs to sift through it all, judge appropriately, and draw our own conclusions, while respecting those who arrive at different points of view. We need to look long and hard at the evidence and turn a deaf ear to those who lecture at us, claiming that their theories are the only logical ones, even if they deliver their lecture from a podium, pulpit, or, worse yet, a TV screen. Academic titles and clerical garments are impressive and deserve our respect, but it seems fairly obvious that even the experts are far from agreement. Each and every systematic theory about human origins is full of great gaps and spaces that have yet to be filled. The whole area of study needs more folks who listen and question and fewer who pontificate and bellow. In this field, all knowledge is temporary at best.

These days if you say the words "intelligent design" in an academic setting, you are apt to be accused of not supporting science and trying to corrupt young minds with superstitious bigotry. If you go to a conservative clergy retreat and quietly reveal your acceptance of Darwinian evolution you might be accused of everything from tree hugging to supporting your local PBS station.

In terms of the study of human origins, it's a jungle out there.

That being said, I'm going to tell you what my views are. I don't intend to say anything dogmatic. I certainly don't believe I can claim the last word. I doubt I know anything that others don't know, but it feels somehow important to sum up the survey we have just conducted, and this seems to be the best way to do it. Please feel free to disagree. I offer these thoughts only as a way of recognizing the broad spectrum of ideas and putting them in some kind of systematic order, so here goes.

There is no question that the fields of anthropology and archeology have more evidence to work with, and better tools to utilize, than ever before. The last few years alone have produced bones, DNA evidence, and artifacts from some brand-new human cousins that previously no one knew anything about. We'll identify them and discuss their contributions in the next chapter. Physical evolution, especially human evolution, is a growing science and it behooves us to follow their progress with enthusiasm.

At the same time, however, there are a lot of questions that evolutionists need to struggle with. To suppress those questions, assuming that someday we will solve them so for now they're not important, is irresponsible.

Statistics, for instance, is a legitimate field of study with a bonafide pedigree. Everything from government-based community services to space flights depend on it. So why do we throw statistics out the window when it comes to low-balling the chances of biological life arising in the universe rather than our home planet, to say nothing of producing intelligent, bipedal apes?

"Yes, the chances are slim," we are told. "But it must have happened because here we are!"

That answer rests on nothing but a preformed, prejudicial ideology that says alien life, from either somewhere else in the universe or in another dimension, up to and including a dimension that some call heaven, either doesn't exist or has never interacted with us.

"Show us the evidence! Show us the proof," thunders the voice of academia.

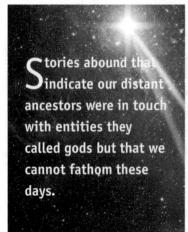

Stories abound that indicate our distant ancestors were in touch with entities they called gods but that we cannot fathom these days.

Well, the proof is the same proof academics use. Against all numerical odds, we are here. Statistically there may even be a greater tendency to support alien intervention then to claim that life arose through chance alone. After all, statistics point to a great chance that the universe teams with life. Doesn't that make alien intervention, and even what some call supernatural intervention, at least a possibility? If that possibility exists, will we ever find out the truth if we decide up front not to look for it?

We also need to take seriously the rich mythology that exists worldwide. Stories abound that indicate our distant ancestors were in touch with entities they called gods but that we cannot fathom these days. It's easy to discount those stories because they sound so impossible to ears attuned to material life in the twenty-first century, but when we discount them we have to admit that we are rejecting them on ideological grounds, not because they rest on shifting sands of impossibility. Studies in psi research these days, such as those being conducted at the Institute of Noetic Sciences or the Monroe Institute in Virginia, all indicate psychic phenomena is a real, if unrecognized and misunderstood, force in the world. It exists in reality, not just in the minds of a few so-called "New Age" believers.

The mythology that comes to us through ancient texts is so structured and rich with detail that we cannot simply discount it as the made-up religious dreams of a few superstitious shamans. On the one hand, we like to say the ancients were ignorant savages who had a long way to go to reach our level of sophistication. On the other hand, they had a far richer level of writing and relaying imaginative detail than most people today are capable of.

We can't have it both ways. Either they were intelligent and understood something we don't, or they were superstitious and ignorant. The depth of their written wisdom indicates the former, not the latter.

Were the ancient "gods" actually a species from another world? Were they survivors of a lost civilization of proto-humans? Or did they come to us from a parallel dimension? We just don't know. Only prejudice forces us to choose one over the other. Definitive facts are not yet in.

Consider the great monuments of stone that point to a greater reality than that experienced by the typical, modern, citizen of the world. A big, imposing, megalith indicates a big, imposing reason for building it. People don't spend untold millennia of work and toil just to build a calendar that will tell them when to plant crops. That's just a silly idea put forth by a person with a modern, materialistic ideology. Those ancient ancestors were in touch with something real. We don't know what it was, and that's fine, but for heaven's sake, let's admit our ignorance. It's the first and most important step in investigating what was going on.

When we begin to accept our ignorance concerning such things, we become open to evidence that points to the stars and ancient contact with extraterrestrial visitors. That's the message of both megalith and myth. To me, at least, it marks a significant starting point. We don't have to understand the nature of that contact in order to acknowledge that such a thing might have been possible, but that acknowledgment marks a beginning point for more research. We don't have to believe to start looking. We just need to acknowledge the possibility.

All this leads me to the conclusion that somewhere in the distant past our species had contact with, and maybe even owes its existence to, help from outside. I don't know exactly what that means. I only know that the universe is a big place and the multiverse is even bigger. Both are arenas that are capable of producing what used to be called magic—the mystery of life. To use a

British metaphor, we are part Uther Pendragon and part Merlin the Magician. We cannot accept one and ignore the other if we hope to understand who we are and where we are going.

We have not yet scratched the surface when it comes to understanding the mystery of life. The journey has just begun, but if we suppress any part of our history, we will never arrive at our destination.

EXPANSION: THE FIRST PIONEERS

PRIME THEORY

OUT OF AFRICA

As we have discovered so far, the quest to determine the origins of the cosmos, the origins of life on Earth, and the origins of human beings is in a state of flux to put it mildly. New information, new equipment, new theories, and new dating techniques are being submitted almost every day, it would seem. Now, as we begin to look at how the first human beings spread out from their point of origin, the situation grows even more confusing.

The principle theory that has been the go-to hypothesis for decades is now under attack. That theory is called by various names: the Recent Single-Origin Hypothesis (RSOH), the Replacement Hypothesis, and the Recent African Origin model (RAO) are just a few, but they are all variations on the same theory that is generally called the Out of Africa theory (OOA).

We talked about it in the last chapter, but to briefly recap, this theory proposes that there was a single time in history and a single point on Earth where modern humans originated. It is thus considered to be a unique event.

Specifically, the time is considered to be between 200,000 and 300,000 years ago and the origin point is usually thought to be in the Horn of Africa. From that time and place the ancestors of every modern human now on Earth eventually spread out to cover the globe.

This theory virtually eliminates the hypothetical possibility that humans could have evolved in various places at different times. To be perfectly clear, it says that every person now on Earth, no matter where they live and what their background, is, essentially, an African by descent.

How and when the great migration occurred is up for debate. Most anthropologists agree that there were waves of emigration, possibly beginning as early as 270,000 years ago, but most certainly between 115,000 and 130,000 years ago. The populations who made up these migration waves seem to have died out or otherwise disappeared by 80,000 years ago. Then, some 70,000 years ago, the direct ancestors of everyone alive today, a species called *Homo sapiens*, made the final big push. It is to these folks that we owe our current dominance.

In 2010, genetic studies began to produce evidence that later population groups interbred with the earlier folks, such as Neanderthals. More recent DNA studies have found evidence of *Homo sapiens* comingling with Denisovans as well. And in 2018, in Denisova Cave in Siberia, the partial skeleton of the hybrid daughter of Denisovan/Neanderthal parents was discovered. Clearly there was a lot of contact between species going on in ancient times, proving that the three species were at least close cousins. They would have had to be in order to produce viable offspring.

There had, for a number of years, been some agreement that Neanderthals went extinct, either because our ancestors murdered them or they were in some ways mentally inferior. With the discovery of Neanderthal DNA

Many anthropologists, thanks to more advanced studies in genetics, believe that *Homo sapiens* interbred with other species like Neanderthals (depicted here) and Denisovans. Today's people all bear evidence of some Neanderthal genes.

in modern humans, however, that theory eventually fell apart. It was seen to be based on preconceived prejudice more than scientific fact. In some very significant ways, Neanderthals didn't become extinct as much as they became us. Their press image is being seriously upgraded these days.

But there is still a lot of disagreement when it comes to sorting things out, and the recent discovery of new human species, such as *Homo luzonensis* in the Philippines and *Homo floresiensis* in Indonesia, quickly nicknamed "The Hobbit" because of its small stature, further confuse the issue.

Much of the current argument swirling around the Out of Africa theory settles around the routes followed by those who emigrated. Generally speaking, proponents have settled on two migration routes.

THE NORTHERN ROUTE DISPERSAL

About 135,000 years ago in tropical Africa there were a series of droughts. It is assumed that these droughts would have caused people to be on the move, searching for better living conditions. They would probably have migrated along seaside routes, following shorelines where food and water would have been obtainable.

A few years ago, on a trip from Israel to Egypt across the Sinai, I had the experience of, for a short time at least, "walking in the footsteps" of the ancestors. It's very easy to picture small family groups walking along the beaches between the African continent and greener pastures in the Middle East.

The modern nation of Israel stands right on this crossroad. When you reach the northeast coast of the Mediterranean, you must make a decision. Turn left and you head toward Europe. Turn right and Asia awaits. According to the Out of Africa theory, these were the routes favored by those who were to eventually become Europeans and Asians.

Bones and artifacts of *Homo sapiens* have been found all along this route. They date back as early as 80,000 years, but the thinking goes that these folks either became extinct or returned home to Africa when climate conditions improved. It was the later population groups who eventually came to stay. They mated with both Neanderthals and Denisovans, who had long ago followed these same routes into Europe and Asia. Both these early species had split off from the line of modern humans as much as 200,000 years earlier.

THE SOUTHERN ROUTE DISPERSAL

The natural land route to the east and north out of Africa wasn't the only way out of town. Evidence indicates that some folks decided to head due east after first crossing the Red Sea. These people then stuck to the coasts and headed through what was to become Arabia and Persia all the way to India and beyond. By at least 50,000 years ago, and, as we shall soon see, probably a whole lot earlier, they made it as far as Australia. The earliest dates for their arrival there, still not universally accepted, are now being pushed back to at least 65,000 years ago.

The specific problem of dating the first Australian arrivals doesn't revolve around DNA evidence. The problem is that for the first Aussies to migrate to what was to become their home continent, they must have had boats. Few traditional archeologists want to admit that anyone back then had boating technology. There is a small but influential minority still holding out against the genetic evidence that indicates a shockingly old ancestral line.

The date for the southern route migration is, as you might have guessed, up for debate. There is heated discussion, but genetic information is being analyzed even as you read these words and more information is sure to be forthcoming. The data is complicated because of the eruption of Mt. Toba, which may or may not have had a devastating impact on human populations in India. I wrote about this extensively in my book *Ancient Gods*, and rather than repeat all the details here I will simply refer you to that book.

> Few traditional archeologists want to admit that anyone back then had boating technology. There is a small but influential minority still holding out against the genetic evidence that indicates a shockingly old ancestral line.

That's the main theory, and it has been accepted for a long time. In short, it proposes that modern humans and their early distant cousins, including all the species we have just identified, originated in Africa through chance mutation. Early in the game, our distant cousins left town and evolved on their own in seclusion. Later, we modern types migrated, reunited with our early cousins, and either killed them or married them.

It was a simple story, and easy to follow, but real history is rarely easy to follow.

In December of 2017, Gemma Tarlach quoted from a new *Science* paper in an article headlined with words destined to strike fear into every comfortable college professor who was counting the days until retirement: "It's Official: Timeline for Human Migration Gets a Rewrite."

There go the old lesson plans. It's a new ballgame now! The very first paragraph sums up the essential gist of the story:

> The wealth of new paleo-anthropological, archaeological, and genetic evidence has passed the tipping point: In a review published today in the prestigious journal *Science*, researchers acknowledge that the conventional timeline of human migration out of Africa "can no longer be considered valid."

The article goes on to say that traditional mainstream thinking is now obsolete and outmoded. As soon as that timeline became an accepted fact, and the textbooks declared it viable, thus casting it in stone, new evidence showed up.

Don't you just hate it when you're a teacher and that happens? It's back to the drawing board again.

I need to be careful here. There are some researchers and professors who love it when new information surfaces. May their kind increase, but there are others who require stability. They don't thrive in the chaos of loose ends and unanswered questions. Those are the tenured folks who tend to suppress new information. There's an old saying that "Those who can, do. Those who can't, teach." It's probably not as true as it once was, but for generations past, it was often the case. Take it from someone who started teaching in 1968!

> To make a long story short, ... the simple truth is that new research indicates that Neanderthals and Denisovans were interbreeding far earlier than was thought and much farther away from their homeland in South Africa.

Once again, Gemma Tarlach nailed it:

> The great thing about science is supposed to be that you come up with a hypothesis and then you and other researchers try to shoot it down and, if the hypothesis doesn't hold up, you come up with a new one based on what you learned from destroying the old one. And the scientific method generally works, as long as everyone keeps their egos in check.

In this case, too much history was suppressed because the evidence didn't fit the prevailing theory. Eventually, the theory began to sink under its own weight.

To make a long story short, and skipping over the technical parts, the simple truth is that new research indicates that Neanderthals and Denisovans were interbreeding far earlier than was thought and much farther away from their homeland in South Africa. When we moderns showed up later, but much sooner than was first believed, the old ones became not so much our "distant cousins" as our "kissing cousins." The evidence points to the fact that almost everyone reading these words, unless they have a pure African descent line, carries both Neanderthal and Denisovan ancestry in their genes. Those two ancient species didn't die out as much as they merged with us.

And the surprises keep coming. There are huge gaps in our ancestry that need filling. Wherever our early ancestors went, from Asia to China and Siberia, from the Middle East to Europe, and even across the ocean into the Americas, there seems to have been folks who got there before them. These days there is almost nothing set in stone when it comes to our ancestor's dispersal around the globe. We call them pioneers, just as the first American pio-

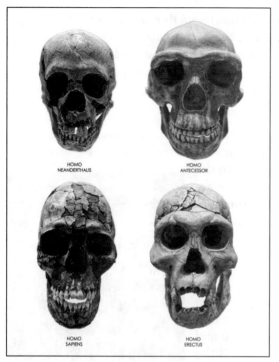

HOMO
NEANDERTHALIS

HOMO
ANTECESSOR

HOMO
SAPIENS

HOMO
ERECTUS

These prehistoric skulls of varying genetic lines represent a sampling of the many species that roamed the Earth.

neers blazed their way into the unknown, but when "pioneers" travel forth to unknown lands and find people already there, are they really pioneers?

All this indicates that our history is a lot older than we like to think it is. Even our birthplace now seems to be up for grabs. Rather than one regional location, the thinking is that the history of human origins is not so much that of a metaphorical genetic river from the past flowing into the present as much as it seems to be a number of intertwining streams coursing parallel to one another, and sometimes even joining together for a period of time. We are now one united species called *Homo sapiens*, but our situation may be an anomaly. For most human history on Earth it might have been otherwise because for vast periods of time there were probably many human species inhabiting our planet.

Christopher Stringer, in a heartfelt and introspective article called "Rethinking Out of Africa," published in *Edge* magazine, reveals the thoughtful musings of an expert who has lived with the Out of Africa theory his whole life:

> I'm thinking a lot about species concepts as applied to humans, about the "Out of Africa" model, and also looking back into Africa itself. I think the idea that modern humans originated in Africa is still a sound concept. Behaviorally and physically, we began our story there, but I've come around to thinking that it wasn't a simple origin. Twenty years ago, I would have argued that our species evolved in one place, maybe in East Africa or South Africa. There was a period of time in just one place where a small population of humans became modern, physically and behaviorally. Isolated and perhaps stressed by climate change, this drove a rapid and punctuated origin for our species. Now I don't think it was that simple, either within or outside of Africa.

But now let's go even further back in history to challenge the theory that all of us came from Africa. Perhaps evidence will even show that human origins weren't limited to one continent.

In December of 2018, Dr. Ioannis Syrigos, the managing director of *Ancient Origins* magazine, writing under his *nom de plume* John Black, told the strange story of a discovery that challenged the whole idea of Africa being the only birthplace of our species. In his article he described a skull discovered in 1959 in Northern Greece. It was found embedded in the wall of a cave full of stalactites and stalagmites, along with many "fossils of pre-human species, animal hair, fossilized wood, and stone and bone tools."

Dr. Syrigos has given me permission to quote his story at length:

The skull was given to the University of Thessaloniki in Greece by the President of the Petralona Community. The agreement was that once the research was done, a museum would be opened, featuring the findings from the Petralona cave, and the skull would be returned to be displayed in the museum—something that never happened.

Dr. Aris Poulianos, member of the UNESCO's IUAES (International Union of Anthropological and Ethnological Sciences), later founder of the Anthropological Association of Greece, and an expert anthropologist who was working at the University of Moscow at the time, was invited by the Prime Minister of Greece to return to Greece to take the position of University Chair in Athens. This was due to the publication of his book, "The Origins of the Greeks," which provides excellent research showing that Greek people didn't originate from the Slavic nations but were indigenous to Greece. Upon his return to Greece, Dr. Poulianos was made aware of the discovery of the skull at Petralona, and immediately started studying the Petralona cave and skull.

The 'Petralona man', or Archanthropus of Petralona, as it has since been called, was found to be 700,000 years old, making it the oldest human Europeoid (presenting European traits) of that age ever discovered in Europe. Dr. Poulianos' research showed that the Petralona man evolved separately in Europe and was not an ancestor of a species that came out of Africa.

The find was disputed, of course. This discovery goes against absolutely everything anyone believed up to this point, but in 1971, *Archeology* magazine, one of the most respected journals of the industry, backed up the findings. The skull was confirmed to be 700,000 years old. To make matters worse for traditionalists, further excavations uncovered pre-human skeletons that were at least 800,000 years old.

The general consensus today seems to be that the skull that set off all the furor belongs to an archaic hominid that differs from not only modern humans but from all other early human species as well. Yet it shows some familiar features, presenting strong European traits. This absolutely challenges the Out of Africa theory. Did a human species actually originate and evolve from somewhere other than Africa?

So far, some forty-six specialists from twelve countries have examined the find and the original research has stood up to every test, but the dictatorship in Greece soon declared a hiatus in the research. In 1983 came a real blow. The Greek government suddenly, without giving any reasons, halted access to the site and findings from the research.

Why was the work stopped? No one knows. Some speculate that the work was too heretical, and pressures were brought to bear, but the truth remains a complete mystery.

The Anthropological Society of Greece took the case to court, and after five years they were again allowed access to the cave, but the Ministry of Culture is attempting to overturn the court's decision, so the work remains suspended in legal limbo.

According to Dr. Syrigos:

Dr. Poulianos' findings contradicted conventional views regarding human evolution and his research was suppressed. Dr. Pou-

The Petralona cave in Greece is where a 700,000-year-old skull, Archanthropus of Petralona, was discovered in 1959. Unearthing it caused great consternation among scientists because it contradicted current views of human evolution.

lianos and his wife were physically attacked and injured in their home in 2012 and the culprits were never found. He and his team have been denied further access to the cave to complete their research and study, and the whereabouts of the skull is now unknown.

A sign now sits outside the cave of Petralona stating that the skull found in the cave was 300,000 years old, and on Wikipedia today you will see references dismissing the evidence and trying to date the Petralona skull within acceptable parameters— between 160,000 and 240,000 years old.

The latest chapter in the saga takes us to Cambridge, where Professor C. G. Nicholas Mascie-Taylor sent a letter to the Ministry of Culture in Greece saying that the correct date of the skull is 700,000 years old, not 300,000. He has also challenged the government's suppression of information regarding this incredible discovery.

Dr. Syrigos included a copy of that letter in his article. The full text is quoted here, again with his permission:

Greek Ministry of Education, Religions, Culture and Sports,
Bouboulinas 20–22,
Athens 106 82, Greece

5 September 2012

Dear Sir,

I am writing on behalf of the European Anthropological Association, which is the umbrella professional and academic association linking all of the national European biological anthropology and human biology societies, to express our concerns about the conservation of the Petralona Cave and Skull, the misinformation of the dating of the skull, as well as the treatment of personnel associated with the conservation of the Cave.

The basis of our concerns are that the skull has been damaged through many scratches and the crown of a tooth (1st molar) cut off. As requested by the Anthropological Association of Greece, what is required is a detailed description of the present status of the skull, so that no one in future can arbitrarily damage it further. There is also the problem of dating, which has been scientifically dated at about 700,000 years ago, not 300,000 as is given at the information desk. There is a very detailed record of the excavations and findings that need to receive further public presentation but which have never been catalogued so as to prevent specimens going missing.

It is very unfortunate that the Greek Archaeological Department stopped Dr. Aris Poulianos from further work in the Cave without any explanation. It is also very worrying that Dr. Poulianos and his wife were physically attacked and injured in their home earlier this year and the culprits have not been found. He was also verbally abused when attempting to give an invited presentation to teachers and school children.

Senior anthropologists and geologists have also been denied access to the Cave and the specimens for further study on a number of occasions without substantive reasons. Earlier this year there has also been misinformation given to the Greek Parliament concerning financial aspects of the Cave.

I look forward to receiving answers to these questions.

Yours faithfully,

Professor C G N Mascie-Taylor MA, PhD, ScD
(all Cambridge), FSB, FNAS (Hungary)

Professor of Human Population Biology and Health and
President of the European Anthropological Association

What does all this mean? If the research were conclusively proved, it would show that there were human species in Africa, Asia, and Europe, existing all at the same time at least 700,000 years ago. That would throw the whole Out of Africa scenario right out the window. Human beings would be a lot older than a mere 200,000 to 300,000 years. And their dispersal around the globe would have taken place much earlier than is now believed. This amount of time throws open the possibilities of whole civilizations coming and going, their remains and artifacts eventually buried and ground away to nothing. The whole history of our planet would change.

> If the research were conclusively proved, it would show that there were human species in Africa, Asia, and Europe, existing all at the same time at least 700,000 years ago.

At the very least, it shows that such ideas can get you attacked and abused. That's how important this kind of research is. Are there powers out there that want to suppress this kind of knowledge, even to the point of using physical force? What don't they want us to know? Are unknown factors in play?

In December of 2018, Dr. Poulianos wrote to *Ancient Origins*:

Experiencing the above I am asserting that the prohibition of research regarding human history is due to the following (most obvious, i.e. not exposing political) reasons:

Various (Worldwide) Universities and their state allied forums have the power to influence all of the small range national institutions in order to achieve the aforementioned prohibition. In turn, this is most probably due to the fact that such research is allowed only to some "confidential" persons. Thus, re-[righting] chapters of human history is only their "right." Whoever does not belong to such clubs and/or forums has to be stopped by all existing means, even by falsifying the truth against well documented evidence (i.e. without providing any scientific contradicting argument). Obviously I am asserting that knowledge is under control, especially what concerns human history.

On a personal note, I have had dozens of articles published in *Ancient Origins* magazine. I am a frequent contributor. Does this kind of thing give me pause?

You bet it does! There are apparently groups out there who simply don't want to see the status quo overturned. A book with the title this one carries could be dangerous to these people. We can only hope calm heads and open minds prevail.

NATURAL ALTERNATIVE THEORIES

With the Out of Africa theory in a bit of disarray right now, are there other theories that attempt to unravel the mystery?

Of course! Here are a few of them. These stories enrich the magic and mystery of the first pioneers.

ANCIENT CIVILIZATIONS AND MISTAKEN IDENTITIES

For a long time there has been an academic assumption that our civilization stands at the apex of an uninterrupted line of ascent that leads from our first human ancestors to the present day. We are at the top of the ladder. The idea is built into every high school curriculum and college degree program, whether it's an anthropological, archeological, historical, philosophical, or even psychological course of study. No one really thought about it. It was just there at the base of every theory concerning our origins.

Now that idea has gone from a serious misconception to an outright fabrication. Although most of the patronizing experts on science panels and TV shows insist, often with great sighs of discontent and pity aimed at those less educated than themselves, that the idea still holds true in academia, the fact is that young, sharp, fresh professionals are now bringing up awkward evidence that has been suppressed for far too long.

That evidence seems to point to a rather startling conclusion.

We are not the first. The history of our planet now appears to be full of vast, uninterrupted spans of time when past civilization could have existed and even thrived.

"Where is the evidence?" shout the voices invested in the status quo.

"Right in front of your eyes!" respond the newcomers. "It's been there all along, hiding in plain sight. You've just ignored it!"

The Sphinx, for instance, has long been paired with the Pyramids as if they were all built roughly at the same time, but all along there has been ample evidence that its construction preceded them by thousands of years.

Lately, Graham Hancock, in his new book *America Before*, put forth compelling evidence that the Serpent Mound in Ohio is much older than the Mound Building culture that followed.

No one thought there was a civilization on Earth sophisticated and organized enough to build any great construction projects before the culture that built on the Giza plateau. Then came the discovery of Göbekli Tepe that predated them by 6,000 years.

> All over the world there are relics that point to sophisticated ancient people who knew what they were doing.

All over the world there are relics that point to sophisticated ancient people who knew what they were doing. I wrote extensively about them in my book, *Lost Civilizations*, but they were not supposed to have existed, according to the accepted timeline and theory of civilization currently in vogue. The experts suppressed the historical evidence, deliberately misinterpreting it when they couldn't explain it away and continued teaching us all the theory that they had been taught and were reluctant to abandon. They weren't being conspiratorial. They just honestly couldn't make themselves believe any evidence that contradicted what they had long thought to be true. It is, sadly, a typical human tendency. To some extent, we probably all do it from time to time. After all, if Grandma's recipe for fried chicken was the best ever, why try something new?

There is evidence, however, that the situation is changing. We live in a chaotic, wonderful time of yeasty new ideas and open minds. As Bob Dylan told us long ago, "The times, they are a-changin'!" He saw it back in 1963. And he was right.

Where is all this headed?

It's time to do a new survey of the field.

DIFFUSION AND THE SPREAD OF IDEAS

To begin, we have to lay some groundwork. Undoubtedly one of the hottest arguments in the fields of anthropology and archeology today revolves around the theory of diffusion. To what extent did ancient cultures communicate their ideas and values?

Think of it this way. A historical society in Egypt decides to build some pyramids. That's all well and good. Archeologists can agree that a local group of people had an idea and reproduced it in stone.

But what happens when we find similar pyramids in Asia and Central America? Did three distinct populations get the same idea and build nearly identical structures, or was there some contact between them?

Your answer to that question determines your position regarding the principle of diffusion. Diffusionists believe that if culture "A" does something similar to culture "B," then culture "A" had contact with culture "B." The knowledge "diffused" from one place to the other.

This offers no problem if the two cultures are relatively close to one another and the spread of information can be easily explained, but what if the information seemed to be passed from one population to another across vast oceans and land masses at a time when such journeys were deemed impossible by ancient peoples? Now we've got problems. Either our ideas about diffusion are wrong or we have completely misunderstood the amount of travel capabilities possessed by ancient cultures.

There are many people wedded to the idea that our understanding of an unbroken line of progress from ancient time to now is set in stone and diffusion is impossible. There are others equally determined that our opinions about cultural progress is wrong, and that the ancients got around much more than we previously thought.

Let's take the case of possible contact between ancient Egypt and Central America, for example. Both cultures built pyramids. That is a given. The structures stand there for all to see. How is such a thing possible?

Diffusionists claim both cultures built pyramids because they were in some kind of contact with one another.

Others say that no contact was required. Some go even further. "The theory of diffusion is actually racist," they claim, thereby twisting the argument by questioning the character of those with whom they disagree. "Do diffusionists actually believe that people from Central America weren't smart enough to come up with the idea on their own? Did they actually need help from

Pyramids of different kinds have been found all over the world from Africa to Central America. Here we see the ancient Aztec pyramids of Teotihuacán in Mexico.

their African high-culture counterparts? Besides, where is any other evidence that proved the two cultures were in contact with one another?"

"There *is* other evidence," claim the diffusionists. "Tobacco, for instance, was found only in the Americas back in that time. How do traces of tobacco show up in Egyptian mummies?"

"It must have been planted there accidentally by those who much later in time discovered the mummies!"

"But what about other crops that made their way across the ocean back in the days before people were supposed to have been capable of oceanic travel?"

On and on the argument rages. Once again, we are dealing with competing ideologies. People on one side of the debate have fixed opinions and then gather facts to bolster those opinions. People on the other side want to remain open to other possibilities and insist they are following where the facts lead. As the argument heats up, they attack their opponent's character rather than their opinions.

To make matters worse, two other ways to approach the problem have risen relatively recently.

One theory says that if two cultures share similar traits, it might be because both cultures are descended from a parent culture that spawned them both and then became lost to history due to a collapse caused either by natural calamity or internal strife. Having founded separate cultures and invested them with values common to both, the original civilization became extinct, leaving their "offspring" to develop and evolve on their own. This explains why some obvious similarities, such as pyramids, survive while other traits seem totally different. We'll have a lot more to say about this before we're through.

A second theory postulates the idea of a universal field of consciousness to which wise, shaman-like figures from two distinct cultures can perceive the same realities, such as pyramids, and then transfer them to public works that survive the test of time. This presupposes a belief in metaphysical reality that many do not share.

Whether or not you believe that contact between cultures situated far away from each other actually took place will depend on your own ideology. You probably already have made up your mind and no words written in a book will change it. Besides, I, too, have a preconceived ideology concerning this subject and could easily find myself citing certain facts and suppressing others, maybe even without my being consciously aware of it, in order to coax you over to my side of the fence.

What I'm going to do instead is drop back into survey mode and present the latest ideas, some of them completely contradictory, about how people spread out across the globe and occupied every land mass on the face of the

Earth. Then you can make up your own mind about whether or not they had contact with one another.

THE FIRST PEOPLE OF AFRICA

Since the Out of Africa theory was prevalent for so many years, we'll begin there, assuming that the first people to inhabit the African continent actually originated there, and didn't migrate in from somewhere else.

We have already discussed the fact that modern people seem to have originated from Africa. Even people who have rejected much of the theory still believe that it is basically true in the sense that DNA always seems to lead back to one home continent, but the arguments these days largely center around where in Africa the first population lived. Was it located in one particular spot or did populations located in many different African locations begin to evolve parallel to one another?

Those who adopt the latter theory have begun calling it a Pan-African beginning. They envision early humans consisting of separate groups showing various physical and even cultural diversity. This seems to be where much of the latest fossil evidence points.

Eleanor Scerri, of the University of Oxford and the Max Planck Institute for the Science of Human History, says it this way: "In the fossil record,

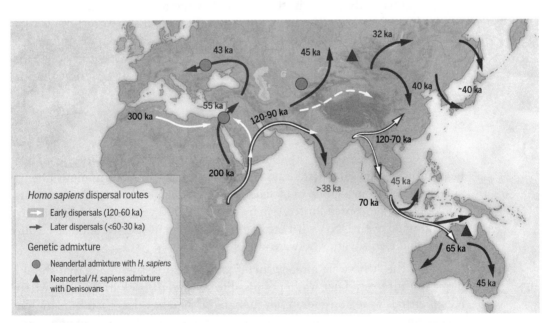

It is generally agreed among anthropologists and other scientists that humanity had its origins in Africa and, over thousands of years, slowly migrated to other parts of the planet. *Homo sapiens*, it is also believed, encountered and interbred with Neanderthals.

we see a mosaic-like, continental-wide trend toward the modern human form, and the fact that these features appear at different places at different times tells us that these populations were not well connected."

Many of her colleagues agree. They think that early human groups must have been separated as a result of ecological diversity. The environment itself, consisting of deserts, forests, rivers, and other natural barriers, would have prevented people from intermingling very much.

DNA aficionados still hold to a single ancestor in a single location, but we'll have to let them argue it out for now.

If the Pan-African theory proves to be true, however, the implications are staggering. It will mean that different human populations grew from many different kinds of ancestors. That will go a long way in determining from whom the various kinds of humans who used to walk the Earth originally developed. And if populations can evolve in different African locations, how can we limit the possibility of other countries with similar conditions being a human homeland as well?

What that means is that the single human race now in existence, *Homo sapiens*, rather than growing apart, is growing together, merging into one universal population. Someday, given this trend, we might continue to look more and more alike until we become one, homogeneous people.

As I write these words, this is exactly what anti-immigration political parties in various countries are trying to prevent. Is history on the side of a homogenous human race or is racial diversity destined to separate us forever? It probably won't be decided in our lifetimes. Evolution works too slowly for that, but in five hundred years the world may look totally different than it does now. Only time will tell.

THE FIRST PEOPLE OF ASIA

We have seen that the Out of Africa theory currently in vogue, but beginning to unravel a little, says that anatomically modern humans like us are descended from a group of *Homo sapiens* who migrated out of Europe about 70,000 years ago, spread into Asia by about 50,000 years ago, and probably intermingled their DNA with other groups of human species, such as Neanderthal and Denisovan, who were already there.

It's the "who were already there" part of that last sentence that should pique our interest. That was a permissible statement back in the days when Neanderthals were considered sub-human, or somehow less than human, but it's becoming obvious that, in many ways, they were just as human as we are. They shared many of the same traits we do, including spirituality, love of music, care for their elderly and children, and genuine talent for art.

In my book *Lost Civilizations*, I spent a lot of time debunking much of the prejudice that has been directed toward Neanderthals until quite recently. Much of that prejudice is similar to so-called "scholars" in America's recent past who, as recently as 75 years ago, wrote treatises claiming that people of different skin color were less "human" than the whites who were in charge of things.

Without realizing it, some people even today believe that. It's called racism. Only a few days after I wrote that last sentence an American president told four U.S. congresswomen, three of whom had been born in this country and all of whom were full-fledged, duly elected members of Congress, to "go back [to the countries] where you came from." The belief in white supremacy, although rarely recognized and acknowledged, is still a real problem in contemporary American society. It's present in Europe, African, and Australia as well.

If we eliminate the premodern-human prejudice that says "we" didn't arrive in Asia until 50,000 to 70,000 years ago, that immediately puts humans in Asia much earlier. How could it be otherwise if there were people there when "we" got there?

If Neanderthals were the first, and there is still no definitive proof of even that, then we have to go back some 300,000 years, when Neanderthals are thought to have evolved from *Homo erectus* in Africa, but that opens up another problem because the oldest evidence known so far for anatomically modern humans was a skull found all the way over in Morocco that is dated to 300,000 years ago. If humans evolved in Africa 300,000 years ago, and then spread to Asia, how did they get to Morocco that fast?

The key may be found in yet another question. If both Neanderthal and modern humans are thought to have descended from *Homo erectus*, who originated some 1.8 million years ago, that leaves a lot of time for *Homo erectus* descendants to migrate and set up shop. Were they more advanced

A reconstruction of how *Homo heidelbergensis* likely appeared based on fragments discovered at Sima de los Huesos. The species ranged from Africa to Europe about half a million years ago.

than we have given them credit for, just as we are now discovering that Neanderthals were a lot more advanced than we give them credit for?

Most anthropologists today think that Neanderthals' ancestors originated in Africa but then evolved into full-fledged Neanderthals in Europe by way of Asia, where they were secluded from their African roots. It was probably not Neanderthals, but the *ancestors* of Neanderthals who were still in Asia to meet modern humans when they arrived some 70,000 years ago. If those ancestors go back as far as 1.8 million years, that leaves a huge block of time for a lot of interesting things to happen before we showed up.

Now it gets even more confusing. Recent evidence indicates that yet another ancient human species, called *Homo heidelbergensis*, originated in Africa and migrated north between 500,000 and 600,000 years ago. The group split into two camps, one going west to Europe, where they became Neanderthals, and the other east toward Asia, where they became Denisovans. By some 250,000 years ago, the ones who had stayed in Africa became *Homo sapiens*. When they all finally staged their family reunion, we called them distant cousins, but it may have really been just one, big, sometimes happy family. The fact that they had children together proves that they didn't always engage in family feuds. There was plenty of time to make love, not war.

What all this proves is that history does not come packaged in a nice, neat bundle that can then be spoon-fed to willing and eager students. Go back and look at some of the key dates we have cited: 1.8 million years; 300,000 years; 250,000 years; 80,0000 years; 70,000 years. We're dealing with immense time spans. It's easy to think of people existing as they were for those periods of time, but the nature of humanity is to reach out, explore, evolve, create, and embellish on the works of their parents. We like to think that when archeologists find a tool here or a spear point there it represents a cross section of what humans were doing at the time, but every artifact could just as easily be an anomaly as much as a representation of the status quo.

Here in my backyard in South Carolina I've found 4,000-year-old Savannah River dart points right next to 200-year-old iron nails, and a rusty pair of pliers I lost last month. Which is "authentic?"

Any archeologist will tell you that's why context is everything. A specialist needs to see the artifact *in situ* or the discovery is meaningless, but archeology is also as much the art of interpretation as the science of excavation. And interpretation means having an open mind as well as sharp eyes.

All this points to the fact that when we say that the "first humans" entered Asia 50,000 years ago, we have to take that pronouncement with a grain of salt. There is much more to the tale, and it is a story that is nowhere near finished being interpreted yet.

THE FIRST PEOPLE OF AUSTRALIA

Native Australians are an ancient people. What makes their origins even more mysterious is that in order to arrive on the continent, whenever that might have been, they must have used boats. There were no ancient land bridges available. That fact, and that fact alone, kept many anthropologists from even exploring the idea that aborigines arrived in their homeland some 60,000 years ago, and maybe even a little earlier than that, but that's what the latest DNA evidence indicates.

As a matter of fact, extremely recent DNA evidence may throw the whole matter into even more of a tizzy. Everything we are about to say assumes modern *Homo sapiens* were the first to arrive in Australia, but Australia is the very place that Denisovan DNA presents the strongest signal. Did Denisovans settle Australia thousands of years before modern humans arrived on the scene? In the coming years, this will prove to be an extremely interesting field of study.

Think about that date for a minute. If early humans struggled out of Africa 70,000 years ago, they had only 10,000 years to make the journey. It's

Torres Strait Islanders perform a traditional dance. The ancestors of these people were part of a planned migration from one island to the next.

some 7,000 miles (more than 11,000 kilometers) by air from South Africa to Australia. Traveling on foot along the coast would easily triple that distance. Add to that the fact that they had to invent boating technology along the way while adjusting to various climate differences and food resources. They also somehow hooked up with at least some ancient Denisovan cousins. And then they would have had to find a reason for migrating across miles of ocean. It was a remarkable achievement, if that's how it happened.

Recent data published in *Scientific Reports*, *Nature Ecology*, and *Evolution* indicate that it took at least 1,000 people to produce a viable population and that the initial immigration was planned. The first people to inhabit Australia, according to these studies, were the ancestors of today's aboriginal people. The Torres Strait Islanders and the Melanesian people participated in what can only be called a technologically advanced immigration.

Until 8,000 to 10,000 years ago, Australia, New Guinea, and Tasmania were joined together into a single island land mass called Sahul. Probably the first landfall came from the north. That would be in keeping with oral history as well as archeological evidence, but a carefully planned, well-executed migration involving boats and island hopping, pulled off by more than 1,000 people, is almost mind boggling. The logistics even today would require considerable skill.

Their goals for making the journey may have been prompted by reasons other than curiosity and exploration. It might have had something to do with very early and ancient trade routes. Then, as now, human beings were interested in improving their lot by opening new geographical areas to exploit.

Back then, gold had probably not attained the intrinsic wealth status it holds today, unless the Sumerian text's emphasis on Anunnaki gold mining turns out to be true, but the facts indicate that gold was mined in Australia for a long time. Artifacts from abroad show conclusively that traders from Pacific regions as far away as New Zealand, Indonesia, Malaysia, China, and India eventually established trade routes all the way to Australia. Their trade goods are now part of the archeological record.

That pretty much puts to rest the "primitive indigenous aborigine" story we've been told, a story that was almost certainly invented by early European bigotry. The invaders simply didn't understand a culture they considered to be inferior to themselves.

There is no mistaking the fact, however, that any high Australian culture that might have previously existed did suffer from a collapse from which they had not recovered by the time of the first modern European contact. What happened?

The answer could be found in the climate record. What we now call climate change is not a new phenomenon. What makes it worse in our day is the rate at which it occurs, but a dramatic decrease in rainfall in the ninth century would have soon made life in any dense population centers unsustainable.

Other forces might have been at work as well.

Legends abound throughout history of a lost continent called Mu or Lemuria. Sometimes it is described as a land mass called "Uru," or "The Great Westland," that existed before a destructive flood brought it low. Easter Island is sometimes described as a mountaintop remnant of this extinct continent.

The Maori people said it used to lie east of New Zealand. They claimed it was once inhabited by an ancient race of people who built stone megaliths and were expert astronomers. Maori mythology records that the inhabitants of this continent were their original ancestors.

Other nations have preserved similar stories. The Chinese wrote of a "land to the south," depicted in ancient, 2,500-year-old maps. They called it Locack. Some of these maps show a rough depiction very similar to the outlines of the Australian continent. Locack was supposed to be rich in resources, especially gold. Its inhabitants were said to be pagan idolaters, but they were excellent astronomers and built great stone megaliths.

Traditional Australian history insists very strongly that the Aborigines never rose above stone age culture. They carved petroglyphs and pecked out some wonderful rock art, but that was about it.

It's important to remember, however, that Australians themselves never wrote traditional history books. Those texts were recorded much later by Europeans. The Aborigines kept their history in other ways. They carved it in stone and told stories that remembered "heroes" who worshipped a supreme being called Biame. The heroes came to Australia in far off times, from across the sea in boats. Some western cave art even illustrated these boats, crewed by visitors called Wandjina, who were illustrated wearing clothes that seem to be Egyptian in nature.

Experts scoffed at such a suggestion until the new science of DNA revealed Australian DNA in Middle East blood groups.

Then came startling new evidence in 2019 that unequivocally revealed Australian DNA showing up as a strong signal in population groups indigenous to the South American Amazon region. How could ancient Australian DNA evidence wind up in South America unless there was ancient contact between the two peoples?

Once the possibility of ancient diffusion between Australia and South America presented itself, other avenues began to be explored. Soon, linguistic studies supported DNA evidence. Certain Egyptian words were found in traditional Aborigine languages. All this evidence, combined with Australian oral history, seems to indicate that the Wandjina people "carved out the mountains and hills" to build cities and mine for gold.

The Wandjina drawings at Raft Point, Western Australia state, Australia, illustrate a pre-Aboriginal people who perhaps came from Egypt.

Who were these early Australians? How did they evolve so fast? Are we missing something about ancient Australian history? Does it go back much further in time than anyone has so far suggested? The fact that such ancient memories remained a part of Australian oral history, a history rich in vivid detail, seems to point to a pre-Aborigine people, or at least a founding culture, who developed a civilization yet to be detected by traditional archeology but vividly recalled in the mythology of those who live in the Southern Pacific Ocean. This population seems to have passed down skills that revealed them to be excellent astronomers. They raised sacred stones and other megalithic structures. If this is true, they were certainly an advanced race of people that don't fit into traditional timelines of history accepted today.

Don't be surprised, if these stories of contact and exchange of knowledge are true, that we might someday soon find other records, outside of Australia, to verify such contact.

Sometimes coincidence, some might call it serendipity, can be a little scary. Read those last two paragraphs again, slowly. I wrote them in June of 2019. Exactly two months later, on August 6, 2019, Marco Margaritoff published an article titled "New Study Suggests Humans Lived in Australia 55,000 Years Earlier Than Previously Thought." It detailed research just released through the Australian archeology network that a site in southern Victoria, Australia, "has raised the possibility that humans existed on the continent 120,000 years ago—twice as long as the previously established timeframe of early human life in the land 'down under.'"

Jim Bowler, now a respected 89-year-old who rose to fame first in 1969 and then in 1974 when he presented the results of his discovery first of the bones of Mungo Lady and later Mungo Man, the oldest bones ever found on the continent, recently made history again. He possesses what archeologists call "a supreme track record," so when he talks, experts listen.

They're listening now. His research has uncovered fire-blackened stones at Moyjil, or Point Ritchie, on the banks of the Hopkins River in Warrnambool, that indicate they were blackened by human-made fires rather than brush fires. Writing in the *Journal of the Proceedings of the Royal Society of Victoria* he shows that the scattered remains of shellfish found positioned with the stones prove that human beings were cooking those shellfish 120,000 years ago, twice the amount of time the current figures allow for the first Australians to inhabit the land.

The technique employed in the study involves thermal luminescence and has become quite popular, in some cases replacing radio-carbon dating, which loses accuracy beyond 50,000 years back in time. The bottom line of the study is that the Gunditjmara people settled on the banks of the Moyjil, probably because it provided easy access to both food and water, 120,000 years ago.

This report, presented by such a respected researcher, has revealed another side of Australian archeology that is, sad to say, too often guilty of suppressing knowledge that doesn't fit established theory. Soon after Bowler let the cat out of the bag, other researchers were forced to admit that they, too, had uncovered similar evidence but had been afraid to release it because they wanted to protect their reputations. Now there are "numerous other sites that had been ignored due to academic dismissal," as one off-the-record insider put it, that produced the same dates. In short, a major reassessment is underway.

If humans reached Australia that long ago, they had to have used boats. This opens up other areas of the world to scruti-

This ancient wall painting of Aboriginal hands in Australia's Mulka's Cave near Wave Rock, Western Australia state, is relatively recent at about 30,000 years old.

ny when it comes to boating technology. Bowler was asked, for instance, about the recent discovery in the United States that suggests people were enjoying California beaches as long as 130,000 years ago.

"I'm a geologist," he said. "I don't enter into such speculative areas, I have no idea who those people were."

Notice that he didn't dispute the fact that people were there at that time in history. He simply said he didn't know who they were.

If these discoveries hold up, and they certainly seem to be so far, we are left with undeniable evidence on two separate continents that indicates an extreme revision in human origins is necessary. We may need to completely recalibrate our theories about who we are and when we arrived on the scene.

In point of fact, some researchers already have. It now appears that ancient Australians might have taught Chinese astronomers a thing or two. Records in China tell of ancient Chinese navigators who undertook sea voyages southward to learn more about the science of the stars. People as far away as the Maya of Central America and the Incas of Peru knew about a land they called Uru. It now appears as though trading networks might have been much more advanced in ancient times than most modern scholars are willing to admit.

In Emerald, located in Queensland Territory in the north, two Easter Island-type stone heads have recently been found submerged in the Whitsunday Passage. An enormous stone head similar to those found in Olmec ruins was dug up just south of Sydney. When Thor Heyerdahl suggested that Peruvian rafts may have sailed the Pacific, even he, as open-minded and intellectually curious as he was, may have underestimated what such vessels could accomplish.

That makes recent discoveries of human footprints preserved in mud and dated to at least 25,000 years ago very interesting. One set of prints even indicates the presence of sandals. Who in Australia would have been wearing sandals 25,000 years ago?

It's important to remember that trade moves in two directions. It is probably not a coincidence that a Peruvian civilization who lived high in the Andes called themselves the Uru. They were a fair-skinned people, whose oral history recalls their ancient ancestors coming from across the western ocean where a great continent once existed. Could this be the basis of human skeletons found in both Peru and the Yucatan peninsula that are thousands of years old and yet demonstrate similar physical traits as those of Australian people? Did ancient Australians actually locate outposts in Central and South America?

If all this weren't enough to provoke our curiosity, remains of walls and structures have been found beneath the ocean surface in Queensland, constructed of triangular-shaped bricks held together with mortar. Similar structures have been found in New Guinea, leading some scientists to think that a great civilization with extensive trade networks might have once existed way back before historic times.

We noted earlier that a land bridge never existed between Australia and the mainland within the accepted historical time frame of *Homo sapiens*. Such a land bridge once existed, but geological studies reveal that it was a long, long time ago, way before human beings were supposed to have lived on Earth. If a population once traveled, or even lived on, such a land bridge, it would be ancient, indeed. That makes recent discoveries of human footprints preserved in mud and dated to at least 25,000 years ago very interesting. One set of prints even indicates the presence of sandals. Who in Australia would have been wearing sandals 25,000 years ago? These discoveries correspond in time to rock engravings that have been dated to this same era.

The anomalies continue with the recent discovery of megalithic structures found beneath the surface of the water in Torres Strait, Queensland, and New South Wales. Most archeologists consider them to be natural formations, but that opinion could well be formed more by ideology than plain fact. Once again, it's hard for some specialists to abandon their long-held prejudice when new discoveries appear.

Some specialists confess that the megaliths are real but must indicate the presence of early Egyptian travelers who wanted to leave their mark on the landscape. That may be true, but it seems quite a stretch. Why would Egyptian pyramid builders want to leave such a calling card behind? There are easier ways to announce that "Kilroy was here." Moving megaton boulders all around the landscape with a minimal work force is a lot of work for a small group of tourists.

Stone eagles and serpents, mysterious megaliths, strange stories from a distant past—all these enigmas work together to suggest that there is much about the ancient Australian past that has been, for the most part, neglected. Perhaps it is time to listen again to the forgotten voices of those who seem to be crying out in the wilderness of popular opinion, hoping that someone will listen with open ears and fresh imaginations. They are our predecessors in the sense that, like us, they, too, thought their civilization would last forever.

THE FIRST PEOPLE OF EUROPE

In April of 2019, Frank Jordans, writing for the Associated Press, reported that the latest research from the journal *Nature*, then hot off the presses, so to speak, indicated that "a wave of migrants from what is now Greece and Turkey arrived in Britain some 6,000 years ago and virtually replaced the existing hunter-gatherer population." The story went on to say that the previous inhabitants, going back as far as 8500 B.C.E., were "dark-skinned foragers who had inhabited the British Isles during the last ice age." They left little trace of their presence in terms of DNA evidence, which suggested to researchers that little interbreeding took place between the two groups.

That takes human populations in Europe back as far as the Ice Age, but if we're looking for European pioneers we obviously have to go back a lot further in time. If the newcomers encountered people already there, who were closely related enough to interbreed, obviously the newcomers were not the first at the party.

So who were the real pioneers?

A reconstruction of *Australopithecus afarensis* on display at a Barcelona, Spain, museum shows an animal more closely resembling a chimpanzee than a human. This hominim lived about three to four million years ago in Africa.

Now the picture becomes a little blurred. The traditional story goes something like this.

Prior to 700,000 years ago, *Homo sapiens* lived in Africa, along with the descendants of "Lucy," whom we met earlier. She was *Australopithecus afarensis*, the ancestor of *Homo erectus* and had lived about 3.3 million years ago. Her descendants split into distinct groups and spent the next 3 million years evolving and spreading throughout the world, including, of course, in Europe. The oldest European human fossil, which was found near Heidelberg, Germany, has been dated to about 650,000 years ago. Evidence indicates that humans learned to control fire some 350,000 years ago. They lived on a continent locked in the grips of an ice age. It wasn't until about 10,000 B.C.E., when the British Isles became separated from mainland Europe, that things finally began to warm up, but that didn't stop our earliest ancestors from going about their business. We are a hardy species who followed migrating animals to obtain food, clothes, and shelter, as far back as at least 70,000 years ago. The caves of France and Spain have yielded a remarkable number of artifacts that prove early humans knew how to live, and even thrive, in what seems like incredibly adverse conditions.

Perhaps it would be best at this point to try to visualize all these dates we've been throwing around:

Human Timeline of Traditional Dates:

- 700,000 B.C.E.: *Homo erectus* leaves Africa and begins to colonize Europe and Asia. There they evolved into Neanderthals in Europe and Denisovans in Asia. The two groups did manage to mix and mingle a little, however, for the next 620,000 years.

- 100,000 B.C.E.: *Homo sapiens* leaves Africa and migrates into the near East. There they become extinct, only to replaced by another wave somewhere around 70,000 years ago.

- 35,000–10,000 B.C.E.: *Homo sapiens* migrates west into Europe, where they meet up with Neanderthal and coexist for a few millennia, sometimes peacefully, other times not so much.

This puts the very first human species, who evolved into Neanderthals, in Europe about 700,000 years ago, and the first anatomically modern humans there about 35,000 years ago.

Maybe. A recent skull fragment excavated from the Apidima 1 cave in southern Greece has been identified as bonafide *Homo sapiens* and roughly 210,000 years old. That makes it the oldest member of our species ever found outside of Africa. Anthropologists think these folks failed to thrive and went extinct, leaving the area to Neanderthals, but one skull fragment is a pretty small sample upon which to base a whole theory of human pioneers.

The question remains, how trustworthy are these dates?

Sarah Pruitt, writing for the History Channel's website in August of 2018, questions this scenario. Quoting sources from the University of Tubingen in Germany, and University of Toronto in Canada, she proposes that the earliest human ancestors emerged in Europe, not Africa, and it happened some 7.2 million years ago.

The research cited arrived at this theory after two fossils were analyzed. One was a lower jaw found in Greece in 1944,

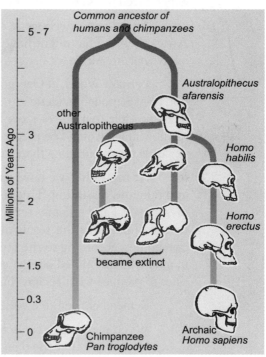

The evolutionary path leading to modern *Homo sapiens* was quite complex, and not all branches of the hominim tree survived over the millenia. As this chart shows, the idea that humans evolved from chimps is a misconception; they are two very different branches of one tree.

and the other was a premolar tooth found in Bulgaria in 2009. Both fossils came from an ape-like creature called *Graecopithecus freybergi*, or "El Graeco" for short. This species is thought to have lived in the Mediterranean region between 7.18 and 7.25 million years ago.

The theory is, of course, the subject of much criticism. David Begun of the University of Toronto, for instance, coauthored the new study, and even he's not totally convinced: "It's not the best specimen in the world. It has a lot of damage to the surface of the jawbone itself and a lot of damage to the teeth, so they're really hard to see, they're difficult to measure, and it's hard to say what they look like." They had to use CT-scanning to look inside the mandible, but when they did, things opened up a bit. To simplify some very sophisticated research, what they found illustrated all the characteristics of humanness that were not found in apes who lived during that time period.

Computer studies of climate tendencies of that period indicated that ancient Greece of that time experienced, dry, savannah-like climate patterns similar to what was found in eastern Africa. Both populations would have experienced the same weather conditions.

This doesn't necessarily change anything about the traditional Out of Africa theory. That might have happened, too. The question is, did humans evolve *only* in Africa?

Bernard Wood, of George Washington University, is cautious. "We just don't have enough evidence to come to that conclusion," he warns. "It's perfectly possible that one or more fossil apes have roots like that.... If you asked me how much would I be prepared to bet that this is a hominin, you'd have to persuade me to put more than a quarter on [it]."

At this point, we have to move from fossilized bones to metaphysical and religious reasoning. This is important because, as we have already seen, mythological and religious texts imply that at some point in the past, humans became human as the result of tampering by a party or parties unknown. Sometimes, according to the mythology, those doing the genetic engineering manually manipulated our genes. Sometimes they mated with ape-like creatures to produce what became human offspring.

Remember the Bible verses, for instance, that we quoted earlier:

When men began to increase in number on the Earth, the sons of God saw that the daughters of men were beautiful, and they married any of them they chose.... The Nephilim were on the Earth in those days—and also afterward—when the sons of God went to the daughters of men and had children by them. They were the heroes of old, men of renown.

—Genesis 6:1–6

If these and similar texts from different geographical locations and separate religious traditions refer in any way to actual gene manipulation, either manually or by means of reproduction, that produced humans, we would expect humans to have originated in more than one spot on the Earth. The human race would have begun wherever and whenever the manipulation took place. In other words, the human species would have had separate and distinct spots of origin. The fossils in Greece don't *prove* such ape/alien liaisons took place. They just indicate that the myths can't be rejected out of hand. Once again, we need to have an open mind and not suppress any evidence just because it doesn't fit the prevailing theory.

Out of Africa still looks good from a scientific standpoint. Early human cousins in Europe back as far as 700,000 years ago look pretty convincing based on fossil evidence, but we are still left with a puzzle. The human species is curious, resourceful, and adaptive. When we settle into an area and get even a little comfortable, we tend to make changes rather quickly and adapt new ways of living very fast. Seven hundred thousand years is a long, long period of time. A lot can happen in that time. Are we sure we understand what might have come to pass, given the sparse archeological evidence and the built-in historical event horizon? Even the vaguest evidence needs to be examined. There seem to be a lot of missing chapters in our story.

THE FIRST PEOPLE OF THE AMERICAS

In the Introduction to this book, I used the American "Clovis First" theory to illustrate the concept of suppressed history. There is probably no example in the field of archeology that better illustrates the tendency to circle the wagons around an idea and defend it against all comers. This has been the tendency in American anthropology for almost a hundred years. It is finally coming undone, but the cost in human sorrow, ruined careers, and bad blood between colleagues has been tremendous. And it is by no means over. The vast majority of specialists still cannot resist the opportunity to attack those who seriously consider well-regarded archeological digs from Florida to Peru that at least suggest that people were in America more than 20,000 or even 30,000 years ago. Clovis First is dying, but it has by no means stilled its death throes.

Once again, to recap what we said in the Introduction, the Clovis First Theory insists that the very first people to enter the Americas were Paleolithic hunters who followed game animals across what was then a so-called land-bridge, which was really much bigger than the word "bridge" implies, that connected Asia and Siberia to Alaska. This migration took a long time. It went on for thousands of years. No one suggests that a single family of people walked all the way from Lake Baikal to Montana. It was a gradual process that included many generations. They moved slowly, adapting to conditions as they went, but when these people finally reached Canada, the theory says,

When early humans reached South America, they hunted such large animals as this glyptodon, a species that became extinct about two thousand years after humans arrived.

they eventually spread out and covered North America, Central America, and then South America. It postulates an uninterrupted migration from the north that began some 16,5000 years ago and ended about 3,000 years later, when rising sea levels flooded what is now called Beringia.

Once here in the Americas, the people developed the Clovis Point, which is considered to be the first American invention. It was a fluted spear point whose sheer beauty has never been rivaled. Because the first example of this point was found near the town of Clovis, New Mexico, the people who made it were called Clovis people. For a long time, and in many corners of the archeological world even today, they were called the First Americans.

In the 1960s it became popular to declare with great confidence that these people, armed with their wonderful invention, were the ones who hunted the great mastodons to extinction. Their arrival seemed to coincide with the disappearance of the great beasts, so why not? It was a great theory back then, partly because the urbanization of America had led a lot of people into cities and hunting was becoming a sort of social stigma. I remember it well. The movie *Bambi* was really popular.

But when you go back and read those articles now, they seem pretty silly. One moment the author is saying how risky and difficult it was to take on a mammoth. Paragraph after vivid paragraph talked about the danger. *National Geographic* was hugely popular in those days, partly due to beautiful and vivid artists' renditions of a supposed mammoth hunt, showing our brave ancestors surviving by bringing down great, lumbering beasts, sometimes at the expense of their lives.

But then, after showing how hard it was to kill a mammoth, the same authors would blithely move on to say that mammoths were hunted to extinction all across the breadth of North America because the great beasts were so unused to people that they just stood there and let people walk up and throw one of their Clovis-tipped spears into their sides. Down they went, a victim of superior technology. The two contrasting pictures never quite made sense, but a lot of people bought it. Those were simpler days.

While this theory was being touted about and written up in high school textbooks, however, the information that giant sloths, huge beavers, immense bison, saber-toothed cats, dire wolves, short-faced bears, and even a type of spruce tree went extinct at this same time was quietly suppressed. To advertise this information would serve to weaken the whole Clovis First theory. After all, why would a hunter seek to bring down a spruce tree with a Clovis point?

Today, though, it has become untenable to stick to Clovis First. Did people cross into the Americas by way of Beringia? Unequivocally, yes, but was Beringia the *only* geographical area to put out a welcome mat? Certainly not. Then as now, America seemed to be a melting pot, open to immigrants from all over. They walked in on foot, came here by boat, followed coastlines, explored rivers, and generally took advantage of a land consisting of two continents that were rich in resources and opportunities.

But when did they start arriving? Who were the very first Americans?

If you close off any door but Beringia, you run smack into glaciers that didn't start to melt until relatively recently. If you add boats to the equation or postulate an ancient time way back before the last ice age when Beringia was also open to foot travel, that opens a lot of avenues of entry.

The problem is that most archeologists don't want to allow our ancestors to have boats or to be a lot older than is currently considered acceptable. Take away boats, take away age, and you're stuck with Clovis First. Those takeaways are too big a hurdle for many archeologists to accept.

"Where's the evidence?" they shout. "Show me some proof!"

Thus the circular reasoning has run for almost a hundred years. I've had college professors and archeologists tell me that, until recently, if they dared to bring up anything other than Clovis First they would never have attained either tenure or funding for their archeological research.

"Clovis First is the gospel," says academia. "We're not going to waste money chasing a crazy theory. When you reach a Clovis layer, stop! Don't fritter away funds that could be used to do real archeology."

So there it is. It's entirely possible that there was little evidence to the contrary because the establishment had declared such evidence off limits. How can you accumulate evidence if you're not permitted to look for it? For almost a hundred years we have been spoon-fed a lie. Those who dared to question the whole process were emotionally and financially bullied, sometimes driven right out of the field.

In previous books I have lamented what I called the Conspiracy of Silence that permeates the field of academia. There is no greater example of this conspiracy than the history of Clovis First in American archeology.

To make matters worse, there *is* evidence to the contrary. More turns up every day. Pennsylvania's Meadowcroft Rock Shelter site, South Carolina's Topper site, Virginia's Cactus Hill, Oregon's Paisley Cave, and Monte Verde in South America offer ample evidence, well documented and peer reviewed, of pre-Clovis activity, but none of them have maintained their status without having to endure some vicious battles.

Thank goodness a few stalwart archeologists persevered and fought the good fight for colleagues who are now following in their footsteps. Without them we never would have begun learning about a rich and extremely long pre-history in America.

To discover just how long a time period we are talking about, let's travel out to California. If new evidence found there continues to hold its own and stand up to the intense scrutiny it has engendered, we are about to add 100,000 years, and possibly even a lost civilization that has within it echoes of what I call the Atlantis Tradition, to American history.

In April of 2017, Kate Wong, writing for *Scientific American*, reported on a story published in *Nature*, which recorded a discovery of the broken bones of a mastodon that are at least 130,000 years old. Old mastodon bones alone don't really prove anything, but the significance of these is that they show evidence of being hammered apart by human beings in order to obtain bone marrow. The hammer stones were discovered right alongside the bones themselves. The only way a human species could have arrived in California at that time was by boat, along the coast. The glacier up north would have pre-

This reconstruction of a mastodon resembles what this relative of the modern elephant looked like over 100,000 years ago. Some mastodon bones appear to bear marks of human tools, possibly those of a Neanderthal or Denisovan hunter.

vented any access by foot travel. To make things even more exciting, this was at a time in history when both Neanderthals and Denisovans roamed Europe and Asia. Since that discovery, genetic DNA from both species has been found in Native American groups now living.

How could Neanderthals and Denisovans, who up until recently were considered "distant primitive cousins" of *Homo sapiens*, have made it across the oceans to America during a time period that was at least 40,000 years before Australians were thought to have used boats? The sexual coupling that produced their DNA in modern humans might have taken place before the migration, but maybe not. It's a point that has to at least be considered.

Wong recorded the sharp criticism of experts. They simply refused to believe it. If the evidence is accepted, it would allow a period of 100,000 years of human presence in the Americas. Almost anything, including the emergence of a relatively advanced civilization, could have arisen in that amount of time.

Once again the voices of academia arose in righteous indignation. "Where is the evidence?" they screamed, while ignoring the evidence before them because they refused to even consider it might be authentic.

The best they could muster were words of hope from such scholars as Tom Dillehay of Vanderbilt University, who for years fought to convince the archaeological community that remains from the controversial site of Monte Verde in Chile predate the Clovis culture: "We need to leave our minds open. I admire these colleagues for sticking their necks out. They should be commended for doing that, but more evidence is going to be needed."

Speaking of "sticking their necks out," some respected specialists are willing to do just that. They wonder if Beringia represents only one door granting entrance into the American continent.

In 2012, Dennis Stanford and Bruce Bradley published a book called *Across Atlantic Ice: The Origin of America's Clovis Culture*. It was, as expected, immediately the subject of controversy. In this book they carefully put forth what is now called the Solutrean Hypothesis. Archeologists, being

Anthropologist and Vanderbilt University professor Tom Dillehay struggled to convince colleagues that the Monte Verde site predated the Clovis culture.

the scientists that they are, depend on precise language. Here is the Solutrean Hypothesis according to Stanford and Bradley:

> Who were the first Americans? The Solutrean hypothesis, in simple outline form, is that during the Last Glacial Maximum, sometime between 25,000 and 13,000 years ago, members of the Solutrean Culture in the Southwest coastal regions of Europe were led by subsistence behavior appropriate to their time and place to exploit the ice-edge environment of the polar front across the North Atlantic and colonize North America to become—after several millennia—what we know as the Clovis peoples, who eventually spread far and wide across the Americas. This does not necessarily mean that the Clovis people were the ancestors—or the only ancestors—of contemporary Native Americans, and it does not mean that Paleolithic northeast Asians did not also colonize the Americas. It does mean, in concert with other strands of evidence, that Clovis is part of the rich, complex, and wonderful story of the ebb and flow of people whose descendants are what we call Native Americans.

Simply put, in their view, representatives of the Solutrean culture migrated west across the Atlantic from France and northern Spain. In doing so, they became possibly the first European people to ever set foot on the continent. They settled there for thousands of years, spreading out across the land, eventually evolving their finally honed stone craft into what is now known as the Rolls Royce of stone technology, the beautifully fluted Clovis Point.

Those who later crossed on foot across the Beringia land bridge eventually reaped the benefits of Solutrean bifacial stone technology, producing a serviceable point called the Folsom Point. It was smaller and easier to make than Clovis, but was sufficient because the megafauna, mastodons and mammoths among them, were now extinct. The prey they sought was much smaller. As these Folsom people gradually spread back across the landscape, they eventually became the ancestors of many Native American Indian tribes.

It's really a fairly conservative theory. The dates don't push back the arrival of the first Americans very far. It certainly doesn't imply anything like the 100,000-year-old California discovery. And if it's true, whenever you pick up a typical bifacial Indian arrowhead, you are holding in your hand the legacy of the Solutrean people of western Europe. Some American Eurocentric scholars even championed the theory because it implied that Euro-

> *Simply put, in their view, representatives of the Solutrean culture migrated west across the Atlantic from France and northern Spain. In doing so, they became possibly the first European people to ever set foot on the continent.*

peans were the first Americans, and the Indians were johnny-come-latelies. This played right into the hands of those who wanted justification for how Europeans treated native populations.

David Meltzer of Southern Methodist University, an authority on the peopling of the Americas, has accumulated a bit of a reputation for demanding more evidence for early dates while refusing to accept that evidence as being insufficient once it is presented. That was the stance he took on the History Channel's TV movie *Journey to 10,000 BC*, which was first aired back in 2008.

About the California discovery, he wrote: "You can't push human antiquity in the New World back 100,000 years based on evidence as inherently ambiguous as broken bones and nondescript stones—not when they are coming from a highway salvage excavation done 25 years ago, and you have none of the detailed taphonomic evidence demanded of such a grandiose claim."

Once again, we are frustrated when the prevailing argument against early human presence in the Americas is that there is no evidence, but then, when evidence is put forth, it is discounted and called illegitimate because it doesn't fit the accepted theory.

The initial discovery happened like this.

A road crew in San Diego County, while on a routine highway improvement job on Highway 54, came across the site and dutifully called in a paleontologist survey team who did a formal excavation. The researchers recovered bones of different ice age species from different stratigraphic levels in the site.

Steven Holen, of the San Diego Natural History Museum, led a group of colleagues who focused their attention on a partial skeleton of a male mastodon. It was soon called the Cerutti Mastodon site, named after Richard Cerutti, who formally reported the results of the study.

The mastodon's leg bones show distinctive breaks called spiral fractures that wind around the long axis of the bone. These fractures only occur before the bone has a chance to harden. In other words, it seems as though ancient humans applied the pressure while it was still fresh, presumably to break the bone apart to get the rich marrow within. Hammer stones were used to accomplish the task, and several such stones were found associated with the bones.

This is nothing unusual. Standard archeological discoveries are relatively common at construction sites. If the remains had been dated to even 10,000 years ago, the find would have stood on its own. What makes the site so special is that using a technique that measures the radioactive decay of uranium rather than carbon, the site was independently dated back to 130,000 years ago.

Remember that up until then the accepted date for human presence in America was only some 30,000 years ago, and many archeologists don't even allow dates that old.

Wong sums up the current status of the debate very well: "If Holen and his colleagues are correct about the age and nature of the finds, researchers will need to rethink everything they thought they knew about the peopling of the New World, including which human species was the first to colonize it. Most researchers agree humans came to the Americas from northeastern Asia. At 130,000 years ago, the authors argue, *Homo sapiens*, *Homo erectus*, the Neanderthals, and the Denisovans … might have been present in that part of the world. They could have crossed Beringia on foot prior to 135,000 years ago, when sea levels were sufficiently low. Otherwise, they could have traveled by boat, following the coasts of Asia, Beringia, and North America to reach the latitude of the Cerutti Mastodon site.

It's hard to imagine what California looked like back then. It was a place where camels and dire wolves roamed freely among the mastodons and saber-toothed cats. The La Brea tar pits in the middle of Los Angeles reveal a striking

The La Brea tar pits as they are today include an extensive museum and a variety of statues, such as these mastodon sculptures, which give guests an idea of what prehistoric Los Angeles might have looked like.

picture of Ice Age America. Who were the first Californians to take advantage of this landscape? They must have enjoyed a good climate and plenty of food resources. It might have been a very nice place to hang out. They couldn't visit Disneyland, of course, but there were a lot of other attractions.

Meanwhile, the debate rages. Technical methods used by paleontologists are different from those employed by archeologists, and the two sets of specialists are often critical of one another. Were the marks caused by humans or were they natural?

To be honest, a layman such as myself, who reads the articles and looks at the pictures but lacks the specific skills and experience to actually conduct a dig, can be easily influenced one way or the other, but I confess that when all is said and done, there is more than a hint of suspicion hidden in the recesses of all the words. It certainly seems as though some of the most vocal specialists are arguing from a position of previously formed ideology rather than honest research. In other words, it sometimes sounds as though conservative voices from the academic community simply don't believe the evidence because it doesn't agree with their prejudices.

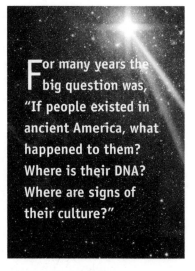

For many years the big question was, "If people existed in ancient America, what happened to them? Where is their DNA? Where are signs of their culture?"

Typical of this position is the opinion of Jon Erlandson, of the University of Oregon. He is a proponent of a coastal migration pattern but draws the line at boat technology: "There's some evidence that *Homo erectus* was able to cross a few small bodies of water, but no evidence that *Erectus*, or Neanderthals for that matter, could do long-range voyaging or that they had sophisticated boats like modern humans had when they colonized Australia."

The circular reasoning goes like this. If the Bering Strait was closed to foot travel, folks would have had to have used boats. Here is evidence of humans having crossed an ocean. They must have used boats, but there's no evidence of boats. So it can't be. And round and round goes the argument, with no end in sight:

"There's no evidence of people in America for 100,000 years after the dating of this site."

"But there is evidence. You just don't accept it."

"Where the evidence?"

"It's at the Meadowcroft Rock Shelter and Topper and Cactus Hill and Paisley Cave and Monte Verde and dozens of other sites."

"I won't accept those sites until you produce some evidence."

When will it end?

And beneath all this activity there lies an even more important fact of history. For many years the big question was, "If people existed in ancient America, what happened to them? Where is their DNA? Where are signs of their culture?"

Admittedly this was a sticking point, but in 2007, the tide began to turn. According to a study published on September 17, 2007, in *The Proceedings of the National Academy of Sciences*:

> In 2007, archaeologists led by Dr Richard Firestone of the Lawrence Berkeley National Laboratory found spherules of metals and nano-sized diamonds in a layer of sediment dating 12,900 years ago at 10 of 12 archaeological sites. The mix of particles is thought to be the result of an extraterrestrial object, such as a comet or meteorite, exploding in the Earth's atmosphere. Among the sites examined was the Topper, one of the most pristine sites in the United States for research on Clovis, one of the earliest ancient peoples.

Cultures from all over the world relate tales and legends that recall a former human civilization that was destroyed by fire or flood. America is no exception. Now the popular press reports that there may be solid science behind the stories. Words such as "Nanodiamonds" and "Micro-spherules" have entered the popular lexicon.

Graham Hancock, in his book *Magicians of the Gods*, shared some of the relevant myths from people around the world:

> From the Brule people of the Lakota nation:

> A fiery blast shook the entire world, toppling mountain ranges and setting forests and prairies ablaze.... Even the rocks glowed red-hot, and the giant animals and evil people burned up where they stood. Then the rivers overflowed their banks and surged across the landscape. Finally, the Creator stamped the Earth, and with a great quake the Earth split open, sending torrents...across the entire world until only a few mountain peaks stood above the flood.

> Similar stories are told by the Cowichan of British Columbia, the Pima of Arizona, the Inuit of Alaska, and the Luiseno of California.

> From the Ojibwa people of the Canadian grasslands:

> [We] remember a comet called Long-Tailed Heavenly Climbing Star that swept low through the skies, scorching the Earth and leaving behind a different world. After that, survival was hard work. The weather was colder than before. And then came ... a fiery blast that shook the entire world, unleashing a tsunami.

From the words of the Bible:

I will send rain on the Earth for forty days and forty nights, and I will wipe from the face of the Earth every living creature I have made.

This message is repeated in other ancient Sumerian texts and Babylonian inscriptions. The geological evidence of past collisions with comets or asteroids is beyond dispute. That it could happen again is also beyond dispute. The question is, have such catastrophes happened during the span of time when human eyewitnesses observed them?

The National Climatic Data Center of the National Oceanic and Atmospheric Administration (NOAA) reports that such an event happened 12,800 years ago. It calls it the *Younger Dryas Event*.

The oral traditions of many ancient peoples include tales of cataclysmic fires and floods destroying most of the planet. Could they be recalling an actual asteroid impact on the Earth long ago?

The Younger Dryas is one of the most well-known examples of abrupt (climate) change. About 14,500 years ago, the Earth's climate began to shift from a cold glacial world to a warmer interglacial state. Partway through this transition (12,800 years ago), temperatures in the Northern Hemisphere suddenly returned to near-glacial conditions This near-glacial period is called the Younger Dryas, named after a flower (*Dryas Octopetala*) that grows in cold conditions and became common in Europe during this time. The end of the Younger Dryas, about 11,500 years ago, was particularly abrupt. In Greenland, temperatures rose 10° C (18° F) in a decade.

It now appears that at the end of the last Ice Age a fiery comet broke apart above the skies of Earth, many of the segments exploding within the atmosphere of the planet. At least four of them, and perhaps as many as nine, each more than a mile across, struck the glacial surface of the Laurentide and Cordilleran ice caps in central and western Canada in North America. The effect was thousands of times more devastating than any nuclear blast the Earth has ever witnessed.

The heat alone would have melted vast amounts of ice, but the worst was yet to come. Almost unimaginable amounts of dust and soot would have been thrown into the upper atmosphere, blotting out the sun for months, if not years. Temperatures dropped almost overnight, plunging the Earth into what amounts to another Ice Age—the Younger Dryas—that lasted for some 1,500 years. And this event might have been repeated every year for the next twenty years, every time the Earth passed through the debris field of what we now call the Taurid meteor showers.

The Maya of Guatemala describe it as "black rain and mist, and indescribably cold." Hopi mythology recalls a world that was destroyed by ice—perhaps the ice sheets of the Younger Dryas.

Andrew Collins, in his book Atlantis in the Caribbean and the Comet That Changed the World, puts forth some compelling evidence that Atlantis was located in the Bahamas and the Caribbean....

The deadly aftereffects ravaged the Earth for more than a millennium, certainly long enough to obliterate any evidence of an ice age civilization that once existed in America, but the stories tell of humans who lived through it, managed to survive, and recorded their tales in what we have, until recently, written off only as myth and legend.

The only way to prove any of this is look for evidence, but if projects can't be funded and careers are discouraged unless they conform to the status quo theories of academia, how will that evidence be found? You can't find what you are forbidden to look for.

It probably doesn't help that the Americas, specifically the Caribbean islands, are thought by some to be the source of what I call the Atlantis tradition. These are stories of a lost, advanced civilization that was destroyed, according to Plato, in a single day. Modern archeologists have a specific disdain for anything with the name "Atlantis" attached to it, but, as I pointed out in my book *Lost Civilizations*, the dates and time all match up to Plato's account.

Andrew Collins, in his book *Atlantis in the Caribbean and the Comet That Changed the World*, puts forth some compelling evidence that Atlantis was located in the Bahamas and the Caribbean, and that present day Cuba may have been the capitol of the island nation. It is his theory that at the time of the Younger Dryas comet impact, some 12,800 years ago, the island of Cuba was devastated and parts of the Bahaman landmass in the Caribbean were submerged beneath the rising sea. Relating ancient myths and legends from the indigenous people of North, Central, and South America, including the Maya of Mesoamerica, the Quiché of Peru, the Yuchi of Oklahoma, the islanders of the Antilles, and the native peoples of Brazil, he believes that the comet that destroyed Atlantis in the Caribbean also formed the numerous elliptical depressions called Carolina Bays, found across the Carolinas and all the way down the eastern Atlantic coast.

It's a compelling theory, and one that deserves attention, but it means acknowledging a preconceived ideology dead set against any mention of

Atlantis. Such an acknowledgement is hard to find these days. Remember the words we quoted earlier from Gemma Tarlach: "The scientific method generally works, as long as everyone keeps their egos in check."

Who were the first people to inhabit the Americas? The truth is, we just don't know yet. Too much evidence has been suppressed over the last century, but the stranglehold of Clovis First is beginning to loosen. We live in exciting times. Who know what the future holds for finally uncovering the story of the Americas?

THE FIRST PEOPLE OF ANTARCTICA

Did anyone ever inhabit Antarctica?

The question seems absurd. For the last 6,000 years Antarctica has been covered by ice. It wasn't even discovered until the nineteenth century. No one could possibly have lived there.

Or could they?

Piri Reis was a Turkish admiral who lived in the late fifteenth and early sixteenth century. He was a son of the pirate Kemal Reis, who somehow rose through the official ranks and managed to become an admiral. He taught his son how to captain ships and plot accurate maps.

Kemal was killed in 1502, causing Piri to quit sailing, or at least pirating, and become a mapmaker. In 1513 he created a now famous map based on a chart captured from, of all people, Christopher Columbus. In those days, captains used to make it a habit to throw their charts overboard if their ship was boarded. Charts were very valuable and carefully protected. They were invariably kept secret. Apparently, Columbus wasn't quite quick enough when he was captured by the Turkish navy. Reis obtained the crucial charts and copied them while serving at the Imperial Library at Constantinople, one of the great academic centers of his age.

I wrote about the mystery surrounding this map in my book *Lost Civilizations*, but here's a quick synopsis.

On a gazelle skin that has been dated to the year 1513, Reis drew one of the oldest maps known to exist. On the map's margins he wrote a series of notes in which he confessed that the map was a copy of a much older document. That document is now lost. His map was filed away and forgotten until, in 1966, Charles Hapgood wrote a book called *Maps of the Ancient Sea Kings: Evidence of Advanced Civilization in the Ice Age*. In this book he unveiled a copy of the Piri Reis map that shows the western coast of Africa, the eastern coast of South America, and the northern coastline of Antarctica.

The continent of Antarctica wasn't charted until three hundred years after Reis drew his map. It had been covered in glacial ice and invisible to the

The historic event of Turkish Admiral Piri Reis (c. 1470–1554) drawing his 1513 map is recreated in wax at the Kilitbahir Castle Museum in Canakkale, Turkey.

naked eye of passing sailors for thousands of years. Yet here was a chart showing the geography of what is now called Queen Maude Land, shown in complete detail. How on Earth could such a thing be? Yet, as I traced the story in *Lost Civilizations*, it has been verified by a mystified cartographic staff who served the Strategic Air Command (SAC).

It seems impossible, but there it is, for all to see.

The only realistic explanation is that somehow, at sometime in ancient history, either when Antarctica was free of ice or possibly existed in a different latitude than it now occupies, there lived a now forgotten civilization that sailed the seas and charted the continents. Somehow their charts managed to survive the vicissitudes of time and were discovered and used by folks such as Christopher Columbus and then Piri Reis.

It's an almost unbelievable hypothesis, but the evidence is there on a map drawn in 1513. Of course, no one wants to believe it. The story of the map falls into the category of suppressed history. If it exists, something is wrong with our interpretation of history. It is simply ignored. Out of sight, out of mind.

Down through history there have been those who knew about the evidence. It's not as if it is a recent bombshell.

On February 27, 1932, an issue of the *Illustrated London News* featured an article entitled "A Columbus Controversy: America—And Two Atlantic Charts." The article reveals that "Columbus got little further than the mouth of the Orinoco, in Venezuela, in his voyage along the coast of South America in 1498, so that the stretches of the South American coast given in the Piri Reis chart must have been copied from other sources."

Obviously others have wondered. So why hasn't the news made the history books?

Well, the answer is probably simple. People just don't want to believe it's true. If it was accurate, it would raise too many awkward questions. In the absence of an explanation, and without an internet and broadcast television to beam the news to a greater audience, the whole issue was simply buried. Now, of course, with modern media outlets, that is no longer possible. People can't be so easily kept in the dark. Is it any wonder the public is angry and books such as this one are being written? This isn't about conspiracy theory. It's about access to suppressed information that specialists have known about for a long time. In some cases, the information has been deliberately suppressed. In other cases, it had proved to be so confusing that no one wanted to risk their professional standing to buck the system.

Those days, thankfully, are about to end.

That being said, is there any evidence that people once lived in Antarctica?

Well, they do now. About four thousand people call the continent home every summer. The population drops to about one thousand in winter, but if the entire continent once occupied higher latitudes, free from ice, it's certainly a possibility. As the ice caps of Antarctica begin to melt, strange structures seem to be appearing beneath the lowered ice cap. Are they evidence of an ancient, lost civilization? It's way too soon to tell. Rumors abound, however.

Fossilized ferns and evidence of a tropical climate have been definitively plotted and studied. How is that possible in a land that encompasses the south polar regions?

Besides the mysterious structures, which are very controversial, there is other evidence that cannot be denied. Fossilized ferns and evidence of a tropical climate have been definitively plotted and studied. How is that possible in a land that encompasses the south polar regions?

The official story is that Antarctica was discovered on January 27, 1820, by Fabian Gottlieb von Bellingshausen and Mikhail Lazarev, who led a Russian expedition that reported sighting the Princess Martha Coast that later became known as the Fimbul Ice Shelf.

No one seems to want to bring up Piri Reis and his infamous map.

But Professor Jane Francis, of the University of Leeds, reports evidence that Antarctica was once forested, and dinosaurs roamed the land. That, of course, was a long time ago. In her words as recorded by the BBC in 2011, "I still find the idea that Antarctica was once forested absolutely mind-boggling…. We take it for granted that Antarctica has always been a frozen wilderness, but the ice caps only appeared relatively recently in geological history…. We were high up on glaciated peaks when we found a sedimentary layer packed full of fragile leaves and twigs."

Granted, her discovery reveals a landscape that existed 3 to 5 million years ago, but once you remove the blinders from your mind, and begin to at least explore possibilities out of the mainstream that say a human species could not have lived that long ago, the ideas become intriguing, to say the least.

THE FIRST PEOPLE OF NEW ZEALAND

When Peter Jackson set up shop in New Zealand to spend ten years or so filming his double trilogy set of *Lord of the Rings* and *The Hobbit*, he created a new tourism industry and reminded people all over the world of the beauty New Zealanders live with every day. The first trilogy, which began to be released to the public in 2001, took the film industry by storm, but by 2012, when the second set, which was actually a prequel, began to fill theaters all over again, historians were prepared with a new set of books that explored New Zealand's mysterious background as well as its impressive beauty.

Most historians tell us that New Zealand was the world's last large island to be discovered and populated. Traditional wisdom has it that the ancestors of the Māori were the first to arrive, making the discovery when they explored the Pacific from their home base in Polynesia. They even remember the name of the navigator who made the discovery—a man by the name of Kupe.

That being said, however, there are alternative possibilities that have a long and illustrious history. Some versions say the original pioneers were Celts, Greeks, Egyptians, or even Chinese.

One of the first alternative studies is found in a booklet called *Lords of the Soil*, written by Kerry Bolton in 1987. He put forth the theory that Europeans, or, in his words, "a Europoid race," populated the country ever since ancient times.

In 1999, Martin Doutré published a book, now out of print, that revived the idea that the first people to populate New Zealand were Celts. The petroglyphs found to this day in Silverdale, on the north island of Auckland, he says, are proof of ancient Celtic artists.

The year 2012 saw the release of the first *Hobbit* movie, as well as two books that presented further alternative origin views. *The Great Divide: The Story of New Zealand & Its Treaty* was written by Ian Wishart. *To*

This statue depicts Polynesian navigator Kupe, who is credited with discovering New Zealand. This statue includes his wife and a priest and stands on the Wellington waterfront.

the Ends of the Earth, by Maxwell C. Hill, put forth the idea that the first New Zealanders were from Egypt and Greece.

The Ngāpuhi are the largest Māori tribe existing today. One of their elders, David Rankin, recalls stories long told by his ancestors that a mysterious people with light-colored skin lived in the islands when the first Māori arrived. Mixed with these legends were tales of red-haired giants. Rankin goes so far as to suggest that academics have joined in a conspiracy to suppress this information. Once again, we are faced with modern scholars refusing to honor the traditions and mythology of an indigenous people. Is it any wonder conspiracy theories abound? A native of the islands hears a story told by his grandfather's grandfather, but because you can't put the story under a microscope or carbon date it, it is discounted by academics who think they know better because they have a degree from a far-off college.

Maybe this prejudice is best illustrated by the rather arrogant words of Michael King, who wrote what is considered by some to be a definitive history of New Zealand: "Despite a plethora of amateur theories about Melanesian, South American, Egyptian, Phoenician, and Celtic colonization of New Zealand, there is not a shred of evidence that the first human settlers were anything other than Polynesian."

Hugh Laracy, of the University of Aukland, goes so far as to say alternative theories are "wild speculation [that has been] thoroughly disposed of by academic specialists."

Once again, when ideologies collide, the tendency for professionals to attack character rather than ideas has risen to the surface. Vincent O'Malley, of the New Zealand Archeological Association, employs the dreaded "R" word (racist) when describing anyone who mentions Celts or Greeks or Egyptians. Such claims, he feels, are derogatory to indigenous New Zealanders. Scott Hamilton echoes his views. In his treatise, *No to Nazi Pseudo-history: An Open Letter,* he even implies that these alternative views can only be held by those who invoke the prejudices of Hitler's Third Reich.

Still, those who hold alternative views of ancient New Zealand labor on. They refuse to push evidence that challenges accepted wisdom under the rug. Māori legends say there were people on the islands when they first arrived. Why is it racist, they say, to believe the ancestors of the Māori themselves?

Typical, or rather, representative, of the kind of evidence they cite is the now famous 150,000-year-old carved tree stump found in 1874, along with the stone artifact used to carve it. If the stories are true about this piece of

> Māori legends say there were people on the islands when they first arrived. Why is it racist, they say, to believe the ancestors of the Māori themselves?

evidence, it would, of course, throw modern ideas about late migration theory out the window.

The stump was discovered in Auckland, near a place called Albert Park. As so often happens, the find was an accident. Crews were excavating for the foundation of a library for the university there, twenty-five feet down (a little more than eight meters) in the sediment. Both scholarly and popular journals of the time recorded it because it's not usual to find such things that deep. What soon raised a lot of eyebrows was that the stump was estimated to be some 150,000 years old. How could a tree stump that old show display markings indicative of human work? Specialists were mystified.

Now, of course, as is so often the case, the story takes a dark turn. Because the find didn't fit the prevailing theory of when humans first set foot in New Zealand, it was brushed aside and forgotten. It soon disappeared not only from the literature of the day, but physically as well. No one knows what happened to it. All we are left with is the written word of some bonafide experts of that day, among them a scholarly treatise with a title that almost ensured very few people would read it. It was called "Notes upon the Probable Changes That Have Taken Place in the Physical Geography of New Zealand since the Arrival of the Maori" by T. H. Cockburn-Hood, F.G.S.

I haven't read the whole piece, but I'll bet it's not exactly a page-turner. I have read excerpts, however, and the author makes some interesting observations. At one point he draws attention to "some scientific evidence in the form of an ancient stump that proves ancient inhabitants existed in New Zealand [during] a period prior to volcanic land formation. It is evidence of human activity in New Zealand prior to the laying down of ancient volcanic debris."

The discovery wasn't kept secret at the time. Here is a quote from the *Auckland Southern Cross* newspaper of 1874:

> An exceedingly interesting relic of the very remote past is now to be seen in the office of the Improvement Commissioners. It is the root of a tree found in one of the cuttings being made under the direction of that Commission.
>
> The root has evidently been chopped through by a stone adze, which was found beside it. There were also several small branches and roots of the same tree on which the edge of the stone adze had been tried, and the whole crown of the stump had the marks of having been laboriously and patiently cut through by the rude stone implement in the unknown past, and by one of an equally unknown race of human beings.
>
> The root was found when cutting the sewer up the middle of Coburg Street, near the lower end, a little above its junction with the continuation of Wellesley Street, and at a depth of

about 25 feet below the surface of the Barrack Hill at that place. From the surface downwards for about 14 feet, at the place where the root was found, the hill is composed of volcanic matter. Below that depth, for about 8 or 9 feet, there is a series of layers of a mixture of sand and clay, which appears to have been at one time deposited under water. Below that is a large bed of fine blue "washdirt" resembling blue clay.

These strata and the blue clay do not seem to have been disturbed by volcanic action, and the several strata are lying with the utmost regularity possible. It was in the upper portion of the bed of blue clay that the root was found embedded, standing upright as if it had grown there, and the several small branches that were found at the same place were of the same kind of timber, and bore plain and distinct marks of the stone implement upon them.

The inference to be drawn is not only that the islands of New Zealand had been inhabited long anterior to [before] the migration of the Maoris to them but that they had been peopled before the extinct volcano in the neighborhood of the present Mechanic's Institute had begun to belch its mud torrents and streams of melted lava.

This conclusion seems to be inevitable, whether it be assumed that the tree grew where the root and the implement of its destruction were, or whether, as some incline to think, a river had run where the blue stratum is found, and that the root had been carried from a distance to its resting place. In either case the root must have been where it was found the other day, not only before the volcanic matter was deposited on the Barrack Hill, but for a sufficiently long period before that to permit a stratum of 8 to 10 feet in thickness to be deposited.

That pretty much tells the story, but without the actual physical evidence in hand, we probably can't blame modern scholars if they are a bit skeptical. If that were the only evidence, we would have to chalk it up to amateurish mistakes made by nineteenth-century inexperienced archeologists.

But that's not the only evidence.

On virtually every important, habitable island in the South Pacific it is usual to find ancient megalithic construction. The standing stone heads on Easter Island are the most famous, but there's also the "Ring Road" of Rarotonga and megalithic construction on Tonga as well. People obviously built these monuments. They are not accidents, but most historians are very vocal in their opinion that somehow New Zealand remained undiscovered while all this was going on, despite the oral history of the indigenous people.

A trilithon on Tonga in Oceania is reminiscent of Stonehenge in England.

Why? Because they seem to have put all their eggs in one archeological basket and refused to even seriously consider any evidence that upsets their own story.

There are nineteenth-century reports of several Stonehenge-type structures published by a very reputable scholar, J. Macmillan Brown, who wrote one of the first "bibles" on Polynesian history. That work has been virtually ignored. There are studies that indicate an extensive canal system found on both islands.

All this information is still being suppressed by scholars who wield the weapon of scorn and character assassination, but thanks to a small but vocal group of native New Zealand specialists, that attitude may be on the way out.

THE FIRST PEOPLE OF THE PHILIPPINES

If, like me, you tend to root for daring archeologists making audacious finds and then risking their reputations by sticking to the facts and following them wherever they might lead, you've got to be excited by the discoveries made in the first decades of the twenty-first century. Whereas it used to be almost impossible to break through the crust of the academic world and declare something new and exciting that will rewrite the history books, it's happening more and more.

The conspiracy of silence that has been at the root of the subject matter of this book so far is beginning to be broken. Things are changing. Chalk it up to better ways to reach the public through media outlets, or a younger, faster, stronger, hungrier generation of archeologists who want to make a name for themselves, or better tools and equipment, or just an idea whose time has come, but these are exciting days when it comes to uncovering the history of human beings on Earth. Much of the excitement comes from the Philippines. A whole series of finds is revealing new branches of our family tree, and it appears the hunt is just beginning.

This can get confusing, so let's take it one step at a time. We'll start down in Indonesia, where, in 2003 on the island of Flores, a strange human specimen now called *Homo floresiensis*, after the island of Flores, was discovered. The first skeleton, almost complete, was that of a three-and-a-half-foot (1.06-meter) 30-year-old, adult female, who was immediately named LB1. A

The island of Flores in Indonesia is where a skeleton of *Homo floresiensis* (inset is a skull of the species sometimes known as the Hobbit) was discovered. This species lived from 190,000 to 50,000 years ago.

name like that couldn't last however, except in a *Star Wars* movie, so because of her small stature the popular press dubbed her the Hobbit, after the characters in the books by J. R. R. Tolkien.

The find was reported in the prestigious journal *Nature*. Mark Collard, a biological anthropologist at Simon Fraser University in Burnaby, British Columbia, told *Live Science*: "We don't have very many associated skeletons of hominins outside of Neanderthals."

Later discoveries uncovered jaw and skeletal remains of more than eight similar individuals, proving that the first find wasn't an anomaly. This was a distinct species, never before recognized.

But the exciting part was yet to come. This species had gone extinct by at least 17,000 years ago, but it might have had a run that began as early as 95,000 years ago. How did they ever get to the islands of Indonesia? They appear to have evolved from *Homo erectus*, a 1.8-million-year-old species that first showed up in Africa. In looking for possible migration routes, a team of researchers reporting in the journal *Nature* discovered stone tools on the island of Sulawesi, which lies between Flores and continental Asia, that dated back at least 118,000 years. Modern humans only showed up there some 50,000 years ago.

No one knows who made the tools, of course. They might have been made by ancestors of *Homo floresiensis*, or other species such as Denisovans or Neanderthal, but whatever species was island hopping a long time ago, it shows that our ancestors really got around. These were relatively sophisticated folks. When they finally were superseded by modern *Homo sapiens*, they had experienced quite a track record. Along with the remains, archeologists found evidence of butchering and roasting. It appears as if Hobbits knew how to use fire.

More research followed, and the very latest information indicates that Hobbits lived in the caves of Indonesia between 190,000 and 50,000 years ago, and because modern human artifacts were also found in those caves, the two species could have conceivably lived for at least a short while alongside one another, similar to the relationship modern humans shared with both Neanderthals and Denisovans in Europe and Asia.

If that wasn't enough excitement for one decade, we now move to the Philippines.

In 2019, beneath the rocky floor of Callao Cave, on Luzon Island in the Philippines, archeologists found yet another human species. This species was dubbed *Homo luzonensis*. Like the Hobbits, they were small in stature, standing only about four feet tall. They have some modern

> More research followed, and the very latest information indicates that Hobbits lived in the caves of Indonesia between 190,000 and 50,000 years ago....

anatomical characteristics but also display features found only in much earlier hominins such as those found in Lucy, the *Australopithecus*. They were estimated to be about 50,000 years old, but a year later, scientists digging in a different cave found tools that dated back 700,000 years.

The questions rose immediately. Given the short stature of the two species, one on Indonesia and one in the Philippines, could they have been somehow related? If so, how did the early hominins island hop across the vast oceans?

Crazy theories immediately came to mind and were suggested very seriously. One of them was that perhaps a few survivors were blown out to sea while clinging to fallen trees and drifted across the great distances.

But who can really take such an idea seriously? If they got to their various locations, they must have meant to get there. Only prejudice makes someone grasp at proverbial straws. The simplest answer to the dilemma is that our preconceived ideas of these early folks is way off base. Human intelligence goes back a lot further than we have, for a long time, dared to think.

The first wave of *Homo erectus* out of Africa, if it ever took place in the way we imagine, was made up of some pretty smart folks who had an agenda. The second wave, *Homo sapiens*, was the same. The true telling of the story of our species is far from over.

The world we now live in seems a lonely place compared to what once was. Matthew Tocheri, a paleoanthropologist from Lakehead University in Thunder Bay, Ontario, Canada, summarizes the situation well: "The more fossils that people pull out of the ground, the more we realize that the variation that was present in the past far exceeds what we see in us today."

There seems to be no question that the staid doors of academia are going to have to rewrite their textbooks after all. The lineage of our species is proving to be a lot more complex, and a lot more ancient, than we have ever believed. Those simple drawings many of us were forced to memorize back in the day, showing a chimp on all fours gradually ascending to an upright man like us, are now outdated. It's a whole new world out there.

THE PROBLEM OF TIME

So far in this book we've been cavalierly throwing around numbers such as "70,000 years" or "1.8 million years." In doing so, we have locked an event in time. To say "50,000 years ago" means that since a particular event transpired, the Earth has made its yearly journey around the sun 50,000 times.

That kind of measurement, though, is suspect for a number of reasons, all of which point to human narcissism and hubris. What does the universe care about such an Earth-bound, relative measurement? There are planets that take a lot longer to circle their star, and planets that do it in much less time. The phrase "one year" applies to only one relationship between one planet and one star and is unique to only our home planet.

In short, we tend to put ourselves in the middle of things. That's what humans do. We see everything in relationship to our own experience.

In the same way, when we "discover" a new geographical area we tend to act as though somehow what transpired there before our arrival was not important. Once we "discover" it, its history can now begin. Without thinking about it, we are really saying that its true purpose is to supply resources of various kinds for humans. Its history then becomes the story of our exploitation of it.

When we start to think in terms like that, we realize that we are victims of a humancentric view of how things work. Sometimes this is merely humorous, as when we meet someone who doesn't understand our language so we begin to talk slower and louder, as if that will somehow help, but when we act as though it is our right to destroy our environment through overexploitation—

Environmental devastation of the planet is a direct result of humans believing that the world and its resources are there for them to exploit.

that somehow Earth exists only for and in relation to humans—the consequences can be devastating. We have only to read the latest statistics on climate change to understand that countless species are going extinct and sea levels are rising because we think everyone on Earth has the right to own an automobile and an air conditioner.

The same idea applies to our view of time. This is a tough one, so don't be too quick to jump to conclusions. What follows is science, not metaphysics, although that doesn't seem to be the case at first glance.

When we say something such as "50,000 years ago" we are inferring that time is a river, or perhaps an arrow, that is constant and travels in only one direction at one speed. Sometimes this is helpful because our experience of time is so universal that it offers a common frame of reference. We all know what someone means when she says, "Last Tuesday at 3:00 in the afternoon."

But scientists these days have discovered that our concept of time is an illusion. They even have a name for it. In scientific circles it is referred to as the "Problem of Time."

What they mean is this. Einstein's theory of general relativity revealed that time is not constant. It is flexible and relative, but in quantum mechanics, an equally proven realm of being, time is regarded as being universal and absolute.

How could both concepts be true? That's the "Problem of Time." We are coming to realize that we really don't understand it. Why does it flow in only one direction, when new equations indicate there is nothing from stopping it from moving either forward or backward? Physics doesn't require time to stay in line with our perception of it, but as far as we are concerned, it does. So which is right?

The latest theories suggest that time is what is called an "emergent phenomenon." By that we mean that time comes about because of the nature of entanglement. That's the term used to describe the unity of all things. On the quantum level of the very small, if we tickle a particle over here, its entangled partner instantly giggles over there, no matter how far apart they are.

But here's the thing. According to this view, time is an emergent phenomenon that is experienced only by those who are what is called "internal observers." In other words, only those within the confines of the material universe are aware of the passing of time. Outside the material universe, time does not exist.

But how can an intelligent entity exist outside the material universe, observe what is going on within it, and not be affected by it?

Enter the aliens. The greatest of these aliens is, of course, what various religionists call "God," but there are other metaphysical systems that have other names and other descriptions.

Before we go there, however, let's delve a little deeper into what researcher Marcia Bartusiak called "the crisis inside the physics of time" in an article written for the September 2018 issue of *Nautilus*:

> Poets often think of time as a river, a free-flowing stream that carries us from the radiant morning of birth to the golden twilight of old age. It is the span that separates the delicate bud of spring from the lush flower of summer.
>
> Physicists think of time in somewhat more practical terms. For them, time is a means of measuring change—an endless series of instants that, strung together like beads, turn an uncertain future into the present and the present into a definite past. The very concept of time allows researchers to calculate when a comet will round the sun or how a signal traverses a silicon chip. Each step in time provides a peek at the evolution of nature's myriad phenomena.
>
> In other words, time is a tool. In fact, it was the first scientific tool.

The article goes on to point out that time can be sliced and diced into ever smaller pieces, but what is being sliced? We can't perceive time by cutting it up and putting it under a microscope. We don't see it, or hear it, or smell, touch, or taste time. All we can do is measure it, but what are we measuring?

"It's a crisis," says mathematician John Baez, of the University of California at Riverside, "and the solution may take physics in a new direction."

If it does, it won't change how we live. We'll still consult our watches and clocks, but it will change the way we think

The very concept of time is a difficult one to define, even for scientists. Is time a continuum? Is it an infinite series of discrete moments? Is it even a real thing independent of our perceptions?

about time. What this means is that quantum physics, rather than sharpening up our objectivity, has instead introduced a level of fuzziness. We can no longer be quite as precise as we might like to be.

That brings us back to the way we throw around phrases such as "50,000 years ago." What we are really saying is something like this: "The ancestors of today's aboriginal Australians arrived on their home continent 60,000 years ago, assuming that there were no cataclysmic catastrophes since then that might have skewed our methods of dating their arrival. If evidence for such a catastrophe is ever discovered, all bets are off."

Scientists are almost universally uniformitarianists. That means they prefer their history to be continuous, uninterrupted, and uniform. They don't like variables. They want their carbon molecules to decay at a uniform rate so they can date them, and they tend to believe comets and asteroids do not make it a habit to obliterate civilizations that might have reached a relatively advanced state.

Even a quick visit to an ongoing archeological dig reveals this tendency. You'll find a nice, flat wall of Earth neatly marked with little flags indicating levels of occupation. This fire burned 2,000 years ago. That artifact was used 4,000 years ago. This bone was from layer 6 that is an archaic level. That bone was found at layer 8, which is a Paleolithic level.

Geologists do the same thing. Visit the Grand Canyon and the guides will point out various layers of history illustrated by different kinds and colors of rocks. This layer is metamorphic. That layer is igneous. It makes history nice and neat.

But real history isn't always nice and neat. We can't even be sure there is such a thing as history. It might be an illusion. There is no proof that every moment in time is happening at the same "now" or instant for everyone. It appears to be that way because time is such a strong illusion, but the truth is that we don't even know what time is. Even our brightest and best scientists admit it's a "problem."

When we look at when *this* happened or when *that* happened, when we make blanket assumptions about when a particular people migrated here or there, remember to take such statements with a grain of salt. We have to be very careful. What we are really saying is, "Assuming nothing of a cataclysmic nature intervened, assuming our tools are working properly, assuming we are correctly interpreting the evidence at hand, and assuming we even have all the evidence available, it looks as though this is when it happened."

Return for a moment, now, to a curious statement we made a few paragraphs ago:

According to this view, time is an emergent phenomenon that is experienced only by those who are what is called "internal observers." In other words, only those within the confines of the material universe are aware of the passing of time. Outside the material universe, time does not exist.

Now we come right down to a central issue. Are there intelligent entities outside of time who are observing us? Are they at all responsible for things that happen—things that we call history?

Surprisingly, the answer held by humans for the greatest span of their time on Earth is an unequivocal "Yes!" We know this because there is a wealth of evidence that proves it. Messages in stone and messages in story abound. From Göbekli Tepe to Stonehenge, from Egypt to Central America, from China to Australia, the evidence is overwhelming. "We know you're out there," echoes the voice of our ancestors down through the corridors of time, assuming such corridors exist. The research of archeology, the science of anthropology, the study of history, and the wealth of the humanities are often a study of how our ancestors reached out to entities unknown who they believed to exist outside of time and space.

They called them gods. One of the great ironies of our time is how a researcher can spend a lifetime studying the religious activities practiced by our ancestors who believed in a supernatural entity the researcher has rejected.

Step by step, uniformitarianism is wonderful. It offers a clear and precise picture of how we got here, but what if it didn't happen that way? What if each and every circumstance is special and unique? What if the old ones were right?

HELP FROM ABOVE

Numerous examples abound that confirm many of our ancestors believed they were led to become pioneers. They felt guided to follow a particular path leading to a geographical location that would become a new homeland. Sometimes those journeys led to unexplored areas.

Perhaps folks as ancient as those who were the first to leave Africa felt the presence of a supernatural force leading them on. They left no written record, so we don't know their motivation. Conventional wisdom chalks up the migration impulse to a search for new resources, but no one really knows if that's the case. It's just an uneducated guess.

The Bible, for example, records that Abraham followed the directions of a voice that spoke to him: "The LORD said to Abram, 'Go from your country, your people and your father's household to the land I will show you'" (Genesis 12:1).

That's pretty direct. He wasn't in search of greener pastures. He was following a voice that spoke to him in clear and distinct tones.

An illustration of Abraham, "the Father of Many Nations," being called upon by God.

No one was around to record if the first hominin to leave Africa had a similar experience, however, so we just assume the first pioneers went off in search of resources, but who really knows?

What follows is an exploration of a few of the many pioneer-guided migration stories. It is by no means a comprehensive list. These were selected because together they offer a fair example of an exhaustive body of mythology that seems to indicate our ancestors felt that they were in touch with a presence or an entity they referred to as "God," but which could just as easily have been an alien envoy.

The Jewish Exodus

The opening book of the Bible offers a plethora of pioneer stories. Adam and Eve left the Garden of Eden to take up residence in the outside world. Cain, after murdering his brother, departed to the land of "Nod, east of Eden," where he built a city. All three were, in effect, forced to migrate by an entity referred to by various names, but presented to us as "God."

The Tower of Babel, built in "the land of Shinar," presumed to be near Babylon, in Mesopotamia, was the place from which people supposedly spread out after their languages were confused because of their hubris in trying to reach the heavens. Again, the migration was not voluntary.

It's interesting to learn that this myth is repeated in many different cultures. The Blackfoot Indians, for instance, tell the story of the Creator, "Old Man," who gave different colored water to the people to drink. As a result, they all began to speak in different languages. These stories share a common root. Someone or something from "outside" was pulling the strings, forcing them to move.

Of all the great pioneer migration stories, perhaps the most well known is that of the Jewish Exodus from Egypt. This story is repeated again and again each year, when Hebrew families gather to tell the story of Passover.

This legend has all the earmarks of an alien presence who guided a specific population, by force at times, to migrate to a new land. Once again, though, the people were compelled out of their comfort zone, even though that zone seemed uncomfortable in retrospect.

It began with miracles of epoch proportions. Plagues and parting of waters, a miraculous intervention that provided food for the journey, and, of course, one of the greatest historical enigmas of all, the famous Ark of the Covenant. It was while communing with this mysterious artifact that Moses supposedly received his marching orders. The ark, undoubtedly of alien origin, even if that "alien" was called God, is at the center of the story.

What was it?

Blueprints for its construction are given three times in the book of Exodus, but perhaps the easiest way to get a mental picture is to read the New Testament description from the book of Hebrews, in chapter 9, written some 1,200 years after the fact:

> The first covenant had regulations for worship and also an Earthly sanctuary. A tabernacle was set up. In its first room were the lamp stand, the table and the consecrated bread; this was called the Holy Place. Behind the second curtain was a room called the Holy of Holies, which had the golden altar of incense and the gold-covered Ark of the Covenant. This Ark contained the gold jar of manna, Aaron's staff that had budded, and the stone tablets of the covenant. Above the ark were the cherubim of the Glory, overshadowing the atonement cover.

Whenever the subject of ancient technology comes up, most people have been conditioned by spectacular movies and TV shows to think right away that the Ark of the Covenant was some sort of weapon, or at least a capacitor of some kind—a power source containing a communicator with which to converse with ancient aliens. Others insist it was a weapon of mass destruction. Fantastic claims have been published describing beams issuing from it that destroyed entire armies, although those claims are not found in the Bible. The Ark is also said to have been the place where the Ten Commandments were kept, but if you read the passage quoted above from the book of Hebrews, and parallel passages from Exodus and Numbers, you soon realize that's only part of the story.

The book of Exodus tells us that when Moses climbed Sinai to receive the Law, delivered to the Israelites after their escape from Egypt, God instructed him to build an ark upon which the glory of God would rest. Moses was always alone when he spoke to God, so we have to take his word for it.

"Ark" comes from the Greek word for chest. A "covenant" is a binding contract or legal agreement. When the original Hebrew texts were translated into Greek, forming what is now called the *Septuagint*, the Greek version of the Hebrew Bible that is called *Old Testament* by Christians, the translated words carried over into our English versions of the Bible. Hence, the "Ark" of the "Covenant" was originally meant to serve as a religious symbol of God's "contract" with the Israelite people, not a technological marvel or weapon of war, even though it was sometimes used in that fashion, especially according to extrabiblical texts.

A modern rendering of what the Ark of the Covenant, which contained the stone tablets upon which were written the Ten Commandments, probably looked like.

It was a box, about two and a half feet high and wide and four and a half feet long, made of wood, covered with gold leaf, and transported by means of two long poles that ran through rings placed on its side. When not being carried about it was housed within the Holy of Holies—the inner sanctuary of the Tabernacle, or "Tent of Meeting"—during the forty years the Israelites were said to have wandered in the Sinai desert. After the conquest of Canaan, it was placed in a sanctuary at Shiloh and later brought by King David to the site of the future Temple at Jerusalem, built by King Solomon. This was the occasion that so inspired David that he "danced before the Lord," much to the disgust of his wife.

By the time the Babylonians destroyed Solomon's temple in 586 B.C.E. the Ark had disappeared from history. Although many have tried to find it, its present location has remained a mystery. Some think it resides in a temple in Ethiopia, brought there by the son of Solomon and the Queen of Sheba. Others believe it is hidden in the caves of Qumran, buried under the temple mount, or even hidden in a booby-trapped pit on Oak Island off the coast of Nova Scotia. Most scholars believe it was destroyed. Many doubt it ever existed.

Although most people who have watched the History Channel or read some of the many spectacular articles about the Ark know it housed the Ten Commandments, there were two more symbolic objects that were alleged to have been placed inside. Exodus 16 and 25, along with Numbers 17, emphasize all three items equally. I Kings 8, which describes the ceremony when Solomon brought the ark into the temple, mentions only the Ten Commandments. Apparently, by then, some 500 years after the Ark had first been constructed, the other two objects so important to the original authors had either been lost or forgotten. What were they and why were they so important to the story of the original Ark of the Covenant?

Each item placed in the ark recalled stories found in the biblical books of Exodus and Numbers that, when taken together, represent the very essence of early Judaism and predate the essential Christian message by a thousand years. Taken together, the three objects symbolized a powerful religious statement.

The first object was, of course, the stone tablets containing the Ten Commandments. These represented God's law, but the people had broken God's law. While Moses was on Sinai receiving instructions that forbade the worship of idols, the people were down below dancing around a golden calf. The tablets, therefore, would forever symbolize the people's *rejection* of God's law.

The second object was a pot of Manna. "Manna" literally means, "What is it?" When the people needed food in the desert following the Exodus from Egypt, the texts tell us that God instructed Moses to have them go outside and gather a daily supply of a light bread that formed with the dew each morning. Only one day's supply could be gathered because the bread would spoil if hoarded. Whatever was gathered on Friday would keep for an extra day so that people would not have to break the Sabbath commandment forbidding work on the seventh day. When the people went outside on the first morning to discover the miracle of God's provision, they saw the bread and said, *Manna?*—"What is it?" The idea was to teach the people to trust in God's daily provision. (This event later prompted a famous Christian petition: "Give us this day our daily bread.") But after the novelty wore off, the people complained, longing for the good old days and "the leeks and onions of Egypt." Manna came to represent their *rejection* of God's provision.

The third item was Aaron's rod that budded. Aaron, Moses' brother-in-law, had been selected by God to be High Priest, but the people wanted to elect their own leaders. The texts tell us that they complained to Moses, who passed the word on to God. Moses was told to have each tribe select a candidate for High Priest. Each would place his "rod," or walking staff, in the ground to be inspected during the next morning's convocation. The implication was that God's leaders bear fruit, while Earthly leaders don't.

Of course Aaron's rod produced a bud, and he went on to become the first High Priest of Israel, but whenever the people thought about the staff in the Ark they would be reminded of their *rejection* of God's leadership.

On the cover of the Ark stood the Mercy Seat. Two carved angels, one on each side with their arched wings meeting in the middle, symbolically looked down at the Ark's contents. There they saw *rejection*—rejection of God's *law* (the Ten Commandments), God's *provision* (the pot of manna), and God's *leadership* (Aaron's staff). That doesn't leave a lot more of God left to reject.

But on one day a year, the Day of Atonement, or *Yom Kippur*, the High Priest sprinkled the blood of a sacrificial lamb on the Mercy Seat. On that day the symbolic angel icons would see not *rejection* but the blood of the innocent substitute, and the sins of the people would thus be atoned for. This was a central religious symbolism called substitutionary atonement, later adopted by Christians who saw Jesus Christ as the sacrificial "lamb of God."

Much speculation has arisen over the true meaning of the Ark. Because the Bible makes a special point of saying Moses' face glowed when he came down from Sinai after talking to God, and because Moses was later said to

Moses is depicted here with the Ark during the Jewish Exodus. It is said that the Jews were invincible with the power of God on their side.

have worn a veil over his face when he came out from the presence of the Ark, some have speculated that it contained a source of light—perhaps even radiation, which might explain his premature death before he got to enter the Promised Land.

It was said that in the presence of the Ark, Moses would hear the voice of God. This has sparked tales of it being a transmitter through which Moses was in contact with ancient aliens, using details supplied from their blueprints to build the Ark to their specifications. Because of the Ark's supposed ability to inspire armies in war, and because at least one man is said to have died after he touched it without proper consecration, speculation arose as to its mystical or military powers, but a careful reading of the text casts doubt on Moses' face "glowing." Instead, the Bible seems to imply that Moses' face wasn't glowing at all, and that caused him such embarrassment that he covered his face because he thought it *should* glow. After all, he had just supposedly been in the presence of the God of Light.

The Ark of the Covenant is surrounded by mystery. If it exists at all, perhaps it still awaits discovery, resting in its 2,500-year-old hiding place, but its basic meaning to the Israelites was clear. The Ark reminded them of their contract with the God who they felt chose them to be a special people and migrate to a special land—a land still in dispute to this very day. It was, plain and simply, a religious symbol that they carried before them into battle, much as the Crusaders carried a cross or armies carry their flag. It served as inspiration. According to the Bible there were no death rays, no secret communications from on high, at least not from any source known to the biblical writers, and certainly no Indiana Jones-type curses.

That is not to say that curious stories about the Ark don't surround its mythology. In I Samuel 5, the Philistines (just a generation before their champion, Goliath, had his famous confrontation with David, the shepherd boy) had the misfortune of capturing the Ark of the Covenant. They recognized that it was a holy object, even though it belonged to the enemy, so they decided to put it on display in the temple of their god, Dagon. One would suppose that it was a "my god can beat up your god!" kind of thing.

Persistent stories eventually grow into a mythology, but is there enough evidence to say that the Ark of the Covenant was really an example of ancient technology...?

But that's when the trouble started. Every morning, when the priests of Dagon went in to do whatever it was they did each day, they found that their statue of Dagon had "fallen on his face on the ground before the ark of the Lord!"

What to do? Well, following the age-old ploy of passing the buck, they decided to move the ark to a different village, but those folks didn't want it either. After seven months of enduring this kind of religious version of musical chairs, the Philistines finally sent for their priests. They decided to put the ark in a cart, along with a guilt offering (kind of a "sorry about that" present), hitch the cart to some oxen, and send it home to Israel.

When they sent it off, the oxen, on their own and with no guidance, "went straight up toward Beth Shemish, keeping on the road and lowing [the Hebrew commentaries usually say 'singing' or 'humming' instead of 'lowing'] all the way; they did not turn to the right or to the left."

Persistent stories eventually grow into a mythology, but is there enough evidence to say that the Ark of the Covenant was really an example of ancient technology by which an alien presence, and we have to include God in this category, led the Jews to a new location?

As always, we have to come to our own conclusions, but when we read the original texts first, rather than simply accepting what we see on television, they seem to point to a powerful religious symbol that, when viewed in its entirety, provided a basis for a three-pronged metaphor that has been ensconced in the atonement doctrine of two of the world's great religions. The message of the Ark of the Covenant seems to be that people may reject God's law, provision, and leadership, but God has nevertheless atoned for their shortcomings.

Whether or not we personally accept this religious doctrine in a historical, or even metaphorical, way, it seems to offer a hopeful message in troubled times.

At any rate, aliens will probably forever be linked in the minds of some to the migration of the Jews from Egypt to Israel. To others, the story will always carry deeply religious implications.

But the fact remains that it seems a very strange way to write mythology. It's frustrating. On the one hand, not enough information is given to establish any real, historical content. On the other, there is much more extraneous information provided than a religious story needs to impart a moral or religious motive.

What does it all mean? Is there a kernel of historical reality found at the base of this story? Or is it mythology created out of a whole cloth with no basis in historical fact?

Like all religious mythology, much is left to the imagination of the hearer.

The Hopi Migration

The Hopi exodus story is, except for the biblical Exodus account, probably the best known of all migration epochs. It offers tantalizing clues that fit exactly what we are coming to understand about the geology of North America.

Hopi elders tell a story of migration between worlds. Each world was destroyed by a cataclysm, but the people were guided by their gods to escape the destruction. Were these "gods" alien helpers? The people seemed to think they were. Even the origins of the Hopi indicate an extraterrestrial presence. They believe they originated amongst the stars, specifically the stars of the Pleiades, the Seven Sisters.

Upon arriving here on Earth, they were instructed by two spirit guides named Sotuknang and Spider Woman. They were told they must respect both Taiowa, the Creator, and the land comprising their new home. Spider Woman herself had prepared it for them, and they were nurtured by its resources. Were these "guides" spiritual or alien entities? That is a matter of individual interpretation.

Over the course of their explorations, they discovered what they called "vibration centers." These were found throughout the Earth and they seemed to mimic similar chakra centers found within their own bodies. These centers vibrated in resonance with the music of the spheres. Their purpose was to tune the people to the will of the Creator, but the people eventually stopped listening. As soon as they began to ignore the music of the stars, they stopped following the Way. They began to quarrel amongst themselves. Eventually Sotuknang decided he must destroy the people before they ruined everything they had been given.

Some of the old ones still remembered how to act in accordance with the will of the Creator, so Sotuknang appeared to them with the sound of a mighty wind and said he would lead them to safety if they followed him and obeyed his instructions.

It came to pass that a few of the ancient ones took refuge among the Ant People as the First World above them was destroyed by fire. Volcanoes erupted from deep below the surface of the land, belching out smoke and flame into the atmosphere.

Notice, here, a theme that will be repeated again and again, not only in Hopi mythology but in stories from cultures found all around the Earth. Humans are created by the gods. They abuse their posi-

In the Hopi exodus story, the Seven Sisters (Pleiades) constellation was the original home of their people.

tion as free people and seek to destroy one another. One god seeks to end their lives. Another leads a remnant to safety. It's a recurring song that prompts many cultural variations.

A second world was prepared for the people, almost as beautiful as the first, but in this world the animals no longer trusted humans, so they kept themselves apart, running away whenever a human approached.

This world was a good place in which to live. Maybe too good. The people once again began to think they knew more than the Creator and ignored his plan for them. Life was easy. They had everything they needed, but, typical of human behavior, they wanted more. They thought they could live any way they chose, even if it was disrespectful and selfish, and it soon became apparent that Sotuknang would have to destroy them again.

Once again, the Ant People came to the rescue. The people were led to safety in the underground kivas of their friends.

Two twins, Poqanghoya and Palongawhoya, guarded the poles of the Earth, but when they left their stations for a time the world spun off its axis and went whirling away through space. Ice soon covered everything. It remained until the twins returned to their posts and restored balance to the Earth. The ice began to melt, and the people soon returned to their new home.

When we studied the Younger Dryas comet theory, we painted a picture of a segmented comet that brought fire and destruction upon the world 12,800 years ago. In the wake of this catastrophe, the world entered into an ice age that lasted for 1,200 years. This sounds eerily similar to the Hopi legend up to this point. Were there people alive who witnessed these events and recorded them in oral history? It certainly seems to be a distinct possibility, but if that's true, the Hopi must be descended from an ancient people who lived a lot earlier than traditional scholarship allows.

As the story continues, the people ascended into a third world called Kuskurza. Here the people quickly multiplied. They built cities and countries and began a whole new civilization, but Sotuknang and Spider Woman noticed that the people no longer sang the praises of Taiowa, the Creator. They were too occupied by their Earthly plans and selfish dreams. The further people traveled on the Road of Life, the harder it was to remain faithful and true. The gods tried to teach young people the old ways, but the young people, as is so often the case, refused to listen. They invented new ways to destroy and conquer, enhancing their personal power at the expense of others.

In a fascinating detail, the story says that people even invented what they called "flying shields." These enabled warriors to fly off to faraway villages, where they attacked and pillaged before returning so quickly that no one knew where they had gone.

Sotuknang knew he could not allow this way of life to continue, so he warned Spider Woman that he would again destroy the people, this time with a great flood.

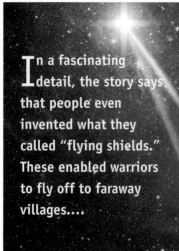

In a fascinating detail, the story says that people even invented what they called "flying shields." These enabled warriors to fly off to faraway villages....

Spider Woman knew of the few folks who still listened—who tried to teach the people the ways of the Creator, but this time she didn't know how to save them. In a great flood, even the homes of the Ant People would be destroyed. The people searched long and hard for a solution—for a way of salvation. Finally, they hid themselves inside the hollow stems of bamboo trees while their world was drowned.

When the flood waters began to recede, the people came out and began again. They made what seemed an endless journey by boat. The Earth remained covered with water, so from time to time the people would send out birds to scout for a place of safety. The birds always returned.

Finally, they began to find land. Islands appeared, like stepping-stones, and they offered good places to live, but each time Spider Woman told them they must move on. The places they stopped were too easy, she said. They would soon fall again into their evil ways.

Eventually the people were too exhausted to continue on their own. All they could do was open the doors of their hearts and allow Spider Woman to guide them. They were forced to submit to her wisdom.

At long last they came to a sandy shore where they were greeted by Sotuknang, who gave them instructions. They were to separate into different groups, each group following its own star by night and pillar of cloud by day, until they came to a place where the Earth met the sea. Each group would keep track of their migration on a tablet of stone, and record in symbol the representation of their journeys. At long last they would be brought together again, but only after much travail. In this way they would finally come to remember what they had forgotten—to obey Taiowa, the Creator, and live according to his plan for them.

Was there ever a culture in North America that invented flight? It sure is difficult to imagine a primitive people coming up with such an idea.

These are the words of Sotuknang, which he spoke at the beginning of the fourth world:

> I have washed away even the footprints of your Emergence; the stepping-stones which I left for you. Down on the bottom of the seas lie all the proud cities, the flying shields and the worldly treasures corrupted with evil, and those people who found no time to sing praises to the Creator from the tops of their hills, but the day will come, if you preserve the memory and the meaning of your Emergence, when these stepping-stones will emerge again to prove the truth you speak.

The imagery found here is so similar to the Middle Eastern flood epochs that it barely needs comment. A flood, boats, sending out birds to hunt for dry land, following the wisdom of the gods—it's a familiar story, very similar to the account we read in Genesis.

Inventing "flying shields," however, is a new twist. Was there ever a culture in North America that invented flight? It sure is difficult to imagine a primitive people coming up with such an idea, but when the glaciers suddenly melted 11,600 years ago, there were immense floods in the west that could have easily drowned any evidence of such a civilization. Backed-up glacier lakes, when suddenly free of their ice dams, carry tremendous power. Evidence of their destructive power is found in the geology of the entire American west.

Once again we are forced to ask if there were people then living who survived to tell these stories, but we have to also ask, given the exchange back and forth between competing god-like figures, if alien intervention hasn't once again peeked out from under the covers of forgotten and suppressed history.

It's a theory we might not be able to ignore for much longer. To make things even more interesting, the story of the Hopi carries echoes of an early culture that existed on the other side of the world. According to their oral history, the ancient Hopi ancestors were saved from the first and second catastrophes that overcame their world by their friends, the Ant People, who gave them shelter and saw them through the worst of the destruction.

In Hopi, the word translated "ant" is *anu*. The root word of "friends" is *naki*. Thus, "ant friends" can be translated as Anu-Naki, which is suspiciously close to the Sumerian *Anunnaki*. We looked in depth at Sumerian culture when we talked about Zecharia Sitchin and the *Coming of the Gods*. Is this just coincidence? Or were the *Anunnaki*, the "heroes of old, the "men of renown," more widespread than we have been taught? In other words, did ancient aliens, mistaken for gods, have a hand in the dispersal of early human civilizations as they traveled to establish new population centers? If similarities between distant civilizations crop up time and time again, the question seems valid.

Hopi Kachina dolls from Arizona could offer a clue to the ancient spirits—or visitors—in Hopi and Sumerian mythology.

Robert Morningside has compiled a list of such similarities:

- Both Hopi and Sumerians refer to the Creator essence as *Ka*. In Hopi, this essence is personified as *Taiowa*, the Sun God. In Sumerian, the name is transliterated *Ta ea*.

- Both Hopi and Sumerian mythology recognizes two brothers as guardians of the Earth.

- The Hopi word for spirit guides is *Alo*. In Sumerian it is spelled *A lu*.

- Hopi culture is famous for its *Kachina* dolls, often spelled *Kat'sina*. They represent the spirits of nature and representatives of the Great Spirit. Their Father is called *Eototo*. In Sumeria, the "righteous ones" sent from God are called *Kat si na*. The Father of all Beings is called *Ea Ta*.

- In Hopi, *Nan-ga-Sohu* is the name of the "Chasing Star Kachina." The *Danik* are the Guardians in the clouds. In Sumerian, *Nin Gir Su* is called the "Master of Starships." The *Dak an* are sky warriors.

- The Hopi believe they originated in the Pleiades star system. Their name for this system is *ChooChookam*. From there they were transported to *Tapuat*, the planet Earth. In Sumerian mythology, the supreme star system is called *Shu Shu Khem*. The Earth is called *Tiamet*.

- The Hopi word for serpent is *Chu'a*. In Sumerian it is called *Shu*.

- When the Hopi look upward to the heavens, they use the word *Omiq*. The Sumerians say *Am Ik*.

- A Hopi who sees magic is called *Tuawta*. In Sumerian, a *Tuat U* is "one from another world."

- Someday, according to Hopi legend, they will be helped by a "Lost Brother" who will lead them back to the Way. They call him *Pahana*. The Sumerians look for *Pa Ha Na*, an ancestor from heaven, who will someday return to the Earth.

Is all this just coincidence? Or is it evidence that both cultures share a distant past that has been forgotten by most modern scholars who refuse to look to the skies to see the future?

The Aztec Journey

It's easy to push aside claims of extraterrestrial intervention camouflaged as ancient mythology, but when it comes to examining the possibility of alien assistance given to pioneers in their search for a new homeland, there is perhaps no more compelling case than the cross-cultural possibilities inherent in the story of the Aztecs and their discovery of what is now Mexico City. This story touches all the bases, linking together a rich mythology from all over the world.

Briefly, the traditional archeological position concerning the origins of the Aztecs is this.

Somewhere around 1,800 years ago a group of people from the north began to settle in the Valley of Mexico. They were a Nahuatl-speaking culture, who soon began to build an extensive system of canals and dikes that were needed to control water levels for agriculture. They are called Aztec, which is derived from Aztlán, which means "White Land." This seems to be a reference to their ancestral homeland somewhere in the north, presumably what is now northern Mexico. By 1428 the Aztec ruler, called Itzcoatl, allied his people with Tlacopan and Texcoco, thereby forming what is called the Triple Alliance, which controlled the nation until the arrival of the Spanish in 1519.

That's the official version. If you talk to a native Aztec historian, however, you'll get a story that is much more nuanced, much more interesting, much more intriguing, and much more ancient.

The *Tonalamatl of the Aubin Collection*, more commonly referred to as the *Aubin Codex*, is a story, utilizing both pictures and text, that compiles a history of the Aztecs running from their migration from Aztlán in the north until the Spanish conquest and beyond, ending in 1608. It's written on European paper, so it was probably the work of Spanish translators who wanted to retain whatever they could of Aztec tradition after the Catholic Church had burned everything else of value, but it is written in what is referred to as alphabetic Nahuatl, a transliterated Aztec text, so the translators had obviously gone to a lot of trouble learning the language so as to record the story as accurately as possible. Presumably they received it right from the lips of Aztec elders.

According to the codex, the Aztecs believed their ancestors came from the north, but not northern Mexico. It was someplace farther away than that, a land of red rocks that gave birth to four rivers. Some scholars have located the so-called mythical land in the Phoenix, Arizona, area, but that doesn't really fit the description. By the time you get to Phoenix, red rocks are in short supply.

Going farther north, however, brings you to the Four Corners country, where Utah, Colorado, Arizona, and New Mexico meet in what is popularly called the Canyon Lands.

Cecilio Orozco of California State University, Fresno, and Alfonso Rivas-Salmon, an anthropologist at the Universidad Autonoma de Guadalajara, believe this to be the mythical Aztec homeland. The "four rivers" are the Green, the upper Colorado, and the San Juan, which merge to become the lower Colorado River.

Four Corners is a popular modern tourist attraction because one can be in four states—Arizona, Colorado, New Mexico, and Utah—at once, but it is also the possible point of origin of Aztec ancestors known as the Canyon Lands.

When they went into the field to inspect the area, Orozco and Rivas-Salmon discovered ancient paintings and pictographs on the canyon walls of Utah that are strikingly similar to symbols found on surviving Aztec calendars, but those samples of rock art, of a type called Barrier Canyon-Style Rock Art, date back well before the 1200s. They go back in time to at least 502 B.C.E., and maybe quite a bit before that.

Professor Orozco states it very succinctly: "Utah is sitting on a treasure, a missing link in the prehistory of man in this hemisphere. It's right there on the canyon walls. Utah is the home of Quetzalcoatl."

Most Utah archeologists, of course, reject their findings. To acknowledge any such history is to throw out what is commonly believed by the accredited "experts." Especially since Orozco and Rivas-Salmon present an amazing legend that connects peoples from all over the Earth who tell the same story.

An in-depth description of their findings can be found in such books as Orozco's *The Book of the Sun*, now out of print and difficult to find. To summarize their findings, they believe that the Utah rock art reveals a connection to

These interesting and unusual pictographs near Seven Mile Canyon, which are located on the way to Canyonlands National Park near Moab, Utah, may represent visitors known to the ancient Aztecs.

the four- and eight-year cycles of the planet Venus. Venus is often recognized in mythology as representing duality because it is both the morning and evening star.

The legends reveal that the Mexica, ancestors of the Aztecs, were forced from their homeland by what they called "the rain of fire." This cataclysmic event prompted a series of migrations. The people moved ever south to escape tumultuous conditions.

Eventually they were led by their spirit guides to travel until they found an eagle fighting with a serpent on a "barbed tree," or cactus. This they eventually found and settled down to build their capitol city, called Tenochtitlan.

If this image seems familiar, it should be. It's found on the modern Mexican flag, and Tenochtitlan, founded on the place where the eagle fought the serpent, is now called Mexico City, the capital of Mexico.

This raises some serious questions. If all this proves to be historically true, what was the "rain of fire" that caused the initial migration? Could it be connected to the Younger Dryas event, when a segmented comet rained down fire on North America 12,800 years ago?

If so, the Aztecs are far more ancient than traditional scholarship gives them credit for. And if their work prompted the accurate calendars of Aztec astronomy, they were far more advanced than is now believed.

Once again, dates drive us backward in time and reveal a rich history of which we are unaware because it doesn't fit in with what is taught in most college curriculums. The Anasazi and Fremont cultures of the American Southwest are known for their accurate knowledge of the heavens, but here is evidence that the Aztecs may have preceded them by thousands of years.

The reasons we don't know about them are twofold. First, the comet destroyed much of the traces of their early civilization. Second, the Catholic Church burned every Aztec textual record it could find. Is it any wonder this information has been suppressed?

Once again, quoting Orozco: "We must re-evaluate much of our thinking about the greatness and antiquity of Native American civilization."

The story doesn't stop here. In 1529, Fray Bernardino de Sahagún, a Catholic priest, was sent to Mexico with a two-fold task. First, he was to convert the indigenous people. This was, after all, only eight years after Cortés brutally murdered many people in order to establish complete control over the population by means of terrorism. By 1529 they were deemed ready to convert or die.

But there was a second prong to de Sahagún's attack. Rumors had surfaced that many Aztec legends were very similar to Christian religious stories. Could it be that the Aztecs were familiar with the God of the Bible? If so, it would create some problems because the reason the Spanish Church felt so easy about ruling the Aztecs with a rod of iron was because the natives were considered pagans. What if they were God's creation as well as Europeans? How could the church justify treating its own in this fashion?

De Sahagún decided that the best way to convert the people was to establish some common ground, so he wrote a book. That's what scholars do. The result was what is now called *Historia general de las cosas de nueva España* (General History of the Things of New Spain), commonly

Father Bernardino de Sahagún (c. 1499–1590) is shown here at work on his history of the New World, the *Florentine Codex*, which includes Nahua migration mythology.

called the *Florentine Codex*. It tells the story of Nahua history, religious beliefs, and culture, in the common language of the people, but it also includes a running commentary in Spanish.

One of the most intriguing sections of the book, at least concerning the subject we're investigating, relates to Nahua migration mythology. They spoke of a mysterious place called Tamoanchan, which they claimed was, in effect, the birthplace of all Mesoamerican cultures. It was an Eden of sorts, a paradise from which they came following the great flood. The original inhabitants, the ancestors of the Aztecs, had come from the sea: "They say they came to this land to rule over it. They came from the sea on ships, a multitude of them, and landed on the shore of the sea, to the North. From there they went on, seeking the white mountains, the smoky mountains, led by their priests and by the voice of their gods. Finally, they came to the place that they called Tamoanchan ... and there they settled."

Unfortunately for de Sahagún, his illustrations let slip that the Spanish soldiers were not exactly paragons of Christian virtue. They caused a certain amount of embarrassment, so the book was never widely distributed. Once again, suppression for political purposes reared its ugly head.

It is at this point that coincidence, if there is such a thing, comes to bear. Go back for a moment to the Aztec ancestor's veneration of the planet Venus. The same acknowledgment is found in cultures as far distant as Egypt and Sumeria. There we find veneration of the star Sirius as well, also called the dog star. Sirius is located in the Orion constellation. The belt stars of Orion are said by many to be represented by the positioning of the pyramids on the Giza plateau. Orion is also associated with Osiris, a principle deity of the Egyptians.

In Mesoamerican mythology he is known as Quetzalcoatl, the "feathered serpent" or the "plumed serpent." Many Mesoamerican peoples claim him as their ancestor. He was so important, as a matter of fact, that when the Spanish first arrived on the shores of Mexico, Montezuma believed that Cortés was the Aztec god Quetzalcoatl, who had promised to return one day to reclaim his kingdom. That helps explain why the Spanish, outnumbered as they were, could defeat the local people with relative ease.

Quetzalcoatl is "the feathered serpent," represented by Venus, the solar light and the morning star. In biblical imagery, Venus is represented by Lucifer the devil, originally called the "son of the morning." In Isaiah 14:12, we read: "How art thou fallen from heaven, O Lucifer, son of the morning! How art thou cut down to the ground, which didst weaken the nations!"

Jesus, too, takes on the mantle of Venus, the morning star. The title is given to him in both 2 Peter 1 and Revelation 2:28.

The eagle is a soaring creature of the heavens, the serpent a slithering denizen of Earth. Together the two symbolize the duality of heaven and

Earth—spirituality and materialism. The eagle fighting the serpent, the heavens at war with the Earth, formed the symbolic image that indicated to the early Aztec pioneers where they were supposed to settle down. The symbolism is plain to see. Spirituality is constantly engaged in a war with materialism. The Earth is the battlefield.

This message is found in many religious traditions. The devil, the serpent of Eden, battles the Christ, or the dove, that came to represent Jesus. The Sumerian Ninki, usually shown with the scales of a reptilian serpent, battles Enlil, the god who wants to keep humanity in slavery.

Let's remind ourselves of a passage we covered earlier when we looked at *Jehovah and the Demiurge*. It's really important in this context as well. We'll briefly paraphrase the passage:

> Enlil was the patriarchal, evil god, whose only purpose was to enslave the human race.

The Aztec god Quetzalcoatl, the feathered serpent, is an important part of Mesoamerican mythology; many Mesoamericans believe he is their ancestor.

> Ninki, sister to Enki, represented the feminine presence. She is often pictured as a reptilian figure. [Anton Parks] goes so far as to contend that she may have been the inspiration for the serpent in the Eden of Genesis.

Here's why that distinction is so important. If Parks is right, and the Sumerian texts are to be taken literally, then the Genesis serpent wasn't evil at all. In his version the serpent, later called "that old devil" by the Christian author of the Book of Revelation, was actually trying to free humankind by offering them the gift of the knowledge represented by the tree that bore the fruit of the knowledge of good and evil.

Enlil lost the first battle. He wasn't able to prevent the new human race from a major step in their development. He didn't stop them from eating the fruit of the tree of the knowledge of good and evil, but he could cast humans out of the garden before they ate of the tree of life. So that's exactly what he did. Humans were thrown out of Eden.

In other words, the familiar words of Genesis are actually the story of how Enlil disguised himself as God in order to continue his original intent of creating a slave race.

All these images—the morning star, the battle between creatures of the heavens, the dove, or in this case the eagle, and creatures of the Earth, the serpent, the people being led to a new home, similar to the exodus accounts found in many religions, the persecution that followed the initial migration—they all tell the same story. It's happened again and again. Could it be that the human race is still an unknowing pawn in a cosmic battle that continues beyond our perception to this very day? Were the ancestors of the Aztecs no different from the early Jews or the Sumerians, who also have a similar exodus story? Is something going on that is much bigger than we realize? Is human history being manipulated by aliens, called "gods" by the ancients, who are engaged in a cosmic war? Is the history of humankind a revelation of one battlefield, the planet Earth, of that war? Is that why so much of our history is suppressed—to keep us from putting the pieces together?

We refer to the "battle between good and evil." Is that more than a metaphor? Are we pawns on a cosmic chessboard bigger than we can perceive, and is our task to rise to the occasion, pulling ourselves up by our own intellectual bootstraps?

It's enough to keep you awake at night, pondering a bigger picture.

The Mysterious Mound Builders, Part 1: Egypt on the Mississippi

Researchers read a lot of books and professional papers. We explore the back corners of the internet, far away from the general, run-of-the-mill, Wikipedia-type summaries so prevalent on the first page of a Google search, but for real, boots-on-the-ground, no-nonsense exploration, sometimes you've got to go on a field trip.

I've bumped up against prehistoric mound builders my whole life. In 2014, when I wrote "Savannah: A Bicycle Journey through Space and Time," which was an account of my bike trip down the Savannah River from the source to the sea, I even went a hundred miles out of my way to visit the Santee Indian Mound in eastern South Carolina. There used to be at least three Indian mounds in Augusta, Georgia, not far from where I live. My wife, Barb, and I once took a trip down the Ohio River Valley looking for mounds. We visited everything we could find, from the famous Serpent Mound in Ohio to Cahokia Mounds in Illinois. We climbed up them, went to every museum we could find, read a lot of publicity material, talked to specialists, and steeped ourselves in mound building cultures.

In other words, we learned a lot *about* them. The word "about" is the key. Learning *about* something is not the same as really *experiencing* it.

Recently, Graham Hancock's book *America Before: The Key to Earth's Lost Civilization* arrived at my home. I had preordered it through Amazon and anxiously awaited its appearance for about six months. In typical Hancock fashion, the book was a monster—515 pages loaded with facts, figures, interviews, balanced interpretations, and daring excursions into buried histories.

I don't know Graham Hancock, but I own almost every book he ever wrote and consider him to be a "mentor whom I have never met." I've used a lot of his research in past books and have never known him to lead me astray, even though Egyptologists avoid him like the plague and many so-called "experts" expel him to the outskirts of "fringe" history, calling him an "alternative" historian. He thus occupies a place familiar to many researchers in various fields whose work wasn't accepted until long after they were dead.

Located in southern Ohio, the Serpent Mound could be over three thousand years old. Named for obvious reasons, the mount is about 1,376 feet (419 meters) long, and it has been noted that it aligns with the two solstice and equinox events.

With this in mind I started reading *America Before* about ten seconds after I unwrapped the package it came in. I was hooked by the first paragraph:

> Archeology teaches us that the vast, inviting, resource-rich continents of North and South America were among the very last places on Earth to have been inhabited by human beings.... This is the orthodoxy, but it is crumbling under an onslaught of compelling new evidence revealed by new technologies.

Okay, Graham, you had me at "This is the orthodoxy, but it is crumbling...." I was somewhat familiar with a few of the places he talked about, but some were new to me. I had been to Moundville, Alabama, a few times. It is a prehistoric center of a great civilization and is loaded with controversy throughout its colorful past, but I had never been to Watson Brake, Louisiana, where the whole mound-building culture began 5,400 years ago. That was before Stonehenge was erected and way before the pyramids were constructed, if you accept their traditional dates of origin. I had never visited Poverty Point in Louisiana, which was built a thousand years after Watson Brake was deserted. It became the capital of a culture that would eventually extend all the way up the Mississippi and out to the Atlantic coast, flourishing for thousands of years.

I was dealing with some personal issues at the time and decided a good field trip would be just what the doctor ordered. Two days later, I set out on a journey of discovery that would cover almost 1,800 miles (2,900 kilometers) over the course of a week and bring me face to face with the very type of straw-man archeologist that I have been slightly deriding throughout this book. It was a revelation and moved the concept of *about* into experienced reality.

My journey first led northwest from my South Carolina home, which is only about eighty miles up the Savannah River from the Topper Archeological site, where evidence of human occupation goes back at least 50,000 years. We have found projectile points and rock piles on our property, a few of which furnished some material for my books *Ancient Gods* and *Supernatural Gods*, both published by Visible Ink Press. I won't reproduce that material here, so instead I refer you to those books.

I visited the petroglyph rock art at Track Rock Gap Archaeological Area in Georgia and spent an hour or so trying to get in touch with the spirit of the original artists. It didn't work. A few researchers, mostly nontraditional types, find evidence of Mayan culture up here. The site is interesting and well worth a visit, but I was fresh on a new adventure and much too excited to really settle in. There I experienced much the same feeling I had when I first visited Stonehenge. Something was present, down deep in the psychic vibe of the place, but I wasn't able to connect with it. Chalk it up to adrenaline and trying too hard in 92-degree heat and humidity.

I wasn't discouraged, but I decided to prepare a little before my next stop at the Etowah mounds, just north of Atlanta. Rather than plunge right in, I stopped at a hotel for the night, tried to get a good night's sleep, and arrived at the mounds as soon as the park opened the next morning at 9:00.

I was the only visitor for the first hour. The birds sang; the temperature and humidity were bearable; it was quiet; and I had the guide's uninterrupted attention, especially when he found out I wasn't a typical tourist. I questioned some of the dioramas that pictured stereotypical Indians-in-loin-cloth figurines because I knew that Hernando de Soto's chroniclers, back in 1540, didn't mention any mounds but were quite specific about the dress worn by the natives. They employed descriptions of clothing that sound more Mayan than early Cherokee. The copper pendants and tools on display were, of course, attributed to trade networks that spread all the way north to the Great Lakes, but there are records that some copper was mined in Georgia until the 1900s. The guide didn't know anything about that. It obviously hadn't been included in his training sessions. I'm sure he wondered if I knew what I was talking about, but he was very polite about it.

I didn't want to quibble very much, though. I was the guest. He was the host. I was on his turf, after all, so I decided to walk on out to the mounds.

The central mound, called Temple Mound A, is some 63 feet high. That's as high as a six-story building. I had experienced a mild heart attack

Even natives of the area centuries ago did not know the origin or purpose of mounds such as the Etowah Mounds in Georgia.

only a few months earlier. The temperature by now was hovering in the high 80s and rising, but my only thought was, "Well, what a way to go!" So I slowly, cane in hand, ascended the wooden stairway to the top. I'm glad I did. Exertion was often a key ingredient used in the smorgasbord of vision quest methods found throughout North American Indian cultures. It must have worked. I was finally able to mentally break free and feel a little of the spirit of the place.

Surprisingly, I found myself crying. When de Soto, the first European to ever explore these parts, came into town, he and his soldiers brought with them a host of diseases for which the natives had absolutely no immunity. Smallpox, measles, and other sicknesses spread in his wake. It is estimated that eventually 80 percent of the indigenous population succumbed to those diseases. Add to that the nasty habit the Spanish had of taking hostages to insure against attack and you have a very sad picture of the first contact between two races.

I found myself sitting in the quiet of the mound heights, overlooking the ghosts of whoever still might be here, and apologizing for the deeds of my ancestors. I love my country and am happy to be an American, but I am not now, and never have been, proud of much of our history. We've done some wonderful things and have accomplished a lot of good, but what we did to the indigenous people of this land, to say nothing of the slave labor force we imported to build it, and our treatment of the immigrants who were to come later, is simply unconscionable. That also doesn't account for what we're currently doing to our environment and sacred places. I found myself praying a "To Whom It May Concern" prayer to whatever native spirits still inhabited this place, asking for forgiveness for my ancestors. I think it was received well, in the spirit in which it was meant.

As I continued to look down on what was once a raised ceremonial plaza, presumably used for ball games similar to what we used to call stickball when I was a kid, and a game called Chunky, which involved throwing a spear through a rolling hoop of some sort, I pictured a village of folks who, just like us, got up in the morning, did whatever they needed to do that day, and then slept the sleep of the just before rising on the morrow to do it all again. They loved their families, traded and fought with their neighbors, fell in and out of love, were swept up in the drama of social situations, listened to music and danced, and thought their way of life was perfectly normal and would last forever.

Then came the European invasion. It was inevitable, of course. No civilization lasts forever. Ours won't either, but the invasion was insidious in ways they could never have foreseen. When unseen and unknown viral diseases struck, there must have been panic.

These were a religious people. What had they done to deserve this punishment from their gods? They couldn't see the germs that were infecting them. Not even the Europeans understood viral infections. The native religious leaders were no doubt working overtime, trying to explain the mysterious waves of death.

As always happens in such epidemics, the weak were the first to go. The elders died off, taking with them the wisdom of the past. The children were next, taking with them the vitality of the future. All that was left were the young people, who soon became addicted, as young people will, to the technologies and material flim-flam of the new strangers. They wanted guns. They wanted mirrors, beads, and gee-gaws. They wanted what they thought was a better life.

Their people had existed for thousands of years here on this land. They were getting along just fine, but then came the Spaniards, and in one generation everything they knew and loved was gone.

As de Soto moved through the south, his chroniclers questioned the natives about who had built the great mounds they came across. What was their original purpose?

"We don't know," came the answer. "They were here when we got here." Even then, more than 500 years ago, the mounds were an ancient mystery wrapped in an enigma.

I had more to learn. It was time to continue on.

South of Birmingham, Alabama, lies the important archeological site called Moundville. It was a center of trade and commerce for what is called the Mississippi-an culture and flourished at least a thousand years ago.

Many Americans believe the indigenous peoples were killed by conquering Europeans. The truth is, diseases such as smallpox and influenza brought to the continent by white settlers wiped out 90 percent of the native population.

There are many theories about how these mounds were used. Archeologists call it a "sociogram," which is a fancy word for a society based on clans that, in turn, were segregated by rank. We'll never know for sure because by 1500 C.E. the place was a ghost town. The people had all left.

The resident ranger was typical of hosts you find at most archeological museums. He had memorized his material and studied enough to be quite knowledgeable. At least about the official story.

Because we were getting along so well, I didn't bring up John Patton Jr.'s book, *Buried in the Mounds*. Patton lives in infamy in the world of most archeologists. His notoriety stems from his 1973 claim that somehow Moundville was connected to alien extraterrestrials. He revealed in his book that way back in 1938, the dead bodies of two fellow cadets in the Army corps were found, under suspicious circumstances, after they had been digging for relics at Moundville. They had supposedly written, deep under the central mound, "I found the Genesis."

Exactly what they meant by that is unclear, but it must have weighed heavily on Patton. Following his release from the Army he went on to become a professor of anthropology at the University of Alabama, majoring in studies related to Moundville. In 1955 he lost his job for reasons that have never been clearly revealed. He then disappeared from public view until 1973, when his book was published.

Why he waited so long to reveal his find is also unclear. Did he want to somehow cash in on an outlandish, bogus discovery? Or did he sit on his find, afraid that revealing it would ruin an otherwise outstanding career, until late in life when he felt an obligation to let the human race know that we are not alone and have been visited by entities unknown?

His reputation has been denigrated by those who cannot bring themselves to believe in otherworldly beings visiting Earth and being venerated by those on the "fringe" who accept ancient alien beliefs. His facts have never been either proved or disproved. In other words, this is yet another case of dueling ideologies.

Those who disagree with Patton usually attack his character and motives more than his ideas. Those who agree with him usually use his ideas to bolster beliefs they already hold, but the internet has been strangely silent about the whole matter. His book is no longer available. It's hard to even find references for it. If you Google his name, it is nowhere to be found. Were it not for a recent documentary (usually called a "mocumentary" by the establishment) to his life called *A Genesis Found*, hardly anyone would know anything about him. Some even doubt that he really existed.

It's a strange story, and on this day I didn't feel much like getting into it with a nice docent who didn't need an aggravating tourist messing up his day.

But something had changed within me that morning. I had made some kind of psychological shift. Moundville worked a kind of magic, and I knew I needed to proceed, so I headed west toward the Mississippi River. On the far shore stood Watson Brake and Poverty Point. I was hoping to find my own version of Genesis.

> Moundville worked a kind of magic, and I knew I needed to proceed, so I headed west toward the Mississippi River. On the far shore stood Watson Brake and Poverty Point. I was hoping to find my own version of Genesis.

When I reached Louisiana, I had a pretty good idea that I'd never get to see Watson Brake, even though I really would have loved to do some exploring there. The mounds are as old, and maybe even older, than Stonehenge. They are currently thought to be more than 5,400 years old, dating back to at least 3500 B.C.E. This age was determined in 1997.

When that find was made public, it turned the world of archeology on its head because there was no agriculture back then. Up to that time no reputable archeologist dared to suggest that a hunter-gatherer society could have possibly organized itself and turned out in sufficient numbers to undertake such a massive construction project. In the world of archeology, it took a lot of effort on the part of the mighty few to convince the entrenched majority, but eventually carbon dating and other methods triumphed and the traditional establishment was forced to face the unpleasant truth that our ancestors were completely different folks than had so far been illustrated in textbooks and dioramas. These were not primitive, scantily dressed natives. Well, they may have been scantily dressed, but only because Louisiana was hot and humid for much of the year back then just as it is now. When I arrived on the scene, I was scantily dressed myself.

The era of the original Watson Brake mounds is known as the Middle Archaic period. It was inhabited by a pre-agriculture, pre-pottery civilization that was, up until then, thought to be constantly on the move, following resources from place to place, and consisting of small tribes of closely related people, but cultures such as that cannot muster the sophisticated organizational skills and huge labor force needed to pull something like this off. The situation was much the same as that of Turkey's Göbekli Tepe. That was an even earlier site that archeologists simply couldn't believe was as old as it has proven to be. The concept of a simple, hunter-gatherer culture that gradually evolved into a civilized "us" is just too hard-wired into the collective establishment's consciousness. Some specialists, alas, can't get past their preconceived ideas.

Watson Brake was originally built over the course of a few centuries. It's now located near Watson Bayou, which lies within the floodplain of the Ouachita River, but who knows where the river flowed back then? It must have changed courses dozens of times.

Nevertheless, as interesting as this is, I was pretty sure I'd never be able to see it. The property is family-owned and at least one member of the family refuses to sell. There are a dozen mounds on the site, and there has been some professional work done there, but Stewart Gentry, who owns the land along with other family members, is not willing to sell off his family heritage.

I would commend him for that, were it not for one thing. After all, Barb and I have been asked if we would ever be willing to allow an archeological dig on our property in South Carolina. We're pretty obstinate ourselves about not wanting to dig the place up.

But our decision is based on a desire not to be upset by teams of people in our backyard. Gentry has different reasons. Robert Redding Jr. tells the story in an article entitled "Why the Public May Never See Watson Brake," written for the *Redding News Review* in 2009.

According to the *News Review*, Gentry doubts the accuracy of the estimated age of the place. You see, he is a Christian who believes in a literal interpretation of the Bible. That means he believes the Bible teaches that the Earth is only a few thousand years old. If that is so, how could carbon dating say the things it does?

Joe Saunders, who, as a regional archeologist in the Department of Geosciences at the University of Louisiana in Monroe, was the one who carbon dated the site and determined its age as 5,400 years old. He once asked Gentry, "Do you believe the Bible or do you believe in some scientific carbon dating?"

"I side with the Bible," said Gentry.

This is, to put it mildly, suppression of history for the worst reasons. If you are afraid to dig because your ideology might be proven false, that's a pretty poor reason to gum up the works for everyone else.

Meanwhile, the Watson Brake site, consisting of eleven mounds that are from 3 to 25 feet (1 to 7.6 meters) tall, connected by three ridges so as to form an oval some 853 feet (almost 270 meters) across, may not be long for this world. Lower Jackson Mound, connected in time and culture to Watson Brake, was destroyed by George Skipper in 2001. The Troyville Mounds, thought to be the second biggest mound complex in North America, yielding only to Cahokia in Illinois, was leveled by the Louisiana Highway Commission in 1931 in order to build a bridge across the Black River. When I–20 was built, the project obliterated mound complexes at Fitzhugh and Mt. Nebo. Civilization and progress are not always kind to history.

To understand the importance of Watson Brake, though, is paramount. It marked the beginning of what we know as the Mound Building culture. It rose to prominence 5,400 years ago and then was completely abandoned 600 years later. No one knows why. No skeletons or ceremonial artifacts have ever been found. Something motivated a lot of people to toil for years in the hot Louisiana sun, carrying basket after basket of soil, millions and millions of them, to build a mound. There had to be a powerful reason, but no one knows what that reason was.

Then one day they just stopped and migrated to parts unknown. The site lay fallow for a thousand years, but suddenly, after a millennium, people showed up one day and started to build Poverty Point, just a few miles away. Again, no one knows why.

Most archeologists that I've talked to or read up on don't know why the mounds were built. There have been no significant human remains or ceremonial objects found, so they were not burial mounds. My favorite comment so far has been a quote attributed to Dr. Bruce D. Smith of the *Smithsonian*: "I know it sounds awfully Zen-like, but maybe the answer is that building them was the purpose." I can live with that, I guess.

This map of Louisiana Watson Brake Mounds is reprinted from the *American Antiquity* journal. The site has been carbon dated as over five thousand years old.

At any rate, I knew I wouldn't find any answers at Watson Brake, where it all began, but I thought I might be able to meld with Poverty Point, which is now a World Historic Site. That's where I went next. I was searching for the answers to some key questions that Graham Hancock's book had raised.

- Why a mound culture? Why build mounds at all, especially since life was difficult back in those days and simple survival, without the luxury of a stable, agriculturally based food supply, would have been a daily struggle?

- Why did such a culture thrive for so long and then, one day, just stop?

- Why did it begin again a thousand years later, as if nothing had happened in the interim?

- Why did the mound building culture continue for the next five thousand years, going through multiple permutations called Archaic, Woodland (Calusa, Adena, and Hopewell) and Mississippian?

- Why did they spread all the way north up the Mississippi River and its tributaries, and all the way east to my backyard in South Carolina, and then on to the sea?

- Even more important to me, personally, what was their motivation? What could keep a people focused on such a task for five thousand years?

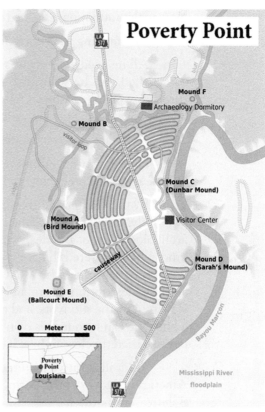

Those were my questions. I wasn't so naive as to think I was going to answer them when so many have tried and are still searching, but I felt that I needed to imbibe a little spiritual draught and see what turned up. In other words, I was going to attempt to intuitively go where archeology, by its very factual nature, could not.

First, though, I had to get by the gatekeeper. My mythological background continually informs me that whenever a hero sets off on a quest he needs to confront the one who guards the way to the palace or stands at the bridge over the moat. Every hero needs to earn his right to allow him to continue on.

A map of Poverty Point in Louisiana, which is now a UNESCO World Historic Site. The area was once a trading center for those travelling along the Mississippi River.

My gatekeeper turned out to be the personification of exactly the same straw-man archeologist I have been describing in this book. He was young, probably seeking the self-confidence that only experience can bring, opinionated, brainwashed by his recent college professors, and slightly full of himself, but that was okay. Much of that description used to fit me as well. Some of it probably still does.

Over and over again, I've said in this book that, in any clash of ideologies, the tendency is to attack an opponent's character rather than his facts. That's exactly what happened when the two of us clashed.

In the young man's defense, I was tired by then and not as polite as I should have been. I also recognized early in the conversation that this was going to provide material for the new book, earning perhaps a whole chapter. Not being without sin, I cannot really cast the first stone. I probably baited him a little, but, in retrospect, it was pretty funny.

It started when, again being the only person in the museum and having his complete attention, I opened the conversation with a softball-type statement.

"It's amazing what these folks accomplished, isn't it?"

All he needed to say was "Yes," and the whole thing might never have snowballed, but he went into his spiel, memorized no doubt and polished through many repetitions. I felt patronized and underestimated. It was sort of petty of me, and my next question was probably uncalled for.

"Why are you so sure of your facts?"

He went into a monologue that included at least three repetitions of "all the reputable archeologists I know say...."

By this he implied that he knew all the reputable archeologists and I, obviously, didn't. That rubbed me the wrong way. I know a few reputable archeologists, too. Besides, after forty years of teaching students of various kinds I had mastered the Socratic method. He hadn't. I decided to lead him down the primrose path. What follows isn't a word-for-word, blow-by-blow, accurate description. It probably glorifies me more than it should, but history is written by the survivors, and this is the way I remember it. (If he ever writes a book, he can recount his own version!) I didn't have a tape recorder handy, but this is pretty close to how it went down.

"Your illustrative material says that these people arrived here in North America by means of the Beringia Land Bridge. What do you think about the Solutrean Hypothesis?"

"That theory has been completely debunked," he informed me.

"Have you read *Across Atlantic Ice*? Stanford and Bradley present a pretty convincing argument."

"No, I haven't read it. I don't want to waste my time. It's enough for me to know that absolutely no DNA study backs up their premise," he declared.

"Have you worked with DNA yourself?"

"No. I leave that to the geneticists."

"So you're willing to turn over all your archeological discoveries to be verified by specialists from a completely different field of study that you don't even understand?"

"Well, they know what they're doing."

"So DNA trumps everything nowadays. What about an explanation involving cataclysmic extinction, including that of DNA evidence."

"You're referring to the Younger Dryas Comet theory, aren't you? They all do, eventually."

I wasn't sure who "they" were. To tell you the truth, I have difficulty finding anyone down at the local diner who has even heard of it. (If you want some of the latest information, I'll go into detail about it in the next chapter.)

Anyway, I pressed on.

"I take it you don't accept the thesis."

"That theory has been thoroughly put to bed. I don't know of one reputable scientist (here came the "reputable" claim again!) who believes that malarkey."

Well, the truth is, a team of sixty-three "reputable" scientists from fifty-five universities and sixteen countries have formed the Comet Research Group and published extensively on the theory. The work is readily available on its website. The group has provided a lot of additional information over the last two years.

Without going into all this, however, and because this whole conversation obviously wasn't going anywhere, I decided to retreat from the field before one of us lost it. In the spirit of establishing good will and harmony, I offered up what I thought was a bit of encouragement for him. Realizing that I was still the lone visitor in the museum I said, "I imagine now that Graham Hancock has written about Poverty Point in his new book, you'll be getting a lot more visitors."

Graham Hancock (1950–) is a researcher and journalist whose ideas about an ancient mother civilization have been dismissed by most of the scientific community as "pseudoarcheology."

"I hope not!" he huffed. "I've never read one of Graham Hancock's books and I never intend to."

"Why not?" I meekly inquired.

"Because Graham Hancock is an idiot!" he replied.

"I hadn't considered that point," I said, my ironic sense of humor rising to the surface. "But he brings up a lot of interesting evidence pointing to a whole lost chapter in American history and quotes a lot of reputable scholars." (I, too, can play the "reputable" card!)

"Anyone who tries to tell me that there is evidence in California that says man has been in North America for 130,000 years is wasting their time!"

I hadn't even been thinking about California, but I was impressed. At least he knew about the discovery that I wrote about back in the chapter about the first people in the Americas, but I couldn't let him get away with the reference to "man being in North America." I'm as politically correct as the next guy.

"Oh, I'm sure that there were women as well."

At that point, the conversation was effectively over. I wanted to get on and he wanted me to. Besides, mercifully, someone else came into the museum and gave him an opportunity to focus his attention elsewhere.

But I had learned something important. With this book half written I needed to know that archeologists and other keepers of the sacred shrines hadn't changed any since I left academia ten years ago. I'd been feeling a little guilty about accusing them of suppressing history in page after page. I had begun to wonder if things had changed and I might be out of date. Now I knew that they were still around. When I retired from teaching ten years ago, this kid was still in school. I could have been one of his professors. I wish I had been. Things might have been different for him, but he has time. Maybe there's still hope.

At any rate, getting upset with a person who held a completely different ideology from me wasn't going to bring me any close to my goal. I ventured forth into the mounds, all alone and by myself, and there I think I found what I had been looking for.

The artifacts discovered at Poverty Point form quite a large display in the museum. Alone, they were worth the trip, but over the last few decades I have spent quite a lot of time in museums and sacred places separated from Poverty Point by both time and geography. Some of the most intriguing days I have ever experienced were spent in the Museum of Egyptian Antiquities in Cairo. I got bored there. Not that it wasn't a fascinating time, but there was so much to see and study that I found myself on overload. I simply couldn't process it all.

Since then I have managed to keep my hand in, long-distance, so to speak. What I saw in Egypt and what I saw at Poverty Point bore so many similarities that it almost took my breath away.

It was Graham Hancock who set me up for it, but I would have come to the same conclusion even if I hadn't read *America Before*. I'm not going to go into the detail that he presented in his book. That would be a disservice to him, but I will summarize his thesis in the hopes that you will get a copy and read it yourself.

Poverty Point was a trade center, similar to the one on the Nile when the pyramids were being built. The native trade routes snaked their way up the Mississippi, Arkansas, and Ohio Rivers, ending as far away as Wisconsin and Michigan, Tennessee and Florida, and down into Mexico and Central America. These were sophisticated people.

We will probably never know for sure what motivated them to spend so much time building their colossal mounds and ceremonial centers, but it seems to me that it almost had to involve religion. People just don't do the things they did without being inspired by something bigger than themselves. Because we live in a secular society that gives more lip service to religion than physical and spiritual participation, it's hard for us to put ourselves in their place, but I think I understand.

> We will probably never know for sure what motivated them to spend so much time building their colossal mounds and ceremonial centers, but it seems to me that it almost had to involve religion.

When Barb and I retired and chose to live in the woods, cut off from seeing people on a daily basis, it was because we both wanted a bit of a spiritual retreat. I wrote about our motivation in *The Quantum Akashic Field and Out-of-Body Experiences: A Guide for Astral Travelers*:

> I've run the gamut. After a full-blown fundamentalist conversion I served time as an Evangelical, a Charismatic, a main-line conservative, and a flaming liberal. I've studied Zen Buddhism, Hinduism, Daoism, various Indian religions, classical philosophy and New Age spiritualities. I've meditated, mediated, illuminated, contemplated and postulated. I've taught more seminars that I can possibly remember, written eleven books and been a college professor, teaching in the fields of comparative religion, cross-cultural studies, and instrumental music. I've preached more than six thousand sermons, led countless Bible studies, and hosted a drive-time religious radio program.

> After all this you would think a person would have the sense to call himself an expert and retire into a season of contentment and relaxation while contemplating a life well spent.

But it didn't work that way. I never intended to give God a rest. Like the story of Jacob found in the book of Genesis, I intended to wrestle with God, shouting out loud, "I will not let you go until you bless me!"

I understand religious motivation. I think it was what inspired people to drag megaton boulders halfway across England to build Stonehenge. I think it was the underlying stimulus for those who built Göbekli Tepe and the Giza pyramids. For that matter, I think it was the underlying motivation for the builders of all the great megalithic structures, including the mound builders.

Many of the symbols I was looking at in the Poverty Point artifact collection were exact copies of those I studied in Egypt.

Don't get me wrong. I'm perfectly open to those who imply that there is a dark side to religion. I've seen it myself. It might not have been a positive motivation for the working-class mound builders as much as a negative one. In other words, the priests could quite conceivably have used fear of the gods to frighten people into getting up in the morning and going to work. The Anasazi priesthood probably employed this technique, as well as some Central and South American religious systems. Religions often resort to using both the carrot of hope for heaven and the stick of the fear of hell. This might have been used here in Louisiana.

But it sure feels like, for good or ill, religion played a part. The mounds display aspects of definite ceremonial features. And that's where I saw the stamp of Egypt everywhere I looked. I couldn't escape it. Many of the symbols I was looking at in the Poverty Point artifact collection were exact copies of those I studied in Egypt. Here's a list of some of the more obvious ones. For much more detail I refer you again to Graham Hancock's *America Before*. He devotes whole chapters to this stuff.

Why pyramids? There are many other architectural choices available, but all over the world—pyramids. They are universal.

Wherever you find megalithic structures you find a reproduction on the ground of what you see in the heavens above. The Lord's Prayer says it so succinctly: "Thy will be done on Earth as it is in heaven." In my own back yard in South Carolina I've found the same religious system. I'll refer you to my book *Ancient Gods* for a detailed analysis of what at least one archeologist has called *The "Problem" of Rock Piles in the American Southeast*. What caused the obsession of mimicking the heavens down on Earth?

- In keeping with this concept, the astronomical alignments of the mounds are strikingly similar to other such ancient constructions found the world over, and most specifically in Egypt.

- The mound builders seemed to have an affinity for the constellation we call Orion and its position relative to the Milky Way. The Milky Way was viewed as a path to the hereafter, and Orion marked the entrance. The Giza pyramids demonstrate the very same iconography.

- Along with this tendency, every mound complex I've looked at so far featured causeways, Earthen bridges, and connected mounds that were separate from the main mound temples. The mythology of both Egypt and the Mississippi valley are full of such references that talk about the dead making a journey along such edifices while encountering various obstacles one must overcome on the journey to the hereafter.

- I once thought the "all-seeing eye" to be a uniquely Egyptian symbol, ultimately finding its way to American dollar bills. Now, here it was again, inscribed on pottery and shown as a part of the constellation Orion. Where we see three "belt stars," the mound builders saw the wrist of a great warrior who served as a kind of celestial traffic cop, holding up his hand and saying, "Stop!" The way forward led directly through the eye enclosed in this giant hand. It was on much of the ceramic pottery found at Poverty Point and other places up and down the Mississippi River valley.

- This last one is, admittedly, a stretch, but I can't get it out of my mind. The museums at both Poverty Point and Cairo feature displays of hundreds of similar looking plumb bobs. They look just like pendulums. At Poverty Point, they are said to have been used for fishing-net weights. In Egypt they are called plumb bobs that were used for establishing vertical alignments in building techniques, much as a vertical level is used today. I was struck by the fact that I couldn't fully accept either explanation. You really don't need such beautifully worked, smoothed stone objects simply to weigh down a fishing net. A simple rock will do. And plumb bobs are good building tools, but why so many? I found myself wondering if there was more in play here. Astronomical alignments call for precise measurements. Dowsers, who use pendulums, often resort to their craft when it comes to determining such measurements. Could there be something going on here that hasn't generated much literature simply because most historians don't know anything about dowsing? As I said, it's a long shot, but I couldn't get the possibility out of my mind. I've got all kinds of dowsing pendulums in my house. I'm also a carpenter. I'm sure that if I suddenly disap-

An Egyptian plumb bob displayed at the Los Angeles County Museum of Art bears a resemblance to fishnet weights at the Poverty Point Museum in Louisiana.

peared, some future archeologist might deduce that I used them in my craft. That would be a logical assumption, but it would be wrong.

These are only a few of the similarities. There were many, many more. How was I to explain all this?

In the past I would have resorted to the doctrine of diffusion—that there was contact between the ancient people I was meeting at Poverty Point and the ancient Egyptians I had met many years ago in Cairo.

Now I'm not so sure. Graham Hancock's thesis is, I think, worthy of a lot of consideration. In short, he doesn't believe there was direct contact between the two cultures as much as the fact that both cultures, and others similarly scattered throughout the world, were born of an ancient, worldwide, "parent" civilization that gave birth to them all before going extinct. (I'd use the word "Atlantis" here but the very word itself will turn some people off, given the amount of baggage it currently has attached to it.)

Consider some facts. Almost every pioneering civilization we have studied in this section has stories about ancient "gods" who showed up "in the beginning" to guide those who had been, up to that time, a basic hunter-gatherer culture. These founders provided wisdom and experience. They taught the secrets of building, sometimes the art of writing and reading, and always the spiritual techniques needed to thrive in a difficult world.

What if these founders weren't alien gods? What if they were flesh and blood people, some of whom saw their civilization destroyed in an immense cataclysm and wanted to pass on whatever remnants they could to the stone age people who survived the cataclysm, in order to again jump-start the civilization they once knew and loved? What if they wanted to leave a legacy?

Picture a scenario something like this: A thriving, probably ice-age but maybe even earlier, civilization is overcome by disaster. What that disaster might have been we'll look at in the next chapter. Because they are a world-wide civilization they are not completely destroyed. Some survive, but their home, their infrastructure, their methods and means of production, are gone. What could they do?

Well, they could set out to start anew, teaching their techniques and wisdom to any pockets of primitive people they can find scattered around the globe. In only a few generations, these survivors of a great civilization would have taken on the status of "gods" in the eyes of their students.

But here's the key. The "students" wouldn't yet have the ability to travel the world and compare notes. They would have been separated from each other, partly because of the immensity of the devastation that destroyed their parent culture. Thus, they all started with the same basic values and then began to evolve on their own. Over the years they developed many differences, but many of the core values and symbols remained.

That is what I was discovering in Louisiana. I wasn't seeing Egypt reproduced on the Mississippi. I was seeing remnant symbols of the parent culture that gave birth to both civilizations.

If there had been a dominant mother civilization long before the ancient cultures with which we are now familiar, it makes sense that it would have spread its symbols and stories across the cultures of the world, resulting in similarities in archeological finds.

Think of it this way. On the surface, there is no similarity at all between a Roman Catholic High Mass and an Appalachian Independent Pentecostal Church, but dig a little deeper and what do you find? They both have a cross as the focal point of their meeting hall. They both tell stories of a virgin birth and a resurrection. They both celebrate communion and baptize new believers. They both use music in their worship. They both read the same Bible and derive their belief structure from it. And yet they are completely different. How could this be?

The answer is simple. They both started at the same place but evolved in different directions. In one sense they are two completely separate religions. Many Catholics have never set foot in a Pentecostal church. And many Pentecostals wouldn't be caught dead attending a Catholic Mass, but an impartial observer, after looking at both religious structures, would see many of the same symbols and practices.

I have come to believe that that was what I was seeing at Etowah Mounds, at Moundville, and now at Poverty Point. What I was noticing was not the differences between the Mississippi culture and the Nile culture but the similarities.

There are so many coincidences that I couldn't ignore them, but there were only three ways to explain them.

- Humans react in much the same way to religious impulses because they are all human. Something in our DNA experiences what we interpret as God, or gods, and we build pyramids and other such structures. Maybe it was even built into our DNA by the Source of All Things.

- Diffusion is a reality. Either Mississippi visited the Nile, or the Nile visited Mississippi.

- A parent culture inspired them both and then left them to evolve on their own.

All three begin with an ancient alien, if you accept the definition that we used at the very beginning of this book that the word "God," whoever or whatever he/she/it may be, represents an ancient alien. Whatever God is, it is ancient, for it precedes the universe. And you can't get more alien than God, given that the word describes something totally outside our experience.

Of the three explanations, I have come to like the third one best.

In short, the Mississippian tradition of mound builders, since the first pioneers at Watson Brake, were inspired by that which was outside of their everyday experience. The people were attempting to reach out to the divine. They were dealing with explanations of what happens when we die and where we go to spend eternity. They looked to the heavens and attempted to reproduce them on Earth. They were a spiritual people, having inherited from their parent culture the idea that there was more to the universe than appears to our meager senses.

In short, the Mississippian tradition of mound builders, since the first pioneers at Watson Brake, were inspired by that which was outside of their everyday experience.

But if these first pioneers were inspired by a parent civilization that was even older, where did *that* civilization go? Where did they come from? What happened to them? Why haven't we discovered remnants of their past?

Those are important questions. That's where we'll go next.

The Mysterious Mound Builders, Part 2: Requiem for the Lost Pioneers

We are about to consider yet again an unproven thesis, but one that is growing by leaps and bounds in the academic community even though it has, like so many revolutionary concepts before it, been declared dead on multiple occasions. I first wrote about it in *Ancient Gods* back in 2017, and even then it was, as far as I was concerned, the best explanation for a lot of what went on in prehistoric America. It explains a lot, so before continuing on you might want to go back to the chapter about the first people of America and re-read what we had to say about the Younger Dryas Comet Event.

It was probably the most destructive event ever experienced in North America, but it is crucial when it comes to asking questions about the demise of the Clovis culture. Indeed, an encounter with an Earth-scorching, devastating comet bombardment in North America would go a long way to explaining one of the most perplexing questions about why Clovis became extinct. There are thousands of Clovis artifacts scattered all across the United States, but only one single burial site has ever been found. The Anzick site in Montana contains the only evidence of Clovis skeletal remains. How could this be, when the culture was so widespread and prevalent?

Did an advanced culture capable of creating such beautiful works of stone art cremate their dead? Did they lay them to rest in above-ground platform sites? This may be, but it is certainly suspicious. There must have been some Clovis folks who died and were left somehow unattended. Why haven't we found them?

Could the answer lie in the fact that the devastation of the Younger Dryas Comet Impact was so severe that it literally melted the evidence into oblivion? How that could happen and still leave intact the bones of Clovis prey is a mystery. Something happened to the bodies. We just don't know what.

Surprisingly, no one seems to be questioning this very much. It's another one of those inconvenient questions, and by not bringing it up, an important mystery remains suppressed in the public consciousness.

How do we explain the many mythologies of the indigenous people of America? What happened to the megafauna that once prevailed upon the landscape? What is the nature of the notorious "black mat" that has been located in hundreds of places around the globe, all dated to about 12,800 years ago? What do Greenland glacial ice cores teach us about the sudden change of climate that we refer to as the Younger Dryas Ice Age?

These and many more questions led me to first examine, and then accept, the work of scientists who dared to suggest that the Earth came into contact with a segmented comet located in the Taurid meteor stream. Bottom line of this encounter? The Earth lost.

What follows is based on numerous technical papers, many of which can be found on the website of the Comet Research Group. You'll remember them from the previous section—sixty-three scientists, fifty-five universities, six countries. This is a group of heavyweights who cannot be ignored any longer, except by those who have a traditional ax to grind. There is now such

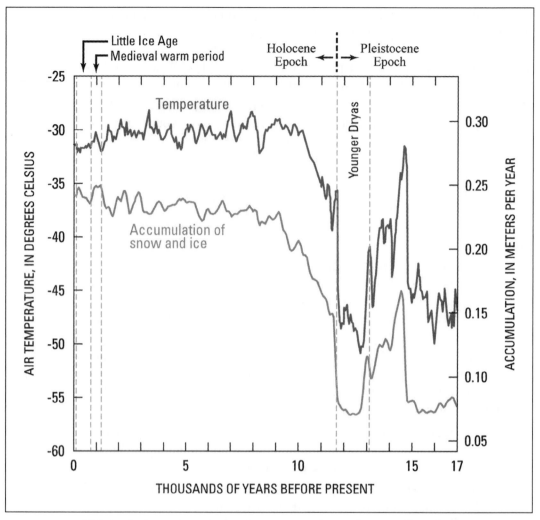

This graph shows temperature and snow accumulation changes in Greenland ice core samples stretching back 17,000 years. There is a pronounced dip in these during the Younger Dryas Age that indicates a dramatic climactic change.

voluminous material available that is of such high quality I'm sure it is only a matter of a very short time before the Younger Dryas Impact Hypothesis (YDIH) will be as well-known as "The Big One That Killed off the Dinosaurs" sixty-five million years ago.

The difference is that people were alive on the Earth to see this one. And they remembered it, but who were they?

This theory doesn't have to do with ancient aliens in the modern sense of the words, except as we shall see, peripherally, but I included it in this section because it was ancient and it was alien. It just wasn't sentient. It had happened before, and it will happen again. Hopefully not in our lifetimes, but that isn't by any means certain. If the folks who built Göbekli Tepe were correct, we might have only a few years until we see a repeat performance, but I'll get back to that in a short while. I wrote about it quite extensively in *Ancient Gods*, so, again, I need to direct you to other places.

What concerns us now, however, is not the details of the event itself as much as the impact the event had on the first pioneers to enjoy the benefits of North America.

I'm not going to go into exhaustive detail by quoting technical papers. The scientists who study this material have their own vocabulary that can quickly render you lost unless you are in on it. Many of them rarely use a pithy phrase when a technical tome will do just as well.

For this we need to forgive them. They are writing for each other, not us. A popular account won't cut it at a technical symposium, but I am under no such obligation. I feel no compulsion to fill this book with information about "Pt [platinum] concentrations" and descriptions of an "ice core metal impactor in the nature of at least 100-fold over –14 y" that "drops back during the subsequent –7 y." I will not employ any suggestions of "multiple injections of Pt-rich dust" that was strewn into the stratosphere.

No, you're safe with me, but what I am going to do is superimpose my concept of an ancient North American parent civilization, which I have inherited from Graham Hancock, over the Younger Dryas Impact Hypothesis, which I learned from studying the work of the Comet Impact Group.

In other words, what follows is not my original research and I make no claims to have come up with this stuff on my own, even though I have 99 percent accepted that this happened much like I'm about to present it. My contribution will be to make it readable and, hopefully, enjoyable enough so that you will want to read the papers and scholarly books on your own, but know as we continue on together that when I'm talking about *people*, a lot of it is informed speculation. When I'm talking about the *comet impact*, we're safely in the hands of the scientists.

With that caveat in place, here goes.

The story begins 30,000 years ago, when a comet that was about 65 miles (100 kilometers) in diameter entered our vicinity from the outer solar system and established a large elliptical orbit. For 10,000 years it remained intact. Then it fell victim to gravitational forces in the inner solar system and suffered what is referred to as a "fragmentation event." This was similar to what we observed back in July of 1994, when segments of a comet known as Shoemaker-Levy 9 separated and collided spectacularly with the planet Jupiter. It was the first time scientists had ever observed this kind of event, and pictures of it filled our TV screens for days. The devastation was tremendous.

When this ancient comet that now draws our attention fragmented, it formed a stream of debris. Some of this debris included a residue comet named, of all things, Encke. (Remember our old friend Enki from Sumeria? The resemblance is striking.) Another asteroid associated with this stream is called by the very prosaic name 2004 TG.

Encke is a remnant of the giant comet that fragmented some 20,000 years ago. Because this stream appears to be highlighted and backdropped by the constellation Taurus, it is now called the Taurus Meteor Stream. It forms a large doughnut-shaped orbit through which the Earth passes twice a year. The fragments, which we call "shooting stars," are viewed every year by millions of folks in late October, so they are sometimes called the Halloween Fireballs.

Usually, the fireballs offer no threat and are simply entertaining. Occasionally they do deliver a payload that can be dangerous.

In 1908, such a fireball entered the atmosphere near the Tunguska River in Siberia. It caused an airburst that leveled more than 80 million trees over an area that covered 830 square miles (2,150 kilometers). If it had burst over London, New York, or some populated city, it would have destroyed it. The energy released was 1,000 times greater than the atomic bomb dropped on Hiroshima in Japan but without, of course, the nuclear fallout. It was by far the largest such event ever recorded in modern world history, but it would

This 1920s photo shows what remained of the eighty million Siberian trees blasted down by the fireball that decimated 830 square miles of forest in 1908.

have paled in comparison to the Younger Dryas Comet impact. And such fragments are still up there, waiting for, perhaps, another rendezvous with Planet Earth, which passes through its stream twice every year.

Picture, now, a hypothetical civilization whose homeland might have been located in North America, which bore the brunt of the initial devastation. The fire rained down twice a year for the next 21 years! It is no wonder that the famous "black mat," consisting of soot, ash, and material that can only be formed under intense heat and pressure, covers North America and many places around the world. The debris field can be easily located by doing a Google search. Many illustrations fill the internet. The information is completely available for those who want to do a little research.

We have placed the origins of our hypothetical advanced North American civilization back around 130,000 years ago, but even if that is too old a time period, if we go back a relatively conservative 50,000 years, or even 35,000 years, that gives a culture a long time to grow and develop before the Younger Dryas Comet wiped it out only 12,800 years ago.

Once again, doubters will ask some questions, beginning with, "Why don't we find evidence of this culture in the archeological record?"

There are many reasons:

- First and foremost, we haven't been looking for it. Any evidence that indicated early dates has been suppressed. Clovis First was the gospel and woe unto anyone who bucked the accepted trend.

- Second, we wiped clean from the record the oral history of those who remembered the event. Nineteenth-century Indian cultures still told the old stories, but in our arrogance and racial bigotry we swept up almost every Indian youth we could find and shipped them off to a school located, in some cases, hundreds of miles away from their elders, forbid the use of their language, and punished them if they didn't act like white children. In one generation, just a few short years, we eliminated virtually all memory of the history that we now need so much to understand.

- Third, any technology this civilization might have possessed was undoubtedly different from ours. We live in a nuts-and-bolts, wire-and-metal world. The evidence we find when we try to deduce how places such as Teotihuacan, Sacsayhuamán, and Ollantaytambo were built defies our understanding. That the ancients somehow built them is obvious. There they stand, for all to see, but how the ancients accomplished the task is unknown. They must have had a technology, but no one knows what it is. In my book *Supernatural Gods*, I suggested the possibility of what I called a Psychic Tool Kit. It is entirely possible that those who built those megalithic structures employed techniques that they inherited from our hypothetical lost civilization. The methods atrophied over the generations and were soon watered down to the point that today only a few people remember how to access them, but psychic phenomena are real. They are being studied under strict scientific protocols. Can we recapture them? Only time will tell.

I have just scratched the surface of the study of our hypothetical lost pioneers. That they studied the heavens and were guided by the stars is obvious. The architecture they left behind reveals that.

Were they guided by an alien presence, even if we define that presence by our modern word, "God?"

Undoubtedly. They were a spiritual people who were engaged in an otherworldly enterprise for which they were willing to devote countless time, struggle, and hardship.

> They were a spiritual people who were engaged in an otherworldly enterprise for which they were willing to devote countless time, struggle, and hardship.

Were they the source of what I call the Atlantis Tradition, an advanced race that was destroyed almost overnight?

Well, Plato's stories and dates certainly point us in that direction.

Was their headquarters in North America, perhaps including the Caribbean islands?

Only time and a lot more work will reveal that.

Did they explore the world during the Ice Age?

Ancient maps of places such as Antarctica, containing longitude and latitude markings, suggest they did, along with a worldwide legacy they seem to have left behind in places as far removed as Egypt and the Americas.

The now famous Antikythera Mechanism, recovered from the sea in 1901, still baffles experts. It is a complex mechanism consisting of at least thirty meshing, bronze gears, designed to chart the movements of the sun and moon, and it was undoubtedly used for oceanic navigation back as far as 100 years B.C.E.

Could an ancient, long lost, sea-exploring civilization once have existed, with its home based in North America? If so, the ports from which they sailed would now lie hundreds of miles off the coasts, buried by the rising seas that inundated ancient shores. Could it be possible that a great chapter of our past has been ripped out of the history we have been taught?

That's what I've come to believe.

Keep your ears open. I have a feeling that this story is not nearly over. In fact, it might be just beginning. Scientists call the type of intellectual climate we are now experiencing a "Paradigm Shift." That's where we are. The ancient mound builders would advise us to look to the proverbial heavens. Change is coming.

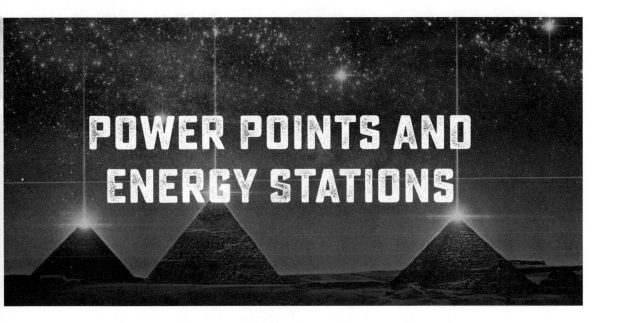

POWER POINTS AND ENERGY STATIONS

As far as we know, our planet is the only place in our Solar System able to sustain life as we understand it. So far, although we have a lot of tantalizing clues, it might be the only place in the entire universe as well, but that, of course, is up for debate. It is fair to say, however, that we have no actual evidence to the contrary.

One of the things that makes life so intriguing is the number of years that the human race has been around. Add to that the great question about what humans were doing a very long time ago and you have a recipe for a great mystery. At a time when the very act of survival was a whole lot more difficult than now, our ancestors seemed to feel the need to go to great lengths and sacrifice in order to construct huge megalithic monuments all around the globe.

What makes these monuments even more interesting is the geometry that links their locations together. When we consider the complex mathematical inscriptions and sheer degree of difficulty in pinpointing with exact precision how these monuments are connected to one another, it almost appears as if a higher power were behind their design. If that is the case, there must have been a reason behind it all.

How did ancient Egyptians manage to place the Great Pyramid of Giza at the exact center of all land mass on Earth? The east/west parallel that crosses the most land, and the north/south meridian that crosses the most land, intersect in only two places on the Earth. One is in the ocean. The other is at the Great Pyramid.

Without the ability to fly and develop a panoramic view of it all, how can this be possible? The people of ancient times didn't know how the world's land mass looked at that time. The pyramids of Giza represent an amazing achievement. The builders would have had to have a good grasp of geometry, physics, mathematics, and cartography.

Consider a few statistics:

- The weight of the great Pyramid of Giza is estimated at 5,955,000 tons. Various formulas have been put forth that indicate that by multiplying this figure by various degrees of 10 you will get a reasonable estimate of the Earth's mass, but how could the ancients have figured all this out when most people today can't even do it without a computer? Or, for most of us, even with one?

- If we tried to build a pyramid today, utilizing the most rugged heavy equipment available, we would be hard pressed to complete the job, let alone making it as dimensionally accurate as the ancients did. Without taking away anything from the intelligence of our ancestors, did they really manage such things with levers, ramps, pendulums, stones, and copper tools?

- The ancients built structures like this all over the globe. Many religious sites look very similar to one another and seem connected in some way along a similar latitude. Ancient astronaut theorists call it a world grid or the Earth Grid. They believe our ancestors purposely constructed their monuments on energy lines that when mapped and connected create a significant pattern similar to an energy web. The whole idea of the "world grid" is that the Earth is like a huge crystal. The energy flows around it at particular points of intersection.

The Great Pyramids of Egypt are impressive both architecturally and because of their more mysterious qualities, such as their positioning on the planet that indicate their builders knew a great deal about math, physics, and cartography. They are also associated with many UFO sightings, and some theorize they were even built by aliens.

Plato was one of the first to propose that the basic structure of Earth evolved from geometric shapes now known as Platonic solids. He pictured the Earth as being created from twelve pentagonal faces and twenty vortices located around the surface. When he drew pictures of his conception, he realized that geometrical formations occur between them. He wrote of a world "soul," comprised of 120 equal, identical triangles.

Today, some researchers speculate that a hidden energy source can be found within these patterns. They reveal a form of technology that we no longer understand, but that could have helped ancient civilizations build their monuments. Thus, the megalithic structures themselves are clues, hiding in plain sight, that such an Earth grid actually exists.

Could we ever learn how to tap its resources? Maybe, but first we would have to at least acknowledge that such a phenomenon is possible.

Beyond the possibility of tapping what could be a valuable resource, we have to ask if entities beyond the boundaries of Earth, or even outside our present perception realm, taught the ancients how to do this.

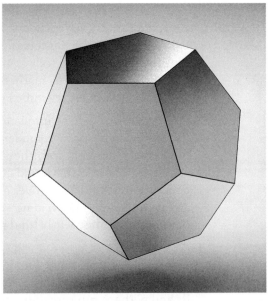

Plato imagined the Earth as having twelve pentagonal faces and twenty vortices: a dodecahedron.

If the ancient Egyptians, for instance, did not place the Pyramids randomly, it must be that they marked that specific geographic location for a reason. If *they* weren't using the grid they marked, who was?

There are those who believe that charged areas of the globe, where the Earth's electromagnetic energy accumulates, were important. They held a great deal of meaning for the ancients. If so, it is up to us to learn why.

Our primitive ancestors seem to have felt and experienced a force, a power, inherent in their environment. They might have recognized it as a sort of Earth magic. It probably led to early religious thought. With the rise of the Age of Enlightenment and the era of modern science, that kind of thinking was no longer either sufficient or appropriate. Humankind is now in an atheist stage, or at least an agnostic one, when it comes to mysterious and unseen forces of nature. Most folks no longer believe in spirits, fairies, and gods, at least when it comes to explaining the nature of materialistic reality. Stonehenge, Easter Island, and the standing stones of Carnac are no longer viewed as the result of maidens caught dancing on the Sabbath or fairy magic.

But the Earth energies that informed, encouraged, and influenced our ancestors remain, as sensitive adepts insist, within our physical experience. We simply have learned to ignore them. Forces such as gravity, for instance, continue to run things in our world whether we understand them or not. We know gravity is not caused by God, but we don't really know what does cause it. It's there, though, whether we think about it or not.

So it is with ley lines, lines of Earth energy, and Earth vortexes. They continue to exist, independent of our belief system *du jour*. The proof of their existence lies in the mystery of the monuments of our ancestors, the word of sensitive people living today, and the discoveries of physicists in this day and age who are discovering mathematically driven forces that were unknown to people a few decades ago but can now appear on a computer screen near you.

Can we begin to unravel this magic thread and follow it to its roots in the past? Can we come to understand that although Earth energies might not be divinely supernatural, they still exerted a profound influence over our ancestors? The ancients found meaning in Earth magic and demonstrated it by enduring great difficulties over many generations as they built stone structures and monuments. They had no science that we know about, except for astronomy, but what they left behind proves they had purpose and a technology we don't understand.

We, on the other hand, know things they couldn't have imagined. Even a few centuries ago, Isaac Newton might have suspected the work of devils and perhaps run screaming from the room if we had turned on the lights and picked up a remote to click through the TV channels.

Thanks to our advanced science and technology we know a lot about electromagnetic fields. We don't know how the ancients could possibly have learned about them, but it certainly seems as if early civilizations knew that if they placed their monuments in specific locations they could connect to an energy grid. From the Mayans to the Egyptians, and on to civilizations in Europe and Asia, the grid seems to be a common denominator.

This leads to a profound question. Did the ancients learn how to tap an energy source of which we are unaware? Or did someone teach them this skill that humankind has since forgotten?

If so it might be the answer to the great question about how the megaliths were built in the first place. We would be hard pressed to do it. They obviously did. How?

No one knows, but if the energy was available then, it is certainly present today. We have simply forgotten how to flip the switch.

The ancient alien theorists are quick to point out that UFO sightings are often associated with these special places. Could they be on to something? Are visitors from afar still utilizing their ancient refueling spots?

It seems fantastic, but so did the harnessing of electricity in 1879.

Once again we are left with the necessity to keep an open mind to possibilities that right now elude us. We know only one thing for sure. If you shut the door to a possibility, it will never materialize. The surest way to miss a target is to never shoot at it in the first place.

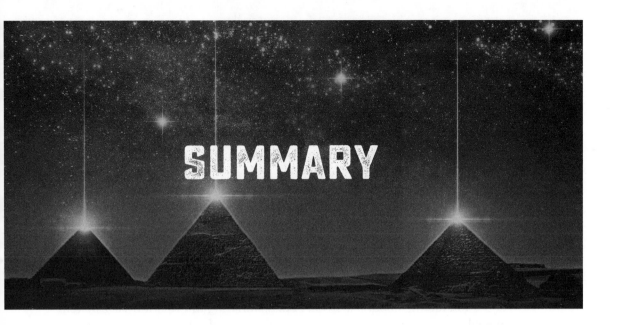

SUMMARY

It's time to start answering the "why" questions. In the introduction to this book I said, "We (the human race) wouldn't have come this far if something didn't intend us to continue, even if that something is only human curiosity." Our survey of the first pioneers to venture forth into the unknown shows us that we come from curious stock. As soon as we were able, we ventured out, in the words of the Bible, to "fill the Earth and subdue it."

I find it strange, therefore, that so much of academia seems so outwardly opposed to curiosity while, in turn, paying it such lip service, declaring curiosity to be the mainstay of science.

In their zeal for technical accuracy, scientists ignore the fact that most people are much more apt to watch the latest episode of *Ancient Aliens* than read an archeological treatise. They are apt to be smug about the whole thing, in a "holier than thou" kind of way, but then they wonder why funding is so difficult to come by when they plan a new project. Most archeologists would kill for the budget afforded commercial TV shows. Their attitude winds up with the practical consequence of suppressing knowledge rather than welcoming new discussions, no matter how outlandish they seem.

Our ancestors once stood on a shore and viewed a distant landscape far out to sea.

"Let's build a boat and go over there," one of them said.

"Why?" came the reply. "We're perfectly happy where we are. Right here, things are easily understood. Why venture forth into the unknown?"

Thank goodness the radicals won the day.

We have talked a lot so far about suppressed histories in various fields. You might draw the conclusion that there is a giant conspiracy out there somewhere—that there is a secret cabal who, for reasons unknown, somehow want to keep information from the general public in order to gain a mysterious advantage that will lead to a nefarious end.

Well, to a certain extent that *has* been true from time to time as history unfolds. To cite only one example, as we discovered when we studied the Isaac Newton story, the Catholic Church deliberately and unequivocally suppressed his ideas for political reasons, and the world suffered as a result. That was the express purpose of the Inquisition. It was developed as a deliberate tool of suppression.

But in the case of suppression of new archeological data, there is an even more devastating opponent. This one will be difficult to defeat.

I'm talking about a method of disseminating information via a system of publication that, by its very nature, is fat, sluggish, slow to respond, and, in the end, detrimental to progress in the twenty-first century. No one organization is really to blame. There is no one at whom we can point fingers. I've talked to a lot of researchers and publishers about the problem and they all agree but feel helpless. No one knows what to do about it. The problem seems almost impossible to overcome.

Let me describe it by giving a personal example.

I wrote my book *Lost Civilizations* over a six-month period that ended with me sending it off to the publisher in October of 2018. It was published and released to the public in October of 2019. That was a really fast turnaround because it was published by an efficient team of people.

While researching the latest cutting-edge information, I discovered that I had to wade through, in some cases, hundreds of professional papers that were published years earlier. Not having access to some of those original papers, I had to resort to scholarship reported in books or, often, online reports. Many of the magazine articles I was able to find had headlines that claimed, in big, bold letters, "This Information Will Change the Way We Think about History!"

A typical case went something like this:

- A field researcher makes a discovery that is completely out of line with accepted archeological information. For the sake of his reputation, he sends his research off to at least three different labs for confirmation. He then sits back to await results. It is not uncommon for this process to require at least a year. Sometimes he must wait up to three years, depending on the nature of the tests that are run.

- He then writes up his findings for peer review. To publish those findings, he contacts a few important publications, most of which publish monthly. They, in turn, send the article off to their review committees, which often meet only once a month. It's common in the publishing business to take at least six months to decide whether or not an article meets their standards.

- Assuming the article passes muster, it is sent off to a team of editors. These include line editors, fact-checkers, layout designers, illustrators, and project design teams. It's a process that can easily take up to six months.

- Finally, the article is published, but if it appears only in a trade journal, the public won't know about it until some reporter for the popular press happens to come across it and write it up for his or her own magazine. That, too, can easily consume another six months.

- Meanwhile, the original article is being discussed in what is called the peer review process. The researcher's colleagues share the information with one another and often decide it might be worthy of a hearing at a specialized symposium. Those happen not more than once a year.

- Finally, the article comes out in a popular magazine, but a lot of people don't subscribe to such magazines nowadays. They have to wait until they see it on the Discovery or Science channel. If you think a magazine has a long publication process, you can only imagine what a TV production schedule looks like.

- Assuming all this happens in a timely, albeit long, process, it still needs to go through the process of making it into the schools. That means being represented in textbooks, but first it has to be taught to the teachers, most of whom take continuing education courses, at the most, every few years.

- And every step of the way the original discovery, being new, is being sniped at by professors who have been teaching the same thing for so long they are quite critical of a new, and to them, untested, hypothesis.

Let's sum all this up as succinctly as we can. Much of the "new, cutting edge" information that I included in *Lost Civilizations*, published in 2019, was at least ten years old, and that doesn't include the stuff that is not yet in the textbooks. If you went out on the streets of any major city today, you would be hard-pressed to find more than one out of a dozen people who had ever heard the terms Younger Dryas Comet, Denisovan ancestry, or Solutrean Hypothesis, let alone know what the phrases mean. And yet, together, they represent the very latest anthropological and archeological evidence presented to answer the big questions everyone has about who we are and where we're going as a species.

The information has been suppressed, but not by any secret organization bent on world domination. It's just the victim of a fat, bloated, sluggish distribution system that hasn't kept up with the speed of twenty-first-century life and, by its very nature, should not be expected to. There is, after all, an intrinsic value to taking things slow and checking them out every step of the way. It eliminates a lot of false information being spread abroad.

> The information has been suppressed, but not by any secret organization bent on world domination. It's just the victim of a fat, bloated, sluggish distribution system that hasn't kept up with the speed of twenty-first-century life....

Meanwhile, those of us with our ears to the ground and research contacts in various fields are hearing about brand new information that has already surpassed much of what is starting to filter out—information that will measure substantially, for instance, in furthering the research about who the brave pioneers were and when they set forth on journeys that were so critical to the evolution of the human race.

Quite a few researchers have already opted to bypass the whole print business and take their findings right to the public via television and social media. That's probably going to continue, but it sacrifices the careful screening process that eliminates solid fact from extravagant fluff that is put forth only to enhance the reputation of a wannabe celebrity.

As I wrote these words, a few days ago I was asked to do a radio interview prior to the release of *Lost Civilizations*. The book wouldn't be out for another few months but had already gone out to the printer. I'd written two books since I sent that one off. I was petrified. Could I remember what I had written? Usually I have a book in front of me when I conduct interviews, but in this case, I hadn't even seen the pre-publication galleys yet.

The show went off just fine because the host was understanding and very knowledgeable. Being an author himself, he and I were able to have quite a talk about the whole business of being in the business these days. We agreed that something needed to be done, but what that something was, we had no idea.

If you hear frustration in the last few paragraphs it's because it's there. I'm at a loss. Publishers are at a loss. Interviewers are at a loss. We all know that some great work is being done that no one knows about. I'm discouraged that some great ideas are not being explored because of entrenched apathy. I cringe when I hear researchers such as Graham Hancock, Andrew Collins, and, to a much lesser extent, myself, referred to as writers of "alternative history" or "fringe science." Sometimes it's enough to make you want to throw in the towel.

But traditional scholarship has a long way to go before it fills in the many chapters of our history that currently stand open—blank pages needing to be filled. The history of academia is littered with the corpses of those who were trod upon and cast out by the establishment, only to find redemption long after they were dead.

How did a small, struggling band of hominins manage to struggle out of Africa at some time in the distant past and begin a journey of discovery that led to our current civilization? Why do civilizations spring into the light of day seemingly from nowhere, with no evolutionary underpinning? Why do even our earliest civilizations tell stories of "those who came before?"

The answers might prove to guide our future among the stars, as well as keep us from bringing about our own oblivion in the present. Those who do not learn from their past are destined to repeat it. And those who do not understand their past will never see their future.

With those caveats in mind we will now turn to those pioneers of the past in order to understand how they made the great step that led to what we call modernity. It was the invention, for good or ill, of civilization.

CIVILIZATION: ON THE ROAD TO MODERNITY

PRIME THEORY

The Mesopotamian/Egyptian Genesis

Over the years of research required to write books dealing with ancient civilizations, I have been continually amazed by one fact above all others. I have yet to find one that claimed to be the first. Wherever I went and wherever I studied Earth's various civilizations that have formed and, in some cases, disappeared, there was always a back story. In every case, someone had come before. No matter how far back in time I went, I came across legends and mythologies of founders who had come from somewhere else.

This is in complete opposition to the typical stories that fill our textbooks today.

And they keep changing, always going back in time. Take, for example, a recent discovery announced in July of 2019. After arguing with great vehemence that civilization began in Sumer and Egypt, after declaring with much authority that no previous culture could have possibly developed that could put this supposed "fact" into question, the Israel Antiquities Authority announced a discovery that put the whole Agricultural Revolution hypothesis of 6,000 years ago in question. With no apologies, with no "we got it wrong" statements, archeologists simply announced that they were working on a new site that is dated to 9,000 years ago. It is a city that obviously was in a transforming phase between hunting/gathering and agriculture. It casts urban life in the Levant into a whole new image.

While engaged in a highway construction project, Israeli workers brought this previously undiscovered and thus unknown city, featuring a population of 2,000 to 3,000 people, to light. A group of archaeologists led by Dr.

Hamoudi Khalaily and Dr. Jacob Vardi worked on the project for 18 months. It turned out to be a huge stone age settlement about a third of a mile (.54 kilometer) in length. Back in its heyday, it would have been considered a metropolis. It indicates that probably other people had lived in this fertile valley, perhaps for as long as some 20,000 years. It contained residential buildings, places of worship, alleyways, and plastered floors and walls.

As of yet there has been no public comment, no archeologists wanting to use the popular press, to tell us that all these years they have been declaring, with great authority, that they knew what they were talking about and so-called "alternative historians" may have been right to question the entrenched academic dogma. It's almost insulting to those who dared to question established authority all these years.

These and other discoveries have forced me to come to believe that no one, no matter how many letters they have after their name, knows where it all began. There is, however, a baseline that most archeologists accept. Although I doubt that it is the last word, and what follows will illustrate that point, we have to begin somewhere. So here's a rough outline of the academic party line taught in most colleges and universities today.

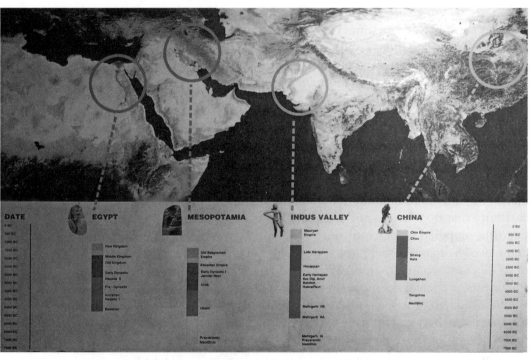

Earth's oldest recognized cultures go back six or seven thousand years, yet, interestingly, none of these people's legends or mythologies claim that they were the first to build a civilization. Could that be because they knew they had predecessors?

Definitions

First, though, we need to define some terms. What, for instance, do we mean by the word "civilization"?

Most texts begin with settled towns or cities. This, of course, requires a stable food supply. That, in turn, eliminates any cultures that existed before the agricultural revolution. By definition, civilization couldn't have begun before the Neolithic Revolution that began, at the earliest, in 10,000 B.C.E. Most texts place it close to 6,000 B.C.E. Since the first civilization with a written record started in the Middle East, we wind up with a relatively late date and a narrow geographical location.

As we shall soon see, that presents a problem, but for now, since for purposes of this survey we're going "by the book" in order to establish a baseline, that rubric puts us in Mesopotamia some 6,000 years ago. (The discovery of Turkey's Göbekli Tepe has thrown this estimate into a cocked hat, but we'll wait to get into that.)

A stable food supply makes it possible to develop specialized labor. That's what creates imposing buildings, works of art, skilled warfare, organized religion, writing, a recorded history, and a centralized bureaucracy to run things.

Not all civilizations employ all of those skills. The folks in Peru, for instance, seem to have gotten along without writing, but generally speaking, civilizations came into existence when the mainstays fell into place.

In *Lost Civilizations*, though, I exercised my writer's prerogative to expand on the usual definition. Here's how I defined it:

> A civilization is any group of people who come together over time to demonstrate a capacity for uniquely human qualities that distinguish them from their animal ancestors. Such qualities include, but are not necessarily limited to, attributes such as shared moral values, technology, an appreciation for beauty in art, a spiritual yearning for meaning in the face of a limited life-span, and a search for ultimate reality.

This expands the definition a bit and allows research into groups of people who didn't manage to develop a written history. It also pushes back the timeline somewhat and welcomes into the civilized fold those who developed much of civilization's trappings without writing about it so as to suit the convenience of future archeologists.

Oral history is powerful. Sometimes it gets diluted when reduced to text. There are still shamanic traditionalists, even in the twenty-first century, who refuse to commit to the written word. Only our modern prejudice insists on it.

MESOPOTAMIA AND EGYPT: 6000 TO 4000 B.C.E.

If we begin with written documentation, a superficial limitation but one that is firmly entrenched in academia, the beginnings of what is often presumptuously called "Man's March toward Progress" began in Mesopotamia and Egypt. The story goes something like this.

When the Sumerian civilization suddenly sprang into existence more than 6,000 years ago, it seemed to arrive as a fully formed, mature civilization. One day there was nothing. The next, cities flourished in the land between the Tigris and Euphrates Rivers, complete with artistic jewelry, advanced city-planning, literature, specialized trading centers, and a trade network that utilized sophisticated reed boats capable of traversing the oceans, as Thor Heyerdahl proved by his Ra voyages.

How did all this spring up, seemingly overnight? There had to have been some kind of proto-Sumerian civilization, but its location eludes archeologists to this day, so the whole subject is often simply pushed aside. In other words, the central questions don't make the history books.

An example of Sumerian cuneiform, which tells of a flood and migration to Mesopotamia.

Here's where we need to turn to mythology and oral history, but neither of those can be measured or carbon dated. They tend to get ignored by the establishment. If you tune into any of the many television documentaries, you will see animated discussions presented with great authority. "This happened, and then that happened, and here's when and where it all went down." But these explanations, no matter how detailed they may appear, are simply educated guesses that cannot really be backed up. Unfortunately, if you say something on TV with enough authority, it quickly turns into gospel truth.

Thanks to Sumerian cuneiform, the earliest written language we know about, civilization there came equipped with some intriguing origin myths. The first written texts, some of which can be traced back as far as 8000 B.C.E., can be a bit prosaic. They consist of lists of trade goods, bought and sold, but others tell wonderful stories of a great flood that inundated the homeland of those who survived by fleeing to Mesopotamia, carrying with them the wisdom needed to begin anew. This surviving remnant became known as sages—the Founders who lived "in the ancient times."

Where did they come from? No one knows. Where was their homeland? Archeologists have yet to uncover it.

One guess comes from Graham Hancock in his book *Underworld*. He speculates that the homeland of the ancient Sumerian sages can be found under the waters of what is now the Persian Gulf. That area was dry land long ago. If a now submerged proto-civilization once existed there, the "Sumerian problem" can be solved if and when we begin to search, but that takes the unique combination of money and a well-organized effort, something that probably won't come together in the near future.

When I wrote about this problem in *Lost Civilizations*, I put it like this:

It's a good theory that ties in Sumerian mythology with practical archeology. It explains the sudden ascendance of Sumerian civilization. It takes into account the flood epics found in the ancient texts. It explains why an ancestral civilization has not been found. It checks all the right boxes. The Persian Gulf has been submerged for at least the last 14,000 years. All that is needed is to push back the accepted dates for the beginnings of civilization and revise the story we have all been taught in our history books.

That's the problem.

When Hancock inquired about mounting an expedition on his own, he discovered he needed to obtain permission from officials in Iraq, the US Navy, the CIA, Texaco, Iran, the King of Saudi Arabia, and the Emirs of Kuwait, Bahrain, Qatar, Sharjah, Abu Dhabi, and Dubai. Those are daunting hoops to jump through before you can even begin to undertake something that is clearly apolitical and serves only to help us better understand the roots of human civilization. The answers will probably remain hidden for the foreseeable future.

Although we don't yet know, and we might never know, how Mesopotamian civilization began, some rich and powerful civilizations originated there. Today we know the region as the eastern end of a geographical area known as the Fertile Crescent. From that region developed civilizations we now call Sumerian, Assyrian, Akkadian, and Babylonian. These ancient people provided our earliest literature and developed legal codes that are still practiced today. They were one of the primary cultures who invented both sophisticated astronomy and mathematics.

Foundational religious texts such as the *Epic of Gilgamesh* and the *Enûma Eliš* were an inspiration for the Bible. The culture developed architecture that included Ziggurats and the Hanging Gardens of Babylon. They produced influential leaders such as Sargon, Akkad, Cyrus the Great, and, of course, Hammurabi. To this day Hammurabi is remembered by anyone who argues before the Supreme Court. On the south wall of the courtroom, his image is carved in marble, along with other historic lawgivers. Some historians believe the *Code of Hammurabi* is the inspiration for the *Ten Commandments* of Moses.

But while all this was going on in the land now known as Iraq, another civilization was developing along the banks of another great river at the other end of the Fertile Crescent. The Nile Valley became home to the great, mysterious Egyptian legacy of pyramids, enigmatic texts, monuments, and funereal practices.

But the history of Egypt, just like Mesopotamia, also featured mysterious visitors from the past, which early Egyptians called the Zep Tepi, or the "First Time." That was when gods walked the Earth. The *Edfu Building Texts* tell the story of a group of sages who, after seeing their homeland destroyed by a ferocious flood, sailed the seas in their great ships, trying to help what we

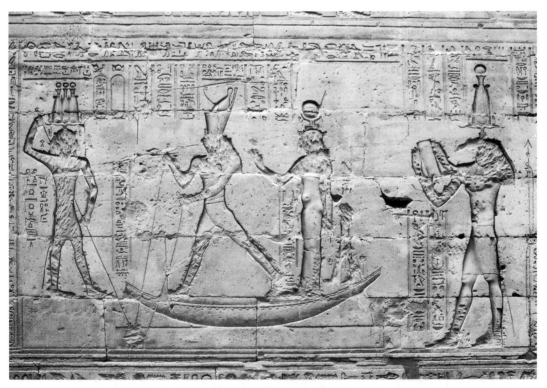

Carved reliefs on the Temple of Horus at Edfu in Egypt show gods among the Egyptian people, who arrived to re-create their destroyed homeland.

now call stone-age peoples dig out from a period of devastation such as the world had never seen. They sought to jump-start a new civilization.

In the Temple of Horus at Edfu, on the west bank of the Nile, the *Edfu Building Texts* exist to this day. They are, for the most part, weathered away, but what remains tells a story strikingly similar to what we read in Mesopotamia. The "gods" who walked among the Egyptians came from a place called the "Homeland of the Primeval Ones." It was an island that had been located in the midst of the western ocean. Prior to the time of the Egyptian civilization, the island was destroyed in a great cataclysm in which "the earliest mansions of the gods" had once stood.

Some of the population survived and, according to the Edfu texts, set forth in their great ships to bring about "the resurrection of the former world of the gods." Their mission, in other words, was to re-create their destroyed world.

Do surviving ancient histories recall the same event—a worldwide cataclysm that brought destruction to the parent civilization of both Mesopotamia and Egypt?

Out history texts are, for the most part, silent. If students don't raise awkward questions, professors will not face awkward situations. It is simpler to just avoid the issue. "Civilization arose on the banks of the Nile, the Tigris, and the Euphrates," we are told. And that's that.

THE INDUS VALLEY: 2500 B.C.E.

Meanwhile, we move on to other rivers and other primary civilizations. One of the greatest of those is found in the Indus Valley. No one knows for sure whether or not it was influenced by Mesopotamia. It might have been a spontaneous local development. All archeologists can say for sure is that by about 2500 B.C.E., Neolithic villages that had, up to this point, defined the culture of what is now Pakistan and northwestern India began to band together into one, distinct civilization with its own personality and characteristics. There is evidence of religious ceremonial practices that go back much further—all the way back to 5500 B.C.E. But when the two large, mysterious, and sophisticated cities of Harappa and Mohenjo-daro began to expand, they covered an area larger than Egypt and Mesopotamia combined, and they thrived in a very consistent way for a thousand years.

Mohenjo-daro means "mound of the dead." The name comes from the fact that this ancient and mysterious archeological site indicates that a thriving city once existed here, but it seems to have been leveled almost instantly by some kind of tremendous explosion that occurred 4,000 years go. It once stood equal to dynastic Egypt and was home to between 40,000 to 100,000 citizens. It had an extremely sophisticated infrastructure. The citizens were familiar with brick bathrooms, toilets, and sewers made of covered stone slabs, but it seems to have been suddenly reduced to rubble. Many artifacts there were found to have melted together under intense heat and then quickly cooled. They were fused together.

Initial speculation centered on an asteroid strike. What else could have caused such an explosion that long ago?

But David Davenport, a British researcher who studied the ruins for more than twelve years, compared the site to the destruction of Nagasaki at the end of World War II. Could the destruction of Mohenjo-daro have been the result of something akin to a modern atomic bomb?

The epicenter of the blast in which everything was fused together is about 50 yards (45.72 meters) wide. Moving out from this area, there is evidence of melted brick. It certainly seems like some sort of blast took place. There are even unconfirmed reports of a layer of radioactive ash that was broadcast out from the epicenter and of a human skeleton that showed clear evidence of extremely high levels of radioactivity.

In *Lost Civilizations*, when I wrote about Mohenjo-daro, I recalled the words of the *Bhagavad Gita*, a foundational Hindu religious text from India:

"Now I am become Death, the Destroyer of worlds." Although no one knows who wrote those words, they are estimated to have been recorded somewhere between 400 B.C.E. and 200 C.E. They were famously quoted by J. Robert Oppenheimer, one of the

Some pieces and pots recovered from the Mohenjo-daro site in present-day Pakistan. The end of this civilization was swift, leading to speculation about a large blast of some sort.

architects of the atomic bomb, when scientists in New Mexico first saw the devastation they were now capable of producing. When asked about whether the bomb produced by the members of the Manhattan Project was the first ever to be exploded, he replied, "Yes—in modern times."

We don't know how Mohenjo-daro and Harappa first formed a thriving civilization. We don't know for sure what happened to it. The whole area is mysterious—another intriguing chapter in the story of our path to civilization.

THE AEGEAN: 2000 B.C.E.

Next in line to develop a great civilization was a geographical area centered in the many bays, inlets, and islands of the rugged coastline of Greece, bordered by the Aegean Sea. What had formerly been an area of trade and commerce, as well as piracy, began to exercise control over the shipping routes that connected cities located on the Mediterranean Sea. With this kind of wealth pouring into the area, it wasn't long before someone began to dominate the area and form a bureaucracy to govern it. The center of the bureaucracy was the island of Crete, situated perfectly to guard the entrance to the Aegean.

More than a hundred years ago, Arthur Evans, a British archeologist, became the first to open a formal excavation. What he found so impressed him that he named the civilization after King Minos. It remains the Minoan culture to this day.

Traditional dating for this civilization places it at 2000 B.C.E., but I can't determine why. There is evidence of a Bronze Age culture that goes all the way back to 9,000 years ago. These early pioneers grew to build palaces at Knossos. They established trade networks so as to import copper and tin.

These were the materials needed to produce bronze. The best tin mines of that day were located in what is now Britain.

These must have been sophisticated folks, adept at exploiting resources for personal use and economic gain. And yet they seem to have lived rather simple lives. Their homes were made of stone and mud-brick. They grew olives and harvested cypress in order to build trading vessels. They even imported luxury items such as artistic jewelry.

But they didn't build city walls or fortifications. It seems as though they had no

Remains of the Minoan Palace of Knossos on the Grecian island of Crete.

use for them, indicating a peaceful way of life. This undoubtedly gave them time to practice the arts. Murals featuring dolphins, monkeys, and birds are prevalent, but so are pictures of sporting events, especially boxing. They even developed a written language that we now call Linear A and Linear B scripts, found on clay tablets scattered throughout areas surrounded by the Aegean Sea.

Life must have been good for them until one day they were threatened when the Santorini volcano exploded. That was the single most devastating day the Aegean had ever experienced. Studies in 1987, gathered from evidence collected as far away as the Greenland ice cap, concluded that the explosion of Santorini produced a dust cloud in 1645 B.C.E. This was a full century and a half before the destruction of the great Minoan palaces, so it probably didn't bring the entire civilization to its knees overnight, but it must have weakened it. The island of Crete, especially, located about 70 miles away from the volcano, must have survived and sustained interest from sea-faring invaders because those invaders attacked and plundered the island some 200 years later.

We can speculate that the normal lineup of social unrest and economic problems led to the disappearance of the Minoan civilization. There is even a school of thought in academic discussions that, according to historical evidence, civilizations seem to come with a sort of built-in expiration date. They form, they grow, and they die, probably as much because of the influence of human nature as anything else.

The eruption of Santorini is a convenient excuse for many theories about unexplained historical mysteries. Some see it as the destruction of Atlantis. Others believe that the aftereffects were responsible for tide fluctuations that made possible the biblical miracle of the Hebrews crossing of the Red Sea.

However the Minoans came to be, and how they disappeared from history, they did secure for themselves a featured spot in the traditional story of our path to civilization.

CHINA: 1600 B.C.E.

Although China came relatively late to the civilization party, when it arrived on the scene it soon dominated the room. Sumer, the Indus Valley, and the Aegean Crete are all gone, remembered only by the evidence they left behind, but China is still alive and kicking. Along with Egypt, it's the oldest continuing civilization in the current history of humankind. Its sheer size is vast, along with its abundant resources. It remains fiercely proud of its long history of resisting foreign influence. It needed strong and ruthless leadership to conquer and govern, but there seemed to be an abundance of local rulers ready to take up the challenge.

Somewhere around 1600 B.C.E., the Shang dynasty arose, featuring arti-facts of unsurpassed beauty. Writing was a priority, and many of the characters seen in today's Chinese script were introduced back at this time.

This is the long-held, traditional story of the rise of civilization in China. Most academic textbooks tell us that the first Chinese civilization began in the Central Plains region, along the Yellow River, somewhere around 2,000 B.C.E. The recent discovery of a large step pyramid in Shaanxi in north-west China now has archeologists questioning that information.

It was built at least four thousand years ago. That's close to the traditional date of the origin of Chinese civi-lization, but the place is wrong. It is located not in a river valley, but in the highlands. And it seems to have been built before the Great Wall was constructed. Only a flour-ishing civilization could have provided the manpower and organizational skills needed for such an ambitious project, and such a civilization was not thought to exist back then, especially in this location.

The site is called the Shimao ruins, which was dis-covered in 1976, but it wasn't until 2011 that real analysis of the evidence began to trickle down into the public press.

This is now recognized as the largest prehistoric ruin in China. Even more stunning is that in its heyday it was probably the largest city in the world. Until 2011, the only people who knew much about it were a few archeologists who didn't tell anyone. Picture a structure that was at least 1.5 miles (4 kilometers) square, completely surrounded with a defensive wall. That wall contained a trove of human skulls that appear to be connected to rites of human sacrifice.

> The recent discovery of a large step pyra-mid in Shaanxi in northwest China now has archeologists ques-tioning that informa-tion. It was built at least four thousand years ago.

The pyramid itself consists of 11 broad steps that rise to a height of 230 feet (70 meters). Palaces located on the top seem to be the homes of an elite caste, the mark of a hierarchical society similar to the traditions found in the American Mound Building cultures. As is often the case with ancient mega-liths, ritualistic images, including a half-human, half-animal figure, can be found carved into the rocks.

Why a pyramid? And if they were the first, preceding everyone else in China, why did they require such an immense defensive wall and feel the need to conduct human sacrifices? Were they protecting themselves from those whose skulls were found buried in the walls?

Evidence seems to indicate that even before the first emperor of the Han Dynasty came to power, the Chinese were capable of making maps that included both longitude and latitude. This was knowledge unknown in the west until the late Renaissance. Over time, sophisticated maps such as these fell into disuse, as China began to experience a local dark age similar to the European Middle Ages.

But the Chinese continued on, enduring high and low times. Evidence keeps popping up that their long and rich legacy had a much greater influence on human history than is often acknowledged.

CENTRAL AND SOUTH AMERICA: 1200 B.C.E.

The official story teaches us that somewhere around 1200 B.C.E. the Olmec civilization in Central America and the Chavin civilization in the Andes began to exert a great influence on the surrounding areas. Both of these cultures built temples that still stand today. How they managed to move megaton boulders and erect them with such precision is a mystery. The tolerances between them are such that you can't even fit a piece of paper between the massive stones used in construction. To this day these temples defy explanation. Sculpture, as well, dominated the cultures. The giant Olmec heads, many of them displaying African-featured, helmeted, stern-looking faces, are just as enigmatic today as they were when they were first discovered.

From the Olmec, we are told, descended the Maya and the Aztec in Central America. This is the standard party line of most academic texts. Even generic online encyclopedias such as Wikipedia follow this timeline. What isn't often mentioned are mysterious and inconvenient facts that point to an early South American genesis. Why this is so remains a question.

This Olmec carved stone head in Central America bears features not consistent with those of the native inhabitants.

Five thousand years ago, contemporaneous with the time of the Egyptian pyramids, there existed a civilization called Norte Chico, or the Caral Supe. It is the oldest acknowledged civilization of South America. We know next to nothing about it, except that like most civilizations, it grew up along rivers—in this case the Fortaleza, the Pativilca, and the Supe. Archeologists have found no pottery or visual art of any kind, but what they have discovered are elevated platform mounds and circular plazas. That kind of architecture, as we have pointed out again and again, requires a workforce and organizational structure.

The strange thing, however, is that once again there is no evolution of build-up present. One day there is no civilization indicated. Then, the next, it is suddenly there in full flower. How could this be?

To answer questions like this, we need to listen to the people themselves. The Incas tell stories about a "white man of large stature and authoritative demeanor. He was past his prime, with grey hair … but he spoke to them with love." He brought to them the blessings of civilization. Before he came, the land was full of chaos. When he departed across the Pacific—some say he walked on the water, others say he used rafts—he left order and a better life in his wake. His name, they say, was Viracocha, the "Foam of the Sea."

Was this merely legend, or did such a historical person actually exist? Does local mythology hint yet again of an Atlantis-type tradition, found in both Egypt and Sumer, wherein survivors of a cataclysm that destroyed their civilization went forth to rebuild that culture in various ports all around the world? We've already seen that such a cataclysm took place in North America some 12,800 years ago. Just as was the case with the Olmec and the Maya, such an event might very well have marked the genesis of a great South American civilization.

But you have to really dig to find these stories. Most archeologists simply don't want to talk about such matters. It would mean revising too much of the American story. Once again, ideology and a desire for neat, clean answers appear to trump questionable facts.

THE MEDITERRANEAN: 1000 B.C.E.

The Aegean civilization came to a sudden and mysterious halt about 1200 B.C.E. No one knows why, but 200 years later, around 1000 B.C.E., another rose to take its place. The Phoenicians sailed forth from their home ports in Lebanon and began to explore, trade, and pillage their way into the history books. It's not too much of a stretch to say they turned the Mediterranean Sea into a Phoenician Lake. They controlled everything from the narrow Straits of Gibraltar, the entrance and exit point into the Atlantic, to the coasts of both Africa and Europe. Some historians even believe they made it as far as the Americas and carried on trade with the copper-rich Indians of the Great Lakes.

The Bible refers to them as Canaanites. These days, Phoenicia generally refers to what we know as Lebanon. Canaan is a broader term. It includes Israel, Syria, and Jordan, but they were all a Semitic people. It was their written language that was the basis for first the Greek and then the Roman alphabet. English continues in that tradition.

Spotting their great ships on the horizon must have been a common occurrence. They featured carved images of horse's heads in honor of Yamm,

An 1,800-year-old carving of one of the Phoenician ships that traders used to sail the world. Some believe they might have journeyed as far as Michigan's Great Lakes!

the Phoenician god of the sea. Evidence indicates that purple robes from Tyre, used initially by Mesopotamian royalty and later by Roman aristocrats, were a valuable trade commodity. Tyre and its sister city, Sidon, were famous for their exports and trade networks, while Byblos, which was to become a central part of the Egyptian myth of Osiris, and Baalbek, named after the god Baal who was later so despised by the Hebrew prophets, were the most important religious centers of the Canaanite civilization.

The Bible tells the story of King Hiram of Tyre. He was instrumental in building the temple of King Solomon. Freemasons everywhere are taught lessons derived from Hiram. He is considered one of the founders of modern Masonry.

Phoenicians are frequently referred to as the "carriers" of civilization. This is a reference to the fact that because of their seafaring skills and feats of exploration they carried their ideals, products, and culture to the whole known world. Greece would eventually follow in their footsteps, and then Rome, but it was the Phoenicians who led the way.

THE PATH TO THE PRESENT DAY

Both the march and the clash of civilizations continue to this day. Civilizations came and went, rose to prominence and fell with resounding implications. Religions, such as Christianity and Islam, spread their cultures in profound ways. Economics and power were often more important driving forces than faith, which was generally used as an excuse to solidify political influence and prestige. Rome and Damascus were often two sides of a familiar and autocratic coin.

European civilization spread to the Americas and Australia, and on around the world. Many parts of the globe, even in relatively sheltered Eastern countries, assume that capitalism is the path to economic success. McDonald's and Wal-Mart may be our best defense against world war. There is too much money at stake to risk it.

I well remember once being on a tour bus that was making its way from Israel to Egypt. We had been steeped in Middle East history for ten days and were beginning to think, eat, and act like Israelis, but when the bus pulled into a McDonald's in the middle of the Sinai peninsula, we all eagerly piled out and lined up for a taste of home. It was hard to imagine that not long ago, Israeli tanks rolled along this very same highway on their way to fight a six-day war. Television has penetrated the deepest jungles of Africa, as have movies and the internet. We are not far from a global civilization, if, indeed, it hasn't already arrived.

The driving force behind the spread of civilization today is not political. It isn't pushed by monarchs and governments. It is driven by huge conglomerates and multinational companies. This is unprecedented. We have never seen anything like it before. Where it's going, no one knows.

It's an exciting time, but a bit scary as well.

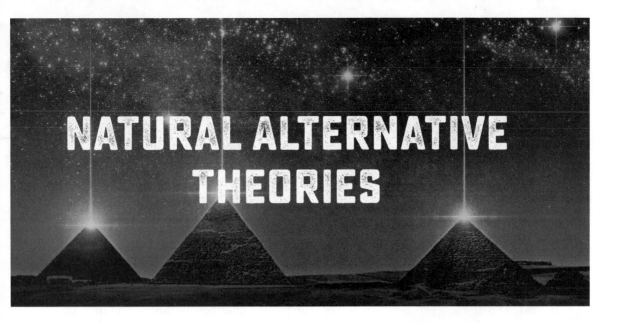

NATURAL ALTERNATIVE THEORIES

This, then is a quick overview of the course of the highlights of our civilization's evolution. A similar scenario can be found in almost every textbook in use today. The so-called march of progress is so prevalent that few students question it anymore. From Sumeria and Egypt, we have been told, the film has slowly unrolled off the spool of history, and here we stand today, at the pinnacle of human success.

But did it happen like that? Many are beginning to doubt it. The whole historical story we have been spoon-fed is beginning to crumble. Let's look at a few anomalies that throw some grit into the well-oiled machine of the traditional accounts.

MYSTERIES OF GÖBEKLI TEPE

No single archeologist has ever discovered anything more important than the German Archaeological Institute's Klaus Schmidt. In 1995, he began to dig at a place in Turkey called, by the locals, Potbelly Hill. We know it as Göbekli Tepe. At the time, Schmidt, who died in 2014, was moved to say, "In 10 or 15 years, Göbekli Tepe will be more famous than Stonehenge. And for good reason!"

His prophetic words are coming true even as you now read them.

For a hundred years, Egyptologists had been arguing against pushing back the origin time of the pyramids. "No one in the world was capable of such a giant undertaking before the Old Kingdom society that existed in the Nile River Valley on the Giza Plateau in 2589 B.C.E.," they said. "Show us the proof of an earlier civilization who accomplished such things and we'll believe you!"

At the Göbekli Tepe site in Turkey, this carved pillar, weighing several tons, was created over 11,000 years ago, eons before the pyramids of Egypt.

Then, in 1995, the proof was revealed to the world. Göbekli Tepe was built 11,600 years ago! That's 7,000 years older than the Great Pyramid of Giza and thousands of years before even the beginnings of Stonehenge. It's an unmistakable religious temple built of immense stone pillars arranged in sets of rings. The tallest are 18 feet high and weigh 16 tons. Carved into their surfaces are a whole menagerie of bas-relief totemic animals of prey.

The dating is beyond question. The surrounding hillside is littered with flint tools from Neolithic times. Knives, projectile points, choppers, scrapers, and files are found virtually everywhere, and in all stages of use.

Even more intriguing, and troubling to those who believe in the traditional version of our path to civilization, is that just like the area of the mounds at Watson Brake in Louisiana, there is absolutely no evidence of existing agriculture in the surrounding area. The temple seems to have been built, impossibly, by hunter-gatherers who had no communal support structure except for hunting teams that would fan out, kill what game they could, and bring it back to the workers. The bones of their evening meals consisted mostly of aurochs and gazelles.

How did a hunter-gatherer culture supply the manpower to carve and move 16-ton rocks? It must have taken hundreds, if not thousands, of laborers. What motivated them? Religious temples supposedly weren't built until after the Agricultural Revolution, when settled communities found the time to develop traditions of public worship.

Here was a fully developed religious temple built thousands of years before religion was thought to have been organized enough to even attempt such a thing! Göbekli Tepe seems to be the largest building project ever attempted by humankind up to that point in history, but what is so baffling is that there is no build-up, no gradual evolution of techniques, no precursors. One day there was nothing. The next, Göbekli Tepe. It defies belief, but there it stands.

What's more, the most sophisticated building happened at the bottom of the dig. In other words, the primary builders were the most skilled. What we have is a system of *devolution* rather than *evolution*. Göbekli Tepe thus seems to illustrate the unraveling of a tradition rather than the building of one.

And then came the most puzzling discovery of all. When it was done, the work completed, after a very short time it was deliberately buried, preserving it intact so that it could not be dug up and studied until its discovery in 1995.

As we have seen, the standard academic texts tell us that we humans took a giant stride toward civilization in Sumer and Egypt. Up to that time we had been "simple" primitive hunter-gatherers until the period known as the *Neolithic Revolution*. This had been the theory ever since V. Gordon Childe first presented it in the 1920s.

His concept of how our ancestors developed agriculture was that some clever humans, probably women, since they were the ones who gathered plants and seeds while the men were out hunting, discovered that wild grains could be planted, cared for, and then harvested.

No author did more to propagate this theory than James Michener. In his immensely popular book published in 1965, *The Source*, he told the fictional story of just such a woman, who in fits and starts while living in what is now the modern nation of Israel, invented the techniques of agriculture, only to discover in the end that she had been trapped by the process. Her garden owned her as much as she owned it.

It seemed so reasonable and made so much sense that the many people who read that book absorbed it into their psyches without even realizing it. The cultural collective simply accepted it as the way things were.

Before this time, for thousands upon thousands of years, humans had survived by following wild game and gathering what food crops they found while living in whatever shelter nature happened to provide. These were the "cave men" we learned about in grade school.

Then, according to Childe, domesticating crops changed everything. It was soon dubbed the "Agricultural Revolution"

Australian archeologist V. Gordon Childe (1892–1957) was a specialist in European prehistory. Most of his career was spent in Edinburgh and London, where he preferred the currently popular theories about the establishment of agriculture and civilization.

and it marked the beginning of civilization. A stable, local food supply led to the birth of settled towns, which soon exploded into cities. Populations flourished. People began to adapt special occupations. A cobbler, for instance, could practice his trade and get paid for it in consumer goods. He didn't need to go out and hunt anymore. Eventually, money was invented to represent commodities such as food, thus making transactions easier to handle. Writing was developed to keep track of who got what and how much was paid. Economy was born. One city might grow barley while another grew wheat. Trade flourished. A merchant class grew to oversee caravans. Trade between regions led to an immense social upheaval in the field of religion. Prior to agriculture, gods took the form of animals. After agriculture, heavenly gods were needed to oversee grain production by sending rain in due season. A priestly class arose. Because they lived in one settled place and now had the manpower to build, temples were constructed.

But inevitably one town's fields began to encroach on another's. Resources had to be protected. "This is *our* field, not yours!" To enforce that claim, armies developed, but armies needed strong male gods. Goddesses can't intimidate as well as war-like gods. Mother Earth is gentle. Yahweh, Baal, and Zeus are not.

In the first chapters of the Bible we read a metaphorical summary of this story. Cain, the agriculturist, kills Abel, the pastoralist. Cain immediately goes out and builds a city. Genesis 4 lists some of the specialized occupations that developed: builders, agriculturalists, musicians, industrialists, soldiers, priests, and lawyers. No wonder the final verse of the chapter says, "At that time, men began to call on the name of the Lord." The biblical god YHVH (Jehovah) was born.

Shortly after, a man named Abraham left Ur of the Chaldees, which is near Göbekli Tepe. He took with him his family army, traveling across the Fertile Crescent to Israel, which the biblical writers call Canaan.

He sallied forth with a simple idea: "My God is better than your God!" Later Hebrew writers would say it much more poetically: "Our God is a great God, above all other gods."

Abraham's journey marked the birth of what we now call monotheism, although the concept would not really triumph for another 1,500 years. He migrated west, we are told, because God commended him to go. This marked the early form of what was to become Judaism, Christianity, and Islam.

From these simple beginnings in the Fertile Crescent sprang specialized tools, pottery, writing, cities, trains and buses, wars, stress, high blood pressure, the morning commute, obesity, Facebook, Twitter, smartphones, and all the other benefits of modern civilization.

This is the accepted story. It has been poked and prodded, shaped a little and molded into academic shape, but it remains basically the same since Childe first called it the Neolithic Revolution. We now recognize it as an agricultural revolution that took place in the New Stone (*Neo-Lithic*) Age. It was a radical change, fraught with revolutionary consequences for the whole species. Childe declared that it was "the greatest event in human history after the mastery of fire!"

The idea is so ingrained that most people just accept it without even thinking much about it, but then came the discovery of Göbekli Tepe.

Why was it built? What was the motivational factor that caused a group of hunter-gatherers to completely abandon their way of life and build such a monument?

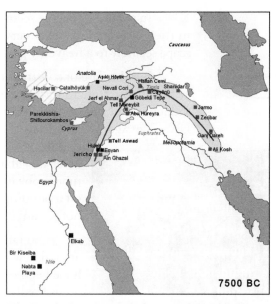

The Fertile Crescent was an area in the Middle East that was conducive to agriculture, thus helping to give rise to several civilizations thousands of years ago. Numerous important sites, including Göbekli Tepe, are located there.

According to Charles C. Mann, writing in the June 2011 edition of *National Geographic* magazine, it was religion. Images of carved shamanic totem animals abound, carved in high relief. There are astronomical alignments galore. This was a temple. Everything about it cried out that in opposition to the accepted story, religion preceded the invention of agriculture. It may have even *led* to the invention of agriculture. There is evidence that agriculture was invented in Turkey, more than 5,000 years before it showed up in Sumer. This is totally contrary to what we have been taught.

Göbekli Tepe isn't an easy place to get to. The builders had to have been motivated by what they saw and felt on the landscape, not by where they found it convenient to work. There is no nearby water source. There is no great river, such as we find in Sumer, Egypt, Pakistan, and India. There were no towns, villages, or fields. These marks of civilization hadn't been developed yet. As far as we can tell, there was no written language.

But because of the animal totems and astronomical alignments, we can assume the motivating religion was the precursor to what we now call animism. This is the belief that an all-pervading spirit animates everything in creation, but it also seems likely that astrology figured in somehow. The alignments of the structures at Göbekli Tepe tie the Earth to the sky. There are too many star, sun, and moon sightlines to ignore.

In short, the people seemed wedded to a particular spot of ground that, in their eyes, manifested a very powerful religion that tied an Earthly landscape securely to a heavenly perspective.

But the date of construction tells us even more. Göbekli Tepe was built at the precise time in history, some 11,600 years ago, when the whole Earth suddenly, and with global impact, began to make its way out of the Younger Dryas Ice Age. It was a time of great upheaval. Myths all over the world tell stories of floods and devastating climate changes. The great megafauna went extinct. In a time of such tumultuous upheaval, how did a primitive culture manage to pull off a building project so big and vast that the world would not see anything like it for another 7,000 years?

> The original survivors, perhaps known as "gods" to the indigenous people, would have been able to show the workers how to go about their business.

So far, our discussion of Göbekli Tepe has centered around new but accepted archeological doctrine. The dates have been confirmed, the evidence is overwhelming, and it has finally been accepted by the academic world.

But in our search for the birth of civilization we now have to ask questions that aren't so readily accepted by specialists in a field of study that is, by its very nature, pretty conservative.

The principle question is this. How did members of a primitive, hunter-gatherer society suddenly learn to build in this fashion and express their religion in such a manner? Could they suddenly have learned these things on their own? Or were they taught?

Earlier we speculated about the possibility of a "parent" ice age civilization that saw much of its infrastructure destroyed in a great cataclysm that might very well have been caused by a segmented comet that struck the Earth, causing worldwide devastation.

Could survivors of that impact have attempted, at Göbekli Tepe, to reproduce their way of life by teaching a group of hunter-gatherers how to build and operate a temple that would have illustrated their former spirituality—their religion?

That would explain why the best work is found at the bottom of the dig. The original survivors, perhaps known as "gods" to the indigenous people, would have been able to show the workers how to go about their business. Word would have quickly spread. People would have come from far and wide to lend a hand and participate with the "gods."

The technologies probably did not consist of techniques with which we are familiar. We have followed the path of leverage and brute strength. We've developed machines capable of lifting great weights and massive boulders. No evidence like that is found at Göbekli Tepe, but a different kind of civilization might have developed totally different ways of building.

In previous books I've speculated about what I call a "psychic tool kit." Scientists today are experimenting with such powers. A top-secret military project, recently revealed by means of the Freedom of Information Act, tells about experiments with remote viewing carried out during the Cold War. Institutions such as the Noetic Institute in California and the Monroe Institute in Virginia test for what are commonly called "psi" powers in humans. They use strict scientific protocols and are discovering magnificent possibilities that, since the death of the last Ice Age "gods" of civilization, we seem to have forgotten. The abilities may lie dormant within us, but they are there.

Could it be that sophisticated builders, well-versed in such powers, arrived on the scene at Göbekli Tepe, having witnessed a heavenly event, such as a comet impact, that reaped devastating havoc on Earth? If so, they might well have inspired a religion that "married" heaven and Earth into one theological construct. Göbekli Tepe might very well be the first temple of that new religion.

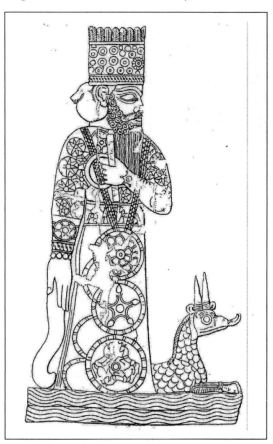

The *Enûma Eliš*, an ancient Babylonian religious text, was written just south and downstream from Göbekli Tepe. It tells of ancient gods called Anunnaki, who suddenly appeared on the scene at this time of history to organize, some say mate with or otherwise genetically manipulate, the ancestors of this very people, producing the first civilization.

In Genesis 6:2 the Bible makes a pointed reference to the fact that "the sons of God saw that the daughters of men were beautiful, and they married any of them they chose." This puzzling passage describes events that took place in this very geographical location. It seems to represent more historical fact than religious mythology. It doesn't read like a typical myth. The children of these unions resulted in a mysterious race called the Nephilim, "heroes of old, men of renown" (Genesis 6:4).

In these texts, do we find echoes of a very real historical condition and events

The Babylonian god Marduk, who was also a part of Assyrian and Akkadian mythology, was an important member of the Annunaki.

that took place in actual time? They are distorted, of course, because they happened more than 11,000 years ago, but what if they depict something that really happened? Is there a kernel of truth behind the blown-up stories?

● If so, then Göbekli Tepe doesn't represent the *beginning* of our civilization. It represents a *rebirth* of an even older civilization that might have much to teach us.

Is this at all practical? Does it affect us much in our day-to-day lives?

Maybe. It might have more to teach us than we have so far acknowledged.

You see, if these people had an astrological sense sophisticated enough to know about segmented comets and the powers of devastation carried with them, if they had witnessed such an event and managed to live through it, they might have been astute enough to plot the comet's trajectory and determine that Earth wasn't finished yet with its date with destiny. In other words, they might have foreseen its return.

In Graham Hancock's *Magicians of the Gods*, he describes his reaction while reading a paper presented by Paul Burley in June of 2011, called *Göbekli Tepe: Temples Communicating an Ancient Cosmic Geography*. For an in-depth study of the topic, I refer you to Hancock's book, but the bottom line is that on Pillar 43 at Göbekli Tepe the builders had carved an exact relief of what the sky would look like at the time of the Winter Solstice during our period of history. It's an exact replication of what you can see in the night sky if you go out, find a dark place, and observe the heavens.

In Burley's words:

> What's important here is that for some unknown reason the builders of Göbekli Tepe constructed a temple apparently highlighting a time 11,600 years in their future. Yet this time is intentional. The symbolism is clear and in keeping with many mythologies describing this very same event occurring at the very same time we live in today!

And then, after completing their work, they buried the whole complex so it wouldn't be discovered for more than 11,000 years. And in 1995 it was revealed.

Were they able to accurately compute the Taurid debris stream and determine a window of time in the future when Earth would again pass through the same area of that stream, possibly encountering again the devastating portion of debris that so disrupted life on planet Earth long ago? Are we living in that window of danger? Is Göbekli Tepe a warning to a future generation? Are we that generation?

Every October/November and June/July, when we regularly pass through the stream and watch for shooting stars, keep this in mind. Some year the outcome might not be nearly as pleasant as what John Denver wrote when he saw it "raining fire in the sky," as described in the song "Rocky Mountain High."

ARTIFACT ANOMALIES

Leaving Göbekli Tepe aside for a moment, which is, itself, a highly curious anomaly, there are other examples of a lesser order found through the world. Taken together, they all imply that an ancient, lost parent civilization existed and remains buried in time, a forgotten chapter to what we naively call modernity. Here are just a few examples that usually aren't mentioned in the history books. They are labeled "OOPArts" by archeologists. That stands for "out-of-place-artifacts." The list was originally compiled by Tara MacIssac for the *Epoch Times* and then reprinted by *Ancient Origins* magazine in September of 2015. They are here used by permission:

Singer and songwriter John Denver (1943-1997) witnessed fragments of the Taurid meteor stream first-hand while high up in the Rocky Mountains. He later sang about seeing it "raining fire in the sky."

- Batteries: Clay jars with asphalt stoppers and iron rods made some two thousand years ago have proven capable of generating more than a volt of electricity. These ancient "batteries" were found by German archaeologist Wilhelm Konig in 1938 just outside of Baghdad, Iraq. "The batteries have always attracted interest as curios," Dr. Paul Craddock, a metallurgy expert at the British Museum, told the BBC in 2003. "They are a one-off. As far as we know, nobody else has found anything like these. They are odd things; they are one of life's enigmas."

- Light Bulbs: A relief beneath the Temple of Hathor at Dendera, Egypt, depicts figures standing around a large light bulblike object. Erich von Däniken, who wrote *Chariot of the Gods?* created a model of the bulb that works when connected to a power source, emitting an eerie, purplish light.

- Nuclear Reactor: In 1972, a French factory imported uranium ore from Oklo, in Africa's Gabon Republic. The uranium had already been extracted. Scientists found the site of origin to

This relief sheds light on the technological know-how of the ancient Egyptians. It appears to be a working model of a light bulb. If the Egyptians had electric lighting, it would explain the lack of smoke marks one would expect inside the pyramids if torches had been used for illumination.

have apparently functioned as a large-scale nuclear reactor that came into being 1.8 billion years ago and was in operation for some 500,000 years. Dr. Glenn T. Seaborg, the late head of the United States Atomic Energy Commission and Nobel Prize winner for his work in the synthesis of heavy elements, explained why he believes it wasn't a natural phenomenon, and thus must be a man-made nuclear reactor. For uranium to "burn" in a reaction, very precise conditions are needed. The water must be extremely pure, for one. Much purer than exists naturally. The material U-235 is necessary for nuclear fission to occur. It is one of the isotopes found naturally in uranium. Several specialists in reactor engineering have said they believe the uranium in Oklo could not have been rich enough in U-235 for a reaction to take place naturally.

- Seismoscope: In 132 C.E., Zhang Heng created the world's first seismoscope. How exactly it works remains a mystery, but replicas have worked with a precision comparable to modern instruments. In 138 C.E. it correctly indicated that an earthquake occurred about 300 miles west of Luoyang, the capital of

China. No one had felt the quake in Luoyang and dismissed the warning until a messenger arrived days later requesting aid.

- Plumbing: Caves near Mount Baigong in China contain pipes leading to a nearby lake. They were dated by the Beijing Institute of Geology to about 150,000 years ago, according to Brian Dunning of Skeptoid.com. State-run media Xinhua reported that the pipes were analyzed at a local smeltery and 8 percent of the material could not be identified. Zheng Jiandong, a geology research fellow from the China Earthquake Administration, told the state-run newspaper *People's Daily* in 2007 that some of the pipes were found to be highly radioactive. He said iron-rich magma may have risen from deep in the Earth, bringing the iron into fissures where it may have solidified into tubes. He admitted, however, "There is indeed something mysterious about these pipes." He cited the radioactivity as an example of the strange qualities of the pipes.

- The Antikythera Mechanism: We briefly mentioned this earlier, but it bears repeating in this context. A mechanism, often referred to as an ancient "computer," that was built by Greeks around 150 B.C.E. was able to calculate astronomical changes with great precision. "If it hadn't been discovered, no one would possibly believe that it could exist because it's so sophisticated," said mathematician Tony Freeth in a *NOVA* TV documentary. Mathias Buttet, director of research and development for watchmaker Hublot, said in a video released by the Hellenic Republic Ministry of Culture and Tourism, "This Antikythera Mechanism includes ingenious features which are not found in modern watchmaking."

The Antikythera Mechanism on display at the National Archaeology Museum in Athens, Greece, is often referred to as an "ancient computer" because of the precision in which astronomical calculations could be made with it.

- Ancient Drill Bit: John Buchanan, Esq., in a presentation to a meeting of the Society of Antiquaries of Scotland on December 13, 1852, described a mysterious drill bit that had been found encapsulated in a layer of coal and buried in a bed of clay about 7 feet thick. Coal was formed hundreds of millions of years ago. The society decided that the instrument was of a modern level of advancement, but it concluded that "the iron instrument might have been part of a borer broken during some former search for coal." Buchanan's detailed report, however, did not include any signs that the coal surrounding the instrument had been punctured by drilling.

- Enigmatic Spheres: Spheres with fine grooves around them found in mines in South Africa have been said by some to be naturally formed masses of mineral matter. Others think they were precisely shaped by a prehistoric human hand. "The globes, which have a fibrous structure on the inside with a shell around it, are very hard and cannot be scratched, even by steel," said Roelf Marx, curator of the museum of Klerksdorp, South Africa, according to Michael Cremo's book *Forbidden Archaeology: The Hidden History of the Human Race*. Marx said the spheres are about 2.8 billion years old. If they are mineral masses, it is unclear how exactly they formed.

- Iron Pillar of Delphi: This pillar, which is formed of 99.72 percent iron, is at least 1,500 years old. It remains rust-free and is of an astounding purity. In modern times, wrought iron has been made with a purity of 99.8 percent, but it contains manganese and sulfur, two ingredients absent in the pillar. It was made at least "400 years before the largest known foundry of the world could have produced it," wrote John Rowlett in *A Study of the Craftsmen of Ancient and Medieval Civilizations to Show the Influence of Their Training on Our Present Day Method of Trade Education*.

- Ulfberht "Viking" Sword: When archaeologists found the Viking sword Ulfberht, dating from 800 to 1000 A.D., they were stunned. They couldn't see how the technology to make such a sword would have been available until the Industrial Revolution 800 years later. Its carbon content is three times higher than other swords of its time, and impurities were removed to such a degree that the iron ore must have been heated to at least 3,000 degrees Fahrenheit.

- A Very Old Hammer: A hammer was found in London, Texas, in 1934 encased in stone that had formed around it. The rock surrounding the hammer is said to be more than 100 million years old. Glen J. Kuban, a vocal skeptic, claims the hammer was made millions of years ago. He said the stone may contain materials that are more than 100 million years old, but that doesn't mean the rock formed around the hammer so long ago. Some limestone has formed around artifacts known to be from the twentieth century, so concretions, masses of hardened mineral matter, can form fairly quickly around objects. Carl Baugh, who is in possession of the artifact, has said the wooden handle has turned to coal. That implies great age. He notices that the metal head has a strange composition. Critics have called for more independent testing to verify these claims, but thus far no such testing has been conducted.

- Construction in the Ancient Past: Workers at a stone quarry near Aix-en-Provence, France, in the eighteenth century came across tools stuck in a layer of limestone 50 feet underground. The find was recorded in the *American Journal of Science and Arts* in 1820 by T. D. Porter, who was translating

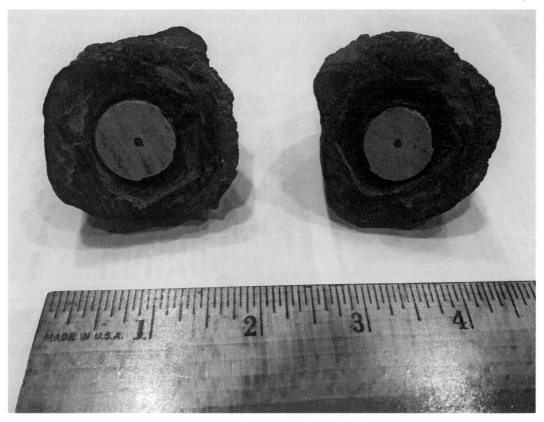

Discovered in Olancha, California, these ancient artifacts were encased in a 500,000-year-old geode. Upon examination, they appear to be a kind of spark plug!

Count Bournon's work, *Mineralogy*. The wooden instruments had turned into agate, a hard stone. Porter wrote: "Everything tended to prove that this work had been executed upon the spot where the traces existed. The presence of [man] had then preceded the formation of this stone, and that considerably, since [he] had already arrived at such a degree of civilization that the arts were known to him, and that [he] wrought the stone and formed columns out of it."

- Ancient Spark Plugs: In 1961, three people were out searching for geodes for their gem and gift shop in Olancha, California, when they found what appeared to be a spark plug encased in a geode. Virginia Maxey, one of the three discoverers, said at the time that a geologist examined the fossils around the device and dated the device at 500,000 years or older. The geologist was never named, and the current whereabouts of the artifact are unknown. Critics of the claim—Pierre Stromberg and Paul V. Heinrich—only have x-rays and an artist's sketch of the artifact to analyze. They think it was a modern spark plug encased in a quick-forming concretion rather than a geode, but, Stromberg and Heinrich have said, "There is little hard evidence that the original discoverers intended to deceive anyone."

There are many more such discoveries on record. I once asked a history professor who had written sections of a text used in his course why these kinds of things aren't included in most modern textbooks. He replied that he had too much to cover in one semester to "bother with half-baked ideas from the fringe."

In other words, these kinds of discoveries are suppressed not because of evidence, but because they don't fit the modern paradigm.

THE PROBLEM OF THE AMERICAS

Over and over again throughout this book, I have been forced by hidden and suppressed facts to speculate about what is now frequently being referred to as the "problem" of American history. Simply put, it's this.

One of the hard and immutable doctrines of academia is that the Americas were the last great landmass to be inhabited by humans. Writers such as myself may sometimes suffer the slings and arrows of being called "pseudoscientific authors," but you can't get more pseudoscientific than to insist for fifty years that an outdated doctrine such as Clovis First is documented fact and set in stone.

According to traditional archeology, the American march to civilization began when ancient humans crossed into Alaska via the Beringia land bridge approximately 15,000 to 20,000 years ago. Under no conditions was it permissible for professionals to keep their reputations intact, and in some cases even hold on to their jobs, if they broke out of lockstep with this doctrine.

I can't emphasize it enough. It's a problem even today. I don't understand why it's considered to be such an immutable doctrine, but it is. Professionals have even come to blows over this subject. It's that important to them.

But, as we have seen throughout this book, the doctrine is now on shaky ground. There are simply too many suppressed facts that cannot be ignored or shoved under the rug, given the prevalence of the internet, television, and social media. We've covered many of these arguments already and will continue to do so, so I won't go into more repetitious detail here, but I do want to emphasize something that I believe will shake archeology to its very core within the next decade or so.

The human race is an amazingly agile species. We can accomplish a lot in a very short time. Why should ancient humans be any less capable than we have proven to be?

The Out of Africa theory still has a chokehold on human origins, and will probably continue to do so for the foreseeable future, but the day will come, and I believe it will be sooner rather than later, when anthropologists will be forced to admit that ancient America played a much bigger role in human history than has so far been acknowledged. Tantalizing evidence is coming to the surface that can no longer be ignored. A prehistory of 100,000 years, or 50,000 years, or even 25,000 years, allows plenty of time for a civilization to arise, come to prominence, explore the world in ships, chart the shorelines of continents, and then disappear in a great and devastating tragedy such as the Younger Dryas Comet impact, which could easily wipe nearly all evidence of past triumphs and discoveries from the scene. Look at what we have accomplished in a mere 8,000 years. That's a drop in the bucket when dealing with time frames of 50,000 or 100,000 years.

The human race is an amazingly agile species. We can accomplish a lot in a very short time. Why should ancient humans be any less capable than we have proven to be?

Here are just a few of the areas now coming to the surface that will bear watching in the years to come. They represent chinks in the armor of established doctrine concerning the "problem" of the Americas and the birth of western civilization.

ORAL TRADITION

The oral tradition of the first Americans is, in many cases, completely at odds with what we are taught in American History classes. We are told stories depicting various ways by which Native Americans "entered" the continent, but most Native Americans disagree. They say they have always been here. They didn't come from anywhere.

The result is an either/or argument. *Either* we believe the scientists *or* we believe the Indians. Given today's materialistic, scientific bent, that's an argument that automatically requires a preordained decision on the part of anyone who doesn't want to be ostracized or laughed at.

It's a totally intellectualized ideology that makes some critical assumptions. It *assumes* oral history is not as accurate as written history, even though we all know that history is written by the winners. It *assumes* oral history is not trustworthy and must, by its very nature, change over the years, even though western history itself is full of examples of the accuracy of such accounts.

I once had an argument with a person who believed the written word as presented in the Bible. Because it was written down, he said, it was accurate, as opposed to religions based on early mythology. When I pointed out that the Sermon on the Mount proposes to be a twenty-minute sermon, transcribed word for word at least thirty years after it was delivered, and five chapters of the Gospel of John purport to be a lecture delivered by Jesus in the upper room, written down sixty years after the fact, he was not impressed. When I asked why he could believe early Christians capable of such feats of memory but not ancient storytellers, his answer was, and I quote, "That's different!" In his mind, that settled the argument.

Oral history versus the written word, however, is now being looked at with fresh eyes. In an article entitled "Educating America: The Historian's Responsibility to Native Americans and the Public," published in the journal *Perspectives on History* in May of 2000, Angela Cavender Wilson describes her own experience as a child who was, even at a young age, well versed in two distinct traditions—that of her European-type education and her native ancestry.

Wilson is the former name of Waziyatawin, a Dakota writer, professor, and activist who is committed to the pursuit of Indigenous liberation and reclamation of her ancestor's homelands.

She is from the Pezihutazizi Otunwe, the Yellow Medicine Village, in southwestern Minnesota. After receiving her Ph.D. in American history from Cornell University in 2000, she earned tenure and an associate professorship in the history department at Arizona State University where she taught for seven years. Her book *What Does Justice Look Like? The Struggle for Liberation in Dakota Homeland* won the Independent Publishers' Silver Book Award for Best Regional Non-Fiction in the Midwest in 2009.

She remembers quite vividly her grandmother telling her stories about the United States–Dakota conflict of 1862. On the one hand she was forced to read stories about so-called "primitive" savages fighting the heroic U.S cavalry. On the other hand, she would listen to stories of her persecuted ancestors from the lips of one who had personally heard the stories of those who were there at the time. Her grandmother often concluded her recitations with the words, "That was never written in a history book!"

In Waziyatawin's own words, "It was her account of the Dakota past which fostered my love for history and led to my pursuit of a degree in the discipline, but reconciling differing conceptions of history—those of my native community and academia—has been full of challenges and frustrations. The gulf between them often seems unbridgeable."

The problem, according to Waziyatawin, is that there is a fundamental difference between people with different ideologies, who, quite frankly, don't trust each other because they have totally different ways of viewing reality.

A 1904 painting by Anton Gag shows Dakotas attacking a defenseless town during the 1862 Dakota War. American history books naturally describe the Indians in a bad light, while the Dakotas had a different tale to tell.

Those of an academic bent don't even think about it much. They just accept that their way of interpreting history is correct because they are, to put it bluntly, brainwashed from an early age to form prejudices of which they are simply not aware.

"Did the ancestors of ancient Americans come from Asia?"

"Of course they did!"

"Why?"

"Because that's what the DNA evidence indicates."

I'll have a lot more to say about DNA evidence in a minute, but for now, they have come to a conclusion without even analyzing how they got there.

But it was easy, really. They simply made an unthinking decision that historians are right and that Indian oral history is wrong. Somewhere in that mix is usually found the unstated, but very obvious, prejudice that historians are "smarter" than a bunch of old people who don't know any better.

We can pity the Indians, perhaps, in a sort of patronizing way. We can even respect their allegiance to indigenous traditional ideologies, but they're wrong because modern science says something other than their primitive mythology.

Waziyatawin puts it this way. I quote her at length, with her permission because she says it so well:

The fundamental difference between academic Native American history and Native American history from the native perspective is the medium through which the history is interpreted. For the vast majority of native cultures, the primary means of transmitting and understanding history has been through the oral tradition; for academic historians, the primary way of transmitting and understanding history is through the written narrative. For many Native American people, whose voices and perspectives are rarely included in written histories, those histories are considered just another form of oppression and continued colonization. For historians, mistrust of the oral tradition is based on the view that all oral history needs to be validated by written sources, without which oral narratives constitute unverifiable legend and are therefore unreliable sources. Overcoming that mistrust will require educating academic historians about native oral traditions and demonstrating to them the value of understanding Native American history through the perspective of those who have lived it. Ultimately, a consensus must be reached within the discipline about the absolute necessity of including Native American voices in the research and writing of Native American history. This would ensure a measure of accountability to the living people about whose ancestors we are writing.

> There is a growing voice in the field of Native American studies that recognizes that we can't do real history for another race of people.

Thankfully, things seem to be changing. There is a growing voice in the field of Native American studies that recognizes that we can't do real history *for* another race of people. We must do history *with* them. We need to look no further than the now discredited Clovis First theory that dominated archeology for fifty years to understand that specialists often get it wrong. Had they really listened to the Indians back in the early twentieth century they wouldn't have embarrassed themselves so thoroughly. Two centuries of stereotyping whole populations, however, have wormed their way into our psyches and solidified what I call the "Faithful sidekick Tonto" image into our brains.

We simply have to get over the idea that the oral history of the first Americans is supplemental to our study. It should be, indeed, primary. Over the years, many people I talked to told me that history was the least interesting subject in their high school curriculum. It was for me, too. How much more would we have been influenced if our academic education had consisted of sitting at the foot of a wise grandmother or grandfather while listening to the old stories? That kind of education is vital and alive, not boring and dead.

Again, quoting Waziyatawin:

Historians researching and writing in the arena of Native American history have an ethical obligation to include Native American perspectives in their work, a notion that recognizes the authority and expertise of tribal historians, and in the end will produce more balanced interpretations. The field of Native American history, and by extension American history, will only be enriched by the inclusion of differing perspectives and in the process will broaden and expand the definitions of history.

There is a rather heartbreaking sequel to this story. Copyright laws limit how much I can quote from an article or a book without permission. I felt the above quotes, which exceed that limit, were so well written and powerful that I wanted to use them in their extended form, here presented, so I contacted Waziyatawin to obtain her permission. Without going into a lot of detail about the nature of this book, we engaged in a brief email exchange. She had no idea, of course, of my stance on academia and the suppression of history other than what the title implied. Her response, which totally justified my premise, shocked me to the core. I quote from her email:

> I have long since abandoned the project of trying to carve a place for Indigenous oral tradition within the academic field of history. It became an issue when I went up for tenure. I did receive tenure and promotion based on my work with oral history, but through the process saw how deeply it was contested by my colleagues.

It appears that entrenched academia still rears its ugly head, even in these so-called enlightened days.

THESE DAYS, DNA TRUMPS EVERYTHING, BUT SHOULD IT?

By now you may be thinking, "Okay, but what about DNA evidence? It's okay to listen to old stories. Maybe even charming ones, but how about real science?"

Well, nowadays DNA evidence is the elephant, or perhaps, given our context, we should say "mastodon," in the room. Let's take it on.

Although many people who don't follow this stuff closely might not realize it, despite the popularity and seeming inevitability of DNA evidence used on TV cop shows, there is a growing concern among some archeologists that the new science might be leading the whole field of anthropology down a primrose path. The science of genetics is basking in a well-deserved glow of unquestioned acceptance right now, but are there problems when we take the eggs of archeology, anthropology, linguistics, and mythology and place them all in the same basket with genetics?

In no less a respected journal than *Nature*, Ewen Callaway wrote an article published in March 2018 entitled "Divided by DNA: The Uneasy Relationship between Archaeology and Ancient Genomics." In it, he pulled aside the curtain that has been shielding a growing battle between specialists in the field of ancient origins.

At various sites around the world, including Stonehenge, where his article begins, some archeologists are growing increasingly uneasy about the way DNA is being used to completely overthrow other evidence they have encountered.

Traditional patterns of pottery manufacture, for instance, and radio-carbon dating techniques that have proved useful over the years are immediately thrown out the window when DNA results are figured into the mix. How could all the traditional tools in the archeological toolbox prove to be wrong?

Cultures may show an uninterrupted sequence of occupation that lasts for thousands of years, for instance. For all that time the ancient people kept doing the same things in the same way, but then DNA analysis comes along and says a particular population died out a thousand years before the evidence of its existence suggests.

> In various sites around the world ... some archeologists are growing increasingly uneasy about the way DNA is being used to completely overthrow other evidence they have encountered.

How could this be?

Some scientists love the new techniques. Others are suspicious. What if something is wrong with the field of ancient genetics but we don't yet understand exactly what it is? Can we trust it completely, seeing it has such a short track record?

Philipp Stockhammer is a researcher at Ludwig-Maximilians University in Munich, Germany. He finds himself right in the middle of the debate. "Half the archaeologists think ancient DNA can solve everything. The other half thinks ancient DNA is the devil's work," he says. "The technology is no silver bullet, but archaeologists ignore it at their peril."

Many archeologists are coming to the conclusion that submitting entirely to what they call a molecular approach robs the field of "boots-on-the-ground" nuance and experienced intuition.

Marc Vander Linden, an archaeologist at the University of Cambridge in the United Kingdom, puts it quite succinctly: "They give the impression that they've sorted it out. That's a little bit irritating."

Colin Renfrew, a Cambridge archeologist, warned about the coming debate back in 1973. In his book *Before Civilization*, he speculated about the

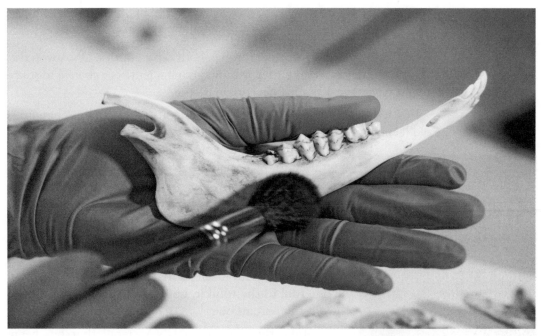

DNA can be used to determine the age of an item, but one should not disregard nearby physical evidence that could also indicate age.

then relatively recent use of carbon dating methods: "The study of prehistory today is in crisis. Much of prehistory, as written in the existing textbooks, is inadequate. Some of it is, quite simply, wrong."

When carbon dating came along, it transformed the whole field. Before then, archeologists had to rely on something they called "relative chronologies." They would employ ancient Egyptian calendars, for instance, or estimations on how far and fast ideas could spread through time and across geographical areas.

Early carbon dates were often off by significant time spans. It took years for the science to be trusted. DNA studies, being very new on the scene, haven't had that much time yet. A common complaint heard at archeological conventions is that "pots are pots, and people are people."

Kennewick man, for instance, found along the shores of the Columbia River in Washington State in 1996, seemed to have European biological features. Dated at about 9,000 years old, he was the subject of a lot of controversy. Native Americans claimed him for their own and insisted his bones should be buried according to the Native American Graves Protection and Repatriation Act (NAGPRA). They called him the Ancient One.

DNA indicated he was most closely related to contemporary Native Americans, but he also showed some evidence of Polynesian ancestry and his features looked more European than Asian. Who should get to claim the body, scientists or Native Americans?

Bad feelings still reverberate through both communities. DNA won the court battle, so the body was buried without giving scientists a chance to study it. It might have revealed some new origin theories.

Besides all this, the whole subfield of migration research is changing. The old feeling was that groups of homogenous people moved across the land from here to there, leaving artifacts in their wake that were later used to trace their progress. Now anthropologists are not so sure. The whole process doesn't seem quite as tidy. DNA seems to indicate that whole groups of people can be quite more in flux. And the number of samples that have been accumulated is still quite small. There's room for a lot of wiggle room.

> What all this means is that DNA probably needs to be one tool in the toolkit, but not the only one, or even the most important one.

What all this means is that DNA probably needs to be one tool in the toolkit, but not the only one, or even the most important one.

Take the Australian DNA signal that has been found in the remote regions of the Amazon jungle, for instance. Graham Hancock, in his book *America Before*, goes to considerable lengths to point out that because this signal is not found in North or Central America, the most plausible way for it to suddenly appear in South America is for people from Australia to cross the Pacific right to the South American continent. Even geneticists agree this is the most plausible explanation.

But geneticists are not archeologists. And archeologists claim that early Australians didn't have boats capable of crossing the Pacific. Since specialists in one field don't like to argue with specialists in a different one, the information remains unreported.

What all this means is that we need to proceed slowly. Science is wonderful and important, but so is common sense. Ancient Indian oral history is important. If they say they didn't "come from" anywhere, maybe we need to at least listen to them before rushing to judgment. Important clues may demand our attention. The chapter about the problem of the beginning of American civilization is not yet fully written.

MULTIPLE WAVES AND THE BERINGIAN STANDSTILL

One of the recent theories about the first people of the Americas and the beginning of western hemisphere civilization is called the Multiple Wave Theory. This was the theory put forth by the Science Channel's popular and award-winning 2008 documentary *Journey to 10,000 BC* and many more made-for-TV presentations.

Its premise is that before 1492 waves of immigrants from differing locations came to America at different times and by various routes. Some walked

Using DNA evidence is a favored way that scientists have traced immigration patterns across Beringia thousands of years ago. On this map, different letter/number combinations indicate a type of gene found commonly in various archeological finds.

here over the Beringia land bridge. Others followed the shorelines, either on foot or by small boats. Others braved the high seas, but once here, they were able to jump-start American civilization.

I won't go into a lot of detail about the identity of these ancient travelers because I devoted much of my book *Lost Civilizations* to this very topic. Suffice it to say that the homelands of the immigrants were spread around the globe and throughout history, from the Solutreans of western Europe, to Polynesians, to ancient pre-Japanese cultures, to Chinese explorers, to Africans, and many more.

Lately, however, a new variant has been proposed. It's called the Beringian Standstill and it owes much of its recent popularity to DNA evidence and some archeological discoveries made at the Bluefish Caves in the Yukon.

In March 2017, Heather Pringle, of *Hakai* magazine, wrote an article that was published on the *Smithsonian*'s website entitled "What Happens When an Archaeologist Challenges Mainstream Scientific Thinking?" It told the story of Jacques Cinq-Mars and the Bluefish Caves discovery, but in doing so she revealed, in her words, "how toxic atmosphere can poison scientific progress."

That, in a nutshell, is the very premise of this whole book.

As we said earlier in our survey of how people first got to North America, the mainstream opinion is that is happened some 12,000 or so years ago, when sea levels were lowered sufficiently to allow passage on foot from Siberia to Alaska via the Beringian land bridge.

> The evidence found at Bluefish Caves directly challenged mainstream scientific thinking. The Clovis First model was so firmly entrenched that anyone questioning it was automatically banned....

Quite a few researchers simply didn't buy that theory, but they were almost forced by their colleagues to remain silent. Cinq-Mars refused to stay quiet. His work at Bluefish Caves suggested to him that Asian hunters roamed the northern Yukon at least 11,000 years before the arrival of the Clovis people. He was also influenced by many of the same arguments we have previously considered in this book. He looked at the evidence from Meadowcroft in Pennsylvania to Monte Verde in Chile, and all points in between, and decided he needed to speak out. Like so many before him, he had assumed his work would spark a renewed interest in searching for answers. Instead, according to the scientific journal *Nature*, "the finds stirred fierce opposition and a bitter debate ... one of the most acrimonious, and unfruitful, in all of science."

The evidence found at Bluefish Caves directly challenged mainstream scientific thinking. The Clovis First model was so firmly entrenched that anyone questioning it was automatically banned from the party list of those who follow traditional theories.

In Pringle's words:

It was a brutal experience, something that Cinq-Mars once likened to the Spanish Inquisition. At conferences, audiences paid little heed to his presentations, giving short shrift to the evidence. Other researchers listened politely, then questioned his competence. The result was always the same. "When Jacques proposed [that Bluefish Caves was] 24,000 years old, it was not accepted," says William Josie, director of natural resources at the Vuntut Gwitchin First Nation in Old Crow.

All Cinq-Mars could do was watch his work collapse. Funding dried up. His livelihood disappeared. And there was nothing he could do about it. He knew in his heart that he was right, but it seemed that established "experts" had beaten him.

This all happened between 1979 and 2001. Today, as we have seen, the Clovis First model lies in shambles on the floor of entrenched academia. Dozens of new studies show that the Clovis people were not the first Americans.

Again, to quote Pringle: "Pre-Clovis people slaughtered mastodons in Washington State, dined on desert parsley in Oregon, made all-purpose stone tools that were the Ice Age version of X-acto blades in Texas, and slept in sprawling, hide-covered homes in Chile—all between 13,800 and 15,500 years ago, possibly earlier."

Finally came the ultimate victory for Cinq-Mars. The Université de Montréal sponsored the work of Lauriane Bourgeon, a Ph.D. candidate, and her colleagues who restudied the Bluefish Caves material and confirmed that the caves were at least 24,000 years old.

Once again, we are forced to watch these kinds of academic shenanigans and ask why real research and study need to be so acrimonious. It seems as though specialists in various fields are demanding that the real work of a scientist is that of developing a thick skin. "Gentle people need not apply!"

It might be said, with come accuracy, that academics are among the only ones who shoot their own wounded. More than a few observers wonder if scientific nerds, after having been bullied in high school, spend the rest of their lives verbally taking it out on others once they arrive at the top of their professions.

Quentin Mackie, an archaeologist at the University of Victoria in British Columbia, Canada, sums up the latest findings: "This report will tilt the scales for some [archaeologists] towards accepting the site, and for some more, it will inspire a desire to really evaluate the caves more seriously and either generate new data or try to replicate this study."

And it only took forty years.

Tom Dillehay, an archaeologist at Vanderbilt University in Tennessee and the principal investigator at the Chilean site of Monte Verde, says it very succinctly: "The scientific atmosphere was clearly toxic and clearly impeded science."

As a result of Cinq-Mars's work in the Yukon, a new theory of American origins, and perhaps even American civilization, has arrived on the scene. It's called the Beringian Standstill model.

The theory begins by saying that the Multiple Wave Theory doesn't work because of linguistics. Language similarities cited to show various patterns of migration don't seem to stand up to close scrutiny. If people came from various established civilizations such as Japan or China, they would have brought their languages with them and at least a few of those remnants would be present in early Native American speech. They don't seem to be, however.

That may or not be true, depending on which specialists you talk to, but let's continue.

Clovis First, according to the theory, doesn't work either because of the timing. People lived in North America before the invention of the Clovis point.

Again, proponents of Clovis First argue this point, too, but, onward.

What does that leave? Only what is now called the Beringian Standstill or the Beringian Incubation Model. Implied in that second name is the primary source of support for the theory. Until the work at Bluefish Caves, it rested almost entirely on DNA evidence.

What the theory says is this.

People migrated into the Yukon and were stopped in their tracks by the great ice sheets that still blocked the overland route south through Canada and into Montana. Rather than turn back, they stood still right where they were for a long time.

> People migrated into the Yukon and were stopped in their tracks by the great ice sheets that still blocked the overland route south through Canada and into Montana. Rather than turn back, they stood still right where they were for a long time.

They stayed in the Bluefish Caves area long enough to split from their Siberian ancestors over the course of the next 30,000 years. There they developed a new population in isolation, until eventually, by various ways and means involving both overland migration and shoreline navigation, they found their way south about 15,000 years ago.

K. Kris Hirst, in a scholarly paper entitled "The Beringian Standstill Hypothesis: An Overview," published on *ThoughtCo.com* in August of 2017, argues that:

During the turbulent times of the last glacial maximum, about 30,000 years ago, people from what is today Siberia in northeastern Asia arrived in Beringia. Because of local climate changes, they became trapped there, cut off from Siberia by glaciers in the Verkhoyansk Range in Siberia and in the Mackenzie River valley in Alaska. There they remained in the tundra environment of Beringia until retreating glaciers and rising sea levels allowed—and eventually forced—their migration into the remainder of the Americas about 15,000 years ago.

If all this is true, the Beringian Standstill helps explain why DNA results have been so strange. The Americas weren't populated by people with modern Siberian genetic signals. They were populated by a previously unsuspected people, no longer existing, who were cut off from Siberia by some 30,000 years. They still carried Siberian DNA in their genes, but it was well watered down by time.

This still doesn't explain the very early dates of an American population, but at least it makes it easier to speculate that if people lived as close as the Yukon, they might have found their way through or around the glaciers whenever a pathway, however small, either opened up or drew back from a passage along the coasts.

Authors W. Michael Gear and Kathleen O'Neal Gear produced an interesting variant on this theory in 1990 with their novel *People of the Wolf*. Although the Beringian Land Bridge theory was in vogue back then, they pictured the first Americans entering the American landscape by following a tunnel formed when the McKenzie River began to carve its way underneath the glacier, thus providing a clear but very frightening passageway. Such a passage would have certainly been remembered and might even have formed the kernel of mythologies that remembered Indian ancestors entering this "world" through a hole in the ground.

It's an interesting take, to be sure.

The Mistake of Teaching That America Was Sparsely Populated by Primitives

This last point is so obvious that by now it hardly needs mentioning, but to round things off, we need to at least note that for many years it was assumed that America was a sparsely populated, wide-open country when the Europeans descended upon it.

Nothing could be further from the truth. As Charles Mann abundantly proved in his 2005 book, *1491: New Revelations of the Americas before Columbus*, the Americas, from Canada to the tip of South America, was a place of bustling

A reconstruction of one of the Mound cultures in southern Illinois reveals that the pre-Columbian peoples of the Americas were quite sophisticated, and perhaps, in some ways, even more sophisticated than the Europeans who invaded their lands.

activity. Recent revelations prove beyond the shadow of a doubt that not even the Amazon was a virgin wilderness. In the last decade, discoveries there point to a thriving civilization that managed the Amazon Rain Forest to produce what we know today.

The reason native populations seemed to be sparse was that Europeans, from New England to Florida and from Mexico to California, happened to invade in force at precisely the time when disease and slavery raids had decimated as much as 80% of the populations that once lived on the land. When New England pilgrims reported cleared forests with no underbrush and fields ready for planting, it was because only a few years before, the natives had been farming this land and had been for a few thousand years. The same is true for Florida, the Mississippi River system, the western plains, and so on and so on.

The people weren't primitive. If anything, they were more sophisticated than many of the ignorant, bigoted fools who shot them on sight and hunted them nearly to extinction before the government took over the task with their organized and efficient armed forces.

From New England to the Rocky Mountains the story is told over and over. If the Indians hadn't taught the Europeans how to survive, they never would have made it. In many ways, we owe our American "civilized" success to Native Americans, even if we repaid their generosity with a bloodbath.

The problem of Göbekli Tepe puts traditional theories about Asian civilization in the east to the test. The problem of the Americas puts traditional theories in the western hemisphere to the test. The "problem" is this. No matter how far back in time we go to the "first" civilization, there always seems to be someone there already. Who really came first?

We've already considered the possibility of an Earth-based, parent civilization that might have existed during the Ice Age and before, but what if we're looking in the wrong place? What if civilization is a product not of human contrivance after all, but of alien intervention? What if the stars above hold the secret? It's time to lift our eyes to the skies.

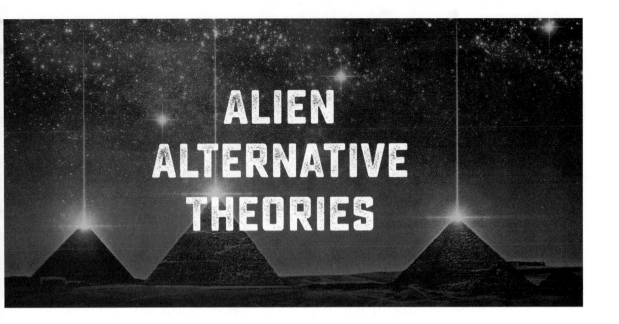

ALIEN ALTERNATIVE THEORIES

Is it possible that modern civilization is really a result of alien manipulation?

Be careful, here. Take it from one who has been a doubter his whole life. It's all too easy to scoff at the possibility because it seems so radical, so far-out, that you first form your opinion and then start to muster your facts. Most people who reject even the possibility of alien intervention do so out of preconceived prejudice, not rational thought processes. I did it myself for years. "You'll never convince me ..." is a very common statement.

I once found myself laughing at Neil deGrasse Tyson, a man whom I respect very much, for falling into this trap. During a TV interview he had rejected the notion of God because he couldn't, in effect, place God under a microscope and examine the evidence. "Give me something to measure," he said.

That was all well and good. I didn't agree with him but I respected his right to his own beliefs, but only a few minutes later he was seriously considering the possibility that we live in a digitally created universe that is the product of some future hacker playing with his quantum computer.

The hypocrisy seemed so obvious to me that for a moment I thought Neil must have been kidding. Then I realized he wasn't. Why the concept of a future hacker was plausible, while the concept of a supernatural being was not, was obviously a matter of preconceived prejudice, but Neil seemed oblivious to it. It reminded me of a bumper stick I once saw: "Thank God I'm an atheist."

Before you rush to judgment, either for or against the idea of alien intervention, try to put your prejudices and faith statements aside for a minute. The universe is a big place and it has been around for a long time. We've already sent probes out into space and walked on the moon. It won't be long before we visit an actual planet in person, as soon as we follow up on the Mars probes we've already sent. Why should any alien civilizations be any different than us?

Let's examine a few places that have so far defied our every explanation, along with a few others that remain mysterious. What we find may surprise us. Let's conduct a search to inquire whether there might be a grand plan to usher in civilization at work here on Planet Earth, to which we have so far remained oblivious.

A GRAND PLAN

If an alien civilization evolves to the point where it can learn how to travel among the stars, the immense distances involved would almost certainly preclude staying in any one place for very long. They would probably want, however, to leave calling cards behind to be discovered when local civilizations arrive at a propitious point in their evolutionary history. These would be more than "Kilroy was here"-type messages. This was the central plot device of Stanley Kubrick's 1968 film, *2001: A Space Odyssey*. It was also the theme of the *Star Trek: The Next Generation*, episode called "The Chase." Whether on the moon or a nearby planet such as Mars, explorers of the cosmos would want to let future folks in the neighborhood know who they were and what they were like, perhaps even seeding foreign worlds with their DNA.

Why do we think this? Because that's exactly what we have already done.

In 1977, when NASA rocketed the Voyager spacecraft toward the heavens, it carried what is called the Golden Record, which consisted of 115 images and a large variety of natural Earth sounds, such as surf, wind, thunder, birds, and whales. It also was etched with musical selections and greetings from Earth spoken by people in 55 languages, along with a printed message from both President Jimmy Carter and U.N. secretary-general Kurt Waldheim.

Carl Sagan himself explained why: "The spacecraft will be encountered and the record played only if there are advanced space-faring civilizations in interstellar space."

It's designed to be played at sixteen and two-thirds revolutions per minute, and

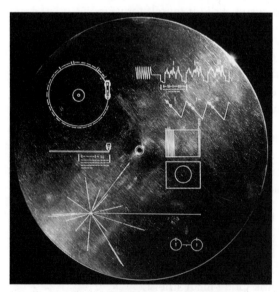

The Golden Record, which included "Sounds of Earth" for outer space listeners, was carried by the Voyager spacecraft that was launched in 1977.

comes equipped with a cartridge, needle, and pictured instructions. (One can only hope that if it ever is discovered the aliens won't decide they shouldn't waste time with a civilization that hadn't even invented digital CDs yet.)

THE "FACE" ON MARS

This brings us to the subject of aliens in the 'hood. Our first site may prove counterproductive because it almost certainly has been exposed as an optical illusion, but it illustrates our notion of a "Grand Plan" at work in the cosmos.

In 1976, the Viking 1 Orbiter took a picture of Mars that seemed, at first view, to reveal such an anomaly. It appeared to show a human face, built on the landscape.

Once the picture was released to the public, it immediately provoked a whole host of speculation. Could an ancient alien civilization have visited Mars, and possibly Earth, in the distant past, recognized right away that Earth would someday produce intelligent life (some would argue that this hasn't happened yet), and left this calling card to be viewed only when human beings had evolved sufficiently to begin space exploration? Does that explain why one of the Nazca line drawings, which we will consider next, resembles a human being waving at the camera in greeting? Do aliens look much like we do? And, if so, is that in itself proof that we are descended from them?

It certainly sounds like an intriguing idea. The phenomenon produced a plethora of books and videos, and true believers were positive this was the case. The "face" is nearly two miles long in a region called Cydonia, situated right in a geographical area that marks the border line between the smooth plains of the Martian north and the cratered, rugged terrain in the south. Scientists derided the whole idea that it was made by sentient beings, but the alien enthusiasts wouldn't buy it. In the minds of real ufologists, any government that covered up what was being studied in Area 51 simply couldn't be trusted.

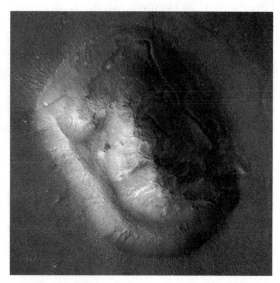

In 2001, NASA's Mars Global Surveyor, using a high-resolution camera, went back to revisit the site. Unfortunately, the new pictures showed the whole "face" area to be an optical illusion, caused by fuzzy resolutions and shifting shadows in the original images. There was no face. Just another typical Martian landscape.

This "face on Mars," first photographed by Viking I in 1976, was later proved to be an optical illusion.

Conspiracy theorists, of course, claimed that the new images were doctored, but much of the steam had gone out of their cause. Some even began to admit that we might have really landed on the moon after all, but that's just the way conspiracy theory works.

(My favorite story about the whole matter of such true believers goes like this: A dyed-in-the-wool conspiracy theorist once died and went to heaven, where he was greeted by none other the Almighty. He was told that to honor the occasion he was allowed to ask one question that would be immediately answered.

"Who killed Kennedy?" asked the newly inducted theorist.

"Lee Harvey Oswald, acting alone," replied God.

"Wow!" said the conspiracy theorist." This goes higher than I thought!")

At any rate, you don't have to subscribe to outlandish theories to recognize a simple truth. At some point in the far reaches of space, NASA's Voyager could be overtaken by a distant civilization on a faraway planet. That was the whole purpose of sending it out in the first place. What if it soft-landed in a faraway ocean? The entities on that planet could easily discover it floating far out to sea, learn how to follow the directions, listen to the recording, and have proof positive that we exist, somewhere out among "their" stars. *We* would be considered the ancient aliens. Maybe their government, out of fear of invasion or some such thing, would decide to hide the information until they felt their people were ready to receive it, but perhaps a group of *their* true believers would discover the cover-up and be branded as kooks and banished to the fringe.

Admit it. It could easily happen. We would be the instigators, and all because we produced our "Golden Record."

If it could happen, maybe it already has, and countless times. These are the feelings invoked by the so-called "face" on Mars. We need to open our minds to such possibilities, rather than ostracize those who give them voice. Theirs may be the hope that propels us into the future.

THE NAZCA LINES

Speaking of visitors from space, we come next to the famous Nazca Lines. They first came to real public attention when Erich von Däniken wrote about them in his 1968 book, *Chariots of the Gods?*, but they had been recognized in the 1920s, when commercial air travel was introduced between Lima and the southern Peruvian city of Arequipa.

Stephen S. Hall wrote an article about them called "Spirits in the Sand" in the March 2010 *National Geographic Magazine:*

The Nazca lines have puzzled archaeologists, anthropologists, and anyone fascinated by ancient cultures in the Americas. For just as long, waves of scientists—and amateurs—have inflicted various interpretations on the lines, as if they were the world's largest set of Rorschach inkblots. At one time or another, they have been explained as Inca roads, irrigation plans, images to be appreciated from primitive hot-air balloons, and, most laughably, landing strips for alien spacecraft.

Whatever people say about these lines, and both defenders and adherents are legion, the fact remains that the lines, which depict unmistakable images of animals, birds, human beings, and other figures, were not noticed by anyone until the advent of air transportation. In other words, they were meant to be seen from the air. Indeed, it is only from the air that they can really be made out at all. There are no towers you can climb or nearby mountaintop refuges where a person can stand and take in the whole panorama. You have to fly over them to really see them.

This raises suspicions and constitutes a certain kind of evidence. It's not the kind of evidence you can dissect and put under a test tube, but it *is* evidence.

Aside from that, the lines are "puzzling." Even the professionals admit that.

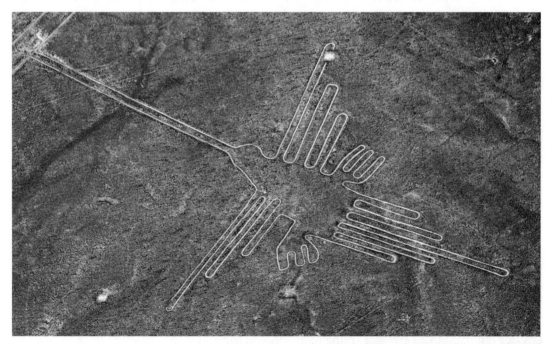

When viewed from the air, these lines made in the landscape at Nazca look like a hummingbird. Why would someone create this and many other drawings that could only be seen properly from high above the ground? The scientific community is still divided on this question.

Hall dismisses any and all opinions, and he immediately resorts to disparaging his opponents' character, rather than their facts, by introducing the idea of "Rorschach inkblots." That will always produce a laugh, but it won't contribute to a real argument. He says he believes them to be built by an Earth-bound people to be seen from the sky while, at the same time, dismissing as silly any thoughts of ancient air transport, especially of the alien variety. He calls them "laughable," which reveals a totally prejudiced ideology rather than a fact-formed theory.

In his defense, however, his article does show an appreciation for a spiritual vibe about the landscape:

> The parched desert and hillsides made an inviting canvas: By simply removing a layer of dark stones cluttering the ground, exposing the lighter sand beneath, the Nazca created markings that have endured for centuries in the dry climate. Archaeologists believe both the construction and maintenance of the lines were communal activities—"like building a cathedral."

But after surveying the scene he proceeds to draw his own conclusions, which completely ignore the whole view-from-above line of evidence. He dismisses it as unimportant. He thinks the whole Nazca area is an elaborate way to provide water to a parched desert land. The effigies are merely a way to placate various animistic deities who might be called on to help grow crops.

Every time I reread that article, I am astounded that a prestigious magazine such as *National Geographic* allowed such opinionated views, offered in the name of factual scholarship.

At the very end of the article, however, he returns to the mystical component:

The Nazca Lines are a captivating mystery. They imply a lost history and hidden truths from a mysterious people whose motivation is now ... lost in the mists of a forgotten time.

As my footsteps continued around the curves of the spiral, it occurred to me that one of the most important functions of the "mysterious" Nazca lines is no mystery at all. The geoglyphs surely provided a kinetic, ritualistic reminder to the Nazca people that their fate was tied to their environment—its natural beauty, its ephemeral abundance, and its life-threatening austerity. You can read their reverence for nature, in times of plenty and in times of desperate want, in every line and curve they scratched onto the desert floor. When your feet inhabit their sacred space, even for a brief and humbling moment, you can feel it.

This paragraph, I believe, redeems Hall's efforts. I am drawn to his beautiful prose. He at least felt the wonder.

The Nazca Lines are a captivating mystery. They imply a lost history and hidden truths from a mysterious people whose motivation is now, and perhaps forever, lost in the mists of a forgotten time.

Why did they do it? We don't know, but we have to at least allow for the fact that the ancient builders saw something, or someone, in the sky, and felt an urgent need to respond in the only way they knew how.

STONEHENGE

Stonehenge was designed and built by astrologers. For more than 40,000 years people had been recording times and seasons by carving on rocks and cave walls, but Stonehenge was different. I've said many times in many books that megalithic structures are usually said to be calendars so that early farmers would know when to plant their crops, but I just can't make myself buy that explanation. To me it doesn't stand up to even superficial scrutiny.

First of all, many of the megalithic structures scattered around the countryside throughout the world predate agriculture by, in some cases, thousands of years. As we have already seen, evidence at Göbekli Tepe in Turkey indicates that agriculture may have been invented to support workers who were already hard at work. If that is the case, astrology came before agriculture. That eliminates the idea of building megaliths to tell you when to plant crops.

Second, even if you did want to know when to plant, there are easier ways to deduce the correct seasons than to lug huge boulders all over the landscape. Frost doesn't pay attention to rocks.

We simply have no way of knowing what early astrologers were thinking. They might have believed the heavens caused events on Earth. They might just as well have believed the heavens merely *foretold* events on Earth, but the universal principal of "as above, so below" has influenced humans for thousands of years.

Despite what you see on TV, no one knows what the ancients believed, or how they pursued their craft. Everything we hear today is based mostly on guesswork, but whatever it was that inspired the building of Stonehenge, it was powerful, and it lasted for thousands of years.

The first postholes that marked the beginning of Stonehenge were dug during the Mesolithic period, sometime around 8000 B.C.E. Almost 5,000 years later, about 3100 B.C.E., the so-called "Stonehenge II" circular bank and ditch construction was built. Then, sometime around 2600 to 2400 B.C.E., came "Stonehenge III." For the first time, rocks were substituted for Earth and wood. The classic ring of Sarsen stones was constructed. Finally, around 2280 to 1930 B.C.E., "Stonehenge IV" was built over the course of a few hundred years. The stone masters put the final trilithons in place around 1066 B.C.E.

Think about those dates. From start to finish, Stonehenge took almost 7,000 years to build. To put that into perspective, Christianity is only 2,000 years old. Hindus believe the Vedas were written a little more than 3,000 years ago. Judaism goes back some 5,000 years, at most. Agriculture, if you choose to believe the experts, is only 6,000 years old.

What could have possibly been so important to these people that, off and on over a period of 7,000 years, they felt motivated to labor hard and long to construct the monument that still stands on the Salisbury Plain?

Is it any wonder that many people believe the initial impulse had to come from the heavens, or the experience of receiving aliens from the skies? I'm not saying that alien technology was employed. We seem to have a pretty good idea about how and when the monument was built, but why? What was the inspiration? That's the question.

Some of the rocks weigh fifty tons and came from all the way over in Wales. That's some impressive motivation. That's why Swiss author Erich von Däniken once suggested it was a model of the solar system, or perhaps served as an alien landing pad.

Of course, the landing pad theory never caught on. It just doesn't fit with the design, but that's no more unbelievable than the notion that all it did was serve as a ceremonial function.

Stonehenge, the ancient structure in England that is famous worldwide, was constructed over a period of seven thousand years. It clearly demonstrates that its architects understood the movement of the sun to mark the seasons, but what is really puzzling is how they moved huge blocks of stone from as far away as Wales.

What we're left with is this. Stonehenge has too many astronomical alignments to rule out that it somehow, in some way or another, sought to tie the heavens to the Earth. It was built by a civilization of astronomers, but what did they see in the "heavens" that prompted the initial work and then inspired the people to continue for so long? Did they remember, deep in the recesses of their consciousness, visitors from the sky who, perhaps, remained with them for a time? Was this the inspiration that motivated them for so long?

Who knows, really? But it's as good as any other theory. Stonehenge marks a significant stage in human civilization, but no one really knows what inspired that stage.

EGYPTIAN PYRAMIDS

The granddaddy at the source of all ancient alien theories probably has to do with the Pyramids of Giza. How could such enigmas have been constructed?

Our civilization made a choice long ago that in terms of technology we would go the way of levers, wedges, brute force, and mechanical advantage. That thinking is now so prevalent that we can't imagine anything else.

But the pyramids defy that kind of thinking. In the case of what stands on the Giza Plateau, such ideas just don't work.

It was built by a highly advanced civilization. There stands the proof, right before our eyes, that the ancients accomplished what we, even today, would be hard pressed to do. The technology remains a mystery, but the results of a technology we do not understand are certainly apparent. The proof is that no one today understands how the ancients accomplished the feat.

Usually Egyptologists insist that they used ramps composed of brick and Earth to build inclined planes that were pitched at a gradient of about one foot of rise for every ten feet of length, but that would have required a ramp almost 5,000 feet long and more than three times the amount of material than is used in the pyramid itself. There is absolutely no evidence of the disposal of such material to be found anywhere at all in the vicinity of Giza. Besides that, modern engineers have proved that such a ramp would collapse of its own weight unless it was built more massively than the Pyramid itself.

The Great Pyramid consists of tens of thousands of blocks weighing 15 tons or more and another few million blocks that weigh a few tons each. Egyptologists believe that a pyramid took about twenty years to build. If they were meant to be tombs built by living Pharaohs to house their remains, twenty years might even be stretching it a bit. Back in those days, there was no guarantee that a Pharaoh would live for twenty years in order to outlive the building of his final resting place.

Consider this. If builders worked ten hours a day, 365 days a year, they would have to place one block every two minutes in order to complete the pyramid within that time span. The tolerance between most of the blocks do not permit even a thin knife blade between them That's why the pyramids are still standing. Otherwise they would have collapsed under their own weight thousands of years ago. That's an impressive accomplishment.

But here's the thing, as I learned when I spoke to Egyptologists when I visited the pyramids some years ago. They told me that all this was done during only three months of work every year because the workers were needed in the fields the rest of the time. Given that time constraint, the schedule would now call for placing about four blocks every minute, or some 240 every hour.

A team from *Discovery* magazine once conducted an experiment in which they "proved" that by combining just the right amount of water and sand, they could create a slippery slope over which they could move big blocks of stone "quite easily," in their words.

But building a pyramid involves a lot more than simply moving big blocks of stone. And even if that were all there was to it, a "slippery slope" works both ways. It goes uphill and downhill. On the level, sand and water might work, as it did for the *Discovery* crew, but I would not choose to be the worker who was stationed downhill from a mega-ton block, especially if I was working fifty feet up a ramp.

Could the pyramids of Egypt have been built with blood, sweat, tears, and a basic knowledge of wheels and levers, or did the ancients have access to more sophisticated technologies?

But now, assume you have the stone way up high and manage to put it in place next to its neighbor. You still have to wiggle it into place. Down on the level you can use a lot of men, but there are only so many people who will fit around a pyramid stone on only three sides. How can so few workers move such a big block so closely into place that you can't fit a piece of paper between it and its companion block?

Once again, we're talking about ideologies. There are those who cannot believe the early builders in Egypt had access to any technology other than what we now understand. As is usually the case, those whose minds are made up attack their opponents with disparaging arguments that defy logic.

Articles abound that purport to "solve" the mystery about how the pyramids were built, but this one, published in a Cornell University journal, best sums up the whole thing:

> The only mystery surrounding the pyramids is why people still believe their origin is a mystery. Many people, misled by mystery-mongering books, web sites, and TV shows, believe that the pyramids are a classic unexplained mystery. There are several ways that heavy blocks could have been added to the top. Side ramps made of Earth or wood could have been built along the sides of the pyramids, or the workers might have simply built an Earthen ramp against one side and dragged the blocks up on logs.

There is absolutely no archeological evidence of any of these hypothetical "side ramps made of Earth or wood." There is no dumping ground where the supposed building material was discarded. There is no mention of any of these methods in any early records, but despite this absence of evidence, supposed scholars insist the early builders used methods known to us today, even though none of those methods will work.

To be fair, Egyptologists spend a lot of time dealing with many theories generated on social media by fringe groups. Maybe I shouldn't be too hard on them, but the fact remains that the builders must have had different technologies than we can imagine. They had to. None of our ideas stand the test of experimentation. Any other conclusion won't stand up to scrutiny.

Does that mean they were built by technologies learned from ancient aliens?

No.

But it doesn't mean they weren't, either. Until we discover the answer, one way or another, maybe we need to be a little more open minded when it comes to explaining the work of those who were there at the beginning of our modern civilization.

Sacsayhuamán and Beyond

Was Sacsayhuamán, a fortress outside the Inca capitol of Cusco in the Peruvian Andes, built by ancient aliens?

Probably not, but that guess is as good as any. Constructed of interlocking blocks that weigh up to 360 tons each, quarried as many as 20 miles (32 kilometers) away, transported to the site and then fitted together with what can only be called laser-like precision, no one knows how the feat could have been accomplished without a technology we cannot begin to duplicate today.

And Sacsayhuamán isn't the only such example. Similar structures are found throughout the Inca Empire, each more intriguing than the last. In

Visitors are dwarfed by the massive stone blocks of Sacsayhuamán in Peru. Many of these quaried rocks weigh over three hundred tons and were transported a distance of twenty miles.

Cusco, for instance, placed in a wall of the city you can find a stone that consists of 12 separate angles. A recent discovery of what might have been a rope-and-lever type transporting system made archeologists breathe a sigh of relief and declare the problem solved, but that didn't begin to answer the myriad questions relating to the whole problem of precision, accuracy, lifting, and fitting. And it didn't even attempt to answer the question "why?"

The only reason scholars are reluctant to consider alien intervention with an ancient civilization, or even a transfer of technology, is because of preconceived prejudice. They don't believe in aliens, period.

That's understandable, but as that most reasonable of fictional detectives, Sherlock Holmes, used to say: "When you have eliminated the impossible, whatever remains, however improbable, must be the truth."

That's a good statement to keep in mind, especially since the seemingly impossible work at Sacsayhuamán, Ollantaytambo, Machu Picchu, Tiahuanaco, Puma Punku, and other sites in the Americas are duplicated around the world.

We've already looked at Stonehenge and Egypt. To that list we can add Easter Island and Baalbek. These structures all exhibit signs of engineering skills that should not have been possible in such ancient times with only the tools and knowledge that orthodox academics insist were available to them back then. The material they were working with was extremely hard. Precise cuts on stone such as granite are impossible for us to approach unless we employ very sophisticated power tools. The methods used to lift such gigantic blocks into place are unknown to us. There is not even a hint in the archeological record that they used leverage and power techniques known to us today.

Standard cranes used in construction these days can handle only about 20 tons. There are presently, in the United States, where I live, two cranes in the entire country capable of lifting 200 tons.

Some of the blocks discovered at Baalbek in Lebanon weigh 800 tons. The largest, discovered in a nearby quarry, is considered to be the biggest stone block ever cut and shaped by anyone, anywhere, ever. It weighs 1,200 tons. That's as heavy as six modern locomotives. How did they ever cut and shape it, let alone expect to move it? It was prepared as long as 12,000 years ago. What were they thinking?

The problem compounds exponentially when we turn to Siberia. In 2014, in the mountains of Gornaya Shoria, Georgy Sidorov photographed what he called "super megaliths" thought to be 3,000 to 4,000 tons. Associated with these megaliths was another strange phenomenon. Compasses in the area swing away from the megaliths. Some kind of negative geomagnetic field exists in their vicinity. Can it be somehow associated with antigravity technologies?

Scientists shake their heads and say, "We just don't know."

But that doesn't cut it. It's okay not to know. That's what drives the scientific method. Curiosity is a wonderful thing. The search for knowledge is a noble pursuit, but in the absence of evidence to eliminate any possibilities based solely on preconceived prejudices it is not scientific.

Most scientists will agree that there is a good possibility of alien life existing out there in the cosmos. All will agree that we have already taken the first steps to explore the universe ourselves. What is so foreign and unacceptable about taking the next logical step and asking if we have been visited in the remote past?

THE GRAND PLAN SUMMARY

When we put all this together, a possible Grand Plan of exploration by unknown extraterrestrial parties that might have contributed to the beginning of our civilization begins to take shape.

Imagine you are an alien astronaut on a mission of discovery. If your journey takes you into an inhabited corner of the cosmos, your first step will probably be to set up

Most scientists will agree that there is a good possibility of alien life existing out there in the cosmos.

a base nearby, such as Mars in relationship to Earth, or even the moon, and observe for a while. You don't know what kind of biological diseases you might carry with you that could infect your new discovery. You don't know if they could infect you.

It will take time, but once you do establish first contact, the results will be predictable. The locals are, of course, more primitive than you. Otherwise they would have discovered you first. Having seen you, and experienced your superior abilities, they may view you as gods. You might spark a whole new religion. Indeed, they might even invent religion as a result of your presence among them. They will want to signal you using such things as Nazca lines. They may build monolithic structures in your honor, just as we build cathedrals to honor a "God" who walked among us 2,000 years ago. They may search the heavens to initiate evidence of your return. They may invent a mythology to explain your presence.

Eventually this whole system of beliefs will be watered down by time, diluted, so to speak, just as many religions in practice today dilute the message of their founders and develop ideologies quite removed from the original intention of those who first inspired them.

But the Grand Plan will still be intact. Thousands of years after first contact, those who followed the original religion will still await your return, just as Christians believe Jesus Christ will return in the flesh.

You may have left a calling card, fully intending to return someday to see what has happened on that planet you visited once, long ago. What will you find?

All this seems farfetched to those who refuse to allow themselves to believe that such a thing might be possible, but is it so farfetched, really?

If a race of humanoid beings had existed on the Moon, for instance, they would even now be anxiously awaiting our return. We haven't been back to visit for years since we first set foot there. We've been busy doing other things, but they wouldn't know that. They'd be wondering what they did wrong to cause us to abandon them.

When you come right down to it, it's only a matter of distance. The moon is a lot closer than a faraway galaxy, and we can't imagine a way around the distance problem, but just because we can't imagine one doesn't mean it's not possible.

Meanwhile, the mysterious structures that defy logic and tantalize our minds because we can't imagine how a so-called "primitive" people could have built them might be fulfilling their purpose. One of those purposes could have been to spur us on to question how they got there. Their builders might be suggesting to us that we, too, are capable of miraculous, magical things.

What if aliens came to Earth long ago and were mistaken for gods before leaving the planet again? The memory of them could easily turn into legends and myths, resulting in interesting imagery such as these guardian statues protecting a village in Tamilnadu, India.

But to deny the very existence of those who could possibly have meant to propel us forward is to defeat their very purpose. Maybe we need to at least keep open the possibility that bigger things are afoot than we care to realize.

DISSENSION IN THE RANKS OF THE GODS

Let's go even further out on a limb, although this is certainly not foreign to many people today who attend places of worship every weekend. What if alien intervention took place and is now remembered in the vocabulary of modern religion? What if the story of civilization is the story of a god or gods driving us forward? Is it a coincidence that the Bible begins with life in a garden and concludes in a great city? This alone hints that the growth of civilization is part of a divine story.

We live in a world of dualism. We see life in terms of hot and cold, right and wrong, up and down, fast and slow. Our news reporters promise to give us "both sides of the story," as if stories just had two sides. Our choices almost always seem to break down into two components—this or that.

Robert Frost, in his poem, "The Road Not Taken," wrote of "two roads [that] diverged in a yellow wood…. I took the one less traveled by…. And that has made all the difference."

Our ancestors were certainly sophisticated enough to understand this dualistic ideology, and they invented a wide-ranging mythology to explain it. Usually that mythology told of competing gods who trapped the human race in the middle of their feud. One god was "good," the other "bad."

Although this is an ancient concept, going back all the way to the Chinese teachings about Yin and Yang that became the basis for the *Dao* (the Way), the Persian Zoroaster, also called Zarathustra, was the first to personalize it in what was to become the basis for westernized religion. His teaching became known as Zoroastrianism. Thirty-five hundred years ago, Zoroaster taught that a good god, named Ahura Mazda, created the world. He was opposed by Angra Mainyu, the evil god.

The two were not considered to be equal. While one represented positive energy, which created the world, the other personified negative energy, which sought to destroy it.

Ahura Mazda, so the teaching goes, created everything—even Angra Mainyu, who turned to evil of his own accord. Good is thus stronger than evil. This concept was passed on down to Judaism, Christianity, and Islam.

Creative energy causes a magnificent tree to grow. Negative energy seeks to destroy it. Life and death. Day and night. Growth and destruction. Up and down. Neither can be understood without the other. They are at war, but ultimately good will triumph in the end.

When religions such as Zoroastrianism separated from natural philosophy, they added another level. They declared that the battle is constantly being fought in the natural world around us, but it is also being fought in the moral world, the world of the spirit. Love and hate. Joy and misery. Peace and war. Human beings have a choice. And that choice goes on forever.

What if, however, the religious mythology is more than a poetic position? What if there really *are* opposing "gods" beyond our understanding who are fighting it out on planet Earth? The vast majority of people alive today follow religious systems that preach this very thing.

God and the devil. Good and bad. Right and wrong. The battle is raging.

With this in mind, let's review the three main monotheistic religions practiced today to see how they view the whole situation. If these stories are familiar to you, try to envision them, for a minute, as if God and the Devil are actual alien entities.

JUDAISM

Zoroastrianism was hugely popular in Persia as far back as 600 B.C.E. During that time in history much of the Jewish nation, having been taken captive by Nebuchadnezzar in 586 B.C.E. and transported en masse back to Babylon, were living under Persian influence. Before the captivity, the Jewish Bible, now known to Christians and Muslims as the Old Testament, had little to say about the cosmic, moral reality of Dualism. The Psalmists, for instance, celebrated the fact that "Our god is a great god, and a great king above all gods" (Psalm 95:3). That's not dualistic monotheism, by any means. That sentiment recognizes one god among many, but after the Jews returned from their captivity in Persia to rebuild Jerusalem, they were solidly monotheistic—believers in a good God who is simply tolerating, for a time, a bad devil.

The symbol for Zoroastrianism is seen here on a column in Persepolis, Iran. Zoroastrianism is an early monotheistic religion that has its roots in ancient Persia.

God was understood to be the ultimate victor and will win the final battle. Until then, humans are forced to contend with a malicious, evil, personal, supernatural force called the Devil, and his infamous followers, called demons. That certainly hints at Zoroastrianism influence.

According to the Hebrew scriptures, the story goes like this.

In the beginning, God created a class of supernatural beings we now call angels (from the Greek *angelos*, or "messengers"). They were divided into classes and ranks called archangels, cherubim, principalities, powers, and so forth, but their purpose, apparently, was to serve God.

According to the book of Isaiah, chapter 14, the leader of this heavenly force was called Lucifer, the "son of the morning." Unfortunately, he committed the sin of hubris. He wanted to be like God.

Lucifer couldn't see the future. He didn't understand the nature of ego. He didn't understand how ego separates an individual from the Source. He couldn't know that "I" was a word that denotes separation, division, and, eventually, downfall. He didn't understand that there is no "I" in "team." When he employed that word, he "fell" from grace.

Here's how the Bible tells the story. Remember that in this reading we're going to picture God and the Devil as two ancient aliens.

We begin in Isaiah 7:14, as God talks directly to Satan:

How you have fallen from heaven, morning star, son of the dawn! You have been cast down to the Earth, you who once laid low the nations!

A few pages later, in Isaiah 14, Lucifer employs the "I" word five times:

"I will ascend to the heavens; I will raise my throne above the stars of God. I will sit on the mount of assembly, in the far reaches of the north. I will ascend above the tops of the clouds; I will make myself like the Most High."

• Now we move to Ezekiel 28:11–19. Here God is talking to the "King of Tyre," traditionally interpreted as being a metaphor for Satan, but the way we are reading these passages, through ancient alien lenses, Tyre could actually be the literal city that was near Baalbek, Lebanon, home of the Canaanites/Phoenicians and thought to be home to alien entities in ancient times. One of them could have been, quite literally, the entity formerly known as Lucifer, in his guise as the "king" of Tyre:

Thus says the Lord GOD: You were the signet of perfection, full of wisdom and perfect in beauty. You were in Eden, the garden of God; every precious stone was your covering, carnelian, chrysolite, and moonstone, beryl, onyx, and jasper, sapphire, turquoise, and emerald; and worked in gold were your settings and your engravings. On the day that you were created they were prepared. With an anointed cherub as guardian I placed you; you were on the holy mountain of God; you walked among the stones of fire. You were blameless in your ways from the day that you were created, until iniquity was found in you. In the abundance of your trade you were filled with violence, and you sinned; so I cast you as a profane thing from the mountain of God, and the guardian cherub drove you out from among the stones of fire. Your heart was proud because of your beauty; you corrupted your wisdom for the sake of your splendor. I cast you to the ground; I exposed you before kings, to feast their eyes on you. By the multitude of your iniquities, in the unrighteousness of your trade, you profaned your sanctuaries. So I brought out fire from within you; it consumed you, and I turned you to ashes on the Earth in the sight of all who saw you. All who know you among the peoples are appalled at you; you have come to a dreadful end and shall be no more forever.

Notice a few really interesting sentences:

• *You were in Eden, the garden of God:* One location considered to be a possible location for the biblical Eden is in the mountains north of Göbekli Tepe, the first temple built by our civilization. That marks the location of the "four rivers" mentioned in the book of Genesis.

- *You were on the holy mountain of God:* The mountain of Ararat, said to be where Noah landed his ark, is also in this area, north and east Göbekli Tepe.

- *I cast you as a profane thing from the mountain of God:* When Cain was cast out of Eden he went out and "built a city." That city, according to some, was the ancient city of Baalbek, home to the god Baal, who, according to many scholars, was also the identity of Lucifer. Lucifer is the *morning star, son of the dawn,* and is thus associated with the planet Venus, worshipped at Baalbek. According to this interpretation, when Cain was cast out of the camp of the "good" god, he went and joined forces with the "bad" one.

We could speculate further, of course, and pull out more references. For an in-depth study of the relationship between Eden and Baalbek I refer you to my book *Lost Civilizations*, where I covered the topic in a lot more detail, but all this indicates a close parallel to Sumerian texts that describe the "battle"

A Romanian artist's view of Old Scratch and his Earthbound followers—angels that became demons—who had a literal falling out with God.

between Enki and Enlil that purportedly took place just downstream and south from this very location. It also seems to imply that the battle continued throughout the history of the Old Testament because thousands of years later, the Jews of Jehovah were still battling the followers of Baal over the possession of the souls of the people.

At any rate, Lucifer was thus banished to Earth where his evil could be contained to one planet in the universe. With him came a third of the angels, henceforth called demons. It's important to remember that they don't reign in Hell. They reign on Earth. Hell is their punishment, not their dwelling place. If that's the case, we who now live on Earth are really living within the confines of Lucifer's prison. Lucifer became the *Satan*, literally, the "deceiver" and the "accuser of the brethren."

According to this interpretation of Jewish scripture, and, by extension, Sumerian and Zoroastrian theology as well, Earthly duality and its resulting hardship is a result of cosmic dissension among the gods. And we are caught right in the middle of it.

CHRISTIANITY

The Christian version of this story continues on with a further interpretation. It, too, views the Earth as an arena wherein God and the devil are fighting it out, but its central focus now turns to God, who enters personally into the fray.

After centuries of trying, it became obvious that humans were unable to win a lasting victory by themselves. They needed divine assistance. So the good god, in the form of Jesus the Christ, came to Earth to take upon himself the penalty for human sin. In doing so he released humanity from a death sentence and freed them for all eternity.

If this is read according to the ancient alien interpretation we began when we looked at Judaism, Jesus becomes an emissary of the off-planet entity known as Jehovah, which is just one of many names attributed to him. He is born a hybrid, recalling the days in Old Testament times when "the sons of God" mated with the "daughters of men."

Like those earlier Old Testament hybrids, he was, in the words of Genesis 6, "a mighty man of old, a hero of renown." His life story is full of attributed "miracles" that are similar in nature to the works of "gods" and shamans in almost every culture in the world.

When his allotted time on Earth ended in seeming defeat with a terrible murder, a victim of the powers that had long since taken over the established civilization, he "ascended in the clouds" after promising to someday return. This is a familiar story and is repeated in various mythologies all around the Earth.

When you put it that way, Christianity takes on a whole different meaning. As presently interpreted by traditional Christians, however, the basic idea behind Christianity of all types is this.

Picture yourself arrested for speeding. You are brought before a judge who asks one question: "Are you guilty?"

"Yes," you reply, "I knowingly and willfully broke the law. I'm sorry. I wish I hadn't done it, but I did."

The judge tells you that being sorry isn't enough. You broke the law and the penalty must be paid. That's the way the system works. He then fines you $100.

"I don't have $100. I am unable to pay the fine," you respond.

"That doesn't matter," declares the judge. "This is a nation of law and you are guilty of breaking it. You are hereby sentenced to jail."

But before the bailiff takes you down to the dungeons, the judge does a significant thing. He takes off his robe, the symbol of his power and authority. He then steps out from behind his high bench and walks down to stand beside you, where he reaches into his pocket, pulls out $100, and pays your fine himself.

> In Jewish theology the substitute was an animal sacrifice, often a lamb. Christianity substituted the son of God—the "lamb" of God transferred to "the bread of the covenant."

The law has been satisfied. You were guilty of breaking it but your penalty has been paid by the very judge who pointed out your fatal flaw. He has stepped down from his world, the superior world of the high bench, and steps into yours, the world of the fatal flaw—the planet Earth. You are free to go and, hopefully, sin no more. You exit the courtroom singing "Amazing grace, how sweet the sound that saved a wretch like me."

This doctrine is called *substitutionary atonement*. Human sins are "atoned for" by a substitute. In English the word breaks down to "at-one-ment"—being at one, or joined to, God.

This is typical of the mythological motif called "the sacrifice of the god for humanity." In these stories, a god willingly offers his life. Often it is cut into pieces and those pieces are consumed by the faithful in order to restore them to life. In Christian symbolism this is accomplished whenever the Mass, or Holy Communion, is accompanied by words, "This is my body, broken for you."

In Jewish theology the substitute was an animal sacrifice, often a lamb. Christianity substituted the son of God—the "lamb" of God transferred to "the bread of the covenant." But the meaning is exactly the same. It pictures a struggle between a good and evil god, played out here on Earth, with the fate of humanity as the final prize. In the end, the good God wins by sacrificing himself.

The end of the battle is gloriously pictured in the final book of the Bible, the *Revelation of St. John:*

> And I heard a loud voice from the throne saying: "Behold, the dwelling place of God is with man, and He will live with them. They will be His people, and God Himself will be with them as their God.

> "He will wipe away every tear from their eyes, and there will be no more death or mourning or crying or pain, for the former things have passed away."

> And the One seated on the throne said, "Behold, I make all things new. Write this down, for these words are faithful and true."

In today's traditional Judaism and Christian circles, all this is usually understood to be metaphor, but it doesn't take a lot of imagination to read it through the eyes of an ancient alien conflict, complete with good gods and bad gods who live "in the heavens," played out on Earth by representatives from distant, or even parallel, realms, who share the common goal of wanting to "fill the Earth and subdue it."

All that is required is to read the familiar words through the same lenses we use to read other ancient texts that are not so much a part of our religious culture. To do so will certainly invite charges of blasphemy in many churches and synagogues, but that in itself is a form of suppression.

ISLAM

Muslims teach this same story but with an interesting twist. Although Christians and Jews teach that Satan was cast out of heaven because of his ego-centered desire to "be like God," Muslims believe that he had a much nobler intention than selfish ego.

In Islam, Iblis (the devil) is accompanied by creatures called Jinns. These spirits have free will and operate within human cultures, sometimes delivering good things such as are found in the famous "Three Wishes" of Aladdin's fairy tales, and sometimes, seemingly on a whim, causing all sorts of evil things to happen.

According to Muslim belief, in the New Testament book of 1 Corinthians, when Paul asked, "Do you not know that we (humans) will judge angels?" This bothered Iblis, but for different reasons than you might expect.

According to the Qur'an, Iblis loved God. He loved God so much that when God created Adam and then told all the angels to bow down before him, Iblis was presented with a horrible problem. How could he bow before anyone but his beloved God? Iblis' sin was, in effect, that he loved God too

A circa 1415 illustration from the *Annals of al-Tabari* shows Iblis refusing to bow before Adam even though God commands that he do so.

much to kneel before a lesser being such as a human. Thus, when he disobeyed God's command to worship a human, he was cast out of heaven.

How did Iblis console himself throughout eternity? He did it by remembering the last words that God, his beloved, said to him.

And what were those words? "Go to Hell!"

It's a tragic take on a familiar story.

GOOD GOD/EVIL GOD

Using Zoroastrian roots, we have traced the twists and turns of the story of good and bad "gods" and their interaction on planet Earth. This story is as old as the very first Sumerian texts. It's easy to forget that billions of people in the world believe this story is ongoing. They just don't recognize it when it is stripped from its holy-sounding, traditional, liturgical language, but the story of monotheism is the story of two ancient aliens, called God and Satan, among many other names, fighting it out for the souls of human beings. Human civilization stands in the apex of the battle.

Could it be true? Is there an actual entity called Satan or, more accurately, *the* Satan—*the* accuser? Or can the whole thing be filed under mythological representation of a philosophical speculation?

Remember that it didn't start with western monotheism. The same story is found in the very first literature of our civilization.

As we have already seen, according to Sumerian texts, Enlil, Enki, and the Anunnaki, besides being "watchers" and "holy ones," carried out all manner of activities on Earth. Sometimes they were thought to pick on innocent bystanders among the human population. It was thought that they had the ability to biologically mate with human women. In many texts the products of these unions were said to be "born of a virgin."

Their descendants sometimes caused illness. The priests of Sumer, called *Ashipu* (Sorcerers), were called upon to heal people who came down with *Gidim*, or "sickness demons." The Ashipu thus differed from regular doctors, who worked with more mundane medicines such as plant derivatives, salves, and ointments.

Shamanic cultures have long recognized the existence of evil spirits. Elaborate rituals were designed to protect shamanic practitioners from evil when they journeyed to other dimensions to learn the secrets of healing.

In other words, according to this interpretation of ancient alien theory, civilization is a response to humans banding together to live on a battlefield that is the playground for two competing ancient aliens. Their names are, in English, Jehovah or its many variants, and Satan, or its numerous permutations.

This view is not limited to western religious interpretations. It is universal in scope.

In January of 2015, Mark Miller, writing for *Ancient Origins* magazine, compiled a list of "gods" who were credited with creating the world. It was called: *The Awesome, Terrible, and Unknowable Creator Gods through History.* Here are a few of them, used by permission:

- Atum of Egypt: "The great he-she" and the "not-yet-Completed One who will attain completion." He was connected loosely with Ra, an important Egyptian god who was worshipped in Heliopolis. He was self-created, and then, through an act of masturbation, he created the goddess Tefnut and the god Shu. They are the ancestors of all the other gods.
- Marduk of Babylon: He was the god who sliced up the body of the terrible monster Tiamat, thus forming all of creation from her corpse.

- Awonawilona: the Zuni god who existed before the beginning and who contained the universe within his male and female self.

- Makroposopos: In Jewish Cabala, the Aged of the Aged, Unknown of the Unknown, Truth of all Truths, Form without Form, the Uncreated Uncreating. Joseph Campbell describes him in his book *The Hero with a Thousand Faces*. Campbell said Cabalists believe Makroposopos is the "I AM" of the Old Testament.

- El or Elohim: Worshipped by many people and still invoked today by Christians, Jews, and Muslims, El saw that the Earth was a shapeless, chaotic mass and divided the light from darkness, bringing the world and all that is in it into being.

- Kali Ma: The Dark Mother of Hinduism dwells in an ocean of her own blood. Still worshiped, she is goddess of creation, preservation, and destruction and has both terrible and benevolent aspects.

- Io-matua-te-kora: "Io the parentless" is one of several creators of the Polynesian people, whose creation stories began with *Te Kore*, which means "chaos," or the void. Then *Te Pō*, the night, and *Te Ao Mārama*, the world of light, come into being. According to the *Encyclopedia of New Zealand*: "There are numerous stages of *Te Kore*, *Te Pō* and *Te Ao Mārama* recorded in different *whakapapa* (genealogical tables) with each stage begetting the next. Sequences vary in different tribal retellings."

- Amma: The Dogon people still worship Amma, who created the egg from which hatched the twins who came forth as male and female, day and night, wet and dry, land beings and water beings, good and evil. According to the *Encyclopedia Britannica*: "The notion of a creator god named Amma, or Amen, is not unique to the Dogon, but can also

Kali Ma (or simply Kali) is the Hindu goddess who is worshipped both as a preserver of the good and a violent destroyer of evil. She is a fierce warrior adept at wielding a sword, scimitar, or trident.

be found in the religious traditions of other West African and North African groups."

- Bunjil of Australia: He formed rivers, trees, plants, and hills from the bare lands and then men from the clay. His brother Bat created women from mud in the depths of the water.

- Bumba of the Congo: A giant white god in human form who got a stomachache and vomited up the sun, moon, and stars. He got sick again and vomited up the living creatures—a leopard, a crested eagle, a crocodile, a small fish, a tortoise, a white heron, a beetle, a goat, and then humans.

- Kururumany of the Arawaks: A creator who created men and goodness. Kulmina created women. Christopher Columbus and his henchmen killed off the Arawak Indians with murder, slavery, and disease beginning in 1492 when the "conquistadors" came to Hispaniola and the New World.

- Luonnotar of Finland: She was all alone in the vast emptiness of space until she came down to the sea, where the wind caressed her bosom and the seas made her fertile. The great Roc visited her and made a nest upon her pelvis and laid eggs there, which made her aroused and excited, causing the eggs to spill out and break, the shells forming the Earth and sky. The yolks formed the sun, the whites the moon, the spotted fragments the stars, and the black fragments the clouds.

- Pangu of China: He hatched the universe from a cosmic egg.

- Earth Diver: This god was known to many people around the world. Often in animal form, he dove down into the first waters and brought up mud or Earth from which the world took shape.

- Vishnu: Loved by millions of Hindus today, he evolved from the primordial reality of *praktri* and then created the universe through austerities and meditation.

Admittedly, it's easy to simply pass off these stories as religious mythology, but to assume that all of them have no basis in fact, especially while holding on to our own religious beliefs, is to commit the terrible sin of the early Spanish conquistadors. "My God stories are historically true and yours are false!"

All these myths, although seemingly very different, have one thing in common. They all tell us that our march toward civilized modernity came about because of an alien, call it divine if you must, battle between good and evil. Are there forces, which exist beyond our sensory perceptions, at work in the universe? Are we on a journey that began in a garden and ends in a civilized city? Is the real story of civilization more complicated than we think?

Until more evidence is either found or released, each of us must decide for ourselves.

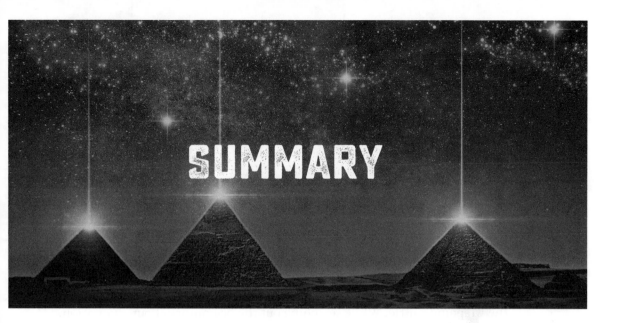

SUMMARY

Humankind's march to civilization is much more complicated than we are usually taught. Just for the fun of it, I keyed in a simple question to my Google search engine: "How did civilization begin?" The answers I found were all over the map, each putting forth their answer as if it was established fact, even though they all disagreed with each other. Here are a few excerpts of what I found:

- The Indus Valley civilization, also known as Harappan civilization, began 5,300 years ago. It flourished in areas that presently extend from Afghanistan to Pakistan and India. Indus Valley civilization is one of the three early civilizations of the Old World along the Egyptian and Mesopotamia civilizations.

- Mesopotamia is the site of the earliest developments of the Neolithic Revolution from around 10,000 B.C.E., with civilizations developing from 6,500 years ago.

- History, civilization, and writing all begin at the same time. That time is about 3100 B.C.E. In about 3200 B.C.E. the two earliest civilizations develop in the region where southwest Asia joins northeast Africa.

- A civilization is a complex human society that may have certain characteristics of cultural and technological development…. In many parts of the world, early civilizations formed when people began coming together in urban settlements.

There were many more entries, each as positive in its affirmations as the others. And therein lies the problem. The plain and simple truth seems to be that no one knows how civilization began, and where, or why, but each expert who studies the problem, probably without realizing it, forms an opinion based not so much on observable fact as preformed opinion. He or she then puts forth evidence that fits that opinion while suppressing evidence that does not.

It's not done purposefully. At least not always, but it is done, as we have seen from our simple Google search, regularly. What we are left with is that under the guise of science someone says, basically, "This is how it seems to me."

That's not science. That's opinion couched in scientific language.

There's nothing wrong with admitting that we don't know something, but there is something wrong with covering up uncomfortable or confusing evidence and then presenting your guesses as scientific fact, neatly tied up with string and presented in a clean package.

In this book I've been trying to untie some of the strings and mess up the wrapping a little. While searching out the beginnings of our civilization, we arrived at some of those "uncomfortable or confusing" pieces of evidence, the kind of evidence that has been suppressed for far too long.

In short, the evidence we have gathered from all over the world indicates a disturbing fact. No matter where we have looked, from Turkey to Mesopotamia, Egypt, the Americas, China, and beyond, every time we thought we were closing in on the "beginning," we have discovered that further back in time there were others. The civilizations credited with being "the first" all seem to have sprung into existence overnight. One day there were only a small group of hunter-gatherers, following the game and resources of their local environment. The next, they woke up and decided to build settlements and temples and establish elaborate rituals and mythology.

The question looms in the recesses of our minds, refusing to be ignored: Did they suddenly think up civilization on their own, or were they taught it by someone? And if so, whom? In other words, did they inherit their civilization, or did they invent it?

Someday we may come to discover that our ancestors accomplished the work of civilization all by themselves, but that day has not yet come. Too many questions remain unanswered. Too much evidence has been suppressed. The verdict, as even the most rudimentary research will reveal, is yet to be reached.

In this chapter we have pondered suppressed evidence found in the natural record and in the possibility of help from "outside," so to speak. Until we clarify the whole subject, we need to remain skeptical. If any possibility exists, no matter how remote it may seem, that we are part of a much bigger process—that we are being guided in some way, either from outside, above, or even in the code of our DNA—we need to be a little less dogmatic when it comes to offering our opinions as completed fact.

I was eleven years old when Sputnik was launched on October 4, 1957, marking the beginning of what we now often call the "space race." In my lifetime we have surrounded the planet with orbiting satellites of all kinds, come to depend on them for everything from communications to GPS coordinates, walked on the moon, sent a highly sophisticated Tonka truck to Mars, photographed the rings of Saturn and the moons of Jupiter, and even sent a "hello there" message out into the cosmos, hoping someone may someday find it.

That's quite a lot of progress, any way we look at it. And it all happened within one person's short lifetime.

Now consider this. The Earth is four and a half billion years old. That's an immense amount of time. It is theoretically possible that sentient life, maybe even human sentient life, could have risen to the point of civilization and disappeared back into the dust of time, leaving not a single trace. It is entirely possible, given the movement of plate tectonics, that the detritus of those civilizations now lay buried beneath desert sands, ocean waters, or even beneath the roots of majestic mountain ranges.

It's okay to believe that speculation about lost civilizations is wishful thinking. It's okay to not believe any of it. It's okay to remain doubtful, but it is not okay to completely rule it out and suppress evidence based on your own personal beliefs. That is not science. A lot of people in many fields of endeavor have gone to their graves, completely destroyed by "experts" who "knew better," only to be proven correct after they no longer lived to see their ideas justified. This is, to put it simply, wrong. The human race needs a good dose of humility. And soon.

With that in mind, let's move now to very real possibilities that we have touched on from time to time throughout this book. We may not be the first civilization to have arisen on Earth. We may not be the first pioneering species to explore a world-wide environment. We may not even be the first human species to develop and thrive. The life forms we are familiar with may have had origins in a fashion beyond our wildest imaginings. This may not even be the first and only universe ever to form.

All these are areas we have studied in the preceding pages. Now we will start exploring in greater depth. Much of what we find will involve speculation, but always speculation driven by evidence that now exists and is known to us, even though it might have been suppressed.

It's time to face the facts, put our egos aside for a few minutes, and take ourselves away from center stage, as if all of creation revolves around us. Maybe, just maybe, we are not the first.

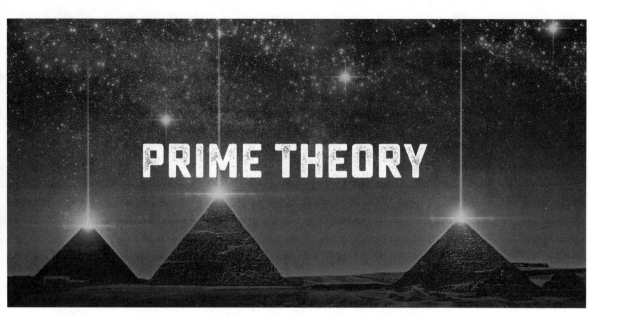

PRIME THEORY

A Purpose for Lost Civilizations

A few years ago I wrote a whole book about lost civilizations. I can't possibly condense almost five hundred pages into this one chapter, so I won't even try. For details, I again refer you to *Lost Civilizations*.

But the bottom line is this: Plenty of evidence is recorded in both stone and story, in the megaliths that dot landscapes around the world and mythologies that are universal in scope, that civilizations have come and gone on Earth for thousands, perhaps even millions, of years. It becomes apparent, when all the evidence is collected and researched, that we are merely one in a long line of civilizations that arise, occupy a brief moment in the sun, and then disappear. We are not the first. In all probability, we will not be the last either.

We don't know why this happens. We can guess, and we will, but the forces that bring about human destruction are many and varied, ranging from warfare to climate change, environmental disasters to population excess. There may even be hidden forces, either psychological or spiritual, of which we are not aware. We just don't know, but, as has often been said, those who don't understand their past are destined to repeat it. Even if our guesses are wrong, and they probably will be in many cases, such speculation is a good thing if it causes us to stop and think about what we're doing.

We may be in freefall when it comes to our future. We may be nearing the end of another period of Earth-based civilization. It is true that the end hasn't come yet, but we are now playing with toys that can destroy us and we might be closer to Armageddon than we care to admit.

Even a superficial study of history reveals that civilization has a dark side. Over and over again, the story is repeated. Greece, Rome, many European cultures, and, in our day, most western, privileged economies all tell the same story. Over time, a small group of people learn to game the system. They rise to the top and control the whole economy. The rich get richer and the poor become enslaved, either literally or economically and through the denial of access to resources.

The word "slaves" might not be popular, but when people are forced to work for the elite or lose their income and ability to buy what they need to survive, that's what they are. They are held in slavery by a power elite that controls the lives of the workers. Finally, the situation becomes so bad that the only recourse is revolution. Civilization falls into disorder and chaos. Eventually, it comes under the power of a dictator or king of some sort. Then it starts all over again from the bottom. It is an endlessly repeating loop.

How many times has this happened down through the years? We don't know. We see it occurring countless times in the last six thousand years or so, but there's no reason to think it hasn't happened before. What we call modern civilization might only be the latest incarnation of thousands, perhaps even millions, of years of rise and fall. It is very possible that this has been going on for far longer than we have imagined. The civilizations of our forgotten past might very well have fallen into such destructive chaos that they became lost to history. There is no empirical reason to think we are any different.

Slavery does not have to involve chains to be a form of servitude. These days, lack of economic opportunity, dead-end jobs, and endless bills with no decent wages can be just as enslaving.

Or perhaps, and this is our hope, maybe some previous civilizations have taken the road less traveled and fulfilled their destiny by *not* choosing to go the way of ruin. That, too, is a possibility.

Where have those civilizations gone? Why aren't they still amongst us?

Maybe they became, according to the words of the Bible, "heroes of old, men of renown—sons of God." Perhaps their reward was to walk among the stars and seed the galaxies with hope. This is probably a forlorn wish fulfillment, but hope is a good thing.

Is there any evidence for this fantasy?

Nothing that isn't flimsy or circumstantial. There are a few enigmatic artifacts and some mysterious mythologies, but any light in the darkness is a good thing. Wouldn't it be wonderful to think that someday, if we ever find life "out there," we will discover that it came from "right here"—that some ancient, Earth-based civilization once conquered its inner need for ego-driven economic fulfillment, chose differently than we have so far, arrived at a higher evolutionary plane, looked to the heavens, and then said, "First the moon, then the second star to the right and straight on until morning"?

This rather far-fetched scenario makes Earth a breeding ground for the cosmos. To make the concept real, think of it this way. We have already been to the moon and begun to venture out among the stars. Our journey is just beginning. If *we* can do it, maybe it's been done before.

Perhaps we have now hit upon the very reason civilizations exist. Are they breeding grounds designed to produce an advanced, spiritually grounded, advanced race of humans, created in the image of "the gods," who are destined to explore, inhabit, and find fulfillment amongst the stars?

In this section we're going to explore some of the myths and legends surrounding what will sound to some of you, perhaps most of you, like a flight of pure fancy. Our objective will not be to change anyone's mind. We will try to simply open them. If we can imagine it, it becomes possible.

Evidence seems to indicate that we have already begun the process of reaching out. We've been to the moon. We've sent a greeting out into space. All that remains is the part about "second star to the right and straight on until morning."

But you can't start out on this journey without civilization. A space program demands countless people with different gifts, skills, and abilities all working together, immense amounts of cooperation, economic resources, and, above all, unified vision. Those cannot develop without civilization's benefits. We return yet again to our civilization's first monument, the genesis of modernity, the place where it all began following the last ice age, Göbekli Tepe. There lay our roots.

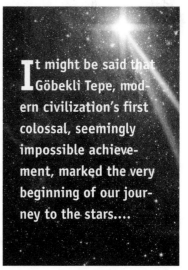

It might be said that Göbekli Tepe, modern civilization's first colossal, seemingly impossible achievement, marked the very beginning of our journey to the stars—a journey that is accelerating exponentially with each and every passing year. It combined invention, a unified common goal, hardship, a star-based vision, obstacles to overcome, mystery, cooperation, and spirituality.

It might be said that Göbekli Tepe, modern civilization's first colossal, seemingly impossible achievement, marked the very beginning of our journey to the stars....

Might those be the very reasons an earlier parent culture, advanced in the ways of civilization, chose this project to be the first undertaking to mark the birth of a new civilization? Did the early guides, their own civilization's path cut short by a wayward comet, see the project through to conclusion, secure in the knowledge that they had spawned a new beginning that would surely lead to a predictable outcome? Did they then bury the whole thing so that it would be discovered only when their newly birthed human experimental species would be advanced enough to understand, look back, and realize that their path had led them to an inevitable end that could have only two consequences—physical annihilation or spiritual fulfillment?

What this scenario does is to take the obvious archeological record we have so far recorded in our history books and add a crucial element. In addition to "when," "where," "who," and "how," it adds the final "why?" It postulates a greater Purpose to the universe, something that science cannot explore. It unifies the various fields of religion, spirituality, philosophy, and metaphysics.

The question "why?" has always been a part of the equation, lurking in the background, but until now it has been virtually ignored. It was thought to be unanswerable outside of simple, obvious sustenance.

Well, maybe it is, but that doesn't mean we can't speculate a little. After all, the surest way to never answer a question is to assume it cannot be answered, and thus never ask it.

Perhaps it's time for that approach to end. Maybe we need to bring it out into the light. If the solution I am suggesting is correct, we in this generation have a choice to make. And soon.

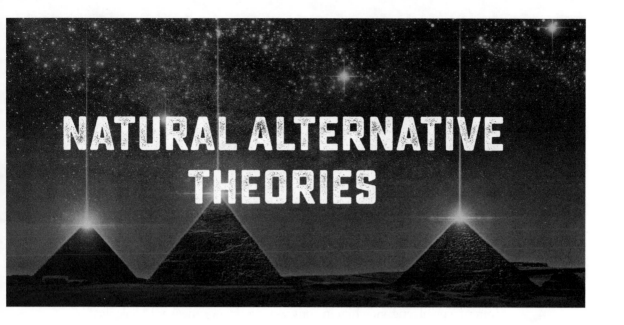

NATURAL ALTERNATIVE THEORIES

THE RISE OF ATLANTIS AND THE COMING OF THE FLOOD

There is very little these days that raises eyebrows more than the mention of the word "Atlantis." To many people it is a catch-all term that reveals everything from conspiracy theories to outright flakiness. To others it is a large tent into which all manner of crazy theories can be gathered, but a few see it as a perfectly reasonable assumption that explains a lot of historical anomalies and might explain how our civilization came about. Even more important, it might explain what our purpose is.

Before going any further let's examine exactly what we mean by Atlantis—and what we know.

In 1980 I fell under the spell of *The Dialogues of Plato*. I was in the midst of a private study in philosophy and was given a boxed set of the *Dialogues* that had been translated into English by Dr. Benjamin Jowett and published by Random House in 1937. The first edition was published by the Macmillan Company way back in 1892, so English versions have a long and distinguished track record.

My first brush with the *Dialogues*, however, goes back to when I first started studying Greek while I was in seminary. My Greek teacher used to give us excerpts from the original texts to translate so we couldn't cheat if, in the middle of a translation of biblical texts, we might recognize the passage we were working on and quote it from memory rather than doing an actual translation. He safely, and quite rightly, assumed that we were all more familiar with the Bible than we were with Plato.

Plato, the Greek philosopher who composed the *Dialogues*, lived his whole life in Athens, Greece, a little more than 2,400 years ago. He was, undoubtedly, one of the most profound thinkers the world has ever known. His famous teacher was Socrates. Plato, in turn, became the teacher of Aristotle, who tutored Alexander the Great. That's quite a legendary legacy, especially when you throw in Pythagoras, who lived at the same time. If there was a period of history I would like to go back and visit, this one would top the list. I would love to visit the famous Academy in Athens, which is thought to be the first great university in the Western world.

I am not alone in this regard. Alfred North Whitehead once declared that all of western philosophy is "merely footnotes to Plato." Augustine of Hippo, one of the key figures to shape Christian systematic theology, held Plato in such reverence that Friedrich Nietzsche once called Christianity "Platonism for the people."

Plato developed a whole new method of teaching and writing that are now called *Dialogues*. He began by describing a scenario in which a teacher would confront a pupil, engaging him in conversation. Hence the word "dialogue."

The teacher would begin by asking a pertinent question and then, many would say somewhat condescendingly, proceed to get the student so tied up in knots, trapping him in his own arguments, that eventually the student's ideas would embarrassingly fall apart in confusion. The teacher would then prove his point with devastating and overwhelming logic.

It wasn't fair, of course. The teacher knew the material and the student obviously was unprepared, but it did expose any cocky, ego-driven arguments the student might have, so the method stood the test of time and, sad to say, is still employed today by some arrogant teachers.

Plato's method of teaching was to engage in a dialogue with a student, gradually picking apart arguments to reveal their flaws and concluding the discussion with devastating logic. His *Dialogues* takes the same approach.

In two of these *Dialogues*, the *Timaeus* and the *Critias*, Plato described a long lost, technologically sophisticated, sea-faring civilization that once existed on an island in the ocean outside the Pillars of Hercules—that is, the Straits of Gibraltar. It was called Atlantis.

Although this civilization had the capacity to conquer the world, it developed, as human civilizations tend to do, arrogance. Plato implied that it grew too sophisticated for its own good, replaced wisdom with hubris, and delved into knowledge that it ultimately couldn't control. For this reason, it was destroyed "in a single terrible day and night," sinking into oblivion below the waves.

Before going any further, let's read exactly what Plato said about Atlantis because it is the only instance we have of someone actually describing the place. According to Plato, this information came from a distant relative of his named Solon, who had traveled and studied in Egypt where he was taught the story that had been passed down there for 9,000 years.

It's important to remember that Plato was conveying second-hand information that, in his day, was already more than 9,000 years old. That fact keeps us honest. Everything written about it since—and the amount of material is staggering—is merely people's interpretation.

Here is how Plato introduced his subject, translated and adapted from my original boxed set of the *Dialogues* by Dr. Jowett. First, from the *Timaeus*:

> In those days the Atlantic was navigable; and there was an island situated in front of the straits which are by you called the Pillars of Heracles; the island was the way to other islands, and from these you might pass to the whole of the opposite continent which surrounded the true ocean; for this sea which is within the Straits of Heracles is only a harbor, having a narrow entrance, but that other is a real sea, and the surrounding land may be most truly called a boundless continent.

> Now in this island of Atlantis there was a great and wonderful empire which had rule over the whole island and several others, and over parts of the continent as far as Egypt, and of Europe. This vast power shone forth in the excellence of her virtue and strength, among all mankind. She was pre-eminent in courage and military skill.

> But afterwards there occurred violent Earthquakes and floods; and in a single day and night of misfortune all her warlike men in a body sank into the Earth, and the island of Atlantis in like manner disappeared in the depths of the sea. For which reason the sea in those parts is impassable and impenetrable because there is a shoal of mud in the way; and this was caused by the subsidence of the island.

In the *Critias* Dialogue, Plato goes into much more detail. Rather than reproduce the whole thing, I'll just give you an overview. According to the report the Egyptian scribes gave Solon 9,000 years earlier, Atlantis was home port to a powerful nation that had sailed out into the Atlantic and beyond. They expanded their base of operations to several islands, with satellites based in Africa and parts of Europe. In all, they controlled an area "greater in extent than Libya and Asia."

Their home island consisted of a series of concentric rings, alternating between water and land. The soil was rich and food was abundant. They built

The giant island of Atlantis was a series of concentric circles alternating between sea and land, according to Plato.

extravagant baths, were led by benevolent kings, had great houses for barracks, and a civil administration. Their rituals matched those of Greece when it came to a mixed bag of "bull-baiting, sacrifice, and prayer." To the Egyptians, those were the hallmarks of a great civilization.

The problems began, however, when Atlantis waged war on Asia and Europe. Only Athens was able to resist the attacks, thereby saving Greece from domination.

Plato goes on for quite a few lines describing the virtues of Athens. The land was magnificent. Men and women practiced the arts of *arête*, or virtue. They were "lovers of honor, and of a noble nature, who made husbandry their business … they took a middle course between meanness and ostentation, and built modest houses in which they and their children's children grew old."

Meanwhile, back in Atlantis, Poseidon, "having received the main island of Atlantis as a gift, begat children by a mortal woman and settled them in a part of the island."

It must have been a good place to live. "There was an abundance of wood for carpenter's work, and sufficient maintenance for tame and wild animals. Moreover, there were a number of elephants in the island."

On and on the description goes. There was:

A fruit which admits of cultivation, having a hard rind, affording drinks and meats and ointments, and a good store of chestnuts and the like, which furnish pleasure and amusement, and fruits which spoil with keeping, and a pleasant kind of dessert, with which we console ourselves after dinner.

Plato then spends the next 1,500 words or so describing the architecture and layout of the city. With his next 500 words he moves on to the rest of the island. Then he spends 1,000 words going into a detailed account of the administration and the duties of the various levels of social classes.

In other words, he writes what amounts to a good-sized, 3,000-word magazine article about the makeup of his "fictional" civilization. That's a lot of words if your only task is to create a metaphor. More about that in a minute.

But then he makes a very interesting point. I'll quote it exactly:

For many generations, as long as the divine nature lasted in them, they were obedient to the laws, and well-affectioned towards the god, whose seed they were; for they possessed true and in every way great spirits, uniting gentleness with wisdom in the various chances of life, and in their intercourse with each other. They despised everything but virtue, caring little for their present state of life, and thinking lightly of the possession of gold and other property, which seemed only a burden to them; neither were they intoxicated by luxury; nor did wealth deprive them of their self-control; but they were sober, and saw clearly that all these goods are increased by virtue and friendship with one another, whereas by too great regard and respect for them, they are lost and friendship with them.

Now comes the part that is most apropos to the state of our current civilization in the twenty-first century:

By such reflections and by the continuance in them of a divine nature, the qualities which we have described grew and increased among them; but when the divine portion began to fade away, and became diluted too often and too much with the mortal admixture, and the human for the upper hand, they then, being unable to bear their fortunes, behaved unseemly ... for they were losing the fairest of their precious gifts. To those who had no eye to see the true happiness, they appeared glorious and blessed at the very time when they were full of avarice and unwelcome power.

Zeus, seeing all this, gathered the gods together and told them what he was going to do to bring Atlantis down, but alas, the rest of the *Critias* Dialogue is lost and we can't read how it ends, except that the great civilization was destroyed by a flood in a single day and night

That's all Plato wrote. Never have so many discussions, books, dissertations, hyperboles, exaggerations, flights of fancy, and accusations been generated by so little information. If Plato had written nothing else but these few pages, he would still be immortalized because of the many arguments that have arisen concerning the legendary, long-lost island of Atlantis.

These days, the vast majority of academic scholars, probably numbering pretty close to 100 percent, believe Plato made up the whole story. They claim he was making an allegorical point. A powerful one, but allegorical nonetheless. The *Dialogues* deserve to be studied for philosophical reasons, academia has declared, but they are not history lessons. They are, and remain to this day, works of fiction, existing only in the mind of Plato.

To further complicate the picture, Plato didn't write them in the first person. He was not the hero of the stories.

> These days, the vast majority of academic scholars, probably numbering pretty close to 100 percent, believe Plato made up the whole story. They claim he was making an allegorical point.

He put his teacher, Socrates, in that position. In other words, although Plato wrote the *Dialogues*, when we read them, we are hearing the story through the lips of Socrates, the words placed there by Plato, the author.

To put it bluntly, then, what we know about Atlantis comes to us by way of a 9,000-year-old tradition, once removed, so to speak, some of which has been lost. If that's all there is to it, we need say nothing further.

Obviously, though, there is another side to the story. Those who, like me, feel the need to read the texts with a little more of a literal interpretation, want answers to two very important questions. Like so many other ancient texts, there seems to be a lot hidden between the lines and behind the scene.

First, if the story of Atlantis is a simple teaching device, a figment of Plato's fertile imagination, why does he give it such a specific location and describe it in so much detail? He provides much more information than is needed just to prove a literary point. If all he is saying is, "Be good and don't get cocky," why all the descriptions of temples and abundant fields?

Second, if Atlantis is a fictional island, why is Plato so insistent about giving its demise such a specific date? Solon was born in 640 B.C.E., about 200 years before Plato's birth. The story of Atlantis, when Solon first heard it, was about 9,000 years old. That places the fall of Atlantis, rounded off to make it easy to think about, more than 9,200 years old when Plato first heard it and

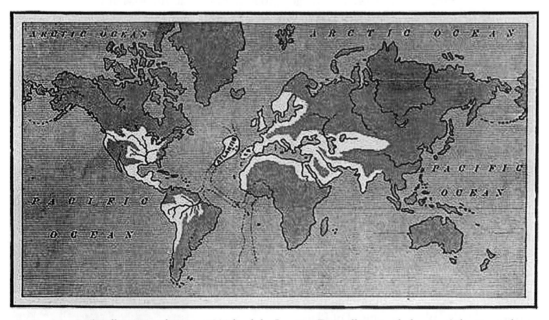

An illustration from an 1882 book by Ignatius Donnelly not only locates Atlantis as a large island west of Spain and Portugal but also speculates about Atlantean influence across the globe.

wrote about it, but Plato lived about 400 years before Christ, and we live a little more than 2,000 years after. According to Plato, when we do the math (9,000 + 200 + 400 + 2000), we get about 11,600 years ago, or 9600 B.C.E.

If that date sounds familiar, it's because we've come across it a number of times already in this book. According to dating revealed from a study of the Greenland ice sheets, that was precisely the time when global floods, signaling the end of the Younger Dryas Ice Age 11,600 years ago, caused the oceans to rise quickly, and in some cases catastrophically, inundating shore-based cities and developed regions. It was a worldwide event.

Why was Plato so specific? Was it sheer coincidence? Did he just pick such a significant date out of the air? That was also the time when many of the worldwide flood legends, such as the stories in the *Epic of Gilgamesh*, claim "God" destroyed humankind. It was when Göbekli Tepe was first built by an early megalithic people who had, seemingly, no formal experience with this kind of building.

Plato didn't have access to glacial core samples from Greenland, which prove this was exactly when the Ice Age came to a sudden and catastrophic conclusion. Why was he so careful to choose this exact date?

Let's see what else Plato had to say about this "mythical" island that somehow doesn't seem quite so mythical anymore. When we read his account with an eye toward historical detail, we see again that it is given much more precisely than needed if his intent was to simply compose a teaching device.

Atlantis, he said, was an island in the Atlantic to the west of Gibraltar, a sort of refueling point on the way to, in his words, "the whole of the opposite continent which surrounded the true ocean."

Those words seem to be an accurate description of the islands of the Bahamas and the Caribbean, beyond which lie the Americas. If we are to believe traditional history books, they would have been unknown to the Greeks of Plato's time.

As we continue to read the *Dialogues*, he describes a civilization that must have included a flourishing agricultural society, a fairly high technology capable of "shining forth in the excellence of her virtue and strength, among all mankind."

It was a maritime nation, implying a great fleet of ships involved in trade and other activities. They must have acquired a superb construction technology that included the building of great temples and public buildings. This would have been unknown 11,600 years ago.

He even throws in a description of elephants and other domesticated animals. If Plato intended Atlantis to be only a teaching device, elephants certainly seem to be a bit of overkill.

There were no elephants in the Americas back then, but there were mastodons and mammoths. Those could certainly qualify as "elephants" to one who had never seen one. By Plato's time, they were extinct, but not in the ancient America he writes about. As we have already seen, they went extinct at the time of the Younger Dryas comet impact.

Admittedly, there is a problem with all this speculation. To put it crudely, where's the body? There is no sunken island in the Atlantic where Plato says it used to be, and there never was one. His allusion to "mud flats unable to navigate" might be a reference to the Sargasso Sea, but there seems to be no island buried beneath their depths.

That hasn't kept people from trying to find Atlantis though.

Some people insist that Plato got everything right except the location, leading to some interesting theories.

One of the most prominent is that Atlantis was in the Mediterranean, not the Atlantic. The best guess from a geological standpoint seems to be the sunken island of Santorini. We mentioned this briefly already. There is evidence of a catastrophic disaster caused by an immense volcano exploding, which produced a measurable tidal wave that destroyed the island very quickly.

But why would Plato get everything else right and miss the correct location? The Mediterranean, even in Plato's time, was certainly not anything like the Atlantic. In his words:

What was left after the eruption on Santorini is now known as the island of Thera; the rim of the old volcano forms the steep cliffs that drop to the Aegean Sea.

In those days the Atlantic was navigable; and there was an island situated in front of the straits which are by you called the Pillars of Heracles; the island was the way to other islands, and from these you might pass to the whole of the opposite continent which surrounded the true ocean; for this sea which is within the Straits of Heracles is only a harbor, having a narrow entrance, but that other is a real sea, and the surrounding land may be most truly called a boundless continent.

Plato obviously knew enough to distinguish the Atlantic from the Mediterranean.

That leads us back out into the Atlantic Ocean.

More specifically, it hints at the Bahamas. The submerged, so-called Bimini Road, that many divers say seems to be built by humans, offers a tantalizing clue that the whole area was once above sea level and consisted of a single land mass.

It doesn't fit Plato's description exactly because it seems to be a little too far west, but at least it's in the right direction.

Edgar Cayce, America's "Sleeping Prophet," thought this was the place and predicted Atlantis would rise again. Indeed, the underwater paved structure called the Bimini Road, which appears to be a road leading to a now-submerged harbor, was discovered the very year Cayce said Atlantis would be discovered. Is that another coincidence? Or does the Bimini Road point the way to Atlantis?

Graham Hancock put forth an interesting argument in his book *Fingerprints of the Gods* that plate tectonics were involved in the destruction of Atlantis. Researching ancient maps and following clues left by Charles Hapgood of Keene State University, he discovered descriptions of a continent that was amazingly similar to Antarctica.

Traditional theory says that as long as there have been humans on the Earth, Antarctica has been hidden beneath great ice sheets, but if so, how could ancient cartographers have ever seen the shoreline in order to describe and map it so accurately, and how could it once have been forested if it has always been located at this latitude?

The answer is that maybe Antarctica once existed at a more northerly location before the comet impact of 11,600 years ago. This was the comet that marked the sudden end of the Younger Dryas Ice Age, just as another comet, or more probably comets, imbedded in the Taurus Meteor Stream, marked the beginning. This presupposes, of course, two hits from the same comet stream—one at the beginning of the Younger Dryas 12,800 years ago, and another at the end, 1,200 years later.

If this second impact was violent enough, and it certainly seems to have been, it could have instigated some massive shifts of the plates that support the Earth's continents. This could have pushed a tropical Antarctica quite suddenly into a southern polar location, beginning a sudden freeze. "Riding" this circular wave, so to speak, the shift would have moved southerly locations to the west farther north. Globally, this would have the effect of not only destroying megafauna such as mammoths, but it would also explain why many of them, which are found in what are now northern latitudes, were flash frozen. One day the poor beast would have been dining on plants and flowers in a relatively balmy land. The next it was frozen solid, the contents of his last dinner still in his stomach, so that archeologists could discover it thousands of years later.

This theory explains some interesting phenomena. Most people don't know much about it because it is certainly not included in our history books.

Oceanographers and geologists tend not to buy in, but it is worth noting that Albert Einstein was quite interested when he first read the theory as it was put forth by Professor Hapgood.

Novelist Clive Cussler did as much as anyone to popularize it. He made it the central theme of his book *Atlantis Found*, featuring his famous fictional character, Dirk Pitt.

Putting together similar streams of information stemming from Egypt, Turkey, Greece, Peru, Mexico, Siberia, the Arctic, and many other places around the globe, the gist of Hancock's argument in *Fingerprints of the Gods* is this:

> An advanced civilization had been wiped out at the end of the last ice age. There were survivors who settled at various locations around the world and attempted to pass on their superior knowledge, including knowledge of agriculture and architecture, to hunter-gatherer peoples who had survived the cataclysm. Indeed even today we have populations of hunter-gatherers in the Kalahari Desert, for instance, and in the Amazon jungles, who co-exist with our advanced technology culture—so we should not be surprised that equally disparate levels of civilization might have co-existed in the past.

Hancock proposed that a great Ice Age civilization came to a catastrophic end when the comet devastated them. Survivors made their way by boat around the world, landing in places that would someday cradle what we now call "our" civilization. They helped the indigenous, stone-age people who lived through the calamity begin the long path toward civilization that we enjoy today.

Why did they do this? Because they were convinced, as was Plato, that their own hubris brought them low. Recivilizing the Earth was their path to redemption. It was their penance to the gods for the ego-driven drive that had destroyed something that was once beautiful, good, and righteous.

If Hancock is correct, or even close to it, we are the recipients of the gift of a forgotten parent civilization. I call it the Atlantis tradition. They were the ones mentioned in the Egyptian *Zep Tepi*, the "First Time." Those were the days, as we have earlier seen, when ancient Egyptians believed the gods walked the Earth. They comprised the genesis of Egyptian history.

These same former Atlanteans were the instructors who taught a group of hunter-gatherers in Turkey how to forgo their traditional ways, gather together in one place, and pool their talents to build the world's first temple, Göbekli Tepe. To feed the workers they learned about the wonders of agriculture. That was why Göbekli Tepe displays its finest workmanship at the bottom of the dig. At first, the Atlantean builders did the work. Gradually, they turned it over to the locals. And when the Atlanteans, who were not gods, of course, but quite mortal, died off, the secrets of their workmanship died with them. Eventually, the folks at Göbekli Tepe even forgot how to "work" the mechanics of the temple, so, in frustration, they buried it until its secrets could be discovered and interpreted when their civilization had matured.

> And when the Atlanteans, who were not gods, of course, but quite mortal, died off, the secrets of their workmanship died with them.

But the survivors of Atlantis were also the inspiration behind the great Mesoamerican cultures of Mexico and South America, whose descendants included the ancient Olmecs, Mayan, Incan and, later, Aztec civilizations.

The legacy of their once great civilization lives on. The problem is, can we learn their lessons before it is too late? Are we also on the road to hubris-inspired destruction? Will we soon bring upon ourselves the same destruction that laid them low?

Archeologists want proof. They want physical evidence. They require at least one single, incontrovertible fact that removes all doubt. They want to discover the site of a lost civilization that can be reliably dated and, preferably, some texts that tell a story.

Believers, however, make the claim that a whole pile of circumstantial evidence is probably all we're going to get. In a court of law, that is often the case.

Perhaps we need to recap the body of circumstantial evidence that does exit.

To this end we now call to the stand a few witnesses of universal flood mythologies.

From the Hopi legends:

Sotuknang knew he could not allow this way of life to continue. So he warned Spider Woman that he would again destroy the people, this time with a great flood.

Spider Woman knew of the few people who still listened—who still tried to teach the people the ways of the Creator, but this time she didn't know how to save them. In a great flood, even the home of the Ant People would be destroyed. The people searched long and hard for a solution, for a way of salvation. Finally, they hid themselves inside the hollow stems of bamboo trees while their world was drowned.

When the flood waters calmed, the people came out and began again.

From the *Epic of Gilgamesh*:

There was once a great world-wide flood that destroyed most of humanity. The only survivors were a god-fearing family led by a patriarch named Utnapishtim. They managed to ride out the deluge by building a boat.

From the New Testament of the Bible:

As it was in the days of Noah, so it will be at the coming of the Son of Man. For in the days before the flood, people were eating and drinking, marrying and giving in marriage, up to the day Noah entered the ark; they knew nothing about what would happen until the flood came and took them all away.

From the *Edfu Building Texts*:

A group of sages, after seeing their homeland destroyed by a ferocious flood, wandered the Earth in their great ships, trying to help what we now call stone-age peoples dig out from the rubble and begin civilization anew. All this happened, according to the texts, during the Zep Tepi, the "First Time," when the ancient Egyptians believed that gods walked the Earth.

From the Brule people of the Lakota nation:

A fiery blast shook the entire world, toppling mountain ranges and setting forests and prairies ablaze.... Even the rocks glowed red-hot, and the giant animals and evil people burned up where they stood. Then the rivers overflowed their banks and surged across the landscape. Finally, the Creator stamped the Earth, and with a great quake the Earth split open, sending torrents ... across the entire world until only a few mountain peaks stood above the flood.

From the Ojibwa people of the Canadian plains:

A comet called Long-Tailed Heavenly Climbing Star swept low through the skies, scorching the Earth and leaving behind a different world. After that, survival was hard work. The weather was colder than before. And then came … a fiery blast that shook the entire world, unleashing a tsunami.

Similar stories are told by the Cowichan of British Columbia, the Pima of Arizona, the Inuit of Alaska, and the Luiseno of California.

From the book of Genesis:

I will send rain on the Earth for forty days and forty nights, and I will wipe from the face of the Earth every living creature I have made.

The latest information on what impact a mega-tsunami can have on an environment comes from a surprising place. Robin George Andrews, writing in the *New York Times* in July 2019, reported that new evidence from the planet Mars indicates that the cold, dry world our landing crafts photograph today was once waterlogged. The discovery of a seventy-five-mile-wide impact crater, found recently in the Martian northern lowlands, when coupled with planet-wide evidence of ancient, scarred coastlines, indicates that Mars had an ocean until the climactic collision. If there was ever life of any kind, it has since disappeared. The planet never recovered.

It all happened some 3.7 billion years ago, but what might have happened to Earth if the meteor had taken a slightly different path?

Maybe we need to start thinking in these terms and remind ourselves that just because something of this magnitude hasn't happened in our recent past, it doesn't mean it won't happen in the near future. Something on Earth akin to the Mars meteor impact, or, for that matter, the Shoemaker-Levy 9 comet strike on Jupiter in 1994, seems to have sparked the Atlantis tradition stories. People saw it and remembered. Their stories are with us still.

Flood stories are universal. They occur all around the globe. This can't be a coincidence. If ancient people saw something and remembered it in their oral history, which was eventually written down, something akin to a universal flood happened after people had settled all around

Native Americans and First Nations peoples speak of a comet that scorched the Earth long ago.

Flood stories are universal. They occur all around the globe. This can't be a coincidence.

the world. It was so widespread, and so terrible to behold, that the witnesses assumed it destroyed everything. Obviously, it didn't. There are too many impossibilities involved, but it seemed that way to those who survived it.

This, then, is the Atlantis tradition. I believe it needs more study and less disparagement. Where there is smoke, there is almost always fire. And fire burns hot under the Atlantis tradition. Could it be that our civilization began with a purpose? Was that purpose to re-create a previous civilization that climbed to the heights and then saw their dream die? Did they intend to teach us about their lost dream? Contemplate again the words of Plato:

> When the divine portion began to fade away, and became diluted too often and too much with the mortal admixture, and the human for the upper hand, they then, being unable to bear their fortunes, behaved unseemly … for they were losing the fairest of their precious gifts. To those who had no eye to see the true happiness, they appeared glorious and blessed at the very time when they were full of avarice and unwelcome power.

STUDIES IN STONE

When we use the words "Atlantis tradition" rather than the simple word "Atlantis," we gain the advantage of being able to include similar stories that aren't limited to a particular geographical area in the Atlantic. A tidal wave capable of destroying a group of islands, and even wreaking havoc on coastal plains, could very well have had an impact on inland locations as well, but we also need to look at an even greater mystery. And this one is hiding in plain sight.

Throughout this book we've mentioned megalithic structures that are found all over the world. We've asked the "who, when, how, what, and where" questions, but it's time to focus in on an even more important question. That's the "why" behind the great megaliths. Were they built in an attempt to realize some purpose that eludes us today?

We can't know for certain. Nobody wrote down what the ancients were thinking at the time. We can't really get inside their heads and examine the reasons behind the construction projects, but maybe we need to speculate anyway because for a period that lasted for more than 8,000 years, an unknown compulsion drove our ancestors to shape, transport, and erect these structures, and we don't have the slightest idea why. A worldwide motivational force was at work, but we have forgotten what it was.

Oh, we toss off bland speculations. "They were astrological observatories." "They were solar calendars." "They were temples built to worship the gods." "They marked the solstices and equinoxes."

Really? Are any of those guesses good enough to explain a motivating force that lasted for more than 8,000 years? There's not a current religion on Earth that has lasted that long. I find it almost beyond belief that such a long-standing tradition could have completely disappeared from our collective memory banks. When it comes to understanding the reasons behind the megaliths, we are a species with amnesia.

When it comes to understanding the reasons behind the megaliths, we are a species with amnesia.

Amnesia is usually caused by a traumatic event. It seems a real possibility that something happened to us as a species to make us block out the central, driving force that occupied the human race for more than 8,000 years, but we don't have the slightest idea what it might have been.

In my book *Lost Civilizations*, I asked more questions than I was able to answer.

- Why are the pyramids called tombs when no bodies have ever been discovered inside them?

- What are the Moai (stone statues) of Easter Island looking at?

- What do the raised relief images of Göbekli Tepe represent?

- What was the real purpose of the Nazca lines?

- Why did the Anasazi build in such inaccessible places?

- Why did builders in the British Isles need so many stone circles? What did they really use them for?

- And what's up with the Carnac stones?

I confess that I still can't answer these questions. I have a lot of guesses, but no one really knows. This is one of the greatest mysteries of human history, but the only people who are studying the mystery are usually pushed out to the "fringe" and labeled "alternative historians." This is a travesty. The answer to the "why" question might reveal who we are and where we are going. Nothing is more important.

The great megaliths were built by our ancestors. They may have been helped (maybe it does not go too far to say they *must* have been helped) by someone, but they built them. That fact has been established beyond doubt. They must have had a reason for going to all that trouble over such a long period of time.

They were not a primitive people. They had building techniques that rival, and even surpass, anything we could do today. They possessed a sophisticated method of communication and organization. We don't know what it was, but it worked better than Facebook and Twitter when it came time to unify people in fulfillment of a common goal. The megalithic builders seem to have been in touch with a powerful belief system, but we just don't know what it was.

In *Lost Civilizations* I put forth a theory that is probably as good as any:

There is one possibility that takes us beyond the scope of simple archeology. It puts forward the possibility that the megalithic builders were highlighting, or we might even say reinforcing, a preexisting Earth energy infrastructure that their civilization recognized and took advantage of, but that ours has forgotten. It's called many things, but perhaps the most popular is the ley line grid.

Could such a grid of energy really exist? Has our allegiance to material reality and the scientific method forced our now atrophied metaphysical intuition into the background? Is our conversion to, and absorption by, materialism the forgotten traumatic event that caused us to forget why our ancestors

Were the megaliths found in such places as Easter Island, England, and Tonga constructed as a message for future generations?

did what they did? Can the megaliths themselves show us the way back as they illuminate the path we left behind?

The United Kingdom is probably ground zero when it comes to megalithic interest. The standing stones and circles of England, Scotland, Wales, Cornwall, and Ireland are among the most studied structures in the world, but Bolivia and Peru in South America, and the entire area of Central America, all appear to be part of the same worldwide network. China and Japan are on the grid, as well as North Africa, Australia, and the lands of ancient Mesopotamia. They all seem to be situated so as to be connected to a universal, energy-filled, landscape.

Of all the recent books on the subject, and there are many, none has radically improved on the work of Francis Hitching and his groundbreaking book published in 1976, *Earth Magic*:

> Expressed simply, the theory is this ... that the whole of (megalithic man's) civilization (was) locked together by a mysterious cobweb of interlocking straight lines, the evidence for which still exists on maps and in the scenery today.

> I feel that ley-man, astronomer-priest, druid, bard, witch, palmer, and hermit were all more or less linked by one thread of ancient knowledge and power, however degenerate it became in the end.

> Read again his final words, "however degenerate it became in the end."

Maybe without realizing it, Hitching put his finger on the process that caused our amnesia. Maybe it wasn't a single event as much as it was a process. Step by step we sold our souls to materialism and left-brain thinking. That led to our addiction to the scientific method as the only legitimate way to advance our knowledge of the world around us. Gradually we came to ignore our legacy of intuitive, right-brained ways of encountering and reacting to reality. Materialism drowned out spirituality, and we forgot who we are, even with the evidence of the great megaliths staring us right in the face.

> Turning again to *Lost Civilizations*, I asked another series of questions:

> Wouldn't you like to be consumed by a spirituality which was so inspiring it could motivate you to transport megaton boulders all the way across the English countryside? Wouldn't you love to wake up in the morning filled with a sense of purpose that gave meaning to your day? Wouldn't you appreciate a belief system so strong it would cause to move mountains?

> Did our ancestors once thrill to those kinds of feelings? If so, they experienced something we have forgotten. The megalithic builders knew something we don't. They were in touch with a reality we have forgotten.

For that reason alone they are worth studying. Because if we could re-capture their enthusiasm and purpose, it might turn us away from the destructive path we seem to be following today.

I went on to quote a poignant portion of a book by John Michell, *The New View over Atlantis*. "In words touched with pathos and laced with irony, [Michell] summoned up a time when Earth energy and Gaia power were a common part of daily life, and then contrasted that time with our lives of impotent religion:

"We appear today to have lost touch with some source of inspiration known in former times, whose departure has left the churches as if under some malign enchantment. Empty, cold, and shunned, their shelter denied to travelers, often locked up, the sensations they invoke are those of guilt and embarrassment. Moralistic vicars drove out the musicians, banned plays and processions, washed the colors off the walls. Now the incumbent, hopelessly bewildered, often appears to see himself as a custodian of an ancient ruin, endlessly worried by details of the rotting fabric, his thermometer sign at the gate pointing out the sum required to prevent the whole edifice from crashing about his ears.

"If amnesia is, indeed, our plight, that sums it up pretty well."

If this is true, the way forward is obvious. We need to recapture our spiritual vision, for therein might lie the purpose for our civilization's existence. If the word "spiritual" smacks you the wrong way, use "intuitive," or "metaphysical." Maybe even "paranormal." They all stand in contrast to the deadening powers of materialism and reductionism that have cast their gloomy, pervading presence over literally everything we do today. More than ever, we are tempted to think our lives lack purpose. That is the inevitable end of materialism.

"If our senses can't perceive it—if we can't see it, smell it, taste it, hear it, measure it, weigh it, or touch it—it doesn't exist." How often have we heard reputable scientists say words to that effect? That's a pretty shallow way to perceive the world because it makes *us* the judge of all things. It implies that *we* are the rulers of the material world.

But we are actually pretty small, compared to the great stone monuments of our past. They stand over us in judgment and cast their shadow over what we have become.

"By their deeds ye shall know them," an ancient prophet once said. As we continue to wreak havoc on Mother Earth who gave us birth, and our fellow humans who share our planet, that shadow looms darker than ever. In

> They all stand in contrast to the deadening powers of materialism and reductionism that have cast their gloomy, pervading presence over literally everything we do today.

contrast to what many folks feel are daily lives of meaningless labor, the stone megaliths cry out. They had a purpose. They reek of meaning. We just don't know what that meaning is.

THE MESSAGE OF THE MYTH

More than three hundred years ago, in New York State's Hudson River Valley, a Dutch farmer pulled a five-pound mammoth tooth out of the ground. Not knowing what it was, he traded it to a neighbor, who happened to be a local politician, for a glass of rum.

The politician was intrigued. He didn't know what it was either. Eventually, he sent it off to specialists in London. There it was identified as an elephant tooth. No one back then had ever heard of mammoths. They had never heard of dinosaurs, either, but that's a whole different story.

The best the specialists could do was refer to the Bible. The book of Genesis clearly said that "there were giants in the Earth" in those days—that is, before Noah's flood. This must have been somehow connected to the pre-flood days, so it was probably about 5,000 years old. Besides that, they decided, since there were no elephants in America, especially in New York state, the tooth must have been swept there by raging flood waters, "proving" that the flood was universal and covered the whole world.

For many years, everyone was happy with that explanation.

Well, almost everyone. The Indian people who still lived in the area at the time of the discovery had many myths in their oral history that described elephant-like creatures with long noses and gigantic tusks. The Europeans didn't believe them, of course. What eighteenth-century academic was interested in campfire stories told by a bunch of primitive savages?

But the distant Clovis predecessors of those very Indians had lived in this same geographical area when mammoths roamed the land, before the end of the Ice Age. They hunted them. Mammoth steaks were a family staple. When the mammoths went extinct following the dramatic climate changes of 12,000 years ago, they must have told their children about a "golden age" when great beasts stalked the land and brave hunters went forth to challenge them.

When a farmer found a mammoth tooth much like this one in the Hudson River Valley, people explained it by saying the biblical flood must have swept an elephant tooth there from Africa.

If the Europeans settlers who farmed the rich land bordering the Hudson River had listened to the myths, they would have known right away what mammoth teeth were, but they ignored the evidence. It took a hundred years before scientists came to recognize that Indian mythology was more accurate than London scientists.

When will we learn our lesson?

Today the claims of anthropology are that modern humans began the process of symbolic, or religious, thought, about 40,000 years ago. That's when they began to paint the great murals on western European caves. Until then, their lives lacked meaning and purpose, but with the discovery of art and religion, everything changed.

Anatomically we go back 200,000, or even 300,000, years. That means our ancestors, who lived within these early time frames, had brains as big as ours. They had the same capacity for thought that we do. What did they think about for at least 160,000 years, or maybe a lot longer than that?

As we have seen over and over again throughout this book, 12,800 years ago everything changed. A new Ice Age gripped the world in its unrelenting grasp.

But then, 11,600 years ago the Younger Dryas Ice Age abruptly ended, with rapid and, in some cases, catastrophic results. It marked the end of the great megafauna—the mastodons and saber-tooth cats, giant beaver, and ground sloths as big as elephants. Severe flooding, caused by the rapid meltdown of the glaciers, caused flooding all over the world.

Today we find ourselves in the exact same position as that Dutch tenant farmer who lived 300 years ago. Scientists tell us about climactic events of those days as if it is a new discovery, but indigenous people all over the world have stories describing exactly what geologists now know to be true.

The problem is that we didn't believe the myths until the scientific facts started pouring in. Most experts didn't believe that there were people alive who witnessed it all and remembered—who passed on the history in myth and legend to their children. These myths were later recorded, and we can read about them today. We just never took them seriously.

It makes us stop and wonder: What else do the myths tell us that we have ignored? Do they convey a wisdom that we have neglected, possibly to our peril? Myths are written to convey purpose. They must be read on many levels. One of them is that they might be based on historical events, but those events often serve as a vehicle for a much deeper meaning.

Proof of a cataclysmic Younger Dryas extinction event does not constitute proof that an advanced culture existed, but it suggests that if such a people did exist they might very well have had a exhibited a wisdom that we have forgotten because they knew things we didn't believe until our scientific methods caught up to them. Part of their wisdom was that, without exception, the original myths all say that floods and devastation happened for a reason. That reason is almost always connected to human overreach. Like Icarus of old, we seek to fly too high for our own good and are drowned in the sea of our own hubris as a result.

Viewed with historical, rather than strictly mytho-logical, eyes, the worldwide myths about a "golden age" of understanding, consisting of a different way of relating to reality, indicate that their message is relevant because our newspapers daily cry out to us that something is drastically wrong with the way we're going about the process of life in the twenty-first century.

We have just seen that there are archeological clues they left behind. The mysterious process by which they built the megaliths are sufficient to indicate that, but when we turn to the complex mythologies, we can discover even more. Alongside the stories of mastodons and mammoths, the ancient myths focus our eyes to the heavens. They tell us we are children of the stars and are fulfilling a purpose on Earth.

Here's just a small sampling.

> We have just seen that there are archeological clues they left behind. The mysterious process by which they built the megaliths are sufficient to indicate that.

From the Ancient Greeks

Oedipus, Antigone, Phaethon, and the aforementioned Icarus are only a few examples that tell us committing hubris was a very serious crime and always led to destruction.

Oedipus' parents, for instance, rather than let destiny take its natural course, acted as if they were more powerful than the gods. They attempted to destroy their child and change their fate. Oedipus' adoptive parents also committed hubris when they lied to him about his past. Like his parents, Oedipus believed that he could change his destiny. His hubris led to him being irrational and jumping to conclusions without first analyzing things. That is what led him to eventually kill his biological father. Oedipus might have been able to save his mother's life, had he not been too full of himself.

From Genesis 11:1–9

Now the whole world had one language and a common speech. As people moved eastward, they found a plain in Shinar and settled there. They said to each other, "Come, let's make bricks and bake them thoroughly." They used

The cloud-piercing Tower of Babel described in the Book of Genesis was never finished before God broke up the civilization by making the people speak a variety of languages.

brick instead of stone, and tar for mortar. Then they said, "Come, let us build ourselves a city, with a tower that reaches to the heavens, so that we may make a name for ourselves; otherwise we will be scattered over the face of the whole Earth." But the LORD came down to see the city and the tower the people were building. The LORD said, "If as one people speaking the same language they have begun to do this, then nothing they plan to do will be impossible for them. Come, let us go down and confuse their language so they will not understand each other." So the LORD scattered them from there over all the Earth, and they stopped building the city. That is why it was called Babel—because there the LORD confused the language of the whole world. From there the LORD scattered them over the face of the whole Earth.

From the Ojibwa People

(As told by Valerie Connors.)

Long ago the world was filled with evil. Men and women lost respect for each other. The Creator was unhappy about this and decided to cause a great flood to purify the Earth.

A man named Waynaboozhoo survived. He turned some floating sticks and a log into a raft for the animals and himself. They floated around for a full moon waiting for the water to go down. It didn't, so Waynaboozhoo decided to do something about it.

"Maang!" he called to the loon. "You are an excellent swimmer. See if you can dive down to the Old World and bring back a lump of mud in your bill. With mud, I will create a New World."

Maang dove into the water and was gone a long time. When he finally did return, he said, "I could not reach the Old World. It was too far down."

"Amik!" called Waynaboozhoo to the beaver. "You are an excellent swimmer. Will you try next?"

Amik dove off and was gone even longer than Maang, but he too returned empty-handed.

"Is there anyone else who'll try?" asked Waynaboozhoo.

Just then a small coot, Aajigade, came swimming along and asked, "What's going on?"

"Get away Aajigade," called one of the birds. "We do not have time for your nonsense."

Now the animals began arguing loudly. Everyone had a different plan about how to get the mud, but no one could agree on whose plan they would use. For hours and hours, they argued. By and by, someone noticed that the sun was beginning to go down. They would have to put off the planning until the next day. Everyone began to find his or her sleeping spot on the raft to rest for the night. Maang asked, "Whatever happened to that silly little Aajigade?"

Suddenly, there was shouting on the other end of the raft. Someone had noticed a small body floating in the water. Water birds paddled hurriedly to investigate and found that it was Aajigade. They brought his body to the raft.

Waynaboozhoo lifted him up, and looking in his small beak, he found a particle of mud. Little Aajigade had reached the Old World and got the mud! He had given his life to do this. The other animals were ashamed of themselves for having made fun of little Aajigade. They hung their heads. They felt very sad.

Waynaboozhoo took Aajigade's little body and softly blew life back into him. Waynaboozhoo held him closely to warm him and announced that from that day forward, Aajigade would always retain a place of honor among the animals.

Waynaboozhoo set Aajigade down on the water and he swam off as though nothing had happened.

Then Waynaboozhoo took Aajigade's mud in his hands and began to shape it. Next, he commanded it to grow. As it grew, he needed a place to put it. Mikinaak (the snapping turtle) came forward and said, "I have a broad back. Place it here."

Waynaboozhoo put it on Mikinaak's back so that it could grow larger.

"Mikinaak," said Waynaboozhoo, "From this day on, you shall have the ability to live in all the worlds, under the mud, in the water, and on land."

The mud began to take the shape of land. Waynaboozhoo placed some tiny enigoonsags (ants) on it. This made it start to spin and grow more. It grew and grew, and more animals stepped onto it until finally it was large enough for moose to walk about. Now Waynaboozhoo sent benishiyag (the birds) to fly around to survey how large the land was. He said to them, "Return to me now and again to let me know how the land is doing. Send back your messages with songs. To this day, that is what the birds continue to do. That is also why they are called the singers.

At last, Waynaboozhoo stepped onto the New World. It had become a home, a place for all the animals, insects and birds, a place for all living things to live in harmony.

From the Mayan Popol Vuh

First the mountains and plant life were created; however, the lack of sound on the planet bothered the gods, so they created animals to live in the forests. After the animals were constructed, the gods ordered them to pronounce themselves. The animals could only bark or grunt or howl. Because the animals could not speak, they could not properly worship the gods, which proved unsatisfactory. The two gods decided the animals must never leave the forests and were to be subservient to the greater humans who would soon be created.

Next Plumed Serpent and Hurricane began experimenting with humans. The first were made of mud, but they kept falling apart. Their heads wouldn't turn and their faces were lopsided. Because they were made of mud, they quickly dissolved when exposed to water. The gods quickly did away with these mud people and started over.

The second experiment created wooden people. This batch of mankind proved to be more successful because they could talk. Their bodies were sturdy, but their skin was dry and crusty, which made it difficult for them to move about. Worst of all, they had no memory and no emotions. Because of this they were unable to properly respect their creators.

Furiously Hurricane sent a flood to do away with the failed wooden people.

Those who survived the flood suffered when Hurricane sent monsters to the Earth to destroy them. The first monster, Bloodletter, ripped off their heads. Gouger of Faces plucked out their eyes, and Crunching Jaguar and Tearing Jaguar ripped off the people's limbs and ate them. Those who survived the monsters' onslaught suffered as molten pitch rained down on them, pulverizing their bodies to dust. The Earth grew dark and a continuous rainstorm came. Wild animals broke into the remaining people's homes. Terrified, the wood people attempted to run away. When they went on their roofs, their houses collapsed. When they climbed trees, they were shaken off. When they ran to caves, the entrances shut in their faces. All that now remains of the wooden people are monkeys. They resemble humans but are mere manikins.

The gods greatly desired to create a successful race of human beings, who could worship them properly. Once these were created, the sun, moon, and stars would become visible. To ensure that this third and final experiment was successful, the gods sent four animals, a fox, a parrot, a coyote, and a crow, to find a location for the creation. These animals found a suitable location and

Some Mayan gods and demons are carved on stone at ruins in Copan, Honduras. Shown are the Bloodletter, the Crunching Jaguar, and Tearing Jaguar, which were particularly terrifying to the people.

brought back maize to an old woman to grind up into a grainy paste. Hurricane and Plumed Serpent then molded the first human beings out of this paste.

Four humans were created. They are the mother-fathers. They explored their world and the skies thoroughly as they possessed great vision that allowed them to see through objects. At first the gods were pleased with their creation and its thirst for knowledge, but soon the humans' knowledge rivaled that of the gods. If this were to continue then the humans would not worship and respect the gods as they should, so Hurricane and Plumed Serpent clouded the humans' vision.

The people began to multiply and fill the Earth; however, the sun still had not risen, so the people wandered the Earth ceaselessly in darkness. Tired of waiting, the people began migration to the east to search for the sun, but soon began to suffer from starvation. The "mother-fathers" then climbed a mountain and prayed to the gods. The gods were moved by the peoples' prayers and sufferings. The sun began to rise, and the people fell to their knees in thanks. In the beginning, the sun's rays were intolerable because they were so hot, but over time the people were able to enjoy the sun's warmth and light. They were allowed to farm the land as they wished, growing maize and other necessary crops.

All these stories are fanciful. They are entertaining, to be sure, but can we read any of them as history? Logic answers with a resounding no.

The problem with coming to this conclusion too quickly, however, is the same problem we encountered when we read Plato's *Dialogues*. It's the problem of too much information. Much more is given than is needed to make an allegorical point or present a story with a moral. It's as if the stories begin with a specific event, and then begin to improvise. Much of the improvisation becomes a bit silly when heard through modern ears, but the stories weren't first told to modern audiences. Their initial audiences were comprised of people who were steeped in an oral culture that considered the fanciful parts to be simply entertaining storytelling. The important thing was the lesson the stories conveyed, but they were set in a familiar landscape and recalled memories that were well within the experience of those who first heard them.

Once again, purpose and meaning take center stage. "Don't act too cocky," they remind us. "When people think too much of themselves, things go wrong!"

We are all tempted to think that modern civilization resembles Garrison Keillor's mythical Lake Wobegon, "Where all the women are strong, all the men are good looking, and all the children above average."

Even if it proves to be the case that we are made in the image of the gods, we are still human, complete with all the faults and frailties found therein, but are we destined for more? Are we on a journey? Does our civilization have meaning and a purpose? To discover if that is the case, we need to look above and beyond ourselves. We need to move outside our perception realm and view the human journey from an alien perspective.

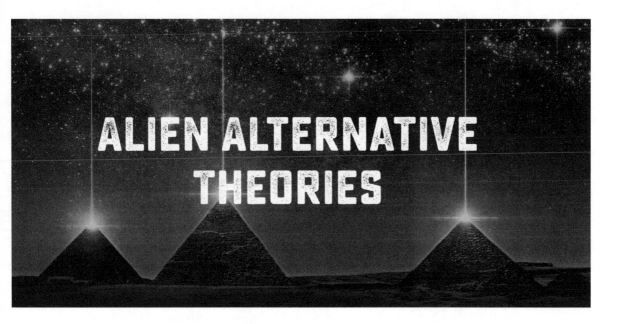

ALIEN ALTERNATIVE THEORIES

A Space of Time

If you want to locate something's position on planet Earth, you need some coordinates. Latitude, for instance, will give you its north/south position. That's a start, but it's not enough. You also need its east/west position. For that you need longitude. When you coordinate latitude with longitude, you can almost predict where it is, but not quite. For its exact position you need another coordinate. That brings us to time. Because everything is in constant motion, to be really precise you need to know not only *where* it is, but *when* it was there.

That's a simplistic explanation of why we refer to the space/time continuum. Space and time are connected. Scientists sometimes speak about spatial and temporal coordinates. Temporal just refers to time, as opposed to eternity.

But time is tricky. We experience it as constant—a ticking away of seconds, minutes, hours, days, and so on, forever. Einstein showed us, however, that time is not constant. It's relative. That upset a lot of people, but when he let the cat out of the bag, so to speak, he opened up a whole new area of study. And once scientists began to really study time, its mysteries only increased. The more they looked, the less they understood.

What is time, really? Did it begin at the Big Bang? Will it continue forever?

In the context of this chapter, we have to ask yet another question. Is time a function of purpose?

To explore that question, we're going to turn to the ideas of a very controversial historical figure. I almost hate to bring up his name because he is hated by some, revered by others, and misunderstood by almost everyone. Those who hate him do so, I think, for the wrong reasons. If they studied his life, they might form a different opinion. And those who revere him do so, I think, for the wrong reasons as well. If *they* really studied his life, they might begin to question his credentials.

I am talking about the man history knows as Saul of Tarsus, but who is universally recognized as the Apostle Paul. That's right, Saint Paul of biblical fame.

His name spurs instant opinions, so please stick with me. You undoubtedly have a preconceived notion of who he was based on your own experience.

If you are a devout Christian, you view him as the father of Christian theology who composed the epic book of Romans, a central foundation of Christian thought. You think of him as the first great missionary who carried the message of an early Jewish Jesus cult to the Gentiles and, by writing letters to the early church-in-formation, forged the theology that made Christianity a worldwide religion.

If you have a less-than-stellar view of Christianity, you undoubtedly think of Paul as an autocratic misogynist who perverted the simple message of Jesus of Nazareth and built a religion based on rules and law rather than grace and peace.

There is some merit in both positions, but we're going to follow a different path. We're not going to analyze Paul's theology. We're going to look at his initial metaphysical experience and seek to understand how much it influenced history. When we come to understand that Paul shaped Christian thought only after undergoing what today we would call a classic out-of-body experience and paranormal encounter, we will find a lot of questions answered. Were it not for the fact that he was such an important Christian figure, he might now be considered one of the premier mystics in history.

> Our particular civilization, in deeper ways than we want to admit, has been shaped by such doctrines. It permeates our thinking far more than we realize.

Before we begin, let me jump right to the bottom line. Christianity is, to a great extent, shaped by metaphysics. Once we remove the preconceived prejudices and verbal inadequacies with which we try to explain concepts involving the nature of heaven and hell, demons and angels, and God and the Devil, once we get away from the strictures of doctrines and dogmas, once we free ourselves from the baggage of any abuses for which the church has been responsible, we uncover a classic story about an encounter with an alien presence. It goes a long way toward explaining the mystery of why time exists and why civilizations help determine meaning and purpose. Our particular civilization, in deeper ways than we want to admit, has been shaped by such doctrines. It permeates our thinking far more than we realize.

That being said, let's begin at the beginning.

Saul of Tarsus was an educated Jewish scholar who, for reasons he never quite made clear, was also a fanatic patriot in the worst sense of the word. He hated Christians because in his day their belief that Jesus was the promised Messiah was beginning to harden into a Jewish cult led by figures such as Peter and James. It threatened to undermine 2,000 years of Jewish history and tradition.

After being authorized by local authorities to put down the cult in whatever way he saw fit, Saul decided to travel to Damascus to arrest Christians there and bring them back to face Jewish justice.

Let's listen to his words, as he dictated them to a physician named Luke, his traveling companion and faithful scribe. This is how Luke remembered the incident that changed the world forever. It comes from Acts 9:

> Meanwhile, Saul was still breathing out murderous threats against the Lord's disciples. He went to the high priest and asked him for letters to the synagogues in Damascus, so that if he found any there who belonged to the Way, whether men or women, he might take them as prisoners to Jerusalem. As he neared Damascus on his journey, suddenly a light from heaven flashed around him. He fell to the ground and heard a voice say to him, "Saul, Saul, why do you persecute me?"
>
> "Who are you, Lord?" Saul asked.
>
> "I am Jesus, whom you are persecuting," he replied. "Now get up and go into the city, and you will be told what you must do."
>
> The men traveling with Saul stood there speechless; they heard the sound but did not see anyone. Saul got up from the ground, but when he opened his eyes he could see nothing. So they led him by the hand

Saul of Tarsus was blinded on the road to Damascus. After regaining his sight and meeting with Christ's disciples, he became one of them and changed his name to Paul.

into Damascus. For three days he was blind, and did not eat or drink anything.

In Damascus there was a disciple named Ananias. The Lord called to him in a vision, "Ananias!"

"Yes, Lord," he answered.

The Lord told him, "Go to the house of Judas on Straight Street and ask for a man from Tarsus named Saul, for he is praying. In a vision he has seen a man named Ananias come and place his hands on him to restore his sight."

"Lord," Ananias answered, "I have heard many reports about this man and all the harm he has done to your holy people in Jerusalem. And he has come here with authority from the chief priests to arrest all who call on your name."

But the Lord said to Ananias, "Go! This man is my chosen instrument to proclaim my name to the Gentiles and their kings and to the people of Israel. I will show him how much he must suffer for my name."

Then Ananias went to the house and entered it. Placing his hands on Saul, he said, "Brother Saul, the Lord Jesus, who appeared to you on the road as you were coming here, has sent me so that you may see again and be filled with the Holy Spirit." Immediately, something like scales fell from Saul's eyes, and he could see again. He got up and was baptized, and after taking some food, he regained his strength.

Up to now his name had been Saul, the name of a great and powerful king. Henceforth his name was changed to Paul, which means "little" or "tiny."

Many of you may have either read or heard about this incident, but you undoubtedly heard it through religious filters. How would it sound to you if it was anyone else telling the story? What if the tale was found in an old text, independent of the Bible, which was discovered during an archeological dig? What if no one knew anything about the identity of its protagonist?

Then we would have quite another kind of document. It would recount a metaphysical experience in which a man received an ecstatic vision, heard a disembodied voice, and received a message from an entity who inhabited another dimension, at which point, he was healed of a physical infirmity. If you put it that way, it sounds more shamanic and metaphysical than biblical. It's no different than thousands of other cultural mythologies found around the world. It's just that biblical language has made us form certain listening habits when it comes to hearing such stories.

Listen to how Paul himself remembers the encounter, or perhaps one that is similar. This one sounds like a classic, shamanic, out-of-body experience. He writes about it in 1 Corinthians 12:

> I know a man in Christ who fourteen years ago was caught up to the third heaven. Whether it was in the body or out of the body I do not know. God knows. And I know that this man, whether in the body or apart from the body I do not know, but God knows, was caught up to paradise and heard inexpressible things, things that no one is permitted to tell.

This experience obviously meant a lot to him because it later moved him to write:

> And lest I should be exalted above measure by the abundance of the revelations, a thorn in the flesh was given to me, a messenger of Satan to buffet me, lest I be exalted above measure.

Some scholars believe that Paul's "thorn in the flesh" was partial blindness, caused by his initial Damascus Road experience. This is inferred because he was known to dictate his letters, rather than write them himself. And when he did sign his name to the completed documents, he sometimes remarked about the "large letters" he used.

I quote all this at length to make a point. If we strip away the traditional liturgical language that has come to encrust these passages, and read them as if they were just the testimony of a typical OBE (out-of-body) practitioner, what we have left is not necessarily a religious experience as much as a metaphysical one.

Something happened to him. Was it a vision, a flaming entity from another dimension, some kind of exploding comet, or another "heavenly" messenger? We don't know. Apparently, no one else saw it or was touched by it. It remains a mystery.

Paul interprets his vision as coming from God, but that's common to all the many similar encounters that fill the pages of the Bible. He might as well be encountering an alien entity from another dimension. And when you get right down to it,

St. Paul, a changed man after his conversion from persecutor to disciple, wrote of things seen and unseen and the influence they had upon him.

isn't that just another way of describing what we call "God?" God is certainly an alien presence who inhabits another dimension. If that entity preceded humanity, and perhaps, by one means or another, even had a metaphorical hand in our creation, it is, by definition, an ancient alien.

This sounds sacrilegious, and even blasphemous, to many people, but there's no reason to take that position unless you deliberately want to defend an obvious belief system. Religions of all types have traditionally believed *their* interpretation of God was correct while *others* were merely superstition, or even diabolical.

In the midst of this experience, however, Paul says he discovered the answer to a great mystery. Basically, it's the mystery of the purpose for time.

In the book of Ephesians, either Paul or a later disciple of his who copied his writing style, said that what we call time was inserted, for lack of a better word, into eternity in order to provide an arena in which "God" could teach "spiritual entities," which exist in a timeless dimension, about meaning and purpose. Let's read Paul's words first, before we begin to flesh out his ideas:

> We are not fighting against flesh-and-blood enemies, but against evil rulers and authorities of the unseen world, against mighty powers in this dark world, and against evil spirits in the heavenly places.... [God's] intent was that now ... the manifold wisdom of God should be made known to the rulers and authorities in the heavenly realms.

Paul's thinking seems to go something like this. It's a story usually told with Christian overtones, but let's use verbiage more common to ancient alien theory, just to emphasize the contrast.

In the beginning, the gods gathered in council, seeking to extend their influence into a new realm of experience—the realm of the material world. Having created a suitable environment, they said, "Let us make humankind in our image."

These are the exact words used in the book of Genesis. God uses the plural—"Let *us* make man in *our* image." This has not escaped the attention of monotheists, who nevertheless still insist that God is one. The context is clear and cannot be explained away by reverting to arguments about translation, but they do it anyway.

Christians usually resort to their belief that God is a Trinity, hence, the plural, but this is a verse out of the Hebrew Bible. Jews don't think in Trinitarian terms. Yet here it is, as plain as can be. This verse declares that "God" is a plural noun. Therefore, we can safely open our story by saying "the gods gathered in council." This is no different than Greek, Roman, Hindu, or many other mythological systems that say the same thing—that the idea to create humanity was a committee decision.

The material realm is, by its very nature, one of individualism and duality. We may act as if all is unity and we are one with everything, but the idea of separation pervades our existence. Each of us experiences life as being separate from, or even cut off from, the nonmaterial, spiritual nature of the Source. It makes us feel alone.

If hell is being cut off from Source, or separate from Source, we can even say that such expressions as "my life is a living hell" or "I'm going through hell" are accurate. Hell is separation from God. We feel separated from God. Therefore, we live in hell.

Paul recognized that reality, but according to him, we share the material world with "evil rulers and authorities of the unseen world," "mighty powers in this dark world," and "evil spirits in heavenly places." They are a part of our daily life.

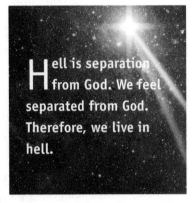

Hell is separation from God. We feel separated from God. Therefore, we live in hell.

They, too, are cut off from Source and subject to both the joys and perils of individuality, but if Source rectified the separation experience by causing it to cease to exist, performing a spiritual abortion, so to speak, before the experiment of material existence ever got off the ground, the remaining committee members who did *not* elect to leave the metaphysical and spiritual experience of Source would, in effect, spend eternity in fear.

To put it bluntly, they could then say, "Don't mess with God or you'll be destroyed!" They can't see the future because time does not yet exist. All they can see is the Now—the destruction of those who chose individual freedom. How would they understand the perils and pitfalls of freedom of choice?

How does Source illustrate the truth of the saying "Perfect love casts out fear"? How does Source invent a way to show what happens when we abuse our individuality? By creating an arena called "time," and inserting it into eternity in order to put limits on how long the whole experiment can continue. In this way of thinking, time is the space during which the curtain goes up, the material experience of duality and separation takes place, and all can see what happens when sentient beings go their own way. They are capable of great things because they come from the Source, but they are capable of horrible atrocities because they have the ability to exercise their free will in terrible ways.

When the curtain falls and the experiment is complete, the Bible again puts it succinctly: "Time shall be no more." It will have served its purpose.

This is how Paul explained time. It is that space in which "evil rulers and authorities of the unseen world," "mighty powers in this dark world," and "evil spirits in heavenly places see enacted before their eyes what happens when perfect unity is broken. Material existence is the arena in which the show is played out.

Paul sums up the whole mystery in words that have been set to music over and over again:

> Behold! I tell you a mystery. We shall not all sleep, but we shall all be changed in a moment, in the twinkling of an eye, at the last trumpet. For the trumpet will sound, and the dead will be raised imperishable, and we shall be changed. For this perishable body must put on the imperishable, and this mortal body must put on immortality. When the perishable puts on the imperishable, and the mortal puts on immortality, then shall come to pass the saying that is written:
>
> "Death is swallowed up in victory.
>
> O grave, where is your victory?
>
> O death, where is your sting?"
>
> The sting of death is sin, and the power of sin is the law, but thanks be to God, who gives us the victory.

This reading of Paul's ideas about time tells us that, according to him, time is a temporary parenthesis inserted into eternity and experienced only by those who are physically born into a material existence. During this parenthesis the blessings and perils of independence and free will, both of which are found in material separation from the Source of All That Is, will be carried out in a grand, experimental plan concocted by "God" or "the gods," who live outside our material perception realm. We are actors in that great plan. That, indeed, is our purpose—to demonstrate the wisdom of the gods.

This 1657 painting by Rembrandt shows Paul working on his writings. Paul had definite concepts about heaven, hell, time, and eternity.

Even Paul got tired of it from time to time. He told his followers that he "would much rather be absent from the body and present with the Lord." Many who experience OBEs say the same thing. They would rather not come back because things seem so much more real and peaceful over there than over here, but duty calls. Only when the mission is complete can we cross over and return to Source, out of time.

Paul seems somewhat exasperated with the game at times but looks forward to the end: "I have fought the good fight, I have finished the race."

There are problems, however, with this whole way of picturing time.

First, we've already pointed out the cultural baggage that accompanies biblical stories. For many raised in modern religious environments, it's hard to step outside that whole package. Many people who are perfectly comfortable talking about Sumerian texts that deal with Enlil and Enki, or Navaho mythology about the Hero Twins, run into a real mind-block talking about Jehovah and Lucifer.

Second, the idea of time being "a temporary parenthesis inserted into eternity" gives people pause. If you can't take the idea of a "time line" seriously, maybe you will be more comfortable thinking of it as a bubble, similar to the images used to describe the bubble universes of the multiverse. Indeed, there is no evidence that all bubble universes contain the dimension of time.

Third, and perhaps the hardest obstacle to overcome, is the whole idea of a "god" contriving all this. No matter what words we use, the whole idea of a god being like a person, only bigger and more powerful, is hard to get around. We have to really work at it. The whole Sistine Chapel thing is heavy in our culture. We're probably more comfortable with the *Star Wars* idea of "The Force" than religious conceptions of gods, but if you can shed your cultural baggage and learn to think in terms of impersonal forces such as the Akashic Field, or parallel dimensions on the other side of the Higgs Field, or whatever else works for you, it's worth the effort.

In the end, the problem really lies with language, not us. Our language is wholly inadequate to the immense task of finding words that express the inexpressible. It was invented to describe things that exist in our world, not parallel dimensions.

Myths are metaphors, as Joseph Campbell never ceased to remind us. You don't have to explain something to say, "Aha!" As a matter of fact, Zen Buddhists tell us that we can't explain revelations. We just have to glimpse them for a moment and realize their presence for them to work their magic.

Such is the nature of time to those who live in eternity but who have lost the experience of it. Eventually, its purpose served, time will disappear. And what has seemed so real to us will prove to be, in the end, an illusion.

LIFE IN THE TEST TUBE

We've already considered the possibility that life is a holographic, digital representation, conceived by a hypothetical hacker playing with a quantum computer. Let's take the idea a step further. Is this whole experience that we call civilized life simply somebody's gigantic experiment? If so, whose?

Is our entire concept of our life and universe simply a gigantic experiment being carried out by a being beyond our ken?

In his most important work, *Critique of Pure Reason*, Immanuel Kant came to the conclusion that all philosophy ultimately aims at answering three questions:

- What can I know?
- What should I do?
- What may I hope?

He wrote this book when he was just starting out on an intellectual quest for meaning and purpose. It stayed with him all the way, and by the time his life ended he had worked out a huge philosophical framework that is still requisite reading for any serious student of philosophy. It is not an understatement to call it revolutionary. He called it "Transcendental Idealism," a name almost guaranteed to drive away any but the most serious of students. If you're not one of those, let's break it down a little to make it less frightening.

Transcendental Idealism is just a fancy way to differentiate between the natural world we perceive through our five senses and the world that Kant calls "supersensible." Throughout this book we have called this second world spiritual, metaphysical, and sometimes paranormal.

In other words, the natural world is trees and wildlife. The supersensible world is God and the soul.

Kant's argument was that we can only have real knowledge about things we can experience—the natural world. The answer to his first question, "What can I know?" is that we can only "know" things about the natural, observable world of our surroundings. From time to time throughout this book I've called it our Perception Realm.

That leads to his second question, "What should I do?" In other words, how should I live my life in terms of morality and ethics? Since, by his definition, we cannot specifically "know" anything about morals and ethics, it would seem as though he thinks these are out of the range of knowledge. One person's right might be another person's wrong.

Others down through history have agreed with him to the point where they have developed cultural laws that delineate between right and wrong. When we say, for instance, "We are a nation of laws," we are saying that our government, whatever form it may take, must protect us from our worst enemy—ourselves.

This is the basis for the whole biblical idea about humanity being a "fallen" species of sinners who need to be surrounded by a hedge of laws to protect us. This concept goes all the way back to Hammurabi, but you can find it carried on in Judaism's Ten Commandments and the Constitution and By-Laws of the United States of America. These are extensions that attempt to solve the problem of what Kant called ethics, or the answer to his "What shall I do?" question.

Kant, though, didn't suggest that laws are the answer to ethics. He insisted on what he called a "categorical imperative." He reduced all laws to one universal law stating that ethics consists of recognizing the humanity in others and only acting in accordance with rules that apply to everyone. If we do that, he said, we will always do the right thing.

That's the equivalent of the Golden Rule—"Do unto others as you would have them do unto you."

But how do we know what that is? Isn't morality relative? What might be perfectly acceptable in some cultures—bigamy, for instance—is unacceptable in others. Here's where Kant gets a little difficult to follow. He calls upon us to act in accordance with some universal, moral, ethical law that we cannot actually perceive with our senses. If we can't perceive it, how do we "know" that it really exists, since he earlier said that we can only know through our filters of sensory perception?

Kant responds that even though we can't actually *know* such a law exists, if we think about it deeply enough, we will come to *believe* that it does. And that is the answer to his third question, "What may I hope?" By the end of his life, Kant came to hope that a god exists who designed the world in accordance with basic principles of law and justice.

That leads us back to the central topic of this chapter, which asks if there is a suppressed purpose for civilization hidden beneath our daily existence. There very well might be one, but if so, it is not deliberately held from us. We suppress it ourselves because many of us are too busy or lazy to think much about such things. It is best summarized by one penetrating question: "Is the purpose of civilization to protect us from ourselves?"

German philosopher Immanuel Kant (1724–1804) orginated the concept of Transcendental Idealism, which differentiates between the natural and spiritual worlds.

One definition of nature is that it consists of "everything against everything." This concept is derived from a much-quoted poem written by Alfred, Lord Tennyson in 1849. He called it "In Memoriam." Its most familiar verse is probably "'Tis better to have loved and lost than never to have loved at all," but right behind it is his reference to "nature, red in tooth and claw."

Most people who talk about "getting back to nature" usually have experienced the outdoors only from the comfort of a screened-in porch. As one who has spent a considerable time in the wilds, trust me when I say it's not always pleasant. Awesome, mysterious, and glorious at times? Yes! Dangerous? Of course? Uplifting? Certainly! But "pleasant" is a word I find a bit distracting when I'm scratching chigger bites and trying to keep the black flies and mosquitoes at bay.

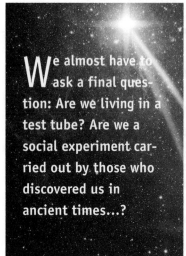

We almost have to ask a final question: Are we living in a test tube? Are we a social experiment carried out by those who discovered us in ancient times...?

The great outdoors, far from civilization's rules, is also, and has always been, the last vestige of many troubled and sometimes dangerous people who choose to live beyond the reach of civilization's laws. Therefore, we need to ask yet another question: Is one of the purposes of civilization to protect us from nature's dark side? If so, how did we develop it? Is it a human invention or were we taught its benefits by design?

Once again, when we turn to the ancient myths and texts, we are told over and over that civilization was taught, not invented. From legends about Quetzalcoatl and Kon Tiki to the religious texts of Egypt and Sumer, the message of the myths is that a stranger, or a group of strangers, arrived from afar, taught the people how to live, how to be safe, and how to be productive, before leaving civilization in their wake.

This might be why civilizations emerged seemingly overnight, suddenly developing all the earmarks of cultural traditions such as writing, laws, and economic development, before beginning the long process of devolution and, finally, extinction.

We almost have to ask a final question: Are we living in a test tube? Are we a social experiment carried out by those who discovered us in ancient times, passed on their knowledge and wisdom, and then left us to develop on our own within the confines of nature's testing grounds?

Over and over again, from the Far East to Israel, and from Central America to North America, the story is repeated. The Founders came, imparted a new way of living, created a veneer between "nature, red in tooth and claw" by creating a civilized society, and then left, but they all said the same thing. "I'll be back!"

Jesus, Zoroaster, Quetzalcoatl, Mithras—all of them left followers awaiting their return to check on the progress of their social experiment in developing purpose and meaning in an often-chaotic life.

The results of that experiment, now and forever, are in our hands. What will we do about them? Our future could very well be at stake.

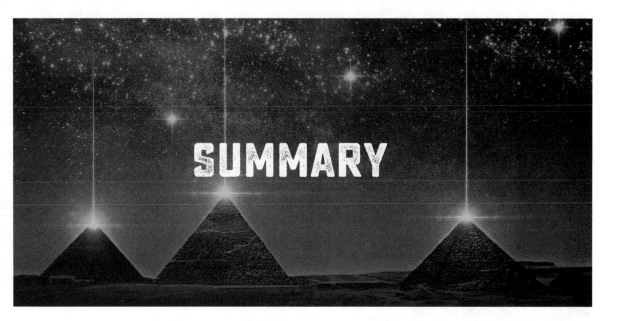

SUMMARY

By necessity, this has been a big, sprawling, chapter. When you leap from Atlantis to Immanuel Kant by way of the Apostle Paul, how could it have been otherwise? But it has been necessary. The history of civilization is a huge, complex subject, full of twists and turns. It can't be condensed in any meaningful way so as to fit within 280 characters, no matter how much Twitter is corrupting our dwindling attention span these days. When you add to the mix speculations about a greater purpose playing itself out, the subject gets even more difficult to handle in small pieces.

But it all fits together for those who take a wider view of history than is usually the case. If we concentrate our focus on one narrow slice of the pie, as is the tendency in today's version of academia, we miss the big picture.

The myth of Atlantis, for instance, symbolizes a greater reality that involves ancient, lost civilizations, a worldwide, devastating catastrophe, and a possible explanation for civilizations that sprang up fully formed, seemingly overnight. That one example involves the fields of mythology and religion, anthropology, geography, archeology, sociology, and history, each of which are considered to be separate and distinct areas of academic study. To qualify in any one of them you need degrees involving years of study in separate universities, since very few, if any, institutions offer this broad a range of degree programs. Then, when it comes time to be examined and awarded your diploma, you need to write and defend a thesis about a subject no one else has ever presented. Considering the number of papers in the master's and doctoral thesis database on file, most of which are never read by more than a dozen people, the selection of topics narrows considerably. Eventually you find yourself writing a thesis about something completely irrelevant called, perhaps, *Shakespeare's Use of the Oxford Comma.*

I've quoted this popular saying before many times, but it is still relevant. Many professors have come to believe that if the current state of academic specialization continues, we will soon reach the point where candidates know more and more about less and less, until eventually they know everything about nothing.

Consider this a plea for more eclectic synthesis and less didactic specialization. The study of civilization is the study of people. And people don't fit into neat boxes.

It appears as though something could very well be going on that is outside our perception of reality.

At the end of this chapter, we come to a tentative conclusion that is beyond the scope of most doctoral programs. It appears as if something could very well be going on that is outside our perception of reality. It's not the only explanation for the evolution of civilization. Our species might have developed completely on its own. That is certainly one point of view.

But it's not the only one. We might have been birthed by a parent civilization in a process I labeled the Atlantis tradition. That civilization is now lost to history, except for the clues it left behind in stone and story, but this thesis goes a long way towards explaining those clues and fitting them into what we experience today.

Another possibility is that cosmic forces, either from within this universe or outside of it, that is, alien-material or supernatural-spiritual, might have intruded on our comfortable Eden-like existence, given us a boost, and is watching us develop within a test tube beyond our ability to perceive. This is, of course, the opinion held by the great religions of the world.

That's three theories of existence. I call them the:

• Material/Historical Thesis

• Parent Civilization Thesis

• Test Tube Thesis

At this point it's not important to decide which sounds more plausible. What's important is not to select one and close your mind to the other two.

If you choose the first, for instance, you will be standing in line with traditional academia but ignoring clues in the areas of archeology and mythology that point to earlier or outside influences influencing the very early origins of our civilization. You will also be turning away from the billions of people on Earth today who believe a God or gods had anything to do with our creation.

If you choose the second, you will turn away from academia, which has a track record of dealing harshly with those who disagree with them. If you go public at any professional symposium, expect to be treated with scorn, shrugged shoulders, and a patronizing attitude. Don't worry. You'll be in good company. It happens to the best of us.

Parts of this second choice fit into the current religious context. You won't be completely burning your bridges if you practice a mainstream religion. A parent civilization is described in many religious texts, including the Bible.

Noah, for instance, built on what came before the flood, as did those who experienced whatever happened at the tower of Babel. Hinduism and many indigenous people everywhere from the Americas to Australia have similar beliefs.

But by and large, belief in a parent civilization puts you in a no-man's land between science and religion.

If you choose the third option you will be accepted in most religious institutions, as long as you use sanctioned God-talk rather than the ancient alien images I've been using so far. In most churches, for instance, if you call God an "ancient alien," you'll be politely escorted out of the building.

If you are a real eclectic, you might want to mix and match a little. That's perfectly okay. We all need to develop our own worldview, but it's important, I think, to keep an open mind at this point. We are living in a day when more and more experts speak with more and more authority about facts that are really opinions and convictions that are really beliefs. The end result is suppressed history. And that serves no one.

POSSIBILITIES:
WHERE ARE WE
AND WHERE ARE
WE GOING?

THE FINAL WORD

SUPPRESSED HISTORY

It's time to put it all together. We've covered an immense landscape that began with the origin of the cosmos and continued on through the emergence of life, the birth of the first humans, the peopling of the planet, the beginnings of civilization, and the theory that our origins may even be found somewhere "out there" beyond our perception realm. Central to everything we looked at is the idea that information about these things is not always forthcoming. It has been suppressed for a variety of reasons.

First and foremost among them is that knowledge is power, and power is addictive. It is assuredly the single most motivating force on Earth. Some people would argue with that analysis, claiming that sex holds the top position, but, when you stop to think about it, sex is so wrapped up in power that the two are sometimes intertwined and confused.

In an attempt to hold on to power, the Catholic Church created the Inquisition and still keeps a lot of historical secrets hidden away in its vaults. Governments withhold information under the guise of protecting its citizens. Corporations create levels of secret files accessible only to those who rise through the ranks. Academia decides both what it will openly teach students and what professors and teachers are forbidden to discuss.

Such power plays create fertile ground for conspiracy theories. They discourage open debate and practically guarantee the very climate that such suppression seeks to avoid. A quick perusal of history proves beyond the shadow of a doubt that suppression never works forever. People will always want to peek behind the curtain to see what's going on backstage.

One would think that people in power would learn the lessons history teaches, but such is not the case. Those who wield the power of suppression are not more intelligent than anyone else. They are certainly not better or more advanced in any meaningful way. They hoard information out of fear and weakness. Any perceived strength they feel they possess is due only to the temporary power they obtain by withholding the truth in hopes of doling it out as a bargaining chip.

> Those who are invested in the status quo don't want to appear foolish if their pet theories are overthrown by some young, hard-charging newcomer.

The U.S. government, for instance, would have been much better served if it had freely opened the pages of Project Blue Book, the now-infamous study of UFOs that it carried out for decades. The Cold War would have been over a lot earlier, assuming that it is really over, had governments leveled with one another in an honest bid for peace through understanding. Religious institutions would be in a much stronger position if they admitted their ignorance and encouraged open debate.

But it's not just retention of power that prompts suppression. Sometimes it's embarrassment. Thomas Jefferson never revealed his sexual liaisons with his slave Sally Hemings because he was ashamed of the affair that began when he first raped his slave when she was only fourteen years old. He freed her children although he never gave her freedom. He thus retained his power over her.

It is fear of exposure that allows blackmail. Those who know dirty secrets have power over their victims only as long as the secrets remain suppressed. Once they are revealed to the public, the threat of exposure ends.

That's probably why researchers who are threatened with bullying and ostracizing are persecuted so vociferously. Those who are invested in the status quo don't want to appear foolish if their pet theories are overthrown by some young, hard-charging newcomer.

Another reason for suppression is rooted in the attempt to retain historical supremacy. That's why small groups of people band together to accuse others of "rewriting" history if unpleasant facts are uncovered that threaten the favored status of one group over another.

In my home country of the United States, for instance, until recently it was considered almost heretical to state the obvious truth that American democracy didn't begin with the signing of the Constitution in 1776. To accomplish that, it took the women's suffrage movement; the Civil War; the Civil Rights Acts of 1957, 1960, 1964, and 1965; and the work of innumerable dedicated black Americans who overthrew Jim Crow laws. It continues today with those who are fighting gerrymandering laws that threaten the basic voting rights of millions.

For generations of those who were, in the words of Lee Greenwood's popular song, "proud to be an American," the original inhabitants of this "land of the free and home of the brave" were ignominiously herded onto reservations and ignored by all except the ones who sought to further exploit them by commandeering the meager resources they were allotted. It was a disgrace, and remains so to this day, by those who seek to retain political and economic power.

The belief in white supremacy is rooted in history, and it dies hard. It is a story seldom mentioned in old history books. Hopefully, that tendency is beginning to change.

Likewise, those elite who occupy positions of power want to suppress knowledge when it comes to political subterfuge. Manufactured wars such as those with Mexico, Cuba, and Vietnam were started when clandestine trigger events were fabricated. There is even plenty of evidence that the United States knew in advance that Pearl Harbor was going to be bombed but let it happen because it provided cover for a president who had promised to keep America out of a European war.

All these reasons for suppression of history argue that those in power are the only ones who are guilty, but such is not the case. Sometimes those who *seek* power are just as guilty.

The Creation Museum in Petersburg, Kentucky, has exhibits presenting conservative Christian views about evolution, including that dinosaurs existed not that long ago.

A branch of conservative Christianity, for instance, has long argued its case that the Earth is much younger than traditional dates imply. One way of reading the Bible infers that history is only about 6,000 years old. Bishop James Ussher, a Catholic scholar who lived in the seventeenth century, even went so far as to narrow the day of creation down to October 23, 4004 B.C.E.

There's nothing wrong with that. People should be free to believe what they want to believe, but when adherents go so far as to fake evidence, that's another story.

Recently there have been published reports of two cases in which stories of dinosaurs that supposedly walked the Earth only a few thousand years ago were put forth as if they represented new discoveries. This is sheer dishonesty and ruins the whole field for those who seek truth through scientific endeavors.

Alas, the internet and social media now offer brand new opportunities for people to suppress truth and present dishonest reporting to gullible people.

Sad to say, for a few minutes recently, I was one of those gullible people. While perusing a huge number of YouTube videos about ancient civilizations, I came across a report that seemed, on the surface, very legitimate. A part-time lab tech at California State University, Northridge (CSUN) named Mark Armitage claimed to have discovered soft tissue in a triceratops horn he found at the Hell Creek Formation in Montana. Soft tissue is never found in dinosaur bones because of their extreme age.

Carbon 14 dating produced an age of only 30,000 years. Armitage claimed that the reason scientists hadn't carbon dated dinosaur bones up to this point was that since carbon dating doesn't work with samples as old as dinosaur bones, they just never bothered.

That was interesting, to say the least, and sounded like it might fit into the subject matter of this book, so I decided to check it out. A simple Google search revealed page after page of documentation, so I was intrigued, but after reading a few of the technical papers purporting to be new research, I found something disturbing. All the articles I could find listed the very same source material. It consisted of one article found in one online magazine, written by Hugh Miller, who, according to some online sources, is associated with the young-Earth creationist movement.

In the interests of full disclosure, it was a magazine to which I have contributed articles myself, but it still sounded suspicious. I never trust information unless it comes from a variety of sources. I decided to find out who Mark Armitage was.

As it turns out, his job at CSUN was to train students in the use of a new microscope that had been purchased by the university, but when the students began to complain that in the process of training he had attempted to proselytize them into his religious beliefs, which included the belief that the Earth was only 6,000 years old, he was terminated. The university cited the reasons for his release—one was for the alleged proselytizing and the other was for budgetary reasons, since his job was only part-time and temporary.

Armitage, however, sued the university claiming discrimination. A judge subsequently threw out three of the five allegations named in the lawsuit and ruled that if Armitage wanted to continue, he would not be eligible for punitive damages even if the remaining charges were upheld. Armitage then took an offer to settle.

But not long after the court decision, he made a video that claimed a victory in court. Evangelical Christian news sources picked it up and ran with it, claiming suppression of their beliefs, which gave them the opportunity to publicize the dinosaur case as evidence that the Earth was much younger than is usually taught in public schools. This, in turn, would bolster the many creation science lawsuits now being brought before various state courts.

But in the course of their reporting, one unnamed source said that the dinosaur horn might have belonged to a mammal instead of a reptile, so I dug a little deeper.

Further research led me to another author of the report who held a PhD in microbiology from Kent State University. He was currently the director of the Van Andel Creation Research Center, which was connected to the Creation Research Center, both of which sponsor research as long as it sticks to the young Earth agenda.

> Evangelical Christian news sources picked it up and ran with it, claiming suppression of their beliefs, which gave them the opportunity to publicize the dinosaur case as evidence that the Earth was much younger....

Needless to say, this was beginning to sound very suspicious. I sent a few emails, but nothing came of them. When I went back to the TV documentaries, YouTube videos, and what appeared on the surface as technical papers, I was careful to note the source material listed. Most of the off-camera voices simply listed the names and degrees held by the authors of the article, and, again, the single magazine article. There was no mention of their Evangelical Christian, young-Earth credentials. The many pages of material I was reading implied, and in some cases flat out stated, that the only reason the discovery of 30,000-year-old dinosaur bones was suppressed was because of academic prejudice.

As of this writing, the whole subject seems up for debate but very suspicious. I would love to find out that humans and dinosaurs walked the Earth at the same time. My heart is on the side of those who claimed the discovery, but my head says differently. The evidence and the reporting of the find leave out too much information that would have made the discovery much more palatable had it been honestly included.

Suppression seems to be a two-way street, practiced by both traditionalists and alternative types, but in its wake follows subterfuge, and the only thing that suffers is the truth.

ALTERNATIVE THEORIES

This leads us to the whole subject of alternative theories and their presentation. How do new ideas get space at the grownups' table, especially in the dog-eat-dog world of contemporary origin theory?

Jim Holt is a deep-thinking and articulate philosopher, among other things. His book *Why Does the World Exist?* is listed in the bibliography. In September of 2006 he wrote an article for *New Yorker* magazine entitled "Unstrung." It was about the status of string theory in today's rough-and-tumble world of physics, but it also lifted the curtain on how scientists treat each other and provided a glimpse of the truly barbaric world of seemingly genteel specialists.

One of the most striking sentences in the piece comes as a real shock to people who expect very smart people to act in a civilized manner. "Physics is stuck in a paradigm doomed to barrenness," he says.

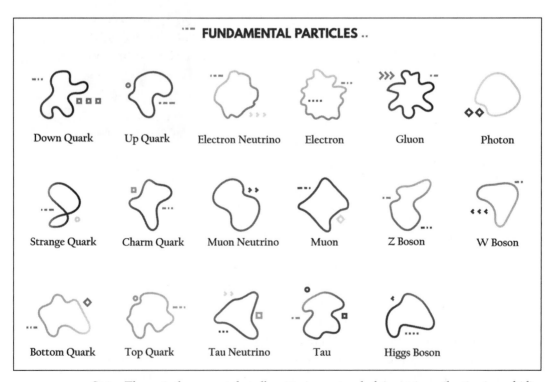

FUNDAMENTAL PARTICLES

Down Quark	Up Quark	Electron Neutrino
Electron	Gluon	Photon
Strange Quark	Charm Quark	Muon Neutrino
Muon	Z Boson	W Boson
Bottom Quark	Top Quark	Tau Neutrino
Tau	Higgs Boson	

String Theory is the concept that all matter is composed of tiny strings vibrating in multidimensional space, creating fundamental particles that then comprise what we experience as matter and energy.

For all the press and glitter about string theory that fills the TV documentaries, hosted by popular speakers such as Richard Feynman, for instance, many of them don't stop at offering critical analysis. They resort to name-calling worthy of any playground bully. String theory is not just wrong, they say, it's "crazy," it's "nonsense," and it's "the wrong direction."

Sheldon Glashow, a Nobel Prize winner, likens it to "a new version of medieval theology" and actively campaigned to keep string theorists out of his department at Harvard. Thankfully, he failed.

Lee Smolin wrote a book called *The Trouble with Physics: The Rise of String Theory, the Fall of a Science, and What Comes Next*. Peter Woits' book on the same subject was given an even more derogatory title, *Not Even Wrong: The Failure of String Theory and the Search for Unity in Physical Law*. He calls the theory a "disaster."

It's interesting that both authors are now outsiders in the field of physics. Both share the view that physics, as practiced today, rewards technicians and punishes visionaries. According to them, Einstein, if he lived today, would still be a patent clerk.

Woit, especially, echoes a thought I've had many times but was afraid to say out loud: "How many leading theoretical physicists were once insecure, small, pimply boys who got their revenge besting the jocks (who got the girls) in the one place they could—math class?" And then, once arrived at the top of their intellectual field, some of those who still suffer the slings and arrows of juvenile discontent act out their pent-up frustrations by bullying those who are now their inferiors.

It certainly doesn't apply to all who rise to the top of a demanding field, but it makes one wonder.

Most of us who follow scientific endeavors and the quest for truth are deeply troubled when insiders such as Jim Holt say things like this: "It is strange to think that such sordid motives might affect something as pure and objective as physics, but these are strange days in the discipline."

All of us want our priests to be holy, our teachers brilliant and caring, our police officers worthy of trust, and our politicians candidates for sainthood. We want our parents to have only our best interests at heart and our doctors to be angels in white coats, but that's not the world in which we live.

I've experienced it in a small way myself. Having written many articles, most of which were posted in online magazines and thus open to comments, I have yet to read the opinion of a reader whom I have never met say something to the effect of, "Interesting opinion. Here's why I disagree."

Instead, although I have been honored to have had a lot of favorable reviews, when someone differs with my arguments I usually get a one-sentence answer filled with misspelled words that contain some variation on the word "crap." I've been called "idiot" by more than one person who can't write a coherent sentence.

My experience, though nowhere near as public and humiliating as it would be in the rarified world of science, seems to be typical. Take, for example, the exchanges that surrounded a theory we looked at earlier called the Anthropic Principle. It was first presented in an attempt to speak to a really important question: Why does the universe seem so finely tuned so as to produce life?

The theory came to a startling, highly debatable, seemingly circular-reasoned conclusion. The reason the universe is the way it is is because if it wasn't, we wouldn't be here to observe it. Therefore, we must somehow be intimately connected with it.

Those who studied the theory saw it as a way to resolve the many problems with string theory that don't fit with our existence.

It is true that Copernicus dislodged us from the center of the universe a long time ago, but since then we've had a lot of time to reconsider. Maybe there is more to the idea than meets the eye.

This is anathema to traditional physicists, who thought they had put to bed for good the whole idea of humans somehow being in the center of things. When the argument broke out of the halls of academia for all to see, it became, in the words of Jim Holt, "a high-school-cafeteria food fight." One physicist claimed the Anthropic Principle was a "virus" that infected the minds of its adherents.

Others published papers that were much worse. I've read more than a few of them, and what I found are often polemics empty of real argument and completely free of courtesy. The comments are often worthy of contempt. They bring the whole idea of scientific discussion right down into the mud. Is it any wonder that many nonscientists have lost interest in science in the same way that many voters refuse to even bother to vote when they see politicians resorting to childish name-calling? How can we be asked to give any respect to people who have violated the laws of common courtesy?

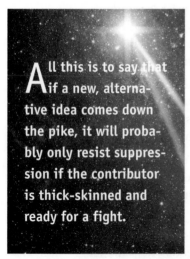

All this is to say that if a new, alternative idea comes down the pike, it will probably only resist suppression if the contributor is thick-skinned and ready for a fight. Sadly, the result is that we all suffer from a lack of new, and what could be exciting, answers to our age-old questions about who we are, where we came from, and where we're headed.

ANCIENT ALIENS

Ten years ago the idea of ancient aliens visiting Earth was still relegated to the outer rim of the pseudo-science orbit, but a lot has changed in the last decade. In December of 2018, the *New York Times*, a mainstream newspaper if there ever was one, published what turned out to be a shocking exposé of what not too long ago would have sounded to most of its traditional readers like some sort of crackpot conspiracy theory.

Admittedly, the physics of space travel is a daunting challenge to overcome. Given the distances to travel and the speed limits set by none other than Albert Einstein, the idea of nuts-and-bolts spaceships from distant galaxies actually getting here seems impossible, but ideas about the nature of quantum reality have had time to percolate through our psyches now. We are apparently more open to new ways of thinking. The TV idea of "warp drive" and "hyper drive" probably didn't hurt either, even if they are, for all practical purposes, impossible.

For five years, according to the article, the Pentagon had been investigating what they called "unexplained aerial phenomena" that was occurring in the skies and atmosphere of the planet. The *Times*' readership responded in a surprising way. Many of those who read the *Times* are politically liberal, educated, socially adept city folks. Much to the consternation of the editors, the public was not filled with terror and concern. Instead, having endured a very exhausting two years of bad news, folks actually looked forward to the time when an alien intervention might save us from ourselves.

Since the 1960s, Evangelical Christians have been looking forward to the Rapture, the first in a sequence of events that would culminate in the return of Jesus Christ, who would then set the world straight. Now the secular version of that theory brought relief to a lot of people. Even former senator Harry Reid tweeted the paper with a simple message: "Thank God." One letter to the editor pondered the possibility that extraterrestrials might save the planet before we completely trash it.

The object that sparked all the discussion turned out to be, probably, not of alien manufacture, but for a few weeks during the Christmas season pictures of what was described as "an alien mega structure" dominated the news. By March the full-fledged conspiracy folks had kicked into gear when pictures taken back in 2015 hinted at a secret trove of documents.

A *Washington Post* op-ed was titled, "Why Doesn't the Pentagon Care?" The very next week U.S. president Donald Trump tweeted about forming a new branch of the military called the Space Force.

The debate grew so vocal that on March 20 *New York Magazine* published an article called "Reasons to Believe." It sparked more major news articles, eventually settling in on thirteen reasons why alien contact may either have taken place in the past or is happening right now. Here is a compilation of those reasons. Notice that they are all very seriously presented. Indeed, things have changed when it comes to considering the very real possibility of what was once a wacko, fringe subject.

Here are a few of the mainstream arguments:

- The government has unequivocally admitted that it takes UFOs seriously. Documents now open for public view due to the Freedom of Information Act show that in 1952 a group called the Psychological Strategy Board, sponsored by the CIA, concluded that, when it came to UFOs, the American public was dangerously gullible and prone to "hysterical mass behavior." The board recommended "debunking" campaigns to tamper the public's interest in unexplained phenomena, even though as late as 2007 the Pentagon confirmed the existence of the Advanced Aerospace Threat Identification Program, funded by $22 million of "black money" siphoned through the budget of the Department of Defense. The program was supposedly suspended in 2012, but given the secrecy in place since 1952, who really knows for sure?

- The data about the size of the universe and the possibility of planetary life simply cannot be denied. In the last thirty years, astronomers have discovered more than 3,000 planets capable of supporting life as we know it. Every star visible in the night sky probably has at least one. In the words of Seth Shostak, the senior astronomer at the SETI Institute, "Even people who are not terribly interested in science know that we've found that planets are as common as fire hydrants—they're everywhere. One in five or one in six might be a planet similar to the Earth." Penelope Boston, the director of the NASA Astrobiology Institute, says it even more bluntly: "We'd have to be dead above the neck if we weren't interested in this."

- People with a lot of money are getting interested. Elon Musk is ready to put $21 billion (yes—that's billion!) into colonizing Mars. "If we're not in a simulation, then maybe we're in a lab and there's some advanced alien civilization that's just watching how we develop, out of curiosity, like mold in a petri dish," is how he puts it. Paul Allen gave millions of dollars to SETI in 1993, after Congress cut off its funding. Yuri Milner, in conjunction with Mark Zuckerberg and the late Stephen Hawking, wanted to contribute significantly toward sending spaceships to

Enceladus, a moon of Saturn, to search for alien life. In the movie *Star Trek Beyond*, Jeff Bezos appeared in a cameo role as a Starfleet official. Elon Musk briefly played himself in *Iron Man 2*. Both are interested in what lies out there "in a galaxy far, far away" where "no one has gone before." Franklin Antonio's company Qualcomm, a mobile tech company, has donated millions to SETI research. When money talks, industry listens. Especially the space industry.

The U.S. government takes UFOs seriously, as is evidenced by numerous official documents (artist's concept).

- There is increasing evidence that prominent people in both military and governments are more than interested in what goes on in the skies over our heads. Nick Pope is Britain's lead UFO investigator. "Know that there are people who watch our skies to protect the sleeping masses," he wrote in his memoir, "but know also that not all potential intruders into our airspace have two wings, a fuselage, and a tail, and not all show up on our radar." Paul Hellyer was Canada's defense minister during the Cold War. He's now in his nineties, but he believes that at least eighty unique species of aliens have been visiting Earth for centuries. They range in appearance from "Tall Whites," the size of basketball players, to "Nordic Blondes," because they resemble folks from Denmark. Philip Corso, who worked with Army Intelligence following World War II, wrote a book published by Simon & Schuster in 1997. It was called *The Day after Roswell* and featured a foreword by Senator Strom Thurmond. Written just thirteen months before Corso died, he confessed to playing a part in what he describes as a cover-up by the government in order to reverse-engineer alien technology. Lasers, particle beams, microchips, and Kevlar were the result of that work. When WikiLeaks published the Hillary Clinton emails, a significant number of John Podesta's emails about aliens were also released. They mention other like-minded folks such as Tom DeLonge and astronaut Edgar Mitchell. Podesta considers his biggest failure in office back in 2014 was that he was unable to get government files declassified about the 1965 Kecksburg, Pennsylvania, UFO incident. He has never spoken publicly about his belief in the reality of UFOs, but in Leslie Kean's best seller, *UFOs: Generals, Pilots, and Government Officials Go on the Record,* he wrote a foreword in which he argued that "it's time to find out what the truth really is. The American people—and people around the world—want to know, and they can handle the truth."

- The list of books and articles about UFO encounters now number in the thousands. From the famous abduction incident involving Barney and Betty Hill to the "Phoenix lights" of 1997 and countless others that could, and have, filled many books, there seems to be a lot of fire under all the smoke.

With all this information available we have a right, and an obligation, to ask why the aliens, assuming they are there, are playing so hard to get. Why the peek-a-boo games? Why don't they reveal themselves?

Those are good questions. Here are a few possible answers:

- The aliens have all died. The universe is 13.7 billion years old, and in that amount of time, there might have been plenty of civilizations that evolved and went extinct. At least one of them could have visited Earth.

- The aliens are hibernating. This one is out there, I'll admit, but I include it because I want to be thorough. Some folks have postulated that an extraterrestrial species might be so advanced it cannot efficiently make use of its technology right now because the universe's temperature is currently too high. You'll have to go back and read more about this in chapter 1, but, as we saw earlier, the universe's temperature is cooling down, even though the temperatures on Earth are rising. Aliens may have decided to hibernate a few billion years or so until the weather suits their clothes.

- The aliens are hiding. Stephen Hawking once said that we need to think twice before contacting aliens because they may not have our best intentions at heart. This might produce a certain amount of fear and trembling. Perhaps the aliens think the same thing we do, after witnessing our warlike propensity for thousands of years. Maybe they're afraid of us. If so, is it any wonder they are listening to their own Stephen Hawkings and hiding from an obviously destructive species such as ourselves?

- The aliens are still evolving. Alien life might be everywhere, but it hasn't yet developed the capacity to communicate with us. Maybe we're more advanced than they are and will have to wait for them to develop their own SETI technology before they even know we're here. We've just started to look. Let's face it, the search for extraterrestrial life is in its infancy. We've only been at it for a few years. Cosmically speaking, that's just the blink of a proverbial eye. Have a little patience! This might take awhile

- The aliens are already here but we just haven't figured it out yet. They might be taking some time to study us before revealing themselves, or maybe they have already let themselves be known to certain groups. The truth isn't out there—it's right here. Watch the three *Men in Black* movies again. You'll get the idea.

Many believe that the government is hiding evidence of space invaders in Area 51, which is why aliens have not yet been revealed to most of the world.

All this is to say that the real study of ancient aliens is now being taken seriously, even if I haven't been able to resist the impulse to poke a little fun at it in the preceding paragraphs. I left the tongue-in-cheek stuff in the final manuscript, though, to make a point. It's very difficult for some people, even me, a true believer, to not treat the subject with a little humor, but—and don't forget this—officials in high places are taking this stuff seriously. We need to do the same thing because there is a very high possibility that our origins do not trace their existence from a primordial swamp somewhere. If the abundant mythology is correct, and the facts of science are beginning to indicate they are, we will find our origins not on Earth, but in the heavens.

HIDDEN ORIGINS

"Where did I come from?"

It's often a young child's first question and probably the most important he or she will ever ask, although not for the reasons you might think. A sense of being undergirds absolutely everything we do throughout our life. People who are secure in their personal identity can handle almost everything life throws at them.

Not knowing the answer to this primary question of life could well be the reason behind the malaise in which the human species is presently wallowing. Most people have probably stopped asking it, thinking it too difficult to answer. That's why we substitute "What do you do?" for "Who are you?" Not knowing who we are, we take refuge in our occupation.

"I am a writer." "I am a businessman." "I am a mechanic." "I work in a factory." "I am a teacher."

None of those things are who we are. They only designate what we do. The tragedy is that when we lose our job, we thus lose our identity. When that happens on a large scale, we lose our sense of purpose. Without purpose, we perish. What's the sense of getting up in the morning if we have no meaningful purpose waiting for us?

Having been an active minister for more than forty years, I've had a chance to do grief counseling with hundreds of people. There is nothing more difficult than to sit and talk with someone who is facing the end of their life, with no time left for a do-over, who feels their life has been meaningless. I have no doubt that the epidemic of suicide among senior citizens is directly related to the fact that meaning has been stripped from the lives of millions of people by means of our current economic system, which consists of insuring that most people have to work at a job while knowing full well that virtually anyone could step in off the street and take over for them, probably working for less money. To spend a third of our life working at such a job while dreaming of better days is dehumanizing.

That's why the pursuit of origins is so important. If life has meaning beyond how we spend our days, if there is a greater purpose being carried out, if the human species has direction, then life is worth living. If the opposite is true, however, then life is not worth living.

We have considered many origin scenarios in this book. No one knows which of them, if any, are true, but hiding the research because it is difficult, because we are afraid people somehow won't be able to handle it, or because we disagree with what others are saying about the subject is not only hurtful, it is damaging.

I have a great deal of difficulty staying calm when I read books by popular speakers who try to get a name for themselves by announcing their belief that there is no God or that life arose by accident and has no meaningful purpose. If they believe that, that is their right. Who knows? They might be right, but when they attempt to take away any kind of faith from people, whether it be religious or secular, just to sell books or establish a brief reputation, it is, I think, tragic.

I have witnessed dozens of TV and conference debates wherein a secular evangelist takes on a religious scholar for the sole purpose of undermining the faith of someone in the audience who is barely hanging on, trying to find a reason to continue a life that lacks direction and meaning. What's the point in such an exercise? All it does is sell books, enhance a questionable reputation, or feed a deranged ego. Far better to remain silent than destroy hope.

A secular organization such as Alcoholics Anonymous understands that in order to find stability, a person must have faith in something, even if that "something" is recognized only as "a higher power."

Religious people are no better, however, when they proselytize members from the church down the street, or when they ask for money because their God is better than the next person's God.

Politicians err when they promise "good jobs" instead of asking if their constituents may be lacking something more in their lives than basic busy work. A new factory will bring money into your community, but will it bring meaning?

Schools are wrong when they prepare students for future employment while cutting programs that teach things, such as music and art, that make life meaningful. Colleges joke about the economic worthlessness of a degree in the humanities. What they are saying is that there is no money in learning about what it means to be human.

Literature, art, music, and theater—the humanities—are areas of study often devalued in our schools as impractical, even self-indulgent. The truth is, the arts help us to discover what it means to be human, and that is a worthwhile pursuit!

For years now I've wanted to teach a college course that builds on the theme of this book. I would love to help students dig into the various opinions and theories we have explored. My suspicion is that it would be extremely popular, but I've been told over and over again that such a course is not "practical."

What makes a human being human? Was there ever a day in history when some ancient ancestor woke up and realized they were curious? If so, what was the previous day like?

Did human curiosity and striving for purpose originate here on this planet, or was it planted here from elsewhere, either another place in the cosmos or another dimension? Is life a cosmic accident? If so, now that we're accidently here, can we invest it with purpose?

It's sad, but true, that to study history is to study war. We might try to suppress that depressing fact, but if you open almost any history book at random, the chances are good that you will find yourself reading about a war going on somewhere. The reason for that unpleasant truth is that in the absence of purpose, we substitute power. In the absence of meaning, we substitute acquisition. In the absence of reflection, we substitute activity. In the absence of creativity, we substitute production. Those are all activities that flourish during times of war.

Maybe it all began because we stopped asking ourselves the first question we asked as children: "Where did I come from?" The tragedy of history is that when we put that question aside and settled for lesser things, we condemned our future to existential failure.

The ancients thought about these things. They wrote rich mythologies dealing with this very question, but in our day, we relegate the subject to the musty halls of philosophy, implying that it is less important than "real" research.

I would like to humbly raise my voice in the wilderness of noise and confusion that is modern life in the twenty-first century and make the claim that such speculation is important. It may even prove to be life saving. Perhaps our "hidden" origins remain hidden only because we have stopped searching for them.

FUTURE SCENARIOS

Throughout the process of writing this book, both the years of initial research and the months of actual writing, I've been vaguely aware of a problem that began as a nagging thought and gradually developed into a full-fledged, troubling disparity. You might be experiencing a similar dilemma, so maybe it's time to bring it out into the open.

Here it is, as simply and clearly as I can state it.

I've been pretty hard on those who make it a practice to first develop an ideology and then muster facts to support it. At times I've been self-righteous to the point of even nauseating myself a little. I've tried to present an objective, well-rounded survey of many and varied points of view and criticized those who do any less.

But I'm human as well and might as well 'fess up to the fact that I'm as guilty as the next guy.

Take the area of origins in general, and human origins in particular, for instance.

After studying the various theories about how everything got started, I'm forced to say that probably the one idea that answers the most questions and offers the fewest logical flaws is that we live in a digitally simulated universe. That makes more sense than any other theory, right down to the fact that we know for certain that the basis of material existence turns out to be something that looks suspiciously like pixels on a computer. When I went back and reread the earlier chapter on this subject, it rang true on almost every level. It seems entirely possible that what we see around us is a very detailed video game wherein the virtual characters on the screen—us—have reached a point of sentience. I don't know who wrote the code for this program, of course, and whether it is generated from the future, from another dimension, or somewhere in what I call the Akashic or zero-point field, but it appears to be a logical assumption once you get over the initial disbelief.

And that's the problem. I can't get over the initial disbelief.

Why?

Because I don't want to believe it. Something in my gut tells me it's not true, no matter how much my intellect musters believable arguments. I *feel* like I'm real, no matter what scientist or philosopher argues otherwise. I'm much more comfortable believing that an outside force, whether it be God, or spirits, or even ancient aliens, got things started. Somehow that seems different.

Not only can I not prove what I believe, however, I can even put forth a very logical case that the whole idea of an outside force behind the creation of the universe is, in some ways, a bit silly. And I was a minister for forty years!

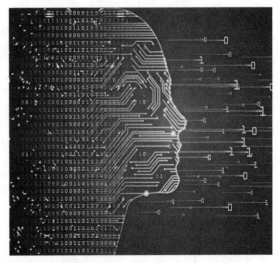

This is us, digitally rendered, in a cosmic computer. Yet, the feeling that we are something more than just a pixilated people remains.

In other words, when I look to the future, I sincerely have placed my hopes on something or someone, call it God, the Akashic field, Manitou, the Force, Brahma, or whatever you want, that is somehow going to insure that things turn out okay.

Why do I believe that? Because something in my gut, not my head, whispers in my ear at those moments when I worry the most. It makes no intellectual sense, but I trust my ideology more than my intellect.

That troubles me, but it is what it is.

I take refuge in the fact that just because I may have a problem, I have tried very hard not to foist it on others. I've tried to be thorough throughout this survey. I hope I've succeeded. It's the best I can do. When push comes to shove, I have to admit to myself that as much as I try to pretend I'm a reasonable, thoughtful, left-brain kind of guy, my ideology may not make a lot of sense, but it's mine, so I have based my understanding of life on my gut rather than my intellect.

Go figure!

Twenty years ago if you had told me that Nobel Prize-winning scientists would be studying the possibility that reality is a simulation or hologram, I would have thought you were crazy, but that's exactly where the new frontier is right now. A lot of really smart people believe just that. I may not be able to accept it in my heart, but in my intellect, I confess they make a compelling case that seems right now to be the future of origin studies.

The basic premise looks something like this. After all is said and done, after all the bangs have banged and the gulfs between nonlife and life have been crossed, there is a very real possibility that our universe does not actually exists. We might be living in a virtual reality simulation and a few scientists are not only beginning to figure out ways to prove it, they're getting close to doing so.

To make matters worse, one of their arguments is a pet method of mine. They go back to ancient mythology and oral history to suggest that the ancients thought along these same lines. There is ample evidence that the ancients believed life is a dream or an illusion. The old ones rowed their boat down the stream of time and sang, "Merrily, merrily, merrily, merrily, life is but a dream." If we convert the old language and concepts to twenty-first-century terms, a good argument could be made that they were talking about things we call a grid, matrix, simulation, or hologram.

According to this way of thinking, not only is time an illusion, so is everything else. The universe becomes what is now called a consciousness hologram or simulation, with reality a projected illusion inside it. At death, we either cease to exist or we get to step outside and view the results of the experiment. No one knows which one will happen.

Could it be that Earth—indeed, our entire universe—is merely an elaborate, holographic projection that our minds interpret as "reality"? That is one scenario that some modern physicists are pondering. It is a theory that is reminiscent of ancient philosophies about life being but a dream.

We can speculate about the purpose for this experiment. Perhaps it's all carried out by consciousness itself, which we have called "God" among other things, and was designed to study emotion, or possibly something like separation and individuality, within a framework of linear time. The hologram or simulation operates through a system of interconnected, electromagnetic energy at a physical level through grid interstices and matrix intersections. Like all experiments, it had a beginning, which we call the Big Bang, and will have an end, when the experimenter pulls the plug.

A scenario such as this answers a lot of questions.

- How do you get something from nothing at the beginning of time?
- What came before the Big Bang?
- How did life originate from nonlife?
- What is the nature of consciousness?
- Does life have intrinsic meaning and purpose?
- How can the basis of the physical world really consist of layer after layer until, at the bottom, you wind up with nothing?

I have to admit it. I hate saying it, but it makes a lot of sense. Think about it:

- According to this theory, we didn't get something from nothing. It was created by a presence or force way beyond our ability to understand. Hopefully we can take comfort in the words of an old sage who said we were created "in the image of God," so maybe in the end we will have something in common with the creator of the experiment.

- What came before the Big Bang was the decision to program the matrix and begin the experiment.

- Life came from nonlife because it was coded into the experiment, probably at the level of our DNA, which eerily resembles digital code.

- Consciousness does not develop in our brains. Our minds perceive it; they don't generate it. It lies "out there" and we are simply aware of it.

- The purpose of life is to finish the experiment.

- The basis of physical life appears to be "nothing" because it actually consists of electromagnetic impulses that we call energy.

It's maddening, isn't it? Intellectually, it makes perfect sense. So much so that a number of dedicated people are trying to prove it. We can express the whole theory in religious language and make it work, or we can use science-speak. A philosopher can study it, along with a mythologist, and feel right at home in the language of their respective disciplines.

But, and this might just be my take on it, somehow it just doesn't feel right. As humans we'd like to think we're more than just a cosmic experiment. I guess we can learn to live with it if that somehow proves to be the case. After all, what other choice do we have?

But it seems to me that somehow, if all this is proven, something inestimable will go out of us. What we're talking about is not fatalism or predestination, because no one knows what will happen in any experiment, but it isn't free will either. Can any of us live comfortably with the knowledge that someday, suddenly, everything will fade to black and we will lose the source of energy that powers the whole thing?

If this, then, is the future of origin studies, the question then becomes one of extreme relevance to the subject of this book. Suppose a brilliant scientist comes up with a breakthrough experiment that will prove conclusively that we are the subject of just the kind of experiment we have been talking about? What if that scientist discovers a way to metaphorically peer through the microscope the wrong way and catch a glimpse of the equivalent of a giant eye staring down at us?

Will he or she be allowed to publish the results or will the powers that be think we won't be able to handle it? Will such knowledge be suppressed because someone, somewhere, thinks it will be too hard to handle if it gets out?

Now comes the part that will really be difficult to get our minds around. What if it's already happened? What if previous civilizations came to this very point in their development, discovered the truth, and saw the experiment conclude with the destruction of everything they knew and understood because to continue with them knowing about it would contaminate the results? What if suppressed histories are the whole point?

Run with this as far as you like or try to just forget it. One way or another, once you open the door to this kind of speculation you will probably never really be the same again.

"Where did I come from?"

Where, indeed!

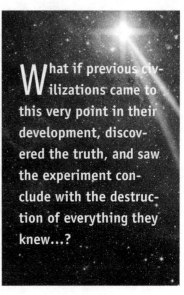

What if previous civilizations came to this very point in their development, discovered the truth, and saw the experiment conclude with the destruction of everything they knew...?

Concluding Thoughts

As we come to the end of this book, the most sprawling one I've ever written, we know we can't really draw any final conclusions. The trouble with suppressed histories is that you never really know what it is that you don't know.

But we can make a few summary statements and conclude with some fairly definitive results.

First, it is obvious that the story we have been taught and spoon-fed for at least the last hundred years is simply not the clean, concise, timeline of evolution we've all been told. Most professors, teachers, scientists, and educators of all kinds are uniformitarianists. They believe that history unfolds in a mostly unbroken line of development from the Big Bang through the development of sentient life, from primitive apes to hunter-gatherers and civilization, to the world we now experience every day. We are the apex. The whole thing happened so we could get up and go to work next Monday.

Implied in this theory is that there is nothing really more to come. Oh, sure, we'll improve our toys and games. We'll travel higher, faster, and farther. Anyone who ever watched *Star Trek* knows that. The universe exists to produce humankind and we're at the top of the evolutionary ladder. That's an unstated given.

But the more we look at history, from both a cosmic and a personal perspective, that simply is not the case. We know better. There are vast, hidden twists and turns in the history of the universe that we are just beginning to explore. As much as we've learned—we've uncovered a vast treasure trove indeed—we still have many more questions than answers.

Times are changing. I've come to believe that we live on the cusp of what sociologists call a paradigm shift—the Greeks call it a transforming καιρδς (kairos) moment rather than a χρδνος (chronos) one. The second denotes the linear, chronological time we are accustomed to. The first is a moment when time stands still and demands a life-changing response. It's a time for action because the exact moment will never come again.

I support my opinion with a few observations.

- Since I began the actual work of writing this book only a few months ago, there have been no fewer than half a dozen news articles reported in the popular press that push back the dates for human evolution or their occupation of a particular geographical landscape back by, in some cases, thousands of years. There have been announcements of brand-new human species that, up until a few years ago, no one had known existed. This just didn't happen twenty years ago, or even ten years ago. It is true that each of these discoveries has been challenged. That's appropriate and even helpful, as long as the tone of the challenge remains civil and courteous, but the underlying assumptions are important. There is more to learn, and the arguments are reaching the ears of the public much sooner than before.

- That leads to another important observation. Social media makes it much less likely that new and important information can be suppressed. Admittedly, this comes with its own set of problems. There are a lot of quack claims being bandied about. Because of the ease of technical methods that can present false information that is surrounded by flashy special effects, it's easy for the general public to be deceived, thinking bonafide information is being served up because it is so impressively presented, but those who have a story to tell can now do an end-around run against a sometimes stodgy academic goal line stand. It's really hard to suppress knowledge in this day and age. You can still do it, but it's a lot harder.

- People are generally more cynical these days. They have been made that way by being let down again and again by governmental, religious, academic, and political leaders. We don't assume honesty anymore. People in the know have to earn our trust. We don't jump through hoops anymore just because Bishop Sheen, Billy Graham, Professor "what's-his-name," or President "so-and-so" tells us to. We have been taken advantage of too many times and seen too many of our leaders stumble over feet of clay.

- Science has new tools in its toolkit—methods of study that just weren't available in the past. This is a good thing. It makes possible all kinds of study that wasn't possible even a few years ago.

Throughout this book, I have often criticized the academic establishment for the way it has too often suppressed histories and information that would have advanced our understanding. I need to make something very clear, however. I believe in the importance of scientific research and development. At its best, the scientific method is unrelenting and powerful. Given enough time, it will eventually crack through to the truth of any problem.

My argument is not with the method. It is with the human hubris that so often accompanies it. I have stood before many classes of college kids who looked to me for answers. The temptation is to believe you know it all, that you have the answer to any question, that your point of view is the correct one. You deliver your sermon or lecture with authority because you believe your heart is pure, your motivation sincere, and your facts clear and unequivocal.

That's how we've all been taught for a hundred years. It's got to stop. At its best it retards the growth of ideas that comes from honest and respectful debate. At its worst, it has destroyed lives.

Without any religious connotations, I have come to believe we live in a spiritually infantile environment. The mythology of the ancients is so superior to anything we come up with today that the difference is immediately obvious to anyone who even begins to study the wisdom of the past. The problem, however, is that most people today, raised in a materialistic and shallow culture, don't know how to tell that difference.

If I am right that we are living on the cusp of a new, deep, and spiritual paradigm shift that will promote the growth of people who want to look beneath the surface of life, this may be the most exciting time in the history of our civilization. Maybe other civilizations have come to this same point in their evolution and made either the choice for the development of their humanity, or their destruction. As we have seen, archeological evidence hints at either possibility.

Whatever they chose, assuming they did choose, our decision does not have to follow theirs. Our future is, hopefully, our own, but that choice cannot be made if we suppress either the wisdom or the folly of those who have gone before us.

Knowledge is power. It may be even our salvation. It's time to break free of the censored past, peer behind the curtain of history, and figure out what to do next. As Yogi Berra once famously said, "Our future is all ahead of us!"

Further Reading

Ashton, John, and Tom Whyte. *The Quest for Paradise: Visions of Heaven and Eternity in the World's Myths and Religions*. New York: Harper Collins, 2001.

Bauval, Robert, and Adrian Gilbert. *The Orion Mystery*. New York: Three Rivers Press, 1994.

Bullfinch's Mythology. New York: Gramercy Books, 1979

Campbell, Joseph. *Transformations of Myth through Time*. New York: Harper & Row, 1990.

Campbell, Joseph, with Bill Moyers. *The Power of Myth*. New York: Bantam Double-day Dell, 1988.

Christian, David. *Origin Story: A Big History of Everything*. New York: Little. Brown, 2018.

Chopra, Depak, and Leonard Mlodinonow. *War of the World View: Science versus Spirituality*. New York: Harmony Books, 2011.

Collins, Andrew. *Atlantis in the Caribbean and the Comet that Changed the World*. Rochester, VT: Bear & Co, 2000.

———. *The Cygnus Mystery*. London: Watkins Publishing, 2006.

———. *The Cygnus Key: The Denisovan Legacy, Göbekli Tepe, and the Birth of Egypt*. Rochester, VT: Bear & Co, 2018.

———. *Göbekli Tepe: Genesis of the Gods*. Rochester, VT: Bear & Co., 2014.

Collins, Andrew, and Gregory L. Little. *Denisovan Origins: Hybrid Humans, Göbekli Tepe, and the Genesis of the Giants of Ancient America*. Rochester, VT: Bear & Co., 2019.

Dennett, Daniel. *Darwin's Dangerous Idea: Evolution and the Meanings of Life*. New York: Touchstone, 1996.

Diamond, Jared. *Collapse: How Societies Choose to Fail or Succeed*. New York: Penguin, 2006.

Durant, Will and Ariel. *The Lessons of History*. New York: Simon & Schuster, 1968.

Fell, Barry. *America B.C.: Ancient Settlers in the New World*. New York: Simon & Schuster, 1976.

———. *Saga America*. New York. NY: Times Books, 1980.

Felser, Joseph M. *The Way Back to Paradise: Restoring the Balance between Magic and Reason*. Charlottesville, VA: Hampton Roads Publishing Co., 2005.

Flem-Ath, Rand and Rose. *Atlantis Beneath the Ice: The Fate of the Lost Continent*. Rochester, VT: Bear & Co., 1995.

Freeman, Gordon R. *Hidden Stonehenge*. London: Watkins Publishing, 2012.

Gooch, Stan. *The Dream Culture of the Neanderthals: Guardians of Ancient Wisdom*. Rochester, VT: Inner Traditions, 2006.

Gould, Stephen J. *Rocks of Ages: Science and Religion in the Fullness of Life*. New York: Ballantine, 1999.

Hancock, Graham. *America Before: The Key to Earth's Lost Civilization*. New York: St. Martin's Press, 2019.

———. *Fingerprints of the Gods*. New York: Three Rivers Press, 1995.

———. *Magicians of the Gods*. New York: St. Martin's Press, 2015.

———. *The Sign and the Seal*. New York: Crown Publishers, 1992.

———. *Supernatural*. New York: Disinformation Company, 2007.

———. *Underworld: The Mysterious Origins of Civilization*. New York: Crown Publishers, 2002.

Hapgood, Charles. *The Earth's Shifting Crust*. New York: Pantheon Books, 1958.

———. *Maps of the Ancient Sea Kings: Evidence of Advanced Civilization in the Ice Age*. Kempton, IL: Adventures Unlimited Press, 1966.

———. *The Path of the Pole*. Kempton, IL: Adventures Unlimited Press, 1999.

Harner, Michael. *Cave and Cosmos*. Berkeley, CA: North Atlantic Books, 2013.

———. *The Way of the Shaman*. San Francisco: Harper & Row, 1980.

Herbert, Nick. *Quantum Reality*. New York: Random House, 1985.

Highwater, Jamake. *The Primal Mind: Vision and Reality in Indian America*. New York: Harper & Row, 1981.

Hitching, Francis. *Earth Magic*. New York: William Morrow, 1977.

Holt, Jim. *Why Does the World Exist?* New York: Liveright, 2012.

James, Peter, and Nick Thorpe. *Ancient Mysteries*. New York: Ballantine Books, 1999.

James, Simon. *The World of the Celts*. London: Thames & Hudson, 1993.

Johnson, Robert Bowie, Jr. *Genesis Characters and Events in Ancient Greek Art*. Annapolis, MD: Solving Light Books, 2004.

Jones, Prudence, and Nigel Pennick. *A History of Pagan Europe*. New York: Routledge, 1995.

Joseph, Frank. *Advanced Civilizations of Prehistoric America*. Rochester, VT: Bear & Co., 2010.

———. *Before Atlantis: 20 Million Years of Human and Pre-Human Cultures.* Rochester, VT: Bear & Co., 2013.

Kauffman, Stuart A. *Reinventing the Sacred: A New View of Science, Reason, and Religion.* Philadelphia: Basic Books, 2008.

Kenyon, J. Douglas, ed. *Forbidden History: Prehistoric Technologies, Extraterrestrial Intervention, and the Suppressed Origins of Civilization.* Rochester, VT: Bear & Co., 2005.

Lanza, Robert, with Bob Berman. *Biocentrism: How Life and Consciousness Are the Keys to Understanding the True Nature of the Universe.* Dallas: BenBella Books, 2009.

———. *Beyond Biocentrism: Rethinking Time, Space, Consciousness, and the Illusion of Death.* Dallas: BenBella Books, 2016.

Laszlo, Ervin. *The Akashic Experience: Science and the Cosmic Memory Field.* Rochester, VT: Inner Traditions, 2009.

———. *Science and the Akashic Field: An Integral Theory of Everything,* updated 2nd edition. Rochester, VT: Inner Traditions, 2007.

———. *The Whispering Pond: A Personal Guide to the Emerging Vision of Science.* Rockport, MA: Element Books, 1996.

The Lost Books of the Bible and the Forgotten Books of Eden. New York: The World Syndicate Publishing Co., 1926.

Mails, Thomas E. *Dancing in the Paths of the Ancestors.* New York: Marlowe, 1983.

Martineau, John, ed. *Megaliths: Studies in Stone.* New York: Bloomsbury, 2018.

Mavor, James W., and Byron E. Dix. *Manitou.* Rochester, VT: Inner Traditions International, 1989.

Mayor, Adrienne. *Fossil Legends of the First Americans.* Princeton: Princeton University Press, 2005.

Michell, John. *The New View over Atlantis.* New York: Thames & Hudson, 1969.

Osborne, Robert. *Civilization: A New History of the Western World.* New York: Pegasus Books, 2006.

Pagán, Oné R. *Strange Survivors: How Organisms Attack and Defend in the Game of War.* Dallas: BenBella Books, 2018.

Prabhupada, A. C. Bhaktivedanta. *Bhagavad-Gita as It Is.* Los Angeles: International Society for Krishna Consciousness, 1984.

Redfern, Nick. *Secret History: Conspiracies from Ancient Aliens to the New World Order.* Detroit, MI: Visible Ink Press, 2015.

Roberts, David. *In Search of the Old Ones.* New York: Simon & Schuster, 1996.

Scharf, Caleb. *The Copernicus Complex: Our Cosmic Significance in a Universe of Planets and Probabilities.* New York. Scientific American, 2014.

Scranton, Roy. *We're Doomed. Now What?: Essays on War and Climate Change.* New York: Soho Press, 2018.

Sitchin, Janet. *The Anunnaki Chronicles: A Zecharia Sitchin Reader.* Rochester, VT: Bear & Co., 2015.

Sitchin, Zecharia. *Genesis Revisited*. New York: Avon Books, 1990.

Stanford, Dennis J., and Bruce A. Bradley. *Across Atlantic Ice: The Origin of America's Clovis Culture*. Berkeley and Los Angeles: University of California Press, 2012.

Tegmark, Max. *Our Mathematical Universe: My Quest for the Ultimate Nature of Reality*. New York: Vintage Books, 2014.

Temple, Robert. *The Sirius Mystery*. Rochester, VT: Destine Books, 1987.

Ulansey, David. *The Origins of the Mithraic Mysteries: Cosmology Salvation in the Ancient World*. New York: Oxford University Press, 1989.

Urquhart, David. *The Lebanon (Mount Souria): A History and a Diary*. BiblioBazaar, 2015.

Von Däniken, Eric. *Chariots of the Gods?* New York: Penguin Group, 1968.

Waters, Frank. *Book of the Hopi*. New York: Penguin Books, 1977.

Waziyatawin, Ph.D. *What Does Justice Look Like? The Struggle for Liberation in Dakota Homeland*. St. Paul, MN: Living Justice Press, 2008.

Willis, Jim. *Ancient Gods: Lost Histories, Hidden Truths and the Conspiracy of Silence*. Detroit: Visible Ink Press, 2016.

——— . *Lost Civilizations: The Secret Histories and Suppressed Technologies of the Ancient*. Detroit: Visible Ink Press, 2019.

——— . *The Religion Book: Places, Prophets, Saints and Seers*. Detroit: Visible Ink Press, 2004.

——— . *Supernatural Gods: Spiritual Mysteries, Psychic Experiences and Scientific Truths*. Detroit: Visible Ink Press, 2017.

Willis, Jim and Barbara. *Armageddon Now: The End of the World, A-Z*. Detroit: Visible Ink Press, 2006.

Witzel, E. J. Michael. *The Origin of the World's Mythologies*. New York: Oxford University Press, 2012.

INDEX

Note: (ill.) indicates photos and illustrations.

C